Paul Collaer

A HISTORY OF MODERN MUSIC

TRANSLATED FROM THE FRENCH

BY *Sally Abeles*

The Universal Library

GROSSET & DUNLAP

NEW YORK

TRANSLATED FROM THE SECOND EDITION OF THE FRENCH TEXT, *La Musique Moderne,* COPYRIGHT ©1955 BY ELSEVIER, BRUSSELS.

With deep gratitude, the translator thanks Rosalie Rebollo Sborgi and Tommye Murphy, whose scholarship and skill gave her invaluable technical and moral support. S. A.

BY ARRANGEMENT WITH
THE WORLD PUBLISHING COMPANY.

LIBRARY OF CONGRESS CATALOG CARD NUMBER: 61-5809

PRINTED IN THE UNITED STATES OF AMERICA

CONTENTS

CONTENTS

A HISTORY OF MODERN MUSIC

INTRODUCTION

IT MIGHT seem presumptuous to write a history of modern music at a time when that period, far from being finished, gives no sign of nearing its end. Without the necessary perspective it is difficult, indeed, to make a definitive judgment on the composers and their works, contemporary as they are, when the ideas they propose and the problems they raise are the object of our daily attention. Because we take part in discussions the composers begin, our tastes and inclinations are focused on the presentation, execution, and interpretation of the music in question. Therefore, our activity is necessarily colored by partisan feelings.

I want immediately to warn the reader, as I have done in other works, that I am neither a musicologist nor a music critic. I have served the cause of modern music as a musician who interprets modern works, or has them interpreted, while they are often still in manuscript and no tradition has been established for their interpretation. The musician who undertakes this task has a responsibility. He is used to studying scores entrusted to him, and judges their meaning and value before presenting them to the public.

Trained by the discipline of his work to acknowledge in his material only the musical realities, the sonorous values that compose it, and often guided in his work by the composers themselves, he is very close to the source of the music, and has the advantage of knowing it before it is deformed by false traditions or surrounded by legends which often are the cause of persistent misunderstandings.

If I have elected to write the history of modern music it is because I am convinced, after more than forty years in its service, that the contemporary period is one of the richest and most beautiful of musical history, and what is more important, that the music of our time participates substantially in the life of today. It is a reflection of the aspirations of modern life and the necessities imposed on it. If only on these grounds, it should be presented as a contribution to the general history of our time.

By "modern music" we mean the music written after Debussy and Ravel in France; after Strauss, Reger, and Mahler in Germany and Austria; after the Five and Scriabin in Russia; after *verismo* in Italy. In short, modern music begins around 1910. Still, it is impossible to place a strict boundary between this and the previous period, for although the evolution has sometimes spurted ahead, it has proceeded smoothly for the most part. A new form sometimes has its roots far back in earlier times.

Earlier periods formed great conceptual wholes, and carry the names impressionist, romantic, classic, and baroque. Modern music differs in that it has no one single trend launched in a given direction. Rather, it is the meeting ground of numerous and divergent trends. Far from showing a unified front, the contemporary period is distinguishable from earlier periods by its great diversity—I would say by a sort of multipolarity, a term which applies equally to general contemporary history. Instead of drawing up a synthesis of the music we are examining, we will therefore have to follow each of the different trends or diverse patterns which have led to the creation of important works and had lasting influence on and brought new and valid elements to music.

Music is a language. But a language is formed and transformed by the weight of interior forces—the conception of life, the nature of feeling and intelligence, and the need for communication.

It would be wrong to treat the history of music in terms of pure philology, because in order to understand the structure of a language we must first of all know to what concepts it corresponds. And yet, despite the diversity of its concepts, contemporary music contributes to the end, or at least the end of the exclusive reign, of the principle of tonality. The reign of classic tonal harmony, as well as the dominion of the bar-measure system over rhythm, is finished.

Johann Sebastian Bach, who has been called the Louis XIV of tonality, followed his inclination to simplify and purify music by making the final break from antique and ecclesiastic modes which insured the unity and solidarity of the musical system until his time. Turning aside from the diversity of modes and differences of expression that their use created, he elevated the *ut* mode [1] (our modern C major scale) and its parallel minor to a position of absolute dominance. Musical architecture gained thereby, but expression lost. The absolute dominance of the *ut* mode was to music what the rule of the three unities was to classical tragedy.

This exclusive rule did not last long. Bach's sons, especially Karl Philipp Emanuel, broke with their father's views. Impelled by the need for strong and flexible expression, Karl Philipp Emanuel Bach opened the romantic period by introducing chromaticism, which consists of multiplying the transpositions of the *ut* mode and passing from one tone to another while still maintaining the principle of tonality. In this way different colors are created whose succession evokes expression, especially at the moment of modulation in the passage from one tone to another. In some of his works, for example *Abschied von meinem Silbermannischen Klaviere,* he clusters modulations closely together, giving the impression that the principle of tonality is tottering.

All of romanticism and impressionism (which is in a way its ultimate phase) developed on the basis of that chromaticism which, from Schumann via Liszt and Wagner to Richard Strauss, moved more and more freely. With their more frequent use and increasing complexity, dissonances ended by not being resolved at all in Debussy's and Ravel's music. The strength of the principle of tonality progressively ebbed in the face of the growing need and desire to express individualism with more refined nuances.

Still, whatever freedom was gained, until the rise of French impressionism musical language continued to revolve around the tonic, its dominant and subdominant. Relationships became more and more subtle; the language, more and more concise, came to

---

1. The *ut* mode is formed by the succession of the diatonic degrees on the fundamental *ut*. It is characterized by two like tetrachords, that is, the succession of a whole tone plus a half-tone. By placing that same order of intervals on the fundamental *re*, *mi*, etc., we retain the same mode, but transposed into different *keys*. Thus we say: the key of D, of E, of F, and not the *tonality* of D, E, or F. Classic tonality is the principle of exclusive use of the *ut* mode.

be understood by a limited audience—it could serve as a vehicle only for people of highly individual and rarefied sensitivity.

It was not until after Debussy and Ravel that contemporary music broke definitively with the principle of tonality as it had been previously understood. No matter what specific current it followed, this new attitude was a logical result of the prevailing outlook at the beginning of the twentieth century. The fact that there are numerous and divergent currents is not surprising, considering the present chaotic state of human society.

On the one hand, artists went to individualistic extremes. On the other, excessive industrialization and standardization in economic areas resulted in a tendency toward social leveling that produced a contradiction between the condition of artistic sensitivity and the general social condition. The many different directions taken by contemporary art reflect the attitude of creative men toward this new social condition. Some disappear into ivory towers and thus retire from all contact with audiences which can no longer understand them. Others abandon their individuality, feeling more at home in the new state of society. A third group submits to official government orders imposed in some countries with the aim of narrowing the gap between creators and the people, whom they are supposed to serve.

We must also consider the impact created by the introduction of such mechanical means of reproduction as the phonograph, radio, and sound film. The development of these methods of communication has enormously changed the relationship between audience and music. Modern society has little rapport with its great artists; fine musicians are as neglected today as they were lionized in times past.

Alban Berg spoke apt words regarding this contemporary disaffection. When asked by a newsman what he thought of Bach and Handel, he answered: "Lucky that Handel and Bach were born in 1685 and not two hundred years later! Today the nationality of one would have been questioned as surely as the music of the other would have been blacklisted as Bolshevik." [2]

2. *"Ein Glück, dass Händel und Bach im Jahre 1685 geboren wurden und nicht zweihundert Jahre später! Denn sonst wäre die Bodenständigkeit des einen ebenso bezweifelt worden, wie man die Musik des anderen für kulturbolschewistisch befunden hätte."* 23: Eine Wiener Musikzeitschrift, March, 1935.

If the present state of music gives an impression of decadence, it is due only to the public's difficulty in distinguishing the various trends. Actually the apparent chaos is teeming with life. If we examine modern music at close range, we are instantly aware of its healthy vitality. It is unimportant that some lines of development lead to an impasse because others provide practicable means. And it would seem that the style of our time will be born of the interaction of these diverse propositions.

To make our examination of this music easier and more accessible, we will begin by describing the concept to which each development corresponds. Then we will see how that particular concept has penetrated musical language. And finally, we will present the composers and their principal works—but not all the composers nor all the works. We will examine only *new music*.

In 1933 Arnold Schoenberg gave a lecture at the Kulturbund in Vienna entitled *"Neue und veraltete Musik, oder Stil und Gedanke"* ("New and Outmoded Music, or Style and Idea"), in which he said: "Only that music which gives expression to a thought for the first time can be called new music, music which will preserve its feeling of newness. Music which does not fulfill that condition is obsolete from birth and cannot expect to get recognition." [3] We will adopt this postulate, for within the limited framework of contemporary music it has already proven itself to be true.

Since the twelfth century all composers of genius in Europe have written new music, be they Pérotin, Roland de Lassus, Monteverdi, Schütz, Bach, Mozart, Beethoven, Schumann, Wagner, or Debussy. It is because of their unique character, their eternal newness, that their works continue to touch us, while the works of their imitators, who through repetition weaken the message already delivered, leave us indifferent and are forgotten.

The history of modern music is the story of the works of those composers who have expressed personal ideas and, in order to give them life, have created a language of their own.

3. *"Als neu und immer neu bleibend wird jene Musik erkannt, die einen Gedanken erstmalig zum Ausdrucke bringt. Musik, die diese Voraussetzung nicht erfüllt, ist schon veraltet zur Welt gekommen und kann keinen Anspruch auf Beachtung erheben."*

1

CHRONOLOGY

THE DIVERSITY of paths followed by composers does not imply that these paths are independent of each other. The influence of one group of composers can sometimes be found in other groups where it would least be expected. Several works have been of such importance that they have affected all subsequent composition.

Certain facts and events have played a prime role in orienting the groups of composers they have touched. Thanks to their opportune timing and the persuasiveness of their demonstrations, theatrical performances and concerts have played an important part in promulgating new music, while musical reviews specially conceived to serve contemporary art have broadened contacts and engendered greater mutual understanding.

It is therefore important to draw up a table of twentieth-century musical activity before studying its most noteworthy works. Though 1910 is the starting point, it is preceded by a short chronological list of works composed earlier that are reference points for the movement of ideas which have governed music since that date. For each year the table lists significant events in modern musical life as well as the most outstanding works composed or published. Only the composers whose works have matured during the last twenty-five years, who have brought to music a new sensitivity, a personal vision, and who have forged for their own use a language appropriate to their expression are listed in this table. It would be useless to point out attempts or experiments which were totally sterile. Reference is made only to those noteworthy works which mark a stage in the composer's own development or bear witness to the general evolution of ideas.

It is impossible to classify composers by nationality. As a matter of fact, in the period we are discussing the phenomenon of *modern music* seems to detach itself from nationalism and become European and American. Neither can we speak of *schools*. There no longer exist groups comparable to the German postromanticists or French impressionists. There are a few dominant personalities who shape certain currents of thinking. Others group around them, drawn to them through a natural affinity. And finally, there are some composers who create a musical world which cannot serve as a basis for anyone else. Even if one can speak of a *Schoenbergkreis* or a group around Erik Satie, the same cannot be said about Stravinsky, Milhaud, or Bartók. Only the surface of their thought can be imitated by other composers.

Webern and Berg have been able to use the idiom created by Schoenberg, for example, without limiting in the least the maturing of their respective personalities. This is so because these composers share the same basic concept and a common viewpoint on the content and role of music. Satie's general principles and philosophy have nurtured works very different from his own in substance. The resonant world of Stravinsky, in its true objectivity, is independent of any specific expressive need. Its superficial aspect can be imitated, but it cannot serve as a rallying point for a group united by a particular kind of spiritual kinship.

CHRONOLOGY

1887

EMMANUEL CHABRIER: Le Roi Malgré Lui.
ERIK SATIE: Sarabandes.

1888

ERIK SATIE: Gymnopédies.

1894

CLAUDE DEBUSSY: Prélude à l'Après-midi d'un Faune.

1897
PAUL DUKAS: The Sorcerer's Apprentice.

1899
ARNOLD SCHOENBERG: Verklärte Nacht.

1902
CLAUDE DEBUSSY: Pelléas et Mélisande.

1903
ERIK SATIE: Three Pieces in the Form of a Pear.

1904
LEOŠ JANÁČEK: Jenufa (1903).*

1905
MANUEL DE FALLA: La Vida Breve.

1906
BÉLA BARTÓK: Ten Hungarian Folksongs.
PAUL DUKAS: Ariane et Barbe-Bleue.
CHARLES KŒCHLIN: Trois Poèmes du Livre de la Jungle.
ARNOLD SCHOENBERG: Chamber Symphony, Op. 9.

1907
Publication of Ferruccio Busoni's Entwurf einer neuen
Aesthetik der Tonkunst.
MAURICE RAVEL: L'Heure Espagnole.

1908
BÉLA BARTÓK: String Quartet No. 1.
GUSTAV MAHLER: Das Lied von der Erde.
ARNOLD SCHOENBERG: String Quartet No. 2.
IGOR STRAVINSKY: Fireworks, Op. 4.
ANTON WEBERN: Passacaglia.

* The date in parentheses after the name of a work is the year a work was
completed but not produced. Throughout the rest of the book, the date given
for a work will refer either to its composition or its publication or production, whichever in the author's opinion is more significant.

1909

First season of Sergei Diaghilev's Ballet Russe in Paris.
ARNOLD SCHOENBERG: Three Pieces for Piano, Op. 11.
Five Pieces for Orchestra, Op. 16.
Erwartung.
RICHARD STRAUSS: Elektra.

1910

ERNEST BLOCH: Macbeth.
FERRUCCIO BUSONI: Fantasia Contrappuntistica.
CLAUDE DEBUSSY: Le Promenoir des Deux Amants.
Trois Ballades de François Villon.
Twelve Piano Preludes (First Book).
GABRIEL FAURÉ: La Chanson d'Ève.
GUSTAV MAHLER: Eighth Symphony.
GIACOMO PUCCINI: La Fanciulla del West.
ALEXANDER SCRIABIN: Prometheus, Op. 60.
IGOR STRAVINSKY: The Firebird.

1911

Death of Gustav Mahler.
Publication of Arnold Schoenberg's Harmonielehre.
IRVING BERLIN: Alexander's Ragtime Band.
CLAUDE DEBUSSY: Le Martyre de Saint Sébastien.
ENRIQUE GRANADOS: Goyescas.
GUSTAV MAHLER: Das Lied von der Erde (completion).
MAURICE RAVEL: Valses Nobles et Sentimentales.
ERIK SATIE: En Habit de Cheval.
FLORENT SCHMITT: Tragédie de Salomé, Op. 50.
ARNOLD SCHOENBERG: Gurrelieder (1900).
Herzgewächse, Op. 20.
RICHARD STRAUSS: Der Rosenkavalier.
IGOR STRAVINSKY: Petrushka.
Le Roi des Étoiles.

1912

CLAUDE DEBUSSY: Jeux.
PAUL DUKAS: La Péri.

NIKOLAI MIASKOVSKY: Second Symphony.
DARIUS MILHAUD: First String Quartet.
MAURICE RAVEL: Daphnis et Chloé.
ALBERT ROUSSEL: Evocations.
            Sonatina for Piano.
ERIK SATIE: Véritables Préludes Flasques.
RICHARD STRAUSS: Ariadne auf Naxos.
KAROL SZYMANOWSKI: Sonata No. 2 for Piano.

1913

CLAUDE DEBUSSY: Poèmes de Mallarmé.
MAURICE DELAGE: Quatre Poèmes Hindous.
GABRIEL FAURÉ: Pénélope.
ILDEBRANDO PIZZETTI: La Nave by Montemezzi.
            La Pisanella.
MAURICE RAVEL: Trois Poèmes de Stéphane Mallarmé.
ALBERT ROUSSEL: The Spider's Feast.
ARNOLD SCHOENBERG: Die glückliche Hand.
ALEXANDER SCRIABIN: Sonata No. 10 for Piano.
IGOR STRAVINSKY: Le Sacre du Printemps.
            Poésies de la Lyrique Japonaise.
ANTON WEBERN: Six Pieces for Orchestra, Op. 10 (1909).

1914

Beginning of World War I.
GEORGES AURIC: Interludes.
ALFREDO CASELLA: Notte di Maggio.
WILLIAM CHRISTOPHER HANDY: St. Louis Blues.
CHARLES IVES: Three Places in New England.
DARIUS MILHAUD: Agamemnon.
            Quatre Poèmes de Léo Latil.
            Sonata for Two Violins and Piano.
GABRIEL PIERNÉ: Cydalise and the Satyr.
SERGE PROKOFIEV: Scythian Suite, Op. 20.
            The Ugy Duckling.
HENRI RABAUD: Marouf, the Cobbler of Cairo.
MAURICE RAVEL: Trio in A.
MAX REGER: Requiem.

JEAN JULES AMABLE ROGER-DUCASSE: Orpheus.

ERIK SATIE: Sports et Divertissements.

ARNOLD SCHOENBERG: Pierrot Lunaire.

RICHARD STRAUSS: The Legend of Joseph.

IGOR STRAVINSKY: The Nightingale.

RALPH VAUGHAN WILLIAMS: London Symphony.

1915

Death of Alexander Scriabin.

First issue of the review The Chesterton *in London.*

Rise of jazz in America.

FERRUCCIO BUSONI: Indianisches Tagebuch.

CLAUDE DEBUSSY: Twelve Piano Etudes.

Sonata for Cello and Piano.

Sonata No. 2 for Flute, Viola, and Harp.

MANUEL DE FALLA: El Amor Brujo.

NIKOLAI MIASKOVSKY: Third Symphony.

DARIUS MILHAUD: La Brebis Égarée.

Les Choéphores.

Second String Quartet.

ILDEBRANDO PIZZETTI: Fedra.

MAX REGER: Variations on a Theme of Mozart.

RICHARD STRAUSS: Alpine Symphony.

1916

Death of Max Reger.

ERNEST BLOCH: Schelomo.

FERRUCCIO BUSONI: Arlecchino.

MANUEL DE FALLA: Nights in the Gardens of Spain.

GUSTAV HOLST: The Planets.

CHARLES IVES: Fourth Symphony.

LEOŠ JANÁČEK: Diary of One Who Vanished.

CHARLES KŒCHLIN: Sonatinas.

Paysages et Marines.

GIAN FRANCESCO MALIPIERO: Poemi Asolani.

DARIUS MILHAUD: Poèmes Juifs.

KAROL SZYMANOWSKI: Third Symphony.

1917

Russian Revolution.
Founding of the Società Nazionale di Musica in Rome.
FERRUCCIO BUSONI: Turandot.
ALFREDO CASELLA: Pagine di Guerra.
ARTHUR HONEGGER: First String Quartet.
                 Le Chant de Nigamon.
HANS PFITZNER: Palestrina.
FRANCIS POULENC: Rapsodie Nègre.
SERGE PROKOFIEV: Visions Fugitives.
                 Sonata No. 3 for Piano.
                 Classical Symphony.
                 Seven, They Are Seven.
MAURICE RAVEL: Le Tombeau de Couperin.
OTTORINO RESPIGHI: The Fountains of Rome.
ERIK SATIE: Parade.
FRANZ SCHREKER: Kammersymphonie.

1918

Death of Claude Debussy.
End of World War I.
First issue of Musikblätter des Anbruch *in Vienna.*
Publication of Jean Cocteau's Le Coq et l'Arlequin.
GEORGES AURIC: Huit Poèmes de Jean Cocteau.
GABRIEL FAURÉ: Le Jardin Clos.
ARTHUR HONEGGER: Le Dit des Jeux du Monde.
GIAN FRANCESCO MALIPIERO: Impressioni dal Vero.
NIKOLAI MIASKOVSKY: Fourth Symphony.
                    Fifth Symphony.
DARIUS MILHAUD: L'Homme et Son Désir.
                Fourth String Quartet.
FRANCIS POULENC: Mouvements Perpétuels.
GIACOMO PUCCINI: Gianni Schicchi.
FRANZ SCHREKER: Die Gezeichneten.
IGOR STRAVINSKY: L'Histoire du Soldat.
                 Ragtime for Eleven Instruments.

1919

GEORGES AURIC: Adieu, New York.
MANUEL DE FALLA: The Three-Cornered Hat.
DARIUS MILHAUD: Le Bœuf sur le Toit.
          Protée.
          Machines Agricoles.
          Les Soirées de Pétrograd.
FEDÉRICO MOMPOU: Cants Magics, for Piano.
FRANCIS POULENC: Le Bestiaire.
          Cocardes.
SERGE PROKOFIEV: Love for Three Oranges.
ERIK SATIE: Nocturnes.
          Socrate.
FLORENT SCHMITT: Sonate Libre pour Violon et Piano, Op. 68.
RICHARD STRAUSS: Die Frau ohne Schatten.
GEORGES MARTIN WITKOWSKI: Le Poème de la Maison (1914).

1920

First issue of the Revue Musicale *in Paris.*
Activity of the Six in Paris.
Founding of the Jean Wiéner Concerts.
PAUL HINDEMITH: Sonata in Eb for Violin, Op. 11, No. 1.
ARTHUR HONEGGER: Sonata for Viola and Piano.
          Pastorale d'Été.
VINCENT D'INDY: La Légende de Saint Christophe.
LEOŠ JANÁČEK: The Excursion of Mr. Brouček (1917).
GIAN FRANCESCO MALIPIERO: Rispetti e Strambotti, for String
          Quartet.
          Sette Canzoni
          (first opera of cycle L'Orfeide).
DARIUS MILHAUD: Five Etudes for Piano and Orchestra.
SERGE PROKOFIEV: The Buffoon (1915).
MAURICE RAVEL: La Valse.
ALEXIS ROLAND-MANUEL: Isabelle and Pantalon.
FRANZ SCHREKER: Der Schatzgräber (1916).
IGOR STRAVINSKY: Concertino for String Quartet.
          Pulcinella.
          Symphonies for Wind Instruments.

1921

Founding of the Donaueschinger Kammermusikfeste, later called the Baden-Baden Festivals.

FRANCO ALFANO: Sakuntala.

GABRIEL FAURÉ: Second Quintet for Piano and Strings.

ALOIS HÁBA: First String Quartet in the Quarter-Tone System.

PAUL HINDEMITH: Mörder, Hoffnung der Frauen.

ARTHUR HONEGGER: Horace Victorieux.
Le Roi David.

LEOŠ JANÁČEK: Katya Kabanova.

ERNST KŘENEK: First String Quartet.

GIAN FRANCESCO MALIPIERO: Orfeo
(second opera of cycle L'Orfeide).

DARIUS MILHAUD: Saudades do Brasil.

SERGE PROKOFIEV: Concerto No. 1 for Violin and Orchestra
(1913).
Concerto No. 3 for Piano.

ALBERT ROUSSEL: Pour une Fête de Printemps (1920).

THE SIX: Les Mariés de la Tour Eiffel.

1922

Death of Felipe Pedrell.

First issue of Melos, Zeitschrift für Musik in Mainz.

Publication of Ferruccio Busoni's Von der Einheit der Musik.

Founding of the International Society of Contemporary Music.

Founding of Pro Arte Concerts in Brussels.

Rise of Fascism in Italy.

BÉLA BARTÓK: Sonata No. 1 for Violin and Piano.

GABRIEL FAURÉ: L'Horizon Chimérique.

PAUL HINDEMITH: Die Junge Magd.
Kleine Kammermusik, Op. 24, No. 1.
Quartet, Op. 22.
Sancta Susanna.

GIAN FRANCESCO MALIPIERO: La Morte delle Maschere
(third opera of cycle L'Orfeide).

DARIUS MILHAUD: Les Euménides.
Sixth String Quartet.

ILDEBRANDO PIZZETTI: Debora e Jaele (1921).

MAURICE RAVEL: Sonata for Violin and Cello.

HENRI SAUGUET: Françaises, for Piano.

IGOR STRAVINSKY: Mavra.

KAROL SZYMANOWSKI: Etudes for Piano.

Hagith.

ANTON WEBERN: Sechs geistliche Lieder.

1923

Founding of La Prora (Corporazione delle Nuove Musiche) in Rome.

Founding of the League of Composers in New York.

BÉLA BARTÓK: Sonata No. 2 for Violin and Piano.

MANUEL DE FALLA: Master Peter's Puppet Show (1922).

GABRIEL FAURÉ: Trio, Op. 120.

PAUL HINDEMITH: Das Marienleben.

Sonatas for Solo Viola, Solo Cello.

ARTHUR HONEGGER: Pacific 231.

ZOLTÁN KODÁLY: Psalmus Hungaricus, Op. 13.

ERNST KŘENEK: Third String Quartet.

Die Zwingburg (1922).

GIAN FRANCESCO MALIPIERO: Tre Commedie Goldoniane.

Stagioni Italiche.

NIKOLAI MIASKOVSKY: Sixth and Seventh Symphonies.

DARIUS MILHAUD: La Création du Monde.

ILDEBRANDO PIZZETTI: Requiem.

VITTORIO RIETI: L'Arca di Noe.

ALBERT ROUSSEL: Padmâvati (1914–1918).

ARNOLD SCHOENBERG: Five Pieces for Piano, Op. 23.

Suite, Op. 25, for Piano.

IGOR STRAVINSKY: Octet for Wind Instruments.

EDGAR VARÈSE: Hyperprism.

1924

Death of Ferruccio Busoni, Gabriel Fauré, Giacomo Puccini.

First issue of Modern Music, publication of the League of Composers.

First concert of symphonic jazz given by Paul Whiteman in New York.

GEORGES AURIC: Les Fâcheux.

BÉLA BARTÓK: Village Scenes.

FERRUCCIO BUSONI: Doctor Faust (completed in 1925 by Philipp Jarnach).

ANDRÉ CAPLET: Le Miroir de Jésus.

ALFREDO CASELLA: La Giara.

GABRIEL FAURÉ: String Quartet.

GEORGE GERSHWIN: Rhapsody in Blue.

PAUL HINDEMITH: String Quartet, Op. 32.
     Die Serenaden.

JACQUES IBERT: Escales.

LEOŠ JANÁČEK: The Alert Fox (1923).

ERNST KŘENEK: Concertino for Flute, Harpsichord, Violin, and Strings.

DARIUS MILHAUD: Salade.
     Les Malheurs d'Orphée.

DOUGLAS MOORE: Pageant of P. T. Barnum.

FRANCIS POULENC: Les Biches.

GIACOMO PUCCINI: Turandot (completed in 1926 by Alfano).

OTTORINO RESPIGHI: The Pines of Rome.

ERIK SATIE: Mercure.
   Relâche.

HENRI SAUGUET: Le Plumet du Colonel.

ARNOLD SCHOENBERG: Quintet for Wind Instruments.
     Serenade, Op. 24.

FRANZ SCHREKER: Irrelohe.

IGOR STRAVINSKY: Concerto for Piano and Orchestra.
     Sonata for Piano.

1925

Death of Erik Satie.

GEORGES AURIC: Les Matelots.

BÉLA BARTÓK: The Miraculous Mandarin Suite (1919).

ALBAN BERG: Concerto for Violin, Piano, and Thirteen Wind Instruments.
     Wozzeck (1922).

ALFREDO CASELLA: Partita.

LOUIS GRUENBERG: The Daniel Jazz (1924).

PAUL HINDEMITH: Kammermusik, Nos. 3 and 4.
     Concert for Orchestra.

ARTHUR HONEGGER: Concertino for Piano and Orchestra.
Judith.
CHARLES KŒCHLIN: La Course de Printemps.
DARIUS MILHAUD: Esther de Carpentras.
Seventh String Quartet.
SERGE PROKOFIEV: Le Pas d'Acier.
MAURICE RAVEL: L'Enfant et les Sortilèges.
VITTORIO RIETI: Barabau.
ALBERT ROUSSEL: Serenade.
ANTON WEBERN: Drei Lieder, Op. 18.

1926

LORD BERNERS: The Triumph of Neptune.
ALFREDO CASELLA: Concerto Romano.
HANNS EISLER: Tagebuch.
MANUEL DE FALLA: Concerto for Harpsichord and Five
Instruments.
LOUIS GRUENBERG: The Creation.
PAUL HINDEMITH: Cardillac.
Konzert für Blasorchester.
JACQUES IBERT: Angélique.
LEOŠ JANÁČEK: Sinfonietta.
LEV KNIPPER: Episodes of the Revolution.
ZOLTÁN KODÁLY: Háry János.
NIKOLAI MIASKOVSKY: Ninth Symphony.
DARIUS MILHAUD: Le Pauvre Matelot.
SERGE PROKOFIEV: The Flaming Angel, Op. 37.
MAURICE RAVEL: Chansons Madécasses.
VITTORIO RIETI: Concerto for Piano.
ALBERT ROUSSEL: Suite in F, Op. 33.
DMITRI SHOSTAKOVICH: First Symphony.
KAROL SZYMANOWSKI: Harnasie.
King Roger.
WILLIAM WALTON: Façade (1923).
Portsmouth Point Overture.

1927

Increased production of sound film.
ALBAN BERG: Lyrische Suite.

ALFREDO CASELLA: Serenade.
CARLOS CHÁVEZ: Sinfonía de Baile, H. P.
REINHOLD GLIÈRE: The Red Poppy.
PAUL HINDEMITH: Five Pieces for String Orchestra, Op. 44, No. 4.
Hin und Zurück.
ARTHUR HONEGGER: Antigone.
ERNST KŘENEK: Triumph der Empfindsamkeit.
Jonny Spielt Auf.
BOHUSLAV MARTINŮ: String Quintet.
Tumult.
DARIUS MILHAUD: Trois Opéras-Minute.
HENRI SAUGUET: La Chatte.
ARNOLD SCHOENBERG: Third String Quartet.
RICHARD STRAUSS: Die Aegyptische Helena.
IGOR STRAVINSKY: Oedipus Rex.
HEITOR VILLA-LOBOS: Chorôs 8.

1928
Death of Leoš Janáček.
Publication of Charles Kœchlin's Traité de l'Harmonie.
BÉLA BARTÓK: Fourth String Quartet.
HANNS EISLER: Zeitungsausschnitte.
PAUL HINDEMITH: Frau Musica.
ARTHUR HONEGGER: Rugby.
LEOŠ JANÁČEK: Glagolitic Mass.
BOHUSLAV MARTINŮ: First Symphony.
DARIUS MILHAUD: Christophe Colomb.
ALEXANDER MOSSOLOV: Iron Foundry.
SERGE PROKOFIEV: The Gambler (1916).
MAURICE RAVEL: Bolero.
ARNOLD SCHOENBERG: Variations for Orchestra, Op. 31.
IGOR STRAVINSKY: Apollon Musagètes.
VIRGIL THOMSON: Four Saints in Three Acts.
ANTON WEBERN: Symphony, Op. 21.

1929
Death of Sergei Diaghilev.
Publication of Egon Wellesz's Die Neue Instrumentation.
BÉLA BARTÓK: Twenty Hungarian Folk Songs.

PAUL HINDEMITH: Neues vom Tage.
    Lehrstück.
LEV KNIPPER: Vent du Nord.
ERNST KŘENEK: Leben des Orest.
CONSTANT LAMBERT: The Rio Grande.
IGOR MARKEVICH: Concerto for Piano.
FRANCIS POULENC: Concert Champêtre.
    Aubade.
VITTORIO RIETI: Symphony.
ARNOLD SCHOENBERG: Von Heute auf Morgen.
IGOR STRAVINSKY: Capriccio for Piano and Orchestra.
KURT WEILL: Threepenny Opera.
    Lindberghflug.

1930

GEORGE ANTHEIL: Transatlantic.
PAUL HINDEMITH: Concerto for Viola and Orchestra, Op. 48.
LEOŠ JANÁČEK: The House of the Dead (1927).
OLIVIER MESSIAEN: Les Offrandes Oubliées.
DARIUS MILHAUD: Maximilien.
SERGE PROKOFIEV: On the Banks of the Borysthene.
ALBERT ROUSSEL: Third Symphony in G Minor, Op. 42.
    Bacchus et Ariane.
HENRI SAUGUET: La Contrebasse.
DMITRI SHOSTAKOVICH: Golden Age (1928).
    The Nose.
WILLIAM GRANT STILL: Afro-American Symphony.
IGOR STRAVINSKY: Symphony of Psalms.
KAROL SZYMANOWSKI: Stabat Mater (1928).
HEITOR VILLA-LOBOS: Bachianas Brasileiras.
WILLIAM WALTON: Concerto for Viola.
ANTON WEBERN: Quartet for Violin, Clarinet, Saxophone, and Piano.
KURT WEILL: Mahagonny.

1931

Death of Vincent d'Indy.
ALOIS HÁBA: Die Mutter.

PAUL HINDEMITH: Concerto for Piano, Brass, and Two Harps.
Das Unaufhörliche.
Concert Music for Strings and Brass.
ARTHUR HONEGGER: Cris du Monde.
Symphony in Three Movements.
IGOR MARKEVICH: Rebus.
DARIUS MILHAUD: Alissa (1913).
MAURICE RAVEL: Concerto for the Left Hand.
Concerto for Piano.
ARNOLD SCHOENBERG: Suite for Seven Instruments.
IGOR STRAVINSKY: Violin Concerto.
WILLIAM WALTON: Belshazzar's Feast.

1932
First issue of 23: Eine Wiener Musikzeitschrift *in Vienna.*
Official statements in Soviet Russia on the meaning of music.
CONRAD BECK: Innominata Symphony.
ALFREDO CASELLA: La Donna Serpente.
La Favola d'Orfeo.
THEODORE WARD CHANDLER: Eight Epitaphs.
IVAN DZERZHINSKY: Poem of the Dnieper.
PAUL HINDEMITH: Philharmonic Concerto.
Plöner Musiktag.
ARAM KHACHATURIAN: Trio for Clarinet, Violin, and Piano.
ZOLTÁN KODÁLY: Spinnstube.
CHARLES KŒCHLIN: Five Chorales in Medieval Modes.
ERNST KŘENEK: Gesänge des späten Jahres.
IGOR MARKEVICH: The Flight of Icarus.
BOHUSLAV MARTINŮ: Špalíček.
DARIUS MILHAUD: Mort d'un Tyran.
Eighth String Quartet.
FRANCIS POULENC: Le Bal Masqué.
HENRI SAUGUET: La Voyante.
ARNOLD SCHOENBERG: Moses und Aron.
IGOR STRAVINSKY: Duo Concertant for Violin and Piano.

1933
Rise of Nazism in Germany.
BÉLA BARTÓK: Concerto No. 2 for Piano and Orchestra.

CARLOS CHÁVEZ: Sinfonía de Antigona.
PAUL HINDEMITH: Second String Trio.
ARTHUR HONEGGER: Symphonic Movement No. 3.
ARAM KHACHATURIAN: Dance Suite.
LEV KNIPPER: Far East Symphony.
ERNST KŘENEK: Karl V.
GIAN FRANCESCO MALIPIERO: Seven Inventions for Orchestra.
DARIUS MILHAUD: First Piano Concerto.
GABRIEL PIERNÉ: Giration.
SERGE PROKOFIEV: Chant Symphonique.
HERMANN REUTTER: Der grosse Kalender.
DMITRI SHOSTAKOVICH: Concerto for Piano and Orchestra.
RICHARD STRAUSS: Arabella (1929).

1934
Death of Frederick Delius, Edward Elgar, and Gustav Holst.
BÉLA BARTÓK: Cantata Profana (1930).
ALBAN BERG: Lulu (suite).
CARLOS CHÁVEZ: Llamadas, Proletarian Symphony.
JEAN FRANÇAIX: Concertino for Piano and Orchestra.
PAUL HINDEMITH: Mathis der Maler.
ARAM KHACHATURIAN: First Symphony.
GIAN FRANCESCO MALIPIERO: La Favola del Figlio Cambiato.
IGOR MARKEVICH: Psalm (1933).
DARIUS MILHAUD: Concertino de Printemps.
           Pan et Syrinx.
SERGE PROKOFIEV: Lieutenant Kije Suite, Op. 60.
           Nuits d'Égypte.
ALBERT ROUSSEL: Sinfonietta for String Orchestra.
VISSARION SHEBALIN: Second String Quartet.
           Third Symphony (Lenin).
DMITRI SHOSTAKOVICH: Lady Macbeth of Mzensk.
IGOR STRAVINSKY: Persephone.

1935
Death of Alban Berg and Paul Dukas.
First issue of Die Musik im Dritten Reich.
First issue of the Boletín Latino-Americano de Música *in Montevideo.*

BÉLA BARTÓK: Fifth String Quartet.
ALBAN BERG: Concerto for Violin and Orchestra.
WILLY BURKHARD: The Vision of Isaiah.
IVAN DZERZHINSKY: Quiet Flows the Don.
WERNER EGK: Die Zaubergeige.
GEORGE GERSHWIN: Porgy and Bess.
KARL AMADEUS HARTMANN: Miserae.
PAUL HINDEMITH: Der Schwanendreher.
ANDRÉ JOLIVET: Mana.
IGOR MARKEVICH: Paradise Lost.
BOHUSLAV MARTINŮ: Second Concerto for Piano.
OLIVIER MESSIAEN: La Nativité du Seigneur.
DARIUS MILHAUD: Ninth String Quartet.
La Sagesse.
SERGE PROKOFIEV: Concerto No. 2 for Violin.
ALBERT ROUSSEL: Aeneas.
Fourth Symphony in A Major.
ARNOLD SCHOENBERG: Suite for String Orchestra.
KAROL SZYMANOWSKI: Fourth Symphony.
VLADIMIR VOGEL: The Fall of Wagadu.
ANTON WEBERN: Concerto for Nine Instruments (1934).

1936

Founding of the Maggio Fiorentino in Florence.
Publication of Ernst Křenek's Über Neue Musik.
AURIC, HONEGGER, IBERT, KŒCHLIN, MILHAUD, ROUSSEL
(joint work): Quatorze Juillet.
BENJAMIN BRITTEN: Our Hunting Fathers.
CARLOS CHÁVEZ: Sinfonía India.
PAUL HINDEMITH: Three Sonatas for Piano.
DARIUS MILHAUD: Suite Provençale.
CARL ORFF: Carmina Burana.
GOFFREDO PETRASSI: Salmo IX.
FRANCIS POULENC: Les Soirées de Nazelles.
Seven Songs for A Cappella Chorus.
SERGE PROKOFIEV: Russian Overture.
Peter and the Wolf.
HERMANN REUTTER: Doktor Johannes Faust.
ARNOLD SCHOENBERG: Concerto for Violin and Orchestra, Op. 36.

DMITRI SHOSTAKOVICH: Fourth Symphony.

KAROL SZYMANOWSKI: Concerto No. 2 for Violin.

1937

Death of George Gershwin, Maurice Ravel, Albert Roussel, and Karol Szymanowski.

Publication of Carlos Chávez's Toward a New Music.

Publication of Paul Hindemith's Unterweisung in Tonsatz (The Craft of Musical Composition), Vol. I.

BÉLA BARTÓK: Music for Strings, Percussion, and Celesta (1936).

ALBAN BERG: Lulu (opera).

CESAR BRESGEN: Maienkonzert.

CARLOS CHÁVEZ: Concerto for Four Horns (1930).

AARON COPLAND: El Salón México.

WERNER EGK: Natur, Liebe und Tod.

JEAN FRANÇAIX: Le Diable Boiteux.

ARTHUR HONEGGER: Second String Quartet.

Third String Quartet.

ARAM KHACHATURIAN: Concerto for Piano.

CHARLES KŒCHLIN: Septet for Wind Instruments.

BOHUSLAV MARTINŮ: Concertino for Piano and Orchestra.

NIKOLAI MIASKOVSKY: Seventeenth Symphony.

DARIUS MILHAUD: Cantata for Peace.

Cantata of the Two Cities.

Nuptial Cantata.

FRANCIS POULENC: Mass A Cappella.

Tel Jour, Telle Nuit.

Sécheresses.

OTHMAR SCHOECK: Massimilia Doni.

DMITRI SHOSTAKOVICH: Fifth Symphony.

IGOR STRAVINSKY: Jeu de Cartes.

ANTON WEBERN: Variations for Piano.

1938

German Annexation of Austria.

Invasion of Czechoslovakia.

GEORGES AURIC: Overture.

SAMUEL BARBER: Essay for Orchestra.

WERNER EGK: Peer Gynt.

PAUL HINDEMITH: St. Francis.
ARTHUR HONEGGER: Jeanne d'Arc au Bûcher.
DMITRI KABALEVSKY: Colas Breugnon.
CHARLES KŒCHLIN: Symphonie d'Hymnes.
BOHUSLAV MARTINŮ: Tre Ricercari.
DARIUS MILHAUD: Médée.
FRANCIS POULENC: Nocturnes.
SERGE PROKOFIEV: Songs of Our Country.
SILVESTRE REVUELTAS: Sensemaya.
HENRI SAUGUET: Les Ombres du Jardin.
RICHARD STRAUSS: Friedenstag.
          Daphne.
IGOR STRAVINSKY: Dumbarton Oaks Concerto.
ANTON WEBERN: Das Augenlicht (1935).

1939
Beginning of World War II.
Emigration to the United States of numerous eminent European
composers.
CONRAD BECK: Cantata for Chamber Orchestra based on Sonnets
          by Louise Labé.
BENJAMIN BRITTEN: Les Illuminations.
RAYMOND CHEVREUILLE: First Symphony.
AARON COPLAND: Billy the Kid.
LUIGI DALLAPICCOLA: Tre Laudi (1937).
HUGO DISTLER: Mörike Chorliederbuch, Op. 19.
TIBOR HARSÁNYI: Christmas Cantata.
DARIUS MILHAUD: First Symphony.
CARL ORFF: Der Mond.
SERGE PROKOFIEV: Alexander Nevsky.
          Ode to Stalin.
          Semyon Kotko.
          Sonatas Nos. 6, 7, and 8 for Piano (begun).
HERMANN REUTTER: Chorphantasie.
HENRI SAUGUET: La Chartreuse de Parme (1936).
ARNOLD SCHOENBERG: Fourth String Quartet (1936).
YURI SHAPORIN: Field of Kullikova.
DMITRI SHOSTAKOVICH: Sixth Symphony.
ANTON WEBERN: First Cantata.

1940

Death of Silvestre Revueltas.

CARLOS CHÁVEZ: Preludes for Piano (1937).

AARON COPLAND: Quiet City.

LUIGI DALLAPICCOLA: Volo di Notte (1938).

WERNER EGK: Johann von Zarissa.

KARL AMADEUS HARTMANN: Sinfonia Tragica.

PAUL HINDEMITH: The Four Temperaments.

ARAM KHACHATURIAN: Concerto for Violin.

CHARLES KŒCHLIN: Les Bandar-Log.

BOHUSLAV MARTINŮ: Double Concerto for Two String Orchestras, Pianos and Timpani (1938).

NIKOLAI MIASKOVSKY: Twenty-first Symphony.

DARIUS MILHAUD: Tenth String Quartet.

SILVESTRE REVUELTAS: El Renacuajo Paseador (1933).

ARNOLD SCHOENBERG: Chamber Symphony No. 2, Op. 38.

RICHARD STRAUSS: Die Liebe der Danae.

IGOR STRAVINSKY: Symphony in C.

MICHAEL TIPPETT: A Child of Our Time.

ANTON WEBERN: Variations for Orchestra.

1941

Publication of Olivier Messiaen's Technique de Mon Langage Musical.

BENJAMIN BRITTEN: Sinfonia da Requiem.

WILLY BURKHARD: Des Jahr.

IVAN DZERZHINSKY: The Storm.

PAUL HINDEMITH: Symphony in Eb.

IGOR MARKEVICH: Lorenzo il Magnifico.

OLIVIER MESSIAEN: Quatuor pour la Fin du Temps.

GOFFREDO PETRASSI: Coro di Morti.

WILLIAM SCHUMAN: Third Symphony.

RICHARD STRAUSS: Capriccio.

1942

Publication of Igor Stravinsky's Poétique Musicale (Poetics of Music) *in the United States.*

AARON COPLAND: Rodeo.

WERNER EGK: Columbus.

ARTHUR HONEGGER: Symphony for Strings.

BOHUSLAV MARTINŮ: First Symphony (1918) (revision).

OLIVIER MESSIAEN: Visions de L'Amen.

DARIUS MILHAUD: Eleventh String Quartet.

CARL ORFF: Die Kluge.

SERGE PROKOFIEV: War and Peace.
Second String Quartet.

HERMANN REUTTER: Odysseus.

VITTORIO RIETI: Concerto du Loup.

HENRI SAUGUET: La Gageure Imprévue.

DMITRI SHOSTAKOVICH: Seventh Symphony.

1943

JEAN ABSIL: Chants du Mort.

BENJAMIN BRITTEN: Serenade.

RAYMOND CHEVREUILLE: Évasions.

LUIGI DALLAPICCOLA: Sex Carmina Alcaei.

LUKAS FOSS: The Prairie.

PAUL HINDEMITH: Second Symphony.

ERNST KŘENEK: Cantata for Wartime.

BOHUSLAV MARTINŮ: Second Symphony.

DARIUS MILHAUD: Bolivar.

CARL ORFF: Catulli Carmina.

VISSARION SHEBALIN: Fifth String Quartet.

DMITRI SHOSTAKOVICH: Eighth Symphony.

IGOR STRAVINSKY: Ode.

1944

SAMUEL BARBER: Capricorn Concerto.

BÉLA BARTÓK: Concerto for Orchestra (1943).

RAYMOND CHEVREUILLE: Symphonie des Souvenirs.

AARON COPLAND: Appalachian Spring.

PAUL HINDEMITH: Herodiade.
Ludus Tonalis.

LEV KNIPPER: Maku, suite based on Iranian themes.

CHARLES KŒCHLIN: Le Docteur Fabricius.

OLIVIER MESSIAEN: Vingt Regards sur l'Enfant Jésus.

SERGE PROKOFIEV: Fifth Symphony.

VITTORIO RIETI: Sinfonia Tripartita.

HENRI SAUGUET: Les Pénitents en Maillots Roses.

ARNOLD SCHOENBERG: Concerto for Piano (1942).
　　　　　　　Ode to Napoleon Bonaparte.

IGOR STRAVINSKY: Ballet Scenes.

1945

Death of Béla Bartók and Anton Webern.
End of World War II.
Important developments in ethnomusicology.

BENJAMIN BRITTEN: The Holy Sonnets of John Donne.
　　　　　　　Peter Grimes.

JOHN CAGE: Book of Music for Two Altered Pianos.

MANUEL DE FALLA: L'Atlantida.

KARL AMADEUS HARTMANN: Des Simplicius Simplicissimus Jugend
　　　　　　　(1935).

JEAN-LOUIS MARTINET: Orphée.

BOHUSLAV MARTINŮ: Fourth Symphony.

OLIVIER MESSIAEN: Trois Petites Liturgies de la Présence Divine.

FRANCIS POULENC: Figure Humaine.

DMITRI SHOSTAKOVICH: Ninth Symphony.

VLADIMIR VOGEL: Thyl Claes.

1946

Death of Manuel de Falla.

BENJAMIN BRITTEN: The Rape of Lucrecia.

JOHN CAGE: Three Dances for Prepared Piano.

LUIGI DALLAPICCOLA: Canti di Prigionia (1940).

PAUL HINDEMITH: When Lilacs Last in the Dooryard Bloom'd.

ERNST KŘENEK: Symphonic Elegy.

FRANK MARTIN: Petite Symphonie Concertante.

BOHUSLAV MARTINŮ: Fifth Symphony.

DARIUS MILHAUD: Thirteenth String Quartet.
　　　　　　　Third Symphony.

SERGE PROKOFIEV: Sixth Symphony.

RICHARD STRAUSS: Metamorphoses.

IGOR STRAVINSKY: Symphony in Three Movements.

1947

SAMUEL BARBER: Medea, Op. 23.
LUIGI DALLAPICCOLA: Marsyas.
LUKAS FOSS: The Song of Songs.
ARTHUR HONEGGER: Deliciae Brasiliensis Symphony.
ANDRÉ JOLIVET: Concerto for Ondes Martenot.
MAURICE LE ROUX: Deux Mimes.
GIAN FRANCESCO MALIPIERO: Fifth and Sixth Symphonies.
FRANK MARTIN: Golgotha.
JEAN-LOUIS MARTINET: Trilogie des Prométhées.
DARIUS MILHAUD: Fourth Symphony.
FRANCIS POULENC: Les Mamelles de Tirésias.
GUIDO TURCHI: Invettive.

1948

LUIGI DALLAPICCOLA: Il Prigioniero.
BRUNO MADERNA: Tre Liriche Graeche.
Concerto for Two Pianos and Instruments.
FRANK MARTIN: Le Vin Herbé (1938).
OLIVIER MESSIAEN: Five Rechants.
MARCEL MIHALOVICI: Phèdre.
MARIO PERAGALLO: La Collina.
HENRI SAUGUET: Second String Quartet.
Symphonie Expiatoire.
Visions Infernales.
PIERRE SCHAEFFER: Étude aux Chemins de Fer.
MÁTYÁS SEIBER: Ulysses.
IGOR STRAVINSKY: Mass.
Orpheus.

1949

Death of Richard Strauss.
HEINK BADINGS: Fifth Symphony.
BENJAMIN BRITTEN: Spring Symphony.
RAYMOND CHEVREUILLE: Concerto for Horn.
KAREL GOEYVAERTS: Tre Lieder per Sonare a Venti Sei.
KURT HESSENBERG: Trio for Strings.

DARIUS MILHAUD: Service Sacré pour le Samedi
Octuor.

GOFFREDO PETRASSI: Il Cordovano.

ARNOLD SCHOENBERG: A Survivor from Warsaw.

1950

WERNER EGK: French Suite after Rameau (1949).

HANS WERNER HENZE: Concert for Piano and Orchestra.

GIAN-CARLO MENOTTI: The Consul.

DARIUS MILHAUD: Barba Garibo.
Eighteenth String Quartet.
Concertinos d'Eté et d'Automne.

JUAN CARLOS PAZ: Dedalus 1950.

SERGE PROKOFIEV: Seventh Symphony.

1951

Death of Charles Kœchlin and Arnold Schoenberg.

HENRI DUTILLEUX: Symphony.

PAUL HINDEMITH: Symphonie der Harmonie der Welt.

ARTHUR HONEGGER: Fifth Symphony (Di Tre Re).

GISELHER KLEBE: Symphony for Forty-two Strings.

MAURICE LE ROUX: Trois Visages.

GOFFREDO PETRASSI: Noche Oscura.
Concerto No. 2 for Orchestra.

IGOR STRAVINSKY: Cantata on Anonymous Elizabethan Songs.
The Rake's Progress.

1952

PIERRE BOULEZ: Oubli Signal Lapidé.
Le Visage Nuptial.

RAYMOND CHEVREUILLE: Concerto No. 2 for Piano.

WERNER EGK: Allegria.

KARL AMADEUS HARTMANN: Symphonie Concertante.

BRUNO MADERNA: Musica in Due Dimensioni.

GIAN-CARLO MENOTTI: Amahl and the Night Visitors.

DARIUS MILHAUD: David.

LUIGI NONO: Epitafio de Federico Garcia Lorca.

KARLHEINZ STOCKHAUSEN: Kreuzspiel.
Kontrapunkte.
BERND ALOIS ZIMMERMANN: Concerto for Violin.

1953
Death of Serge Prokofiev.
Founding of the Concerts du Domaine Musical in Paris.
ELLIOTT CARTER: Quintet.
HANS WERNER HENZE: Boulevard Solitude.
OLIVIER MESSIAEN: Livre d'Orgue (1951).
DARIUS MILHAUD: Fifth Symphony.
GOFFREDO PETRASSI: Récréation Concertante.
ADNAN SAYGUN: Kerem.
IGOR STRAVINSKY: Septet.
DAVID VAN DE WOESTIJNE: La Belle Cordière.
YANNIS XENAKIS: Anastenaria, for Chorus and Orchestra.

1954
Death of Charles Ives.
BENJAMIN BRITTEN: The Turn of the Screw.
ANDRÉ JOLIVET: Symphony.
ROLF LIEBERMANN: Concerto for Jazz Band and Orchestra.
OLIVIER MESSIAEN: Four Rhythmic Etudes.
MARIO PERAGALLO: Concerto for Violin.
HENRI SAUGUET: Les Caprices de Marianne.
ARNOLD SCHOENBERG: Moses und Aron (1932).
DMITRI SHOSTAKOVICH: Tenth Symphony.
KARLHEINZ STOCKHAUSEN: Four Pieces for Piano.
IGOR STRAVINSKY: In Memoriam Dylan Thomas.

1955
Death of Arthur Honegger.
BORIS BLACHER: Concerto for Viola and Orchestra.
PIERRE BOULEZ: Le Marteau sans Maître.
FRANK MARTIN: Etudes for String Orchestra.
LUIGI NONO: Incontri.
PIERRE SCHAEFFER: Symphonie pour un Homme Seul.
YANNIS XENAKIS: Metastasis.

1956

PIERRE HENRY: Le Voile d'Orphée.
HANS WERNER HENZE: König Hirsch.
DARIUS MILHAUD: Quintet No. 4.
FRANCIS POULENC: Dialogues des Carmélites.
KARLHEINZ STOCKHAUSEN: Gesang der Jünglinge.
IGOR STRAVINSKY: Canticum Sacrum ad Honorem Sancti Marci
Nominis.
RALPH VAUGHAN WILLIAMS: Eighth Symphony.

1957

Founding of Incontri Musicali in Milan.
WERNER EGK: Der Revisor.
IGOR STRAVINSKY: Agon.

GENERAL SURVEY

Several important facts come to light from this chronological listing. Musicians and composers were very active during the first half of the twentieth century. The number of composers who, for various reasons, have come to the attention of the international public is considerable. Their work has been rich and generally of remarkable technical quality. But more time is needed before we can give most of the music a fresh critical examination, unaffected by novelty or aesthetic school.

Composers of talent no longer come exclusively from countries with a long, uninterrupted musical tradition, like Germany, Austria, France, Italy, Russia, Spain, as they did in the nineteenth century. It is true that almost all the leading figures of twentieth-century music were born in these countries, but important musical activity is developing in other lands—Holland, Switzerland, Belgium, England, the United States, Brazil, Mexico, Hungary, Czechoslovakia, Poland, and still others—either because old traditions have been revived or because musical life has recently been introduced.

Drawing up a list of contemporary composers in the order of their dates of birth reveals four distinct generations: the oldest prepared music's new mode of being, the second brought it to fruition, the third exploited its resources without new creation, while the fourth generation, whose work did not begin to become public until after World War II, has presented entirely new ideas.

DATES OF BIRTH OF COMPOSERS DISCUSSED

1824 Anton Bruckner
1839 Modest Mussorgsky
1841 Emmanuel Chabrier
     Anton Dvořák
     Felipe Pedrell
1844 Nikolai Rimsky-Korsakov
1845 Gabriel Fauré
1851 Vincent d'Indy
1854 Leoš Janáček
1857 Edward Elgar
1858 Giacomo Puccini
1860 Isaac Albéniz
     Gustav Mahler
1862 Claude Debussy
1863 Frederick Delius
     Gabriel Pierné
1864 Richard Strauss
1865 Paul Dukas
     Jean Sibelius
1866 Ferruccio Busoni
     Erik Satie
1867 Enrique Granados
     Charles Kœchlin
     Georges Martin
       Witkowski
1868 Granville Bantock
1869 Hans Pfitzner
     Albert Roussel
1870 Florent Schmitt
1872 Alexander Scriabin
     Ralph Vaughan Williams
1873 William Christopher
     Handy
     Henri Rabaud
     Sergei Rachmaninoff

     Max Reger
     Jean Jules Amable
       Roger-Ducasse
1874 Gustav Holst
     Charles Ives
     Arnold Schoenberg
1875 Reinhold Glière
     Maurice Ravel
1876 Franco Alfano
     Manuel de Falla
1877 Ernö Dohnányi
1878 Franz Schreker
1879 Frank Bridge
     André Caplet
     Maurice Delage
     John Ireland
     Nikolai Medtner
     Ottorino Respighi
1880 Ernest Bloch
     Ildebrando Pizzetti
1881 Béla Bartók
     Georges Enesco
     Nikolai Miaskovsky
     Heitor Villa-Lobos
1882 Zoltán Kodály
     Gian Francesco Malipiero
     Joseph Marx
     Igor Stravinsky
1883 Arnold Bax
     Lord Berners
     Alfredo Casella
     Josef Hauer
     Alexander Krein
     Karol Szymanowski
     Anton Webern

1884 Louis Gruenberg
1885 Alban Berg
     Edgar Varèse
     Egon Wellesz
1886 Oscar Esplá
     Daniel Ruyneman
     Othmar Schoeck
1888 Irving Berlin
     Louis Durey
1889 Yuri Shaporin
1890 Jacques Ibert
     Alexander Jemnitz
     Frank Martin
     Bohuslav Martinů
1891 Arthur Bliss
     László Lajtha
     Serge Prokofiev
     Alexis Roland-Manuel
     Paul Whiteman
1892 Giorgio Federico Ghedini
     Arthur Honegger
     Darius Milhaud
     Germaine Tailleferre
1893 Jean Absil
     Eugene Goossens
     Alois Hába
     Fedérico Mompou
     Douglas Moore
1894 Willem Pijper
     Walter Piston
     Bernard Wagenaar
1895 Jakov Gotovac
     Paul Hindemith
     Carl Orff
     Karol Rathaus
     William Grant Still
1896 Roger Sessions
     Virgil Thomson
     Vladimir Vogel
1897 Juan Carlos Paz
     Alexandre Tansman
1898 Lili Boulanger
     Hanns Eisler

     George Gershwin
     Roy Harris
     Tibor Harsányi
     Lev Knipper
     Marcel Mihalovici
     Vittorio Rieti
1899 Georges Auric
     Carlos Chávez
     Francis Poulenc
     Silvestre Revueltas
1900 George Antheil
     Henri Barraud
     Willy Burkhard
     Aaron Copland
     Rodolfo Halffter
     Ernst Křenek
     Alexander Mossolov
     Hermann Reutter
     Kurt Weill
1901 Conrad Beck
     Raymond Chevreuille
     Werner Egk
     Marcel Poot
     Henri Sauguet
1902 Theodore Ward
       Chandler
     Vissarion Shebalin
     William Walton
1903 Boris Blacher
     Aram Khachaturian
1904 Luigi Dallapiccola
     Dmitri Kabalevsky
     Goffredo Petrassi
     Nikos Skalkotas
1905 Ernesto Halffter
     Karl Amadeus Hartmann
     André Jolivet
     Constant Lambert
     Alan Rawsthorne
     Mátyás Seiber
     Michael Tippett
1906 Dmitri Shostakovich
1907 Heink Badings

	Wolfgang Fortner	Benjamin Britten
	Camargo Guàrnieri	Werner Meyer-Eppler
	Roman Palester	1914 Jean-Louis Martinet
	Adnan Saygun	1916 Henri Dutilleux
1908	Elliott Carter	Guido Turchi
	Hugo Distler	1918 Bernd Alois
	Kurt Hessenberg	Zimmermann
	Olivier Messiaen	1919 Michel Ciry
1909	Ivan Dzerzhinsky	1920 Bruno Maderna
1910	Samuel Barber	1922 Lukas Foss
	Rolf Liebermann	1923 Karel Goeyvaerts
	Mario Peragallo	Maurice Le Roux
	William Schuman	Sergei Nigg
1911	Gian-Carlo Menotti	1925 Giselher Klebe
1912	John Cage	1926 Pierre Boulez
	Jean Françaix	Hans Werner Henze
	Igor Markevich	Luigi Nono
1913	Cesar Bresgen	1928 Karlheinz Stockhausen

The first generation was born between 1862 and 1873, and kindled a movement in France which, with its direct ramifications, has been named *impressionism*. This first group includes Erik Satie, Claude Debussy, Paul Dukas, Charles Kœchlin, Gabriel Pierné, Albert Roussel, and Florent Schmitt. We will not concern ourselves here with impressionism. Nonetheless it is important to realize that the root of the most recent French movement can be traced to the composers of that period; there is no rupture between this generation and those that follow it.

In Germany the composers of this period—Richard Strauss, Hans Pfitzner, Max Reger—started a movement which marked the end of nineteenth-century romanticism. Reger, however, insured the continuation of the polyphonic spirit which still predominates in German music.

The second generation, born between 1874 and 1895, witnessed the spread of this movement throughout Europe. In German-speaking countries, Franz Schreker, Josef Hauer, Arnold Schoenberg, Alban Berg, and Anton Webern sought to enlarge the scope of their music with hyperchromaticism or atonality. Ferruccio Busoni experimented with new or ancient modes, other than major and minor. Paul Hindemith worked to discover the classic harmony of natural bases. Alois Hába, among others, explored the use of quarter-tones. A mass of experimental compositions of purely momentary interest saw the light of day alongside many less adventurous works. Atonality became the instrument of expressionist art.

In Russia Igor Stravinsky created a singular concept of tonality, breaking the too-narrow frame of major and minor keys but preserving the basis of harmonic reference provided by a tonic key. He freed rhythm from the shackles imposed on it by two centuries of bar-measure. The more traditional Serge Prokofiev brought his distinctive personality to bear on relaxing the concept of tonality.

In France, where academic and scholastic rules were less imposing than in Germany, and where the preceding generation had paved the way for harmonic liberation, it was less a question of revolution than of a natural evolution. Maurice Ravel, Maurice Delage, and André Caplet developed chords of elevenths and thirteenths without resolutions, creating a sort of postimpressionism based on great refinement of harmonic perception. But for Arthur Honegger and Darius Milhaud, this evolution did not fill their needs. Honegger sought a compromise between the inclinations of Schoenberg and Stravinsky while retaining nineteenth-century symphonic forms. Milhaud, more radical and more imaginative, created a very new language from polytonality —but a language which follows nonetheless from a harmonic trend already initiated by Ravel and Kœchlin. Honegger and Milhaud introduced a contrapuntal way of thinking into French music which had not been part of its character since Lully.

Spain was developing its national art along with Manuel de Falla as its protagonist. Italy began to break with *verismo,* the deteriorated state of operatic music. Franco Alfano, Ottorino Respighi, and Alfredo Casella appeared on the scene as eclectic musicians; and Ildebrando Pizzetti, Gian Francesco Malipiero, and Giorgio Federico Ghedini worked for greater musical purity. In Hungary, Béla Bartók and Zoltán Kodály sought the elements for a new language in folk music. A national renaissance grew in Poland with Karol Szymanowski, in England with Gustav Holst, in Romania with Georges Enesco, and in Bohemia with Bohuslav Martinů. However, these national movements were not like similar movements in the nineteenth century. This was by no means purely folklore art, but rather a search for a style based on the melodic and rhythmic structure of folk song.

The most significant artists of our time belong to this second generation. Their perceptions and art correspond to a social revolution without precedent in breadth and depth.

Following this generation, which had enlarged and revitalized musical thought and language, came a third, born between 1899 and 1912, which moved with ease in the framework built by the innovators. Greater liberty had been acquired, and they could meet their needs by the variety of expressions available to them. This new condition in music contrasted strikingly with the traditional pattern: in any prior period, only one single type of language was used for the most diverse expressive aims. Relativist ideas had now replaced dogmatic conceptions.

This third generation, including such musicians as Georges Auric, Francis Poulenc, Ernst Křenek, Henri Sauguet, and Dmitri Shostakovich, worked out the balance between the different trends of the preceding generation. While it brought nothing new from the point of view of technique, and did not enrich the language or enlarge the horizon, the third generation profited by the inheritance from its elders. It did include some original artists, whose main concern seemed to be to establish a new classicism in the midst of the new freedom. This was true of Georges Auric, Francis Poulenc, Henri Sauguet, Jean Françaix, Carl Orff, Raymond Chevreuille, Luigi Dallapiccola, Goffredo Petrassi, and even Olivier Messiaen.

Several Englishmen—Benjamin Britten, Michael Tippett, and William Walton—belong to this group. Creative activity in America progressed with Aaron Copland, Walter Piston, Roger Sessions, and Samuel Barber. Spain outgrew the folklore phase of its evolution, and Mexico gained full stature with Carlos Chávez and Silvestre Revueltas. Moreover, we should take into account the hidden activity in Nazi Germany and Soviet Russia where adherence to a state aesthetic was practically required.

The fourth generation of musicians were born after 1912, and have insistently sought entirely new modes of expression. Their restlessness corresponds to the incoherence of the postwar world, since 1945. Some have built a more or less rigorous, and sometimes even academic, dodecaphonism based on the experiments of Schoenberg and Webern. Bruno Maderna, Luigi Nono, Mario Peragallo, and Pierre Boulez followed this current, each in his own way, while the liberated German composers thought along lines of extending Hindemith's system of construction. What is new, however, is the search for expressions and means which differ from everything thought and developed before, like Pierre Schaeffer's experiments in concrete music and Meyer-Eppler's electronic music. Musicians like Karlheinz Stockhausen and Karel Goeyvaerts are at this moment the most representative composers of a period which is still in its analytic phase.

The classification of composers into four generations is not precise. Some older artists have produced "newer" works than some of the younger men. Considering only the evolution of language, Charles Kœchlin is obviously more advanced than Henri Sauguet and Shostakovich is less modern than Stravinsky. For another thing, musicians from all four generations have composed simultaneously; some have produced mature works while others are still in a trial period. And there is no proof that the older generation always influences the younger—the reverse can be true. Furthermore, there are contacts and spiritual exchanges between artists of different ages which combine to create a spirit of the times that is independent of the spirit of a given generation or of an individual personality. For example, in 1920 Albert Roussel's *Pour une Fête de Printemps,* Stravinsky's *Symphonies for Wind Instruments,* Milhaud's *Studies for Piano and Orchestra,* and Georges Auric's *Les Joues en Feu* were composed. Aside from the differences in expression of the composers' own personalities as well as their respective ages, these works are related by certain common characteristics of the time.

Having made a classification of composers by age and having given a short description of the character of each generation, we must next extract from the chronological listing information about the characteristics of the period. Let us try to describe the times in perspective.

1909-10

In Paris, the first season of Sergei Diaghilev's Ballet Russe makes a deep impression. A new dramatic technique is revealed which calls for close coordination of music, choreography, and painting. The impression is created that the plastic, architectural, and lyric aspects of the musical performance are more concerned with current problems than are the dramatic and philosophic concept of musical drama. In Germany, *Elektra,* by Richard Strauss, enlarges the horizon of musical tragedy (Greek tragedy with its universal thought and human sensitivity). Compact action. Vienna witnesses the first works of expressionism in music: Schoenberg's *Erwartung* and *Five Pieces for Orchestra.* New orchestration, opposing Wagner's and Strauss's massive orchestra with treatment by groups of soloists.

1910-11

Orchestral color as the dominant element; *fauve* music (by analogy with painting). Stravinsky's *Firebird,* Florent Schmitt's *Tragédie de Salomé.* Beginning of Debussy's last period; end of impressionism. Trend toward more sustained sentiment, clearer and more unified form. Trend toward economy and concentration of methods of expression in Gabriel Fauré.

1911-12

The techniques of impressionism reconciled with the concern for construction. Postimpression as in Roussel's *Evocations.* Decline of *fauve* music: *Daphnis et Chloé, Petrushka.* Fauré's austerity attracts Satie, as demonstrated in *En Habit de Cheval.* In Russia, the movement begun with Scriabin continues in Miaskovsky. In Vienna, Schoenberg takes relativism into consideration in appreciation of harmonies.

1912-13

Final major work of impressionism: Debussy's *Jeux.* Postimpressionism: Dukas, Roussel. Symphonic constructions with rhythmic base (influence of ballet). Satie adds to the concentration of expressive techniques certain harmonic short cuts: superimposition of remote keys, an in *Véritables Préludes Flasques.* In Schoenberg's work the accent on expression becomes more important than rhythm, and motif more important than melody. Strict application of atonality: *Pierrot Lunaire.* Use of solo instruments by the orchestra: Schoenberg's *Pierrot Lunaire,* Strauss's *Le Bourgeois Gentilhomme.*

1913-14

Echo in France of Schoenberg's innovations in compositions by Ravel, Delage, Stravinsky. *Le Sacre du Printemps,* central work in the European musical crisis—peak of *fauve* music as well as a return to elementary forms of music. The *polar* note instead of classical tonality. Return to richness and liberty of rhythm. Darius Milhaud begins *Orestie,* a work of musical theater more lyric than dramatic, with the text subordinated to the principle of lyric drama. Visionary music of Schoenberg, who also breaks with lyric drama: *Die glückliche Hand.* Italian music develops rapidly and shares the concerns of European music (Casella).

1914-15

Postimpressionism turns toward a more constructive ideal, a new classicism (which is not an academic imitation of historic classical models): Ravel, Auric. Diatonism and melody reaffirmed: Milhaud, Prokofiev. Busoni composes by creating new modes and using exotic keys.

1915-16

Milhaud brings polytonal counterpoint and harmony into focus. Pizzetti reacts against *verismo* with *Fedra.* Busoni produces his theatrical ideal: *Arlecchino.*

1917-18

The desire for conciseness has led Satie and Schoenberg to say only the essential: *Sports et Divertissements; Sechs Kleine Klavierstücke.* Limiting himself to the elementary action of the music, Satie composes "background music": *Parade.* Influence of cubism and carnival music. End of Stravinsky's "Russian" period. For him as well, condensation of expressive means becomes most important; *Noces, Renard.* In general, rhythmic and harmonic gains are directed toward compact forms. Melody predominates; music denuded of literary intentions. Pure music in the theater.

1918-19

Jazz takes shape in America and makes an immediate and profound impression with its free rhythm and its orchestration. Jean Cocteau, the spokesman of young French musicians, sums up current activity in his *Le Coq et l'Arlequin.* Break with impressionism, creation of a style of music described as trenchant. Close rapport among musicians, poets, and painters: Auric, Poulenc; Stravinsky's *Histoire du Soldat.* Development of the use of orchestras of solo instruments. In the sonata, French music tends to reduce or suppress the *Durchführung* (Kœchlin, Milhaud) and to create new balances in form. Ballet makes its influence felt in French opera: *Padmâvati,* by Roussel.

1919-20

German operas by Strauss and Schreker reflect recent increase of freedom in harmony. *Fauve* music makes its last appearances with Schmitt, Ravel, Bartók. In France, musicians detach themselves from jazz after assimilating its essence; Auric, Stravinsky. The question of movies begins to be noticed by composers; Milhaud's *Le Bœuf sur le Toit.* Orientation toward a new classicism (Satie, Stravinsky) by suppression of individual expression.

1920-21

Postimpressionism, such as in Roussel's *Pour une Fête de Printemps,* is influenced by experimentation in polytonality. The Six form. Polytonal radicalism of Milhaud, Auric, while Satie creates a perfect example of a new classicism with *Socrate.* Igor Stravinsky is mostly concerned with instrumental specificity and the search for a form divorced from any scholastic spirit. Honegger and Hindemith work on modernizing the sonata. Malipiero takes interest in the sources of Italian music. Every detail in the reconstruction of musical language is examined and treated separately. After semi-intuitive discoveries, attempts are made to organize these discoveries with a view to returning to form.

1921-22

In Germany, the annual festival of Donaueschingen is established to give voice to proposed solutions for current problems. In France, Fauré supports classicism. Honegger presents his most radical work, *Horace Victorieux*, and also his most eclectic, *Le Roi David*. Stravinsky simplifies his language and begins to lean toward Tchaikovsky and the nineteenth-century Italians with *Mavra*. Prokofiev shows increased balance: *Third Piano Concerto*. Having started with nationalistic music, Bartók progresses toward universalism. In Italy, the new form of opera, divorced from *verismo*, wins recognition: Alfano, Pizzetti, Malipiero. In general, individualistic music with its development based on the unfolding of a psychological drama has disappeared; it has been replaced by "objective" music.

1922-23

In Germany, Pfitzner carries on in the romantic tradition. Hindemith leaves it entirely and returns to an objective basis: *sachliche Musik*. In Vienna, the Schoenbergian movement moves toward an even more intransigent radicalism. In Paris, Milhaud's *Les Euménides* marks the end of polytonal radicalism. Music is following a distinct trend to incorporate polytonality in normal harmonic language; Ravel, Milhaud. Recognition of predominantly consonant music; Sauguet. In Poland, Szymanowski reaches the peak of his development. In Spain, De Falla marks the end of postimpressionism.

1923-24

Hindemith counters the radical atonality of Schoenberg, Křenek with a system based on old German contrapuntal techniques modernized by an extension of harmonic principles; *Marienleben*. His orientation toward a new classicism becomes more marked. Stravinsky also moves toward a new classicism: *Octuor*. Auric's and Poulenc's classicism is basically a revival of seventeenth- and eighteenth-century French sense of proportion, revitalized by Stravinsky's influence. Honegger experiments with dynamic construction: *Pacific 231*. Milhaud's talent becomes more and more difficult to classify with any given movement or current. He participates in the general trend toward classicism in the simplicity and suppleness of his language. On the other hand, his temperament is romantic in some lights. Manuel de Falla introduces recently won freedom into Spanish music. Young English composers begin to feel the impact of the new French spirit; Walton.

1924-25

In France and Germany, there is a general return to form and a classical conception. End of trenchant-style music like that of Satie. New Stravinsky works provoke discussion of a return to Bach. Schoenberg maintains his atonal radicalism. The influence of jazz on American music develops.

1925-26

Schoenberg examines the problem of form. For his atonal language, he invents a system of development with the twelve-tone row: *Suite,* Op. 25. Alban Berg uses Schoenbergian principles, but less radically. Trends in Soviet art begin to appear through Prokofiev, Shostakovich.

1926-27

De Falla moves in the direction of a Spanish classicism with *Concerto for Harpsichord.*

1927-28

Specific subjects are broached: that of popular musical education by Hindemith and that of chamber opera by Hindemith, Milhaud, Weill.

1928-29

Important works illustrate various trends. Period of maturity for contemporary music. Berg's *Wozzeck* becomes the best example of expressionist opera.

1929-30

Schoenberg shows himself less radical with *Von Heute auf Morgen.*

1930-31

Development of choral music and modern oratorio by Stravinsky, Bartók, Szymanowski, Hindemith, Honegger. Adaptation of modern music to sound film. Performance of an opera in quartertones, *Die Mutter*, by Hába. Igor Markevich composes *Rebus*.

1932-33

Soviet declarations on the meaning of music. This art form is directed toward popular tastes by the state. First real blow to freedom of artistic thought.

1935-36

Dramatic and secular oratorios contain the best of contemporary lyric expression. Among them are works by Vogel, Honegger, Milhaud, Markevich. Active work in chamber and concert music. First publication of Nazi music in Germany: Werner Egk. Schoenberg and Hindemith leave Germany.

1936-37

Pure music, solely or predominantly concerned with construction, such as Webern's *Variations*, Stravinsky's *Jeu de Cartes*, Bartók's *Music for Strings, Percussion, and Celesta*, Sauguet's *La Chartreuse de Parme* proves that traditional, consonant music can produce great modern compositions. In Germany, the music allowed for public consumption shows a spiritual and technical decline. Carl Orff, however, proposes an interesting solution in the spirit of music conceived for the people with *Carmina Burana*.

1937-38

Hindemith publishes a work on modern harmony: *Unterweisung im Tonsatz* (*The Craft of Musical Composition*), Vol. I. His system of harmony is applicable to all principles—modal, tonal, or atonal. Dallapiccola adapts Schoenberg's theories to the Italian temperament. Poulenc's and Milhaud's lyricism flower with cantatas and collections of melodies.

1938-40

The present status of modern music is extended. Trend toward simplification in Hindemith. Emigration to America of numbers of European composers: Schoenberg, Hindemith, Bartók, Milhaud, Stravinsky, Rieti, Martinů. Schoenberg regains his true romantic temperament. He abandons the strict application of the twelve-tone system and begins to use a harmonic language resembling Alban Berg's, in which tonality is always easily perceived although present only in a latent state.

1940-45

Tendency to purify and simplify the language, corresponding to a desire for serenity: Hindemith, Bartók, Stravinsky, Milhaud. Birth of the interest in authentic folk music. From 1945 on, recording of folk songs in their authentic form becomes very important. Growing interest of the European public in ethnomusicology.

1946-53

All the leaders in music, including Schoenberg, feel the need for stronger affirmation of the tonal foundation. However, many young composers are in opposition and rally to dodecaphonism. Others, taking notice of the technical advances of recording and electronics, seek in them the basis for a completely new language and expression.

TO SUM UP: The history of modern music developed in two phases:

The first, from 1909 to 1923, is the period of harmonic and rhythmic discovery, the period of spiritual and technical liberation. These battles are won by 1923, and a new period begins in which the problem of form takes the spotlight, while the freedom acquired in the first phase is prudently exercised.

One can claim that no schools really exist. But there are leaders in music—Schoenberg, Hindemith, Satie, Kœchlin—who guide and attract other composers, and work out certain solutions without imposing them on their disciples or supporters. They define a general trend, both spiritual and technical; and the newly invented technique is preferred to academic techniques. The present diversity in techniques corresponds to the diversity in spiritual states. There is no universal technique.

Thus, Schoenberg's influence has given rise to an expressionist trend, atonal language, and a system of development according to the twelve-tone series. An antiromantic and antiexpressionist current, directed toward German classicism, has formed around Hindemith. Satie's influence appears in the French movement to simplify music, to do away with over-refinement, and to seek simple forms and conciseness of expression. The influence exerted by Kœchlin in the contrapuntal-harmonic domain—less well known by the general public but no less important—puts polytonality on a firm footing and supports the idea that language must be related to content.

Aside from these European currents, national movements have started which intend to free national music from its folklore aspects in order to Europeanize it. Such is the case in Italy, Hungary, Spain, and certain areas of Russia.

However, other nations are in a less advanced state of evolution and are still in the process of developing folk music. This is true of certain American and Balkan countries and the Republics of Soviet Russia.

Apart from these trends, some musicians of exceptional talent have appeared who, like leaders, follow only their own law, but whose art is so individual and independent that they alone know how to utilize it. Stravinsky and Milhaud are such composers. Their successors can at least imitate only certain external qualities of their art.

Despite this diversity and the sometimes contradictory aspects of contemporary music, there is a general movement, as much at the heart of influential trends as in isolated personalities. It consists of a complete break with postromanticism and postimpressionism, and a search for a language divorced from the harmonic and orchestral traditions of the nineteenth century.

This experimentation provoked an aura of increasing tension in music from 1909 until 1923, a tension maintained until 1928. By that time there had arisen a widespread desire for tranquillity and balance in expression, glimpsed in the early attempts, from 1923 on, to establish a new classicism.

During this entire period, all genres of music have been under continuous cultivation: opera, ballet, oratorio, and secular cantata, symphonic music, chamber music, and art song. Relatively little religious music has been produced, although it has enjoyed something of a revival since about 1930. The symphonic poem, psychological and dramatic in essence, has been abandoned. Music is no longer a confession, a psychological drama, as it was in the time of the romantic movement, nor is it the echo of individual reactions to contact with the outside world, as in the time of the impressionist movement, except for Schoenberg's and Alban Berg's expressionism. Generally, music has either detached itself from the individual to become more largely human, or it has become objective—a pure play of forms.

New genres have been created: movie music, choreographic music, chamber music with solo instruments, music for the people.

Let us conclude this general review with an opinion from Luigi Dallapiccola:

> The movement of music is not and has never been in a period of confusion. Or else it always has been. If, in the midst of the most disparate current trends, we stop to look at a few specific works—Alois Hába's *Klageweiberquartett* (from the opera *Die Mutter*), Malipiero's *Torneo Notturno*, Béla Bartók's *Fifth Quartet,* Anton Webern's *Das Augenlicht,* Milhaud's *Christophe Colomb,* to cite only a few—and if we note in each of these the clarity of the idea, the proportion between intention and realization, the intimate poetry, we are convinced that today as in the past a few great musicians have been able to express the world which surrounds them through their personality, with accents we do not forget, once we have heard them. If one day we can speak of a general trend instead of diverse trends, that day will mark the end of art.[4]

Since 1940 contemporary music has evolved into a third phase. This is partly the result of the extension of musical knowledge to very old periods and distant lands—Messiaen's orientalism in *Petites Liturgies*, for example. It is also the result of the development of electronic methods for producing sound, which has stimulated a search for new forms required by the creation of new sounds—the sounds of indeterminate percussion in the music of John Cage, *musique concrète,* and electronic music.

4. *Revue Internationale de Musique,* I/4, 1938.

2

ARNOLD SCHOENBERG, ANTON WEBERN, ALBAN BERG

AROUND 1920, when German musicians realized that music had resolutely stepped out along new roads, the composer and musicologist Egon Wellesz wrote:

When the art of the madrigal reached its apex around 1600, a trend toward a monodic form began which put an end to the dominance of choral music. A period of primitive homophony followed the mid-eighteenth century, when contrapuntal music reached its apex. Today an analogous phenomenon is occurring: the nineteenth century created a harmonic system and developed it to an unbelievable level, at the expense of other factors in composition. But when chromaticism was in full swing (and a decomposition of forms had thereby resulted), the new generation announced its intention to build.

It is difficult to discuss things that are still growing and refuse to be assigned to one category or another. We do not even know where they will lead us or what their final aim is. One thing is certain: after the upheavals of recent years, more definite paths are being laid out.

Absence of feeling for form is responsible for the chaotic development of music during the last several generations, and that absence is a heritage from romanticism and the currents it gave birth to. It is characteristic that the second romantic period created a dominant form: the symphonic poem, which is based not upon a musical architecture but on literary construction. Composers scattered their talents, and wandered off trying to imitate the sounds of nature with an orchestra, to portray objects that cannot by their very nature be translated into music. Augmenting the strength of the orchestra, considered until then as the best means to express a rise of emotions, came to be a necessity and lost its effectiveness as it became an overworked device.

However the romantic work is envisaged, the point was always to outdo, to try to amplify what had gone before. A marvelous excitement pervaded that period: men believed themselves like unto gods, and a moment of doubt brought complete collapse. It was the destiny of the artist, who had to live in a world deprived of gods, to isolate himself from this world and to create. His philosophy was to flee the world and be resigned. He was thus a stranger even to what was best in his own time. There were only a few artists, who went unnoticed, to commend the union of the artist and the world in the heart of which he lived.

There are now increasing signs that the anarchy of recent years will be followed by a period of synthesis. We cannot say that a new form is already developing, for example, to replace the symphony. The essential contribution of the new spirit, however, is not the invention of a new form, but rather the desire to restore the close rapport between form and content.[5]

According to the testimony of Central European composers themselves, German romanticism, which gave us so many masterpieces, carried the germ of its own destruction. There is no doubt that the progressive surrender of form was fatal. Johann Sebastian Bach had perfected the fugue, the form so excellently suited to the tonal system; and Karl Philipp Emanuel Bach struck the first blow at the omnipotence of the tonal principle. He multiplied modulations, made them follow each other at brief time intervals, modulated into remote keys, and abandoned strict form for the sake of expression. We need only leaf through certain pages of the *Freie Phantasien und Rondos für Kenner und Liebhaber,* or a piece like *Abschied von meinem Silbermannischen Klaviere* to recognize this.

The form—the strict governing principle of all the parts of a work, the outline determining the relation of the notes to a fundamental of reference—the form, an end in itself, moved in a framework whose homogeneity, unity, logic, *Geschlossenheit,* as the Germans say, disappeared little by little. The concentration of the idea that all strict forms presuppose gave way to dispersion and disintegration of musical energy. Romanticism looked willingly to literature to buttress the unity and logical development of the musical work, whence came the symphonic poem and lyric drama. Wagner, subordinating music to words, gave the *coup de grâce* to the spirit of form. Constant modulation was needed to maintain the listener's attention, create dynamism—a perceptible increase of musical force—and expose and

5. *"Das Problem der Form,"* in *Von neuer Musik.* 1924.

accent the drama it was supposed to evoke; thus the principle of tonality foundered and chromaticism, of which Richard Wagner is the last exponent, rose to its apex.

Classical harmony based on the diatonic scale, that is on the seven-tone scale, major or minor, had achieved the most complete freedom. Modulations to remote keys had trained listeners to perceive more and more complex relationships, which allowed for an increase of passing tones, appoggiaturas, and suspensions—in brief, the simultaneous sound of diatonic tones and tones "outside the harmony," as they were still called. French impressionism did away with the resolution of dissonances. Ultimately the point came when all twelve notes of the chromatic scale were heard in chords. Even if these chords were left unresolved, they were related to a dominant note in context; an art of allusion, of reading-between-the-notes, was born with the first measures of *Tristan und Isolde* and finally arrived at a very complex and subtle level with Maurice Ravel, as, for example, at the end of *Surgi de la Croupe et du Bond* [*Example 1*].*

This tonal uncertainty made possible several interpretations of a single chord. But the note of reference was still present, and the tensions created were extremely delicate and provocative.

Only one step remained to be taken: to detach the twelve notes from all bases of reference, make them independent of the principle of tonality, and suppress the difference between notes proper to the harmony and those that are foreign to it. Considering the twelve tones as equal in value would project us into a new sonorous realm with no further relationship to the tonal world which succeeded the modal world of antiquity and the Middle Ages and served as the basis for musical language from the sixteenth century on.

Arnold Schoenberg was to take this decisive step. He approached it progressively by force of circumstance and pressures, logically completing a curve that started with Karl Philipp Emanuel Bach and was extended by Mozart, Schubert, Wagner, Strauss, and Mahler. The role of Strauss and Mahler in this development is perhaps not very clear. Here is what Maurice Ravel says about it:

* The musical examples will be found following page 405.

I am very much in sympathy with Schoenberg and his followers; they are equally romantic and severe. Romantic because they want to break the old tablets; [6] severe because they impose new laws on themselves and mistrust that detestable sincerity which is the mother of loquacious and imperfect works.

It is curious and sad that there are almost impenetrable barriers between their tendencies and those of our musicians. Even where there would seem to be kinship, it is more likely due to the common influence of Richard Strauss. . . . Mahler—ardent, talented, and awkward—whom they love, they esteem as an unpolished genius—a little like Berlioz. They detest Strauss (who returns the compliment), but they owe a great deal, if not to Strauss the artist, at least to Strauss the technician.

The bold approach in contrapuntal composition is as old as the organ or violin. The false decorative note, too, dates from the old masters (Scarlatti, for instance). But Strauss was the first to superimpose harmonically incompatible lines. There is a chord in *Salomé [Example 2]* which strongly resists any analysis of cadence whatever—or is at best definable as the simultaneous use of different modal articulations. This is indeed one of the roots of Schoenberg's so-called atonal system.[7]

Mahler's role is, properly speaking, indefinable. Contemporary Viennese musicians, at least those grouped around Schoenberg, seemed to consider Mahler the ultimate heir of the Beethoven-Schubert-Bruckner tradition. Beethoven was not content with considering the symphony as a mental trick. With him it became a metaphysical expression or a profession of faith. Mendelssohn, Schumann, and Brahms are thought to have pursued symphonic musical idiom with more or less virtuosity, while Bruckner and Mahler followed in the footsteps of Beethoven and Schubert.

Mahler seems to be considered the last exponent of an exhausted art form, although he was venerated by the younger generation because of his desire for spiritual purity and form after a chaotic period.

On the other hand, certain melodies from *Des Knaben Wunderhorn* and the *Kindertotenlieder* were written on a purely musical, and not literary, foundation, and the last work of the master, *Das Lied von der Erde,* incorporates aspects of the new musical language. Mahler's orchestration, as well, sometimes

6. Note that the Ravel examples cited above are essentially *tonal.*
7. *Revue Internationale de Musique,* XII/113.

forecast new concepts. Although he used enormous orchestral and vocal masses (his Eighth Symphony is called the "Symphony of a Thousand") he professed that orchestration should serve only to expose an idea clearly, and should not aim at creating color. This principle is strictly applied in the *Kindertotenlieder,* in many symphonic passages (in the Fourth, for example), and in *Das Lied von der Erde,* in which he uses only one part of the orchestra to convey his thought.

It would therefore seem to be as much the example of Mahler's artistic conscience as his work itself which influenced Schoenberg in his first efforts, and above all his determination to pursue his own course and perfect the development of his own genius—a concern that might seem slight to a Frenchman but which created a serious problem for the Viennese artist, working without privacy in the middle of a city where music has an immensely important place but where the musical spirit is particularly narrow and conservative.

In defining Mahler's influence on Viennese musicians, the aspect of local atmosphere is so subjective that it is difficult to get across to a foreigner.

There is a certain affinity between Mahler and the younger generation, either because it carried out similar experiments using different means, for example, the *Ländler* scenes in certain of Mahler's symphonies and in Alban Berg's *Wozzeck;* or because similar means are used to express different things, as Mahler's developments are based on the development and variation of motifs. Schoenberg is the direct heir of that technique, which Mahler specifically applied in the Sixth Symphony and in *Das Lied von der Erde.*

ARNOLD SCHOENBERG was born on September 13, 1874, in Vienna. He studied briefly under Alexander von Zemlinsky, but was mainly self-taught. In 1899 he composed a sextet for strings, *Verklärte Nacht,* Op. 4. In 1900 he wrote an enormous secular oratorio, the *Gurrelieder*—"a paroxysm of every romantic exuberance," Erwin Stein called it—using a gigantic orchestra containing eight flutes, seven clarinets, ten horns, and seven trombones. In 1902 he composed a symphonic poem, *Pelleas und Melisande,*

Op. 5. With it Schoenberg's postromantic period ended. The *String Quartet No. 1,* composed in 1907, inaugurated a period of musical objectivity (*die neue Sachlichkeit*), during which his interest in form began to dominate the empirical aspect of earlier works. This tendency was accentuated in the *Kammersymphonie,* Op. 9 (1906), and especially in the *String Quartet No. 2,* Op. 10 (1908).

Schoenberg modified his use of polyphony during this period. Erwin Stein, who was one of his disciples, wrote on the subject:

Multiple parts on a single harmonic foundation, such as we find in *Tristan* and in Richard Strauss's work, and the perfect polymelody in Schoenberg works like *Gurrelieder* and *Pelleas,* serve to intensify expression. After *Pelleas,* these lines become independent, and are further and further removed from the common foundation in subsequent compositions. Melody is made more and more "pure" and "nonharmonic," in opposition to melody with either latent but distinct harmony, or harmony formed by successive intervals. Polyphony becomes a sheaf of real and independent voices that are more intended to intensify expression than to obey a principle of economy—the concentrated exposition of the musical discourse.[8]

With reservations on the use of the term "pure melody," we should remember that henceforth Schoenberg did not use the word "melody" in its traditional sense. Consequently, his melody will no longer have characteristic properties; it will possibly acquire new ones. We will return to the question later.

The *Quartet,* Op. 10, is in F♯ minor. However, no definite tonality can be heard in the last movements of the work. This is the advent of the music called atonal, a term which itself must be used with reservations. Note that Schoenberg and his disciples find it even "offensively improper." To this new, third period belong the collection of songs, *Das Buch der hängenden Gärten,* Op. 15, on poems by Stefan George; *Three Piano Pieces,* Op. 11; *Five Pieces for Orchestra,* Op. 16; two dramatic works, *Erwartung,* Op. 17 (1909), and *Die glückliche Hand,* Op. 18 (1913); and *Pierrot Lunaire,* Op. 21, a suite, in *Sprechengesang* ("speechsong"), based on poems by Albert Giraud, with an accompaniment of a group of solo instruments.

All trace of romanticism has disappeared in these works. Some

8. *Ibid.*

Viennese musicians find them impressionistic. We find them much more expressionistic in character. Impressionism is the musical expression produced by impressions of the outside world. Expressionism, following on romanticism, is an expression of the *I*, of the individual, but is both more concentrated and more extremist than romanticism.

When he had freed himself from the confines of tonal harmony, Schoenberg held in his hands the elements of a new language that now needed to be organized. Thus he entered a fourth period, a "form-finding" one, and built the "system of the twelve-tone series" (*Zwölftonreihe*) in order to create a new form for the new language.

From this period come the *Five Pieces for Piano*, Op. 23 (1923); the *Serenade for Several Instruments*, Op. 24 (1924); the *Suite for Strings, Clarinets and Piano*, Op. 29; and the *Third Quartet*, Op. 30. These are the works most often discussed and recognized as the most difficult to understand, so essentially different are they from what the ear is accustomed to. For here not only is there a new technique, but a new conception of music as well, a new meaning attached to all the elements of its language. Schoenberg is like a mathematician who has passed from Euclidean to non-Euclidean geometry. A solitary art has been born for which, according to certain fanatic devotees of Schoenberg, no audience is needed—it is sufficient unto itself. It is an art that provoked endless polemics, and above all in Vienna, where a new periodical, *23*, appeared in its defense, expounding the essentials of Schoenbergian aesthetics.

Later works, such as the *Variations for Orchestra*, Op. 31 (1928); the opera *Von Heute auf Morgen* (1929); *Musique pour une Scène Filmée;* and *a cappella* choruses, come in the formalistic period that some have called "classical." But these works are generally less uncompromising. They show an attempt to reconcile new discoveries with the habitual meaning of music. They seem to draw closer to the public.

Let us see now what Schoenberg's system of composition—since there is a system—consists of, and how he arrived at it.

By his background and his situation in the Viennese world of music, the composer of *Pierrot Lunaire* was a hermit. Yet, his methods and teaching are followed with passion by very independent and inquisitive minds. In *Probleme des Kunstunter-richtes,* he wrote:

> What sense is there in teaching how to resolve situations encountered every day? The student learns to use methods he would do well never to learn if he wants to be an artist. But what is more important cannot be given to him: the courage and strength to perceive things in such a way that everything he examines becomes an exceptional case.[9]

This attitude he demands of a musician can obviously be adopted only by really creative minds. It is not for the ordinary musician, for whom the problem of music is limited to acquiring sufficient technical skill to get along. "Belief in technique as a sole support should be combated," he says. "Rather should we encourage any sign of an inclination toward true sincerity."

The outline of his conception of music and of the application he envisages already appear in his *Harmonielehre* (Treatise on Harmony) written in 1911, the essentials of which follow.

Schoenberg's *Harmonielehre* is not a handbook, but it does set forth a system of composition. A true theory of the phenomenon of music must start from the listener who receives the impression of sound. In his *Farbenlehre,* Schopenhauer says that colors are physiological phenomena: "They are states of modifications carried to the eye." The same is true for the relationships that tie sound to ear. As an art, music consists in the association of sound, ear, and emotion. Thus music cannot be based solely on the purely physical phenomenon of sound. Schoenberg was not interested in the physical theory of sounds and harmonies; he concentrated on applying certain artistic methods.

The concept of consonance-dissonance is false because it sets these two notions in opposition to each other. Between the two there are only degrees of habituating the ear and consciousness to the perception of more or less remote harmonic sounds.

Schoenberg attempts to explain chords and their relationships

9. *"Was hat es also für Sinn, die Bewältigung alltäglicher Fälle zu lehren? Der Schüler lernt etwas anwenden, was er nicht anwenden dürfte, wenn er Künstler sein will. Aber das Wichtigste kann man ihm nicht geben: den Mut und die Kraft, sich so zu den Dingen zu stellen, dass alles, was er ansieht, durch die Art, wie er sie ansieht, zum aussergewöhnlichen Fall wird."*

by beginning with the notes of the diatonic major scale. But he can explain the perfect minor chord only by reference to the rather feeble principle of imitation. He finds that it would be simpler to take the twelve half-tones of the chromatic scale as a basis for melody as well as for harmony.

He stresses the fact that composition can only be taught satisfactorily if instruction is limited to a sort of musical craftsmanship, without regard for a "natural system" or any aesthetic system whatever. Such instruction must recognize that the notions of consonance and dissonance are relative, and that from one to the other there is a gradual transition, not a fundamental opposition; that the three laws for the treatment of dissonances—to make them descend toward a consonance, to make them ascend, or to leave them in place—are superseded by a fourth law: to let them escape; that the theory of sounds that belong outside of the harmonic framework is false, and is only a system.

The twelve-tone system includes the following considerations:

1] The material for all types of musical composition consists of a series of twelve tones. (The notion of alteration must therefore be obliterated, and the twelve tones given different names to show their independence.)

2] Ecclesiastic modes, major and minor modes, exotic modes, and various chromatic modes have been constructed using this material. In the final analysis, one arrives at a single chromatic mode.

3] For reasons of style and in the interests of form, the particular characteristics of each scale have been clearly elaborated and developed to their final consequences—hence the laws of tonality for major and minor keys.

4] The principle of tonality can be enlarged:

    A. By imitating the treatment assigned to them, the different modes come to resemble each other more closely.

    B. What is similar is considered as related and is eventually treated in the same way (e.g., different chords built on the same fundamental).

5] The reduction of ecclesiastic modes into major and minor keys and the development of these twenty-four keys among themselves is accomplished as follows:

Horizontally

A. Relationship based on the resemblance of the chords divides ecclesiastic modes into major and minor species.

B. Reciprocal imitation of cadences lets the single major species absorb all the characteristics of major ecclesiastic modes. The same holds true for minor modes.

C. A great many of the three-note chords in ecclesiastic modes, made up of the same sounds, are related to a limited number of keys. As a result, the chords that remain are attached to two of these keys (the diatonic major and minor).

D. The relationship of chords as stated in A. above, and

E. the joint possession of a fundamental causes notes that are one, three, and four degrees removed in the cycle of fifths to draw together.

F. The most remote tones (second, fifth, and sixth degrees of the cycle of fifths) are likewise brought closer by the reduction of the number of boundaries between modes and the simplification of their characteristics; by the multiple significance of chords and parts of scales; by chords diminished to three notes and chords of corresponding sevenths (an open imitation of the perfect natural chord) and their imitation in other degrees.

Vertically

The vertical construction relieves the horizontal construction of chords of four and five notes. A seventh chord, using four notes of the scale, adds one-third to the tonal characterization; a ninth chord adds two-thirds.

6] Movement of the twelve major tones and the twelve minor tones toward twelve chromatic tones. The transition is made in Wagner's music.

7] Establishment of the one polytonal chromatic scale.

Up to the fifth point, the *Harmonielehre* examines the evolution of musical language as presented from this angle. It goes no further; what follows cannot yet be synthesized. Only application and experiment in composition will clarify the situation. Modern music, which uses chords of six and more notes, seems to have reached a stage comparable to the first period of polyphonic music: these chords need no justification other than the direction of their parts. The horizontal, melodic principle predominates.

Here in summary is what the *Harmonielehre* teaches us. After its publication, Schoenberg brought his atonality—which we would prefer to call his absolute chromaticism—into focus. In *Komposition mit zwölf nur aufeinander bezogenen Tönen* he suggests ways of applying his twelve-tone series. Examining some of his works will give us an idea of his discoveries.

Before leaving the *Harmonielehre,* we should note that the author refuses to accept the word *atonal*. All music, he says, is in a given tone, whether it is referred to a single tonic or whether the successions of chords are justified by more complicated relationships or references.

He also emphasizes the fact that the use of chords of six or more notes requires a very extensive type of composition and sufficient instrumentation to soften the effect of dissonances by making them sound as they really are: concurrences of distant harmonies. He cites an example drawn from his monodrama *Erwartung [Example 3]*.

Schoenberg's tonality, nevertheless, is not exactly like Bach's. Schoenberg avoids the perfect chord, precisely because using it would require using the whole procession of satellites bound to it, which would mean reverting to Bach's form of tonality. From another point of view, Schoenberg considers the chords formed by passing notes as independent. He calls them "vagabond" chords.

The misunderstanding that has arisen on the subject of tonality is due to the fact that the term is used to designate two quite different things. Classical tonality is a principle; all the chords in a given piece of music tend toward the perfect chord on a given fundamental by cadential progression. When Schoenberg says that his music is tonal, he means that each chord has its own fundamental, independent of the context. Each chord is in a certain key. But according to Schoenberg, four successive chords, for example, will be in four different keys. The speed at which one key passes to another and the complexity of each chord do not leave the ear enough time to take in the different keys and their relationships. Since there is no continuity in establishing a given key, apparent atonality results.

Schoenberg's music is thus tonal and atonal at the same time, depending on the light in which it is examined. Stoessl's ideas on the subject are worth noting. Atonality is comparable to prose, and tonality to poetry. Poetry and tonality are founded on unification through a particular rhythm, particular sounds of reference which directly attract the ear. Prose is created by writing and can do without these mnemonic devices, and links ideas in relation to the mind. The same holds true for atonality.

Every change in system involves a loss of certain properties and the acquisition of new ones. Modal diversity was abandoned in favor of major-minor duality at the expense of melodic richness, but with benefit to harmonic potential. If in its turn major-minor duality is abandoned, we may lose certain harmonic effects, especially the powerful effect of harmonic tension and release, but the scale of twelve independent tones contributes other possibilities.

Harmonically, this mutation enriches music. For dissonant chords can now develop with no reserve whatsoever. They have risen from slavery to masterhood. Classical harmony, that of Rameau, included only a few dozen admissible chords. Atonality utilizes more than two thousand. Added to that number is the diversity of inversions and groupings of parts within sonorous space. (This is much spoken of as a second dimension after time, from the influence of physics. Actually, the term *sonorous space* is improper. What is meant is the distance between the lowest and highest vibrations in sound frequencies.) This variety in the distribution of chords is of prime importance in Schoenberg's language. Increasing the number of possible chords is no assurance that the music will be enriched. In fact, the greater the number of notes contained in each chord, the less the chords will differ in degree of tension. Many of these greatly exaggerated chords will be so similar that they will show only negligible differences of importance. Variety of distribution within sonorous space compensates for the diminution of differentiation in the chords.

A form for this new musical material had not yet been established when Schoenberg was writing his *Harmonielehre*. According to him, that order will probably not be found in the vertical, harmonic idiom, but in the horizontal, linear, melodic line. We should note in passing that in this same way dissonances took their proper place within classical tonal language: i.e., through the progression of parts. The dissolution of tonality actually unbalanced all the constructive principles of musical composition, for tonality dominated them all, including rhythm, dynamics, and timbre; and so much the more did it determine melody, thematic execution, and the development of motifs. Harmony regained its position of primacy, with rhythm second in importance. The melody, says Erwin Stein, was a sort of façade for the music, a beautiful façade organically woven into the whole structure. To enrich harmony, melody and rhythm were relegated to the background for purposes of maintaining clarity and allowing the ear and brain to perceive complex harmonic treatment. Increasing harmonic instability diminished architectonic possibilities; counterpoint was needed to fill the breach.

The new technique is still too young to accommodate large forms, which explains the predominance of short pieces like the songs in *Das Buch der hängenden Gärten, Pierrot Lunaire,* and the *Six Short Pieces for Piano* (these last do not exceed a dozen measures each). Such short pieces allow remarkable concentration of musical thought. (Satie's piano works, for similar reasons, have this same brevity and concentration, although they differ in style and development.) At this point, harmony and melody no longer exist as architectural ends for Schoenberg; they are purely means of expression. Brevity allows their meaning to be caught, even without repetition. These pieces nonetheless do contain a formal element: unity of idea. And polyphony, more so than harmony, makes the listener grasp the function of the dissonances; this can be seen in *Example 4.*

It is easy to distinguish the contrapuntal essence of atonality, and what makes this counterpoint different from tonal counterpoint. " 'Tonal' counterpoint," writes Frederick Goldbeck, "is the art of lines in a cluster, whereby at any place, point *contra* point, harmonic division can be made. So-called atonal counterpoint is the art of interbuttressed lines, each innervated by latent cadences and modulations within the weave of the musical texture; its logic is justified, not point *contra* point, but line *contra* line." Cohesion in form is achieved above all by the development of the motif. The rhythmic motif is less important than the melodic; the melody is no longer engendered by melodic variations of the rhythmic motif, but by rhythmic variations of melodic motifs. Harmonic freedom requires the melody to protect its own expression. Faithfulness to relationships between intervals has always been requisite for the existence of contrapuntal forms.

At this point Schoenberg turned his attention to the question of form. These considerations prodded him to work from a foundation on the twelve-tone row. The twelve tones, mutually related but not related to a fundamental tone, produce uniformity and equality of value and treatment. If all consonances are avoided in order to do away with a preponderant note, for the same reason a specific note is not allowed to recur several times in a series. Repetition and symmetry are similarly avoided in rhythm. Avoiding repetition and symmetry in rhythm is practically equivalent to doing away with rhythm, just as changing tonality with each chord is equivalent to doing away with tonality. In the twelve-tone series as it was conceived in the beginning, then, we can recognize only very limited constructive properties.

To work out new constructive principles with the twelve-tone row, the series needed to be diversified and have certain limits imposed on it. A specific fundamental note can be replaced by an inalterable succession of the twelve tones; the series thus established becomes the regulating pattern for construction. *Example 5* shows several complete twelve-tone series.

The series will thus be analogous to melodic motifs, but will differ from them in that each note should be considered only in its relationship to the note preceding it and that which follows it. Such an arrangement gives the chromatic scale the specific quality it lacked—a disposition to form.

In building a series of less than twelve notes, it is even possible to introduce notes into the development which do not belong to the series, just as, in the classical style, notes outside the harmony were introduced. The importance and significance of the notes can then be assessed in relation to the series which, in turn, assumes the function formerly filled by the tonic [*Examples 6a and 6b*]. Requirements of form explain the grouping of these alien notes as countermotifs (or, in common parlance, counterweights). Transposition of the restricted series opens up further possibilities of injecting alien tones.

What is essential, therefore, is to compose a fundamental musical entity, which Schoenberg calls the *Grundgestalt*. In this way repetitions become organic, as in the fugue. The *Grundgestalt* is consequently essential to the whole structure of the piece. It is determined by the order of succession of the intervals, but the rhythm remains free. This rhythmic liberty is necessary since the melodic order is invariable. And since rhythm is at least as important as melody in determining the character of the music—"melody" is used here to designate only relationships of intervals (Schoenberg's school uses the term in this sense)—freedom of rhythm creates great potential for variation. Rhythm is therefore no longer the backbone of music; it has only the value of a factor in the development. Since it is no longer a support, another mainstay must be substituted: the expressive accent, with its psychological, extramusical basis.

In Schoenberg's concept the *Grundgestalt* differs from traditional melody in that it can be heard from the first to the last note as well as from the last to the first, or in the inversion of these two schemes, since only the relationships of intervals count. "Looking at a hat from underneath and from the side perhaps changes its immediate appearance, but it is nonetheless the same hat." This saying indicates great similarity between Schoenberg's thinking and cubism as conceived by Pablo Picasso. For Picasso, the real object is the *Grundgestalt*. He does not paint an object from a single perspective but exhibits all its faces, seizes its structural elements, and produces a composition in which the first aspect of the object, which has served as point of departure, is often no longer discernible. Schoenberg also accepts a certain number of treatments which the *Grundgestalt* can undergo without modifying its properties. The four usual methods are shown in *Example 7*.

Subordinated to these four treatments are methods of varying the fundamental idea: changing intervals while respecting rhythm; changing rhythm while respecting intervals; eliding one or several notes; and interpolating one or several notes [*Example 8*].

It is always preferable to use the complete series of twelve tones in composing a piece of music, if not in a single motif, at least in several consecutive or simultaneous and complementary motifs [*Example 9*].

This arrangement gives the series a particular articulation, due to the specific position of each note. To repeat, the function of each note, which formerly was harmonic, has now become contrapuntal. Chords only rise from the melody, while in homophonic style the melody rises from the harmony.

Nonetheless—and this is new—the notes chosen can be introduced simultaneously as well as successively. The chords thus produced are still of melodic origin. It is a fundamental principle of Schoenberg's polyphonic style that the musical thought appears not only when it is stated horizontally, or articulated rhythmically in time, but also when it is expressed instantaneously, vertically, in sonorous space.

There is a resemblance here to tonal language. This is particularly striking in the canon and stretto forms, in which parallel and simultaneous interpretation is audible. In this way, by a melodic detour, the chords become elements of construction but still avoid their former, i.e., harmonic, meaning [*Example 10*].

It would be a mistake to think that any series whatever can be used; the four methods of treatment must produce valid forms by superimposition. In the same way, not all melodies are suitable for use as the theme of a fugue. Some latitude still exists in the course of the composition in putting notes into other octaves and, naturally, augmenting or diminishing them and treating them in acrostic form, that is, for each note to be a possible point of departure for the exposition of a series [*Example 11*]. The notes of the series can also be distributed among a number of voices, provided that they retain their order when heard, to underline the fact that the series does not necessarily have thematic significance. An exposition of the series can be interwoven with another exposition by alternating the notes of the two [CF. *Example 9*].

In a word, the *Grundgestalt* is omnipresent; it is a building material. It is unnecessary and sometimes impossible to recognize it in all its combinations on hearing, just as contemplating a cathedral does not reveal to the eye the plan that has served as the blueprint. Nevertheless, its role is sensed in the feeling of cohesion it evokes. Its mission is to create unity, no more and no less.

When strictly applied, all the notes used figure in the *Grundgestalt*, and if alien notes are introduced they appear in the role of secondary motifs. This is the case of the notes B and A in the *Variations of the Serenade*, Op. 24 [CF. *Example 8*]. In loose application, besides the combinations already described, variations and a progression of voices are used which have less connection with the *Grundgestalt*.

Schoenberg's exposition of his art of composition is, we realize, perfectly logical. His art is serious, exacting, generally strict, and is not intended to confound the uninitiate, an accusation too often read in published critiques of the period we are examining and one which cannot seriously be directed at any of the composers discussed in this book. Atonality and the twelve-tone system bring music into a new phase, just as did the *ars nova* in the fourteenth century.

The Schoenbergian system can be criticized for the speciousness of certain arguments, notably that the transformation of modal into tonal music is attributable to imitation. Certain postulates, such as those on the efficacy of the twelve-tone series, and Schoenberg's denial of certain physical and psychological facts concerning the tonic-dominant relationship, are also questionable.

But after all, it is not a composer's explanations that count, but the result he has achieved in music in putting his own principles—invented for his own use—to work. We can find fault with the principle of superimposition of thirds in Rameau's harmonic system, but this system produced *Hippolyte et Aricie*. And we can refute parts of Stravinsky's earlier point of view, but it has given us *Noces*.

Schoenberg has written many beautiful compositions, and the fertility of his system is apparent in the constructive influence it has had on the work of many other composers—Ravel, Roussel, Stravinsky, and Milhaud, to name only some of the celebrated musicians who are not his disciples and who do not adhere to his aesthetic; and on others who follow him strictly—Berg, Webern, and Křenek, for example, or members of the younger schools.

The sextet *Verklärte Nacht,* Op. 4, and *Gurrelieder,* a great lyric poem written under the direct influence of *Tristan und Isolde* and Mahler's music, are both romantic works; neither contributes anything new or remarkable. However, the *Kammersymphonie,* Op. 9, for fifteen solo instruments, reflects Schoenberg's temperament and has real beauty. In character it is halfway between romanticism and expressionism. The chromatic features are still those of *Tristan* [*Example 12*].

But already chromaticism has ceased to be the guiding force of the composition. The work is based on a theme in successive fourths stated at the opening by the horns, the first indication of the movement to emancipate harmony. The tendency to accord the same importance to vertical statement as to horizontal exposition [*Example 15*] is already apparent. The work also shows a tendency to include very large intervals in the melody [*Example 16*].

This characteristic of Schoenberg's music is explained by the need to establish strong tensions. On the one hand, great tension is a quality of all expressionist music, which seeks to achieve an intensity, an extravagance of expression which disfigures normal, peaceful lines, or, psychologically speaking, "balanced" lines. The balanced, tranquil state, the static state, are foreign to expressionism. Continuous movement and unremitting dynamism, on the other hand, are essential characteristics.

This melodic style obtrudes more and more upon Schoenberg's art, to the point that the tonal base of the harmonic tensions disappears. For the chromatic series in themselves are almost devoid of tension and do not offer a wide scope of expression. Large intervals thus partially compensate for this lessening of tension caused by abandoning tonality.

The *Kammersymphonie* marks an important date in the history of music because of its orchestration. After the massive effects of the great Wagnerian orchestra and those of Strauss and Mahler, this music displays the clarity and ludicity required for communicating polyphonic thought. The best technique to achieve this communication consists in using solo instruments with different timbres which bring out the concurrent lines of melody clearly. The *Kammersymphonie* is the first experiment with this technique. It still often gives the effect of harmony, but in many passages the voices are effectively differentiated. The instruments are the flute, oboe, English horn, small clarinet in D, clarinet, bass clarinet, bassoon, contrabassoon, two horns, solo string quartet, and double-bass. The orchestration still shows a propensity toward the old method of grouping. The differentiation of timbres is more radical in later works as well as in innumerable chamber-orchestra compositions by Ravel, Stravinsky, Webern, Milhaud, Hindemith, and others who have felt Schoenberg's influence.

The flaw in the *Kammersymphonie* is that it is too long. Its content does not require such extensive development. Let us not lose sight of the fact that at the time it was composed the main concern of musicians was to cast off habits inherited from post-romantic composers who delighted in long elaboration.

The *Quartet No. 2, Op. 10,* launches the composer's definitive work. We will point out only that the quartet's structure shows absolute mastery, and draws specific attention to the perceptible progress in condensation of musical material. The passionate lyricism of the first of the two opening movements (which are still tonal) is kept in proper bounds with irreproachable taste. The main theme is presented without any introduction from the beginning of the first measure. [*Example 13*]. The second theme introduces one of the melodies of *Pierrot Lunaire* [*Example 14*]. A rhythmic second section is developed on a condensed treatment of the motifs. The third and fourth movements, in which the quartet is joined by a soprano voice singing two poems by Stefan George, forecast Schoenberg's future technique of composition. *Litanie,* the third movement, is built on the two themes of the first section, the first stated by the viola and the second by the second violin and the cello. This second melodic idea is characteristic of Schoenberg's feeling at that time; it begins with a descent by disjunct degrees, and after a reascent, terminates on the lull of a descent by conjunct degrees. These two motifs are complementary and furnish all the material for the melodic and harmonic construction of the composition. Note in passing the acrostic formed by the two violins [*Example 17*] and further on [*Example 18*] the chord formed by the second violin, viola, and cello, as well as the tremolo of the violins, superimposing the second motif on the first, stated by the cello.

The *Quartet, Op.* 10, is one of the richest, most passionate and tender works in contemporary music.

The new period that Schoenberg next entered is called impressionist by some and expressionist by others. To this period belong *Three Pieces for Piano, Op.* 11; *Mélodies, Op.* 12 and 14; *Das Buch der hängenden Gärten, Op.* 15; *Five Pieces for Orchestra, Op.* 16; two dramatic works, *Erwartung, Op.* 17, and *Die glückliche Hand, Op.* 18; *Six Short Pieces for Piano, Op.* 19; *Herzgewächse, Op.* 20; *Lied for Soprano and Three Instruments; Pierrot Lunaire, Op.* 21; and *Orchesterlieder, Op.* 22. These important works were produced between 1909 and 1914, a period marked by a particular and refined taste.

The music is somewhat impressionistic, but not according to the concepts of French impressionism. Whether in painting, poetry, or music, French impressionism consists of the penetration of the outside world; the subtle play of nuances is captured through abstraction from the particular. The artist stands face to face with nature without thinking of himself; he receives everything from it, lets himself be impressed by it without afterthought, and abandons himself to the joy of contemplation. Thus it is in Monet's cathedrals or water lilies, or in Debussy's *Ibéria* or *La Mer.* The German impressionist also opens himself to nature, but he chooses only those harmonies that suit his psychic state of the moment.

In *Das Buch der hängenden Gärten,* Stefan George writes:

> *Das schöne beet betracht ich mir im harren,*
> *Es ist umzäunt mit purpurn-schwarzen dorne*
> *Drin ragen kelche mit geflecktem sporne*
> *Und sammtgefiederte geneigte farren*
> *Und flochenbüschel wassergrün und rund*
> *Und in der mitte glocken weiss und mild*
> *Von einem odem ist ihr feuchter mund*
> *Wie süsse frucht vom himmlischen gefild.*

French impressionism is generally objective; German impressionism is always profoundly subjective. Listening to the *Rapsodie Espagnole,* we hear a sonorous atmosphere, and do not think of Ravel; listening to the *Three Piano Pieces* or *Das Buch der hängenden Gärten,* the atmosphere created envelops Schoenberg's soul alone. Such is the balance between the impression and expression of the soul of the individual undergoing the experience that the listener is suspended between impressionism and expressionism. From the moment impression is subordinated to intensity and insistence on individual expression, the art form will be expressionist. Pure impressionism is a French phenomenon; pure expressionism, a German—or rather, Austrian.

The *Three Pieces for Piano,* Op. 11, approach the *String Quartet,* Op. 10, in order of beauty. As in the works which will follow it, up to *Pierrot Lunaire,* the intensity, logic, and development of the psychic action are not those of a conscious, wakeful mind, but of a mind in a dream state with its subtle association of images and rapid transition from the most exquisite beatitude to the most violent agony and terror.

The first piece seems to be formed of caresses, murmurings, and a desire that is excited and resolved in a vaguely troubled sleep. The second unfolds in a long crescendo and gradual decrescendo, in an atmosphere of somber uneasiness. The third oscillates between terror, the most powerful outburst of sound acting sometimes like an electric shock, and the most profound silence.

Interpretation of the polyphonic expression of these pieces requires a piano that will differentiate the almost imperceptible nuances. It demands of the interpreter a very legato rendition, even in the leaps he must make between the largest intervals; absolute independence of timbre, color, and dynamics among the superimposed lines; and finally, scrupulous attention to all interpretative markings.

The piano scoring of these pieces has deeply enriched the instrument's potential for expression. Note, in the first piece, the effects of the soft-pedal and the harmonics, where the keys must be depressed without hitting the strings, to make sound with harmonic resonance alone [*Example 19*]. In the second piece,

the leaps of two octaves and more in the theme must be played
without hiatus [*Example 20*].

Impressionism predominates in *Das Buch der hängenden
Gärten* and *Five Pieces for Orchestra*. The atmosphere Stefan
George creates in the former is comparable to that of Maeterlinck's *Hothouses*—a rarefied and exotic climate that is very
oriental—and a love is portrayed which itself is more imaginary
than real. Schoenberg took fifteen poems from this collection
and set them in a suite for voice and piano which gives a feeling
of restraint and fine balance and which contains no excesses.
Great leaps between intervals are rare, and the singing voice
usually advances by conjunct degrees. The chromatic effects are
exceptionally delicate and move in an environment of latent
tonality [*Example 21*]. Schoenberg proves that leaps of sevenths
can express sweetness and do not only, as has been said too often,
convey violence [*Example 22*]. *Das Buch* contains exquisite
atonal phrases, such as the one in *Example 23*, which impressed
Stravinsky to such an extent that he used it as the basis for the
third act of his *Le Rossignol*.

It would be good to see this admirable collection included in
the repertoire of singers, as it would be to hear the pieces of
Op. 11 played more often. But unfortunately interpreters are
little interested in modern works if they are difficult and demand
some effort on their part and on the part of the audience.

Just as the *Three Pieces for Piano,* Op. 11, mark a milestone
in the history of the piano, *Five Pieces for Orchestra*, Op. 16, are
of outstanding importance in the evolution of the orchestra. The
great orchestra as Wagner, Strauss, and Mahler knew it is no
longer used for massive effects, but for great diversity of colors
by division of parts and frequent use of groups of solo instruments, giving it the clarity of a chamber orchestra and the
means of continuously renewing combinations of sound. This
arrangement became common in the Viennese school and in
those foreign works that have felt its influence—Stravinsky's
Rossignol, among others.

The third piece, *Der wechselnde Akkord* (*The Changing
Chord*), is totally impressionist. Written in very short motifs, it
is composed of chordal agglomerations differentiated by timbre,

which give it a unique pointillist effect and demonstrate an incredible refinement of ear. It can be said that this piece goes beyond Debussy's *Jeux* and marks the most extreme point reached by impressionist art.

The last piece is entitled *Das Obbligato Recitativ*. A dominant voice (*Hauptstimme*) runs throughout, which is henceforth indicated by the letter *H,* as the secondary voice (*Nebenstimme*) is designated by an *N* in the orchestral score. In execution, not an accent, but particular eloquence must always be attributed to this principal voice. The voice is not confined to a single instrument. As its curve progresses, its expression is underlined by continually changing timbres, which create a rainbow effect and suggestive power that have not been achieved with other methods.

More than ever before, the music is conceived orchestrally. The dosage of intensities and timbres is administered so minutely that scores which seem complex in the extreme on reading, sound clear when played. All that seemed problematic on reading disappears as if by magic. This is why reducing scores by Schoenberg and Alban Berg to piano transcription is impossible. Such transcriptions are only useful as guides for interpretation, and are admittedly incapable of giving even an approximate idea of the real character of the work.

Schoenberg adds a note in the score of the third piece:

It is not the business of the conductor to bring out the lines in this piece which he thinks should dominate, or to try to modify certain complexes which do not seem balanced to him. Where a voice must stand out, it is instrumentalized accordingly, and its sonority should not be muffled. On the contrary, care should be taken that each instrument play precisely the indicated shading, exactly (subjectively) as it corresponds to its proper instrument, and not (objectively) with a view to subordinating it to the sonority of the ensemble.

The spirit of the new music gave birth to extreme precision in orchestral scoring. Stravinsky himself came out with this bit of whimsy: "My music must be executed like a notary's certificate."

In *Erwartung,* Op. 17, and *Die glückliche Hand,* Op. 18, the orchestral technique introduced in the fifth of the orchestral pieces is fully developed. The richness of timbre accorded to the principal voice is not for the sake of color; it tends to compress expression further, to determine and characterize it at every turn. Spoken language does the same thing. The timbre of a voice, varying ceaselessly according to the expression given it, makes conversation live.

The transition from impressionism to expressionism is distinct. The methods developed in the impressionist stage were preserved and put to work for individual expression.

Of Schoenberg's two expressionist dramas, the first, *Erwartung,* is a monodrama based on a text by Marie Pappenheim. There is no dramatic action. The subject is a woman who discovers the corpse of the beloved she was waiting for. But the drama takes place as in a nightmare; the event is unreal and permeated with all the quiet and all the terrors of the night. The work is simply a development in time of a psychic state evoked in a single moment by an unforeseen catastrophe, as rapid and brutal as a lightning bolt.

Die glückliche Hand is the counterpart of *Erwartung.* In this drama the destiny of a life in its entire span is condensed into a few decisive and supreme moments. There is no realism here either, and we are again transported into that dream-state which reflects the almost visionary state Schoenberg lived in for the whole period from 1910 to 1914, when he was closely associated with the painter Oskar Kokoschka. The aura of catastrophe in his two dramas evokes the contemporaneous *Sacre du Printemps;* the social unrest and individual uneasiness which preceded the outbreak of the First World War find expression in these works.

Die glückliche Hand places a man on the scene. Behind him is a mythological monster holding him under his paw. A chorus sings its pity for the victim, or rather murmurs it mysteriously in half chant, half speech. The man aspires to terrestrial happiness, although he knows that the aim of his life is celestial bliss. A woman is the figure of earthly happiness. She abandons the man, who is the symbol of spiritual power, for a stranger, who seems to be an incarnation of the power of money. Abandoned a second time, the man stops to think, and understands that if he masters his own destiny he will be the woman's master, not bodily but spiritually. This scene is followed by a struggle to conquer gold. The man is once more the victor. But since his dream pursues a new vision of the woman, he again falls under the beast's power. And the chorus murmurs: "Must you again suffer what you have so often endured? Do you not know the meaning of sacrifice? Are you insatiable?" The music is even more unreal than that of *Erwartung*, and is lit with almost heavenly colors. The listener finds himself thinking that the sound of the orchestra has no material basis left.

Die glückliche Hand achieves, even more completely than *Erwartung*, the ideal of dramatic expression: all motion is confined to the spirit. Because it is so difficult to perform, it is rarely staged. Written in Prague in 1924 and performed a little later in Vienna, it was a decided success in 1928 at Breslau, in Duisburg in 1929, and in New York in 1930.

Pierrot Lunaire, Op. 21, written in 1914, has done the most to spread Schoenberg's name. This chamber-music work profits from the addition of a sung-spoken voice to the instrumental music, and from being set to poetry by Albert Giraud, translated into German by Otto Erich Hartleben. Schoenberg's expression is visionary still, but the fantastic has given way to the tragic and horrible and to a humor which is sinister and light in turn, and whose meaning reveals the composer's outlook. The poems should rather be spoken than sung. Their declamation must adhere strictly to the rhythm of the music, and the voice must begin on the notes indicated but take care not to hold them as they are held in a song. On the contrary, it must abandon the note as soon as it hits it and take the undetermined timbre of a spoken voice. There can be no question of sung declamation; what must be created is a nonrealistic language halfway between song and speech.

This voice is combined with a chamber orchestra comprising flute (and piccolo), clarinet (and bass clarinet), violin (also viola), cello, and piano. The chamber orchestra, which Richard Strauss was the first to use in *Le Bourgeois Gentilhomme* and which Schoenberg perfected in the *Kammersymphonie*, is, in the opinion of Strauss himself, ideal for the composition of lyric and dramatic works. In a 1929 article, the composer of *Elektra* wrote: "The orchestra of the future is the chamber orchestra. With the sharp, crystalline definition it gives the dramatic action, it is the only means capable of clearly achieving the composer's intentions when a setting for a sung voice is needed." This opinion is possibly too absolute, but the striking point is that a composer who utilized the largest orchestral masses arrived at the same conclusion as younger composers. Remember, by the way, that Mahler too used a chamber orchestra in his *Kindertotenlieder.*

Pierrot Lunaire captures the spirit of the chamber orchestra very successfully. Its motifs are conceived according to the specific character of each instrument. Instrumental imagination guides the music, as in Stravinsky's work.

A single example drawn from *Pierrot Lunaire* will explain the nature of the chamber orchestra [*Example 24*]. In it the piano is treated as a staccato, not a melodic, instrument. Stravinsky and even Busoni, the great interpreter of Chopin and Liszt, follow this tendency. The piano is not in fact a proper instrument for translating polyphonic music; it lacks the means to mark different lines strikingly. This explains why piano composition has progressed very little in modern German art, while it continues to be prominent in France, where a harmonic tendency prevails.

We will say no more about the condensation of musical material; we have already given an example of the conciseness of style Schoenberg displayed in composition after writing this score, which was his last expressionist work.

The atmosphere of *Pierrot Lunaire* is one of biting, lashing, mocking irony, and, as in *Erwartung* and *Die glückliche Hand,* mysterious nocturnal clarity. Schoenberg's expressionist music is a music of the night. His expressionist period ends with this perfect work; a new series of compositions are to rise from a concern with form.

We can follow this new spiritual orientation in the *Five Piano Pieces,* Op. 23. Here the theory of the twelve-tone series is put into practice for the first time. We have already sufficiently discussed the new form to dispense with detailed analysis of this important composition. The first piece is a creation in three voices. Three themes, stated simultaneously, are submitted to rhythmic variation from the beginning of the first measure, constantly producing new groupings of notes, new chords. The second piece, built on two themes, contains a final stretto which is built on an inversion of the first theme. In these two pieces, the *Grundgestalt* plays a thematic role. It dominates melodically and imposes its character on the expression.

From the third piece on, the concern with form relegates all other considerations to the background. The *Grundgestalt* becomes organic, like the theme in a strict fugal form. Transposition, cancrizans, inversion, rhythmic variation, canon—all possible combinations are put into operation.

The fourth piece is formed of three *Gestalten,* each with six tones. Finally, the fifth, a waltz, uses a complete series of twelve tones, recalled continuously in the same order and direction, without transpositions. It too has no thematic meaning, for the notes are dispersed among different voices. Rhythmic repetitions occur more often than in all preceding works, and guarantee clear articulation.

Henceforth Schoenberg's new principles of form are debatable. There are grounds for wondering if it is necessary to build complete series of twelve tones which act so despotically. Does form demand such radical asceticism and self-denial? Does music not need greater freedom of action? And must this freedom won by modern music, a victory Schoenberg helped win, once more be curtailed, and much more strictly than by older disciplines?

These objections have not been overlooked, and we are inclined to second them. But Schoenberg did not seem to be disturbed by these reservations concerning his works of the formalist period. He seemed to be seeking the limits of the world he discovered, and evaluating the constructive power it possesses, with no intention of expressing anything at all. His music is absolute and entirely objective, and cannot as yet be pronounced upon definitively.

The fugue is the apex of tonal art, the ideal form for carrying the constructive force of the tonal form to its extreme. An atonal fugue is not feasible; it would be only an imitation, stripped of deep meaning, of a tonal fugue. It therefore seems strange that Schoenberg, who did not write fugues, tried to apply his principles of form to obsolete forms (minuet, gavotte, gigue, etc.) which are produced by the tonal system and contradictory by the nature of their composition to the spirit of the twelve-tone series.

This is nonetheless what Schoenberg did in his *Suite,* Op. 25, and his *Serenade,* Op. 24. The *Suite* is arid. The *Serenade,* on the contrary, overflows with very real and communicable life.

The *Quintet for Wind Instruments,* Op. 26, and the *Third String Quartet* are undeniably perfect compositions. But like the *Suite for Piano and Sextet* they have such an ascetic quality that they seem no longer to communicate with listeners. In all these works analytic reading brings a certain pleasure, but it is a pleasure not revived when they are heard. The Schoenberg school speaks of the *Third String Quartet* as a great masterpiece, and explains this admiration by the fact that this quartet alone sums up "all that can be done" in the spirit and framework of atonal music and the twelve-tone series. It would seem then that form has become an end in itself and is no longer considered a means.

This is not the first time that such a thing has occurred in the history of music. The Renaissance had Willaert, and, at the end of the Baroque period, Johann Sebastian Bach wrote the *Musical Offering.* This work, and Willaert's *Ricercari,* were long considered to be solely theoretic works. Only in the last few years has it been understood that contemplation of pure forms in music, form stripped of all emotional elements, can also give great joy. An abstract joy, of course; but there are abstract works in literature and painting which are not thrust aside because of their abstraction, although they can only be appreciated by a limited elite. Such is the case for the art of Willaert, Frescobaldi, and for *The Art of the Fugue.* A similar destiny may be in store for the works of Schoenberg we have just discussed.

We still have one reservation to state, because it seems objective. For the reasons we have explained, Schoenberg never worked with consonant chords. As a result, he deprived his music of points of repose. One consequence of his system is perpetual and necessary dynamism; such a state is perfectly admissible in expressionist aesthetic, which is based on unalleviated tension. The artist's taste has moreover limited the duration of these tensions; *Erwartung* and *Die glückliche Hand* are no more than about twenty minutes long. But a formalist art, or at least an art based more on form than on expression, requires an opposition of the static and the dynamic, repose and movement. The question can well be asked whether Schoenberg's art, by its very nature, lends itself well to such a conception. The doubt is valid, although a rebuttal to this objection is still possible: that until the present, music was considered as moving in two dimensions—the scale of wave-lengths (improperly called sonorous space) and time; Schoenberg's search for form tends to contribute a third dimension to music which removes it from the action of musical gravity, from the "weight" of chords.

Schoenberg's later works, those since Op. 29, give the impression of greater freedom and fantasy although he applied his principles as strictly as ever. After the *Third String Quartet,* he generally used transpositions of the *Grundgestalt* in addition to all the combinations heretofore described. This practice enriched his music with new and multiple colors. Under a melodic line, transposed notes of the *Grundgestalt* can now be heard simultaneously, in chords. Schoenberg's art acquired a good deal of suppleness from this procedure. And so gracefully are the notes in the series divided among different voices that the themes are even more varied. More air now circulated in his works; the music was made more transparent, clearer, and at the moment of hearing, the fabric of the series passes unperceived. "The question of the twelve tones is my own affair," the composer said, suggesting by this that the audience has no business with it, does not need to notice it or above all to try to follow its path in listening.

At the same time, the orchestra, already so enriched, has gained a sparkling, translucent lightness. These methods seem to have provided the composer of the *Suite,* Op. 26, with what he was lacking to give life to his form. Later works are obviously more expressive than those of the transition period. The *Variations for Orchestra,* Op. 31, are splendid, and very rich in orchestral invention. A complete series of twelve tones is used here both constructively and thematically. The theme, stated very clearly by the cellos, is treated soberly throughout the variations—the composer does not yield to the temptation to abandon himself to orchestral virtuosity, nor does he incorporate

color as an accessory. The color of the orchestra stays closely
related to the meaning of the theme at all times, and the orchestration aims only at clearness of musical diction—hence its
gracefulness. The *Variations,* Op. 31, are a complete and perfect
expression of Schoenberg's aesthetic and technical ideal—a personal entelechy. Finally, the gay opera (*heitere Oper*) *Von Heute
auf Morgen,* Op. 32, was an enormous and almost uncontested
success from the moment of its first performance in Frankfurt
in 1930. Still without concessions, without relaxing his system
of organizing material, Schoenberg creates by purely musical
means a climate that varies according to the personalities of his
characters and the dramatic situation, moving in the dream
which—this time—is a happy one, full of crystalline resonance.

After 1935 Schoenberg lived in California, where he died in
1951. His last period shows an inclination toward greater affirmation of tonality, which is translated into repetition of the
same note in the theme and insistence on certain chords and
successions which allow the ear to grasp the tonality easily. This
tendency became sharply defined in his *Violin Concerto,* Op. 36,
written in 1939, and is even more evident in the *Ode to Napoleon Bonaparte,* Op. 41, composed in 1944 for string quartet,
piano, and soloist, as well as in the *Piano Concerto.*

Schoenberg's art is magisterial. Although it passed through a
rather rigid period, which is understandable in the case of a
phenomenon so radically new, his last works show that it can
be modified and widely applied.

The work of Webern and Berg has proved from the beginning
that the potentialities of dodecaphonism can be realized by artists other than Schoenberg; and the influence he has exercised
on younger composers like Dallapiccola and Vogel, and on numerous other European and American composers, gives ample
evidence that his principles can be assimilated by different
creative temperaments. Still, it would be shortsighted to consider Schoenberg's art as the only possible route open to the
new musical era. It can properly be considered as one aspect of
modern thought. Schoenberg himself held, after 1945, "that
there are still a good many things to be said in C major." In
articles published in 1949 and 1952 in the Mexican review

Nuestra Música, he again protested against the tendency to dogmatize atonality and serial composition, affirming the right of each composer to organize his language according to his own desires and especially his right to make use of the perfect chord if he sees fit.

ANTON WEBERN was the artist who followed Schoenberg's methods most strictly. Born in Vienna on December 3, 1883, he was a student of Guido Adler in musicology and Schoenberg in composition. An unusually reserved man, he lived a retiring life at Mödling, near Vienna, where Alban Berg and Schoenberg also lived. It is not generally known that Anton Webern was a conductor of great talent. Neither personal inclination nor his ideas or character led him toward a genuine career. But he directed the choirs and orchestra of the Arbeitersbund until the Anschluss, and formed groups of exceptional value. He directed works by Bach, Schumann, and the moderns with equal fire and power of understanding. His concerts were not exhibitions of conducting talent, but musical events; he carried on in the great tradition of Gustav Mahler.

Anton Webern was an expressionist, as was Schoenberg. But while his master's temperament was composed of mystery and revolt and Berg's of resigned magnanimity, Webern's was all angelic gentleness. In that famous triad of composers, Webern incarnates celestial happiness and the peaceful contemplation of higher joys. Alban Berg told us one day that Webern made him think of Flemish painters like Memling and Van der Weyden in the freshness of his notations, the detail of his renditions, and his capacity for saying only the essential.

His art is "all made of little pointed ogival arches, spellbinding and sadistic," says Frederick Goldbeck. Ogival arches, perhaps, but I see no trace of sadism in the man the Viennese call "the master of the pianissimo."

His work includes thirty-odd compositions, almost all conceived in chamber-music form, several collections of *Lieder* accompanied by a few instruments, and some choral pieces. Theodor Wiesengrund-Adorno says that one can mark out the literary boundary Webern's music touches on, and which disappears the moment Webern begins to compose: expressionism, in the most "striking" sense of the word, morally bordered by Strindberg's expiatory characters, lyrically absolved as in Trakl's verses.

Webern's work of creation derives from a desire to communicate thoughts so tender and impressions so sweet that they can only be expressed by sounds. This explains why his music has an air of rejoicing about it. Webern also condenses his musical expression into a single moment, sometimes a single chord or more often one or two successive notes, an opposition of timbres, a tension in intervals. His pieces are necessarily very short, and are such a powerful condensation of thought that they take on the character and qualities of Japanese haiku. The perfection of his language is not an aesthetic concern but the result of the most effective and compact use of language. In this he concurs with the poets Karl Kraus and Paul Valéry in their ideas on language. And Schoenberg, in his preface to Webern's *Six Batagelles for String Quartet,* Op. 9, enlightens us: "Any glance can be developed into a poem, any sigh into a novel. But to express a whole novel in a single gesture, or happiness in a single breath—such concentration is found only where the desire to indulge oneself is absent in the same degree."

The frequently laconic sound of contemporary music is explained by the fact that repetition, pure and simple reiteration, has become intolerable. Perhaps we have learned to understand more quickly. Classical development, intended to comment on and clarify an idea, has been replaced in modern art by other harmonic, rhythmic, and orchestral means whose greater diversity allows more rapid penetration and says a great deal in little time. The brief spans of time are heavier with meaning and more laden with musical material.

Webern develops these characteristics to the fullest degree. The result is an art that was inaccessible to most of its interpreters and audiences from the outset. Executing this music requires a sort of divination, or at least an active faith, which is rarely found. Perhaps more than even with Schoenberg, it is important to grasp the spirit of counterpoint in this music.

French counterpoint [says Goldbeck], a counterpoint of themes (of things *set down*), leaves from the tonic chord and then returns to it, although after many tonal, bitonal, or even polytonal adventures. Viennese counterpoint, all in motifs (element of *movement*), abhors the perfect chord which quiets lines. Its rests and holdings of notes are prancing leaps. Hence the predilection of that school for tremolos, glissandi, and sudden checks—for any effect that recalls movement, even in immobility.

Of Webern's eleven collections of art songs, several are based on poems by Stefan George and Georg Trakl. Two of them are religious songs. Webern had a partiality for mountain dialect and Latin, and generally for basic, simple, and intense languages. All these songs must be interpreted in a spirit of contemplative intimacy, by a voice able to embrace the greatest intervals with no sign of strain and with great tenderness. Most of them are accompanied by solo instruments chosen in such a way as to surround the song with delicately vibrant resonance. Well executed in the presence of a quiet audience, these songs carry the listener into an unreal, supranatural world where he feels untouched by any material contingency.

In the instrumental works as well, the material is compressed to a minimum. Following the *Five Pieces,* Op. 5, and the *Six Bagatelles,* Op. 9, both for string quartet, the *Trio for Strings,* Op. 20, marks the end of a period during which Webern concentrated his efforts on greater and greater simplification. He achieves his ideal in the *Symphony* (for clarinet, bass clarinet, two horns, harp, and solo string quartet), Op. 21, and in the *Quartet* (for violin, clarinet, tenor saxophone, and piano), Op. 22.

This simplification does not aim at severity. It has nothing in common with the asceticism of Schoenberg's transition period. Webern seeks—and successfully—to achieve a detachment from matter. Chords and polyphony seem to have disappeared; they are used so discreetly that only a single curve sounds, almost each of whose notes is assigned to a different instrument to give it a different expressive value. This curve is not itself thematic. All meaning, in the usual sense, is absent. There remains a constantly changing sonority. The *Farbenmelodie* transports us into a jubilant, almost ecstatic state.

All of the first part of the symphony moves, so to speak, only among the interior nuances of *piano*. Rarely does a slightly louder note sound. All the notes are written without *sforzando* and without accent, so that they emit their specific sonority but not the material noise of attack. The exact duration of each note must be scrupulously respected for the liaison of all these successive and differently distributed notes. A good instance is the beginning of the first movement of the *Symphony* [*Example 25*].

The *Variations for Piano,* Op. 27, are even more bare, if such is possible. The twelve-tone system is applied in it as in the trio, quartet, and symphony. It is not directly audible, but its effect on the unity of the material can be felt.

The second variation is very unusual. Everything revolves around the note A, which appears only in the first, ninth, thirteenth, and nineteenth measures. The other notes are so divided that two successive notes are at a remove from the same interval, one above and the other below. This makes for a canon in contrary motion, but what is most interesting is that the A thus becomes a sort of symmetrical pattern, or the axis of a perfectly formed crystal [*Example 26*].

We are touching here on a side of Webern's artistry which is the most difficult to explain. The physicist and the chemist know the joy of watching a crystal grow through a microscope—its formation, the lengthening of its edges, the extension of its faces, by virtue of the constancy of its angles; the pleasure of seeing it pierced by light which leaves the material invisible and reveals only its edges by a difference of refraction. A marvelous spectacle, which causes the purest emotion, an emotion completely detached from any affectation—a splendor of number in movement.

Webern's mature music transmits a joy of the same order. To feel it, the listener must be attuned to it as for Palestrina's *Ricercari.* Webern's marvelous talent and the perfection of his art can perhaps be most fully appreciated in *Das Augenlicht,* a cantata for chorus and orchestra.

The music of Schoenberg and Webern poses not only a technical problem. Theirs is not simply a new way of writing music, but a new way of thinking as well. Their music has a new spiritual orientation. In this respect, its position in contemporary evolution is exceptional. It moves in a world unknown to other composers.

ALBAN BERG, the third great composer of the Viennese triad, leads us back into more familiar territory. Born in Vienna on February 7, 1885, Berg became Schoenberg's student; the disciple became a friend, and the friendship was then extended to include Anton Webern. The cohesion of this group, today famous, is due in great part to that friendship, to the qualities of heart, and to the faithfulness and unselfishness that distinguished the three artists. Their devoted friendship was to them no less important than their devotion to purity. It furnished for each of them a solid pillar that helped them keep intact their faith in the *ars nova* they created amid almost general hostility, until the day when their worth became evident. Their literary tastes united them as well, a taste for subtlety which put them at odds with all-powerful academic groups. At the same time their yearning for individual freedom incited them to exasperation with their social environment, which threatened to exterminate or overwhelm the individual, and tended to make man a machine, a robot, a passive being subjugated to the state. Expressionism is in part the outcome of that revolt against the mounting tide of collectivism.

The character of Alban Berg, so fascinating and charming for all who had the privilege of knowing him, is also a natural product of that tragic time when flights of spirit and personal intuition battled desperately with the indifference of the masses. His destiny was to disappear in full maturity, after succeeding in expressing man's distress so fully and giving the last shout for individualism, before transmitting all he had to pass on to us and before achieving the peace of untroubled happiness. For such was Berg's ultimate aim.

One day we were listening together to Milhaud's *Fifth Chamber Symphony* (for ten wind instruments); delighted and overjoyed, he said to me with that passionate gentleness and that look of tenderness so typical of him: "How I would like to be able to create music as happy as this!" He died in 1935, as he was finishing his second opera.

He knew the world [wrote Hektor Rottweiler] and he sidestepped it. He was melancholy and proud, dreamed of happiness and sought pain; fear, and the malice it hides behind, could be read in his eyes. His temperament was gentle, but it had a stamp of steel. Every thought that rose from one of these traits he considered from the angle of the opposed trait. He was like a seer, with the seer's slow-wakening look and great eloquent gestures. After the triumph of the first performance of *Wozzeck,* he had to be consoled all night long for the acclaim. That such a work (conceived, like Wozzeck himself when he has a vision in the field in response to his own nature, so removed from the real world) had won public approval was incomprehensible to him, and seemed to be an argument against the real worth of his opera. His whole attitude would lead one to believe that material reality did not touch him, even from a distance. He wanted many things, but hoped for none, so alone was he. And he who has no hope has nothing to lose and even less to fear; yet the world belongs to him who possesses the profound knowledge of despair. If there is any truth in the attempted comparison so often drawn between Wagner and Berg, we will find the key in the Wotan of *Götterdämmerung.* He, too, rejected worldly desires. He read the world's negativeness in the despair of his fantasy; he turned it around and mastered it in the fullness and essence of Viennese pessimism. . . . So, as in the Chinese saying, the greatest gentleness triumphs through the greatest hardship. . . . He lived between sleep and death. . . . He resembled Oscar Wilde, and knew it. . . . He was not an ascetic artist; to the contrary, he cultivated that sensuality of ear which was to produce the admirable orchestral sonority in his last works. But he considered his sensitivity and sensuality only as further materials for building his works. Confronted with these works he withdrew from his own person as easily as he did from the rest of the world. He swept out this image of his own soul by dint of composing; he had good reason to be particularly attached to Proust, who was for him the ultimate literary revelation.

He treated his own person with the prudence and indifference of the musical instrument he was for himself. This clarifies a mysterious paradox in Berg's life: he was totally egocentric, and yet entirely detached from himself. He spoke willingly of his works, but without a shadow of vanity. "It is only when I compose," he said, "that I believe myself to be Beethoven; but not after having composed."

Berg wrote music for the poetry he carried in himself. His art is not just a development based on a certain technical facility and virtuosity in composition, as in Hindemith's case. His literary sense is always perceptible in his works. It is apparent in his choice of texts for his *Lieder* and in the mastery he displays in adapting the texts of his operas. He was intuitive, but forced himself to follow a pitiless discipline—a result of meeting Schoenberg. In consequence, the number of his works is restricted. He produced slowly, except his last completed composition, the *Violin Concerto,* which he composed in six weeks. Never did he accept the easiest solution; he sought the exact solution, the most difficult to achieve. As well and clearly as did Proust, he recognized his indebtedness to Baudelaire. For him the secret of form was heavier than the secret of death, and the concert aria *Der Wein,* composed on three poems from the *Fleurs du Mal,* is not only a prologue to his unfinished opera *Lulu* but also the most striking evidence of an elective affinity.

Perhaps these reflections will define what the nineteenth century meant to Berg. If he adopted its qualities, he modified their function. He did not liquidate this inheritance, but fitted it to his inner feelings.

The texts of his two operas belong to that period—but he illuminates and salvages them. In this he is like Karl Kraus. Berg composed upon Büchner's work (*Wozzeck*) as Kraus quoted Claudius and Göcking, and the perspicacity with which Kraus defended Wedekind's *Pandora's Box* gave birth to music in the character of *Lulu.* The nineteenth century survives in Berg because it is condensed into a style. Wedekind made the remark that *kitsch* was today's gothic or baroque. Taken seriously, it defines a good part of Berg's constructive principle. It is brought out in the *Variations* for the Casti-Piani scene in *Lulu,* which Berg considered particularly successful. Nothing is more false than to think of these variations as a parody; Berg detested parody.[10]

Berg's penchant for transforming an exterior aspect by integrating it with his own concepts, a penchant that defines his affinity with the nineteenth century, could only be exercised in terms of exaggeration: he magnified extreme traits, which destroyed the bourgeois propriety of that century's aesthetic. The erotic motive principle that animates *Tristan* exceeds the limits of individual psychology; it is amplified to the point of chaos. This threat of chaos inherent in Berg's personality is frightening, and has been from the start. The greatest scandal of the Schoenberg group was provoked by one of Berg's art songs set to a poem

10. Regarding the Hussar's refrain in *Mavra,* Stravinsky said to us: "Faking is awful. But when it's done deliberately and well, it can be beautiful."

by Altenberg. There is chaos in the *Lied, "Der Blaue Reiter,"* in the second part of the quartet. Only once has this chaos burst out in full force—in the march from the *Three Pieces for Orchestra.*

When he showed me the score [says Rottweiler], I thought: It sounds as if Schoenberg's *Orchestral Pieces* and Mahler's *Ninth Symphony* were being played together, and I will never forget the enormous joy on Berg's face when he heard my opinion, which would have offended any civilized ear. "Yes," he said vehemently, "there had to come a day when we could hear how a chord of eight tones really sounds in the brasses," as if he were convinced that no audience would survive such a concert.

The quality in some of Berg's work described here as "chaotic" deserves our attention for a moment. This chaos, produced by combining seemingly irreconcilable musical elements, is also a powerful motive force. It had already been felt and forecast by the futurists. For comparison's sake, let us quote a passage from F. T. Marinetti's passage on futurist aesthetics, published in *Noi futuristi: Teorie Essenziali e Chiarificazioni* (Milan, 1917):

By imagination without bonds I mean absolute freedom from images or analogies. Until the present writers have abandoned themselves to the immediate analogy. For instance, they range an animal with a man or another animal, which results in an almost photographic reproduction of the original. *I* compare a fox terrier with boiling water. I want a larger and larger scale of analogies, deeper and more concrete relationships, even when they are very disparate. An analogy is nothing more than the profound love that links seemingly distant, diverse, or hostile things. Only by using very broad analogies can polychromatic, polyphonic, and polymorphous orchestral style translate the life of matter.

This somewhat verbose statement contains truths that Berg's "chaos" or the *Sacre du Printemps* demonstrated.

To quote Rottweiler again:

If Berg's technique of composition is the offspring of Schoenberg's *Kammersymphonie,* he nonetheless preferred—and passionately preferred—*Erwartung* and *Die glückliche Hand.* A certain lack of form in music did not displease him; he only regretted that in this case the music did not dare be more resolutely bare and chaotic. We find this blind force again in the street scene from *Wozzeck,* in the rondo of the *Double Concerto,* and in many passages in *Lulu.* For he did not cast this chaotic substance in a mold; he took it by surprise. For Berg, to form was always to combine, to superimpose things disparate or irreconcilable. He proceeded no differently in the finale of his *Double Concerto,* where he counterpoints the two first movements. From this point on, all Berg's methods of construction are ruses for trapping amorphous material. By crabwise repeats he tricks time as he tricks sonorous space with his contrapuntal constructions. Berg is unwilling to relinquish anything in his music. He wants to unite expression with construction, the shocks of chaotic language with the rapture of sonority, autobiographic confessions with an objective architecture. His thirst for happiness, desperate and overwhelming, is transformed into a mysterious need for security; he wants his music to be so sure that it can stand its ground against all the criteria one could use to measure it.

He may have dreamed of a work which could simultaneously satisfy his friends and the most narrow-minded Beckmessers. Such a deception, and so extreme a deception, is in itself chaotic and mythological. So did Polyphemus close in his cave. Fortunately, Berg did not achieve that security. Until he died he remained equally attached to the demands of the nineteenth century and to the requirements of the new art, Polyphemus and Ulysses at the same time.

Of all contemporary composers Berg is perhaps the only one whose personal life explains and justifies his works. This is why we have borrowed so lengthily from the penetrating study by Hektor Rottweiler, which deserves credit not only for painting an excellent likeness of the composer of *Wozzeck,* but for showing us at close range the intercommunication between the twentieth-century musician and nineteenth-century music. This communication is close and frequent; we will continue to analyze it in discussing Stravinsky. What Wagner is for Berg, Tchaikovsky and Rossini are for the composer of *Jeu de Cartes.*

Friedrich Sieburg once wrote that the French do not have a feeling for nature, but that what they mean by *nature* is a garden laid on the French design. Such a statement would surprise a French reader; nor is it exactly true that the French are devoid of a sense of nature. But a German who thinks he has this sense has only a partial idea, too. For the Frenchman, nature is a paradise, he sees great trees gracefully leaved; he pictures the perfect symmetry of a flower or fruit; he imagines mountains with lovely slopes and ice caps, and takes for granted the functional balance between plant and animal life. He sees all that because his native

earth shows it to him; his culture has sprung from the harmonious environment that makes the Mediterranean basin an
enchanting and peaceful place where life unfolds with ease.
Germanic culture, founded on an ungiving soil, sees such
harmony as only an exceptional state of affairs. For a man of
that culture all is combat, struggle to the death for the right to
live; he envisions the horror of a virgin forest and the tangled
reach for light of overabundant vegetation; he thinks of can-
nibals and the defensive instinct of man mistrusting man. For a
Teuton, nature is ruled by bestiality; for a Latin, it is super-
intended and controlled by man.

Neither of these divergent viewpoints can be dismissed. Both
correspond to reality, and both express partial, but complementary, aspects. French and Flemish painters portrayed the
delights of a temperate nature; Dürer sketched *danses macabres,*
Hieronymus Bosch painted nightmare visions, Lucas Cranach
deformed the human body. France is the home of the *Chevaliers
de la Table Ronde;* Germany, the *Nibelungen.*

Contemporary German expressionism naturally presents itself
in turn as an analysis, then as a synthesis, of a corrosive, destructive spirit, and puts all the horrors of that spirit on display. Its
only conception of joy is an enormous need for tenderness
and goodness, and it seeks refuge in slumber and dreaming.
Kokoschka's and Grosz's art express this state of mind. In drama,
expressionism is the child of Strindberg, of his bitter pessimism
and misogyny. Everything good, noble, and beautiful is stifled
by the crushing forces of the destructive instinct. These views
had already been aired in a famous drama in Germany, Georg
Büchner's *Wozzeck,* and were carried to the extreme in Frank
Wedekind's tragedies. At its highest pitch, expressionist art offers
a vision of a shattered, pulverized world that ends in destruction
and returns to nothingness. This is the chaos Alban Berg expresses in his music.

This conception might offend French taste. But it is equally
understandable that the temperate expression of the French, reflecting tranquillity and happiness, seems futile to those whose
souls are ravaged by violence. Both outlooks can lead to beauty,
but of different types. European art and thought owe their richness to this diversity.

Alban Berg wrote only about fifteen works, but they are almost all of exceptional value. Like Paul Dukas he devoted the utmost care to the smallest detail, and gave much thought to his over-all plan. Again like Dukas, he thought that "One should know a great deal and make music with what one does not know." The works of his first period are still completely tonal and clearly show the chromaticism of *Tristan*. These are the *Piano Sonata*, Op. 1 (1909); *Four Melodies*, Op. 2; *String Quartet*, Op. 3 (1910), and *Sieben frühe Lieder*, written in 1907 but not orchestrated and published until much later (in 1928). Then, in a very brief transition period during which he assimilated Schoenberg's language, Berg produced *Three Pieces for Clarinet and Piano*, Op. 5, in 1913, and in 1914 *Three Orchestral Pieces*, Op. 6.

Having reached the height of his powers, Berg proceeded to compose a series of masterful works: the opera *Wozzeck*, Op. 7 (1917-1922); the *Chamber Concerto for Piano, Violin, and Thirteen Wind Instruments* (1925); the *Lyric Suite for String Quartet* (1927); a concert aria, *Der Wein* (1929); a second opera, *Lulu* (which appeared in 1937); and very shortly before his death, a *Concerto for Violin and Orchestra* (1935).

Without pausing over the first works, except to indicate the intimate quality of the *Sieben frühe Lieder*, delicate love songs set to poems by various authors, and the sometimes provocative character of *Three Orchestral Pieces* (prelude, dance, march), we will go on to examine the score of *Wozzeck*, an opera in three acts and fifteen scenes based on Georg Büchner's drama. Büchner wrote the play around 1835. It was strikingly ahead of its time, if we remember that Strindberg did not begin to write his plays until 1887 (*The Father*).

Wozzeck is a soldier, poor and weak. The world around him pushes him to the limit of his endurance: first he is driven to despair by a girl, Marie, who bears him a child but who is herself weak and lets herself be seduced by the first drum major who happens by; and then by his captain, who heckles and picks on him relentlessly. To earn a little more money for Marie, since his pay is ridiculously small, Wozzeck puts himself at the service of a doctor who is interested in following the evolution of his state of mind, as he goads him little by little to madness. The miserable Wozzeck struggles against these snares, wavering between submission and impotent rage. He finally kills Marie and drowns himself in a marsh.

A résumé of the action can give no real idea of the interest or the value of the play. Dramatic tension is produced by the atmosphere in which the plot develops and by the power of condensation of the action. Like Debussy's *Pelléas et Mélisande, Wozzeck* contains scenes where what is not said is more important than what the words convey, as for example the scene where Wozzeck and his friend Andres are in the fields cutting reeds, and Wozzeck sees in the setting sun a portent of the twilight of the world; the scene with the soldiers, harassed and brutalized, asleep on their beds of planks while Wozzeck sits awake and weeps; the scenes on the edge of the marsh, in the evening mist; the unconcern of the orphan when the other children bring the news of his mother's death. This is poignant and violent, and sheers away from naturalism to take on a semi-mystical atmosphere. Wozzeck and Marie alone are human. The doctor, the captain, and the drum major are only puppets. The tale is perfect for setting to music, and especially Berg's music. This combination was bound to produce a masterpiece.

Its musical beauty cannot be explained in words. At best, we can only point out how the listener should be disposed to be receptive to that beauty. The marsh, the scene where the drama unfolds, impregnates the whole score with the ferment of its putrid waters. Everything is stagnation and boundless despair. The dialogue of most of the characters is a display of cynical brutality, contrasting with the prolonged sob, resigned and impotent, of Wozzeck and Marie. The beauty of the score comes from the force and perfection with which atmosphere is invoked. This is the type of beauty found in Dostoevsky's novels, not a Racine-like beauty. The quality of the score is high from beginning to end. There are outstanding moments, of course: in the first act, Wozzeck's discomfort when he is afraid of the silence of the country and tries to read omens in the sky and earth; the military march and the lullaby sung by Marie; in the second act, the extraordinary tapestry of dances, songs, and cries of distress, the cabaret scene that makes us think of certain scenes in Gorky's *The Lower Depths;* then the soldiers' sleep; and finally,

almost the entire last act, Marie reading the Bible, the terrible
scene when Wozzeck drowns himself in the marsh after the murder, and the pitiful conclusion of the children's indifference.
Noteworthy as well are all the interludes which, as in *Pelléas et
Mélisande,* tie the scenes together and sustain the atmosphere by
condensing the material of the scene just ended.

Begun in 1917, the score of *Wozzeck* was finished in 1922.
The twenty-six scenes of Büchner's drama are condensed into
fifteen. Berg retained only the essential, and his music creates
an atmosphere that is lacking in the spoken drama.

Büchner's work, thanks to Berg's conception of it, has become
larger and more human, and has gained in persuasive force.
The score was written with scrupulous care, following the discipline of the Schoenberg school. Berg denied having tried to
revive old-style opera. And in fact there is nothing in this work
that replaces or modifies its theatrical aspects. What makes it
very strong dramatically is the manner in which Berg organized
his music to give the stage work qualities it needed. He avoided
dividing the audience's attention between action and music.
To achieve unity, he made the music itself the action, and did
not allow motifs and themes to be dictated by the entrance of
the characters or by any element foreign to the natural musical
flow. Dynamics, color, timbre, rhythm, and melodies are all
arranged as in a symphony, the music follows its own laws alone,
and the movement of the dramatic action corresponds to the
movement of the music. On the one hand Berg takes the Wagnerian principle of symphonic development in the drama as his
point of departure; on the other, he adopts an attitude opposed
to Wagner's. Wagner subordinated music to drama; Berg subordinates drama to music, to such a degree that even stage direction is involved in the music. The gestures of the actors are
directed with the exact timing the music requires: when Wozzeck stamps his foot in impotent rage, it is at precisely the moment when a certain chord or accent is sounded which had been
heralded and prepared measures before and which had therefore
become musically inevitable. That chord and that accent do not
interrupt the music because the action calls for them.

Wagner had translated the symphonic development section
into the dramatic domain. Berg goes further and uses the com-

plete sonata form. The leading motif, the Wagnerian leitmotiv, which comments on the ideas of the text and introduces
the characters, is replaced by another principle: the leading
theme, whose function is symphonic only, as are the themes of
fugues or of a cycle of variations.

The motif, a group of several notes, has no particular expression. The theme, a more important formal element, carries an
expression that it imposes on the whole development dependent
on it. With its organizing power, assuring the unity of the musical matter, it also assures the expressive unity of the musical
drama. It imparts the same unity to the melody, harmony, and
rhythm.

Paul Dukas, in *Ariane et Barbe-Bleue,* also makes use of a
uniting theme. He built his drama as symphonic movements.
Berg extends the application of this method: the score of *Wozzeck* includes a passacaglia (twenty-one variations), fugues, a
chorale, and variations. Yet the architecture stays hidden from
the audience, whose attention must not be drawn to the outlines, the skeleton of the work. The only thing it should see
is the fate of the soldier Wozzeck.

At the same time that he uses the large forms, Berg calls on
all the resources of Schoenbergian counterpoint. He applies
them to his passacaglia, variations, and chorale. He establishes
a sort of ideal proportion, a golden mean between Wagner and
Schoenberg.

We shall not go into detail on the contrapuntal composition
of *Wozzeck* or Berg's other works. What we have said about it in
speaking of Schoenberg will suffice to guide the reader in these
scores. Let us pass directly to what is distinctive about *Wozzeck.*
Wozzeck, the character, is statically conceived. There is no development of a personality or the action. From the beginning of
the drama, Wozzeck is in the last throes of despair. There can
thus be no progress, and the music remains in the state it was
in at the opening. As we have already said, the music is dominated by stagnation, which is attained by numerous passages
where the harmony is static, due either to a sort of balancing of
the chords [*Example 27*] or to a succession of chords with the
same, or almost the same, degree of tension [*Example 28*]. These
two examples also show that Berg did not adopt Schoenberg's

integrally contrapuntal method. The style is often harmonic, with the use of unresolved appoggiaturas in the tradition of Debussy and Ravel. The tonal center is audible: the first excerpt is composed of unresolved triple appoggiaturas in the perfect chord of G major; in the same fashion, the second begins and ends in C major. Another way of broaching harmonic immobility is shown in the famous passage when the marsh mist is rising and enveloping Wozzeck: a chromatic succession of identical chords on each step of the twelve-tone scale [*Example 29*]. Moreover, there is general use of the frictions caused by minor seconds, which establishes tonal uncertainty [*Example 30*], as do the tritones and fourth-chords [*Example 31*]. Complexes of sound are always so written as to be clearly understandable by their own specific sound. Complicated chords are often introduced by an arpeggio, by the successive entry of the notes [*Example 32*]; the harmony is also very often caused by the meeting of voices, and contrapuntal language occurs as frequently as harmonic.

Willy Reich notes correctly that the unity of the work is based in part on what he calls "the exchange of dimensions." The melodic line, the chord, and the rhythm continually interchange roles: chord becomes rhythm, rhythm jells into chord, the rhythmic motif becomes melodic, and the melody is distilled into a rhythm; melody congeals into chord, and chord is resolved into melody. These are transformations we have met in studying Schoenberg's technique.

The orchestration is unusual. *Three Orchestral Pieces* had already revealed the assignment of long solo melodies to the horns, trumpets, and trombones, and scarcity of chords set down all at once—and these not grouping the voices which introduce one instrument after another into the chord, thus modifying the timbre as the chord is built up. This caused extraordinary activation and intensification of orchestral color which was to find its highest development in *Lulu*.

In *Wozzeck*, the complete orchestra is utilized chiefly in partial groupings constantly rearranged. Solo string instruments are often used in combination with solo winds. A military band, a cabaret ensemble (two violins, clarinet, accordion, guitar, and bombardon), and a chamber orchestra (the same instruments as in Schoenberg's *Kammersymphonie*) are isolated from the main orchestra but also combine with it. *Example 33* shows the combination of the cabaret group with the orchestra and illustrates that reconciliation of the irreconcilable which expresses chaos, here made possible through orchestral differentiation. *Example 34* shows another dramatic effect of exceptional power: a dizzying cadence by the main orchestra on which the chamber orchestra imposes a rapid abatement.

The slides of chromatic chords during the marsh scene, treated with the same rich orchestral inventiveness and the same care to make everything plain with the clarity of the sound, create an indescribably impressive moment.

We cannot finish this appraisal without citing the famous example of the unison that ends the second scene in Act 3: all the instruments, one after the other, begin in *ppp* and guide the shading toward *fff*—a crescendo in nuance and timbre which sounds like the trumpets of Judgment Day.

Wozzeck was a triumphant success. On February 9, 1930, the Prussian Academy of Art elected Alban Berg an associate member. On that day twenty German-language theaters and the Vienna State Opera played *Wozzeck*. The work has now been produced all over the world, and has entered the repertory of many opera companies.

Since the days of Wagner, opera has become what was called not long ago an exceptional work. It is quite true that repertory opera, daily opera, belongs to the nineteenth century. This genre, aimed at the general public, has today been replaced by the movies. But almost all the great composers are still drawn to the theater. Their works are not the kind to be included in popular repertories, due sometimes only to difficulty of staging. These are works that are the focus of the great annual festivals like Salzburg and Florence, festivals that have grown in number since 1945.

Berg's last works display a more definite melodic and harmonic conception. Without becoming melodic in the proper sense of the word, they are composed with more and more well-defined themes. To understand this evolution, it is essential to remember the distinctions among motif, theme, and melody. A motif is very short, and has its own characteristics, but alone it lacks expression. It is simply a formative element. A theme is more important and has a specific expression. It too can well be used in construction, because it is not so fixed that it cannot undergo broad transformations of rhythm and intervals. Melody is a being unto itself. With no aid from contrapuntal lines or supporting harmonies, melody is endowed not only with its own expression but also with complete meaning, achieved through its rhythmic structure and the stress produced by the succession of notes, in a given order, whose tension is measured in relation to a fundamental. Melody is a polarized being that will not tolerate inversions, cancrizans, or rhythmic modifications without changing the meaning it carries. It is a creation of the modal or tonal system. Berg stopped at the theme, the art of which dwells in contrapuntal construction.

The work immediately following *Wozzeck* is the *Concerto for Violin, Piano and Thirteen Wind Instruments,* which is dedicated to Arnold Schoenberg on his fiftieth birthday (1924). The three key elements on which its construction rests are anagrams of the names of the Schoenbergian triad (Schoenberg, Webern, and Berg), which show the common characteristic of the tritone as their dominant interval [*Example 35*]. The first movement is a *tema scherzoso con variazioni* for piano and wind instruments. In the movement, the theme takes form in successive strides as if the composer's imagination were pushing it each step a little closer to full bloom, a trait also found in *Lulu* and in the *Concerto for Violin* [*Example 36*]. The second movement is a deeply pathetic adagio, tender and voluptuous, played by the violin and the winds without the piano. The center of its main theme is formed of the motifs of themes A, B, and C with the tritone interval [*Example 37*]. It unfolds gently until, after 120 measures, it attains a culminating point, and is then repeated as a whole in varied cancrizans. This system of development might seem arbitrary at first sight; and it would be in tonal music, but not in music conceived in the system of twelve tones related only to each other with no relationship to a fundamental. The crabwise movement of this adagio is as expressive as its *recto* direction and produces calm to the same degree that stress has been built up. The adagio is the loveliest movement in the work. The flow of tenderness which it is intended to evoke can be considered an homage to Webern, and the variations as a song in honor of Schoenberg. A splendid cadence for piano and violin, a fireworks of all of the work's themes, leads into the final rondo ritmico, a diabolic fantasy in which Berg counterpoints the elements of the variations and adagio movements in every possible way.

A repetition of the whole piece is hinted at, but it is superfluous. Better that it pass unnoticed (and the composer agrees) and the attention focus directly on the magnificent coda, within which all formal elements draw together progressively, boil down to the essential, form a dizzying stretto, and end with a pedal chord in the piano on a four-note motif sounded from the beginning of the introductory cadence, a final explosion leaving all the elements exhausted, to fall into abrupt silence [*Example 38*].

Lyricism reaches fruition in this chamber concerto, as in the *Lyrische Suite,* written in 1926. Like the concerto, the *Suite* is based on a latent program: a portrait of the composer, the sensitive and bizarre musician. Six movements unfold. Their titles describe their moods: allegretto gioviale, andante amoroso, allegro misterioso (containing a trio estatico), adagio appassionnato, presto delirando (with a tenebroso passage), and at the end, largo desolato. It is a beautiful masterpiece and one of the favorites of quartet musicians. The initial allegretto takes the form of an undeveloped sonata. "The joining of the parts," says Erwin Stein in the preface of the score, "is just a little loose; the internal and reciprocal affinity of the movements is only vaguely marked, despite all the skill applied to thematic relations and other relations of form." The alternation of the three rapid movements with the slow movements creates a dynamic gradation: allegretto—allegro—presto. The three slow movements produce an expressive gradation: andante—adagio—largo. A number of the movements are built on the twelve-tone system, and the six movements are joined by the reappearance in each of one of the themes of the preceding movement. *Der Wein* (1929), a concert aria based on three poems of Baudelaire, returns to less hidden expression, and reveals a feeling that prepares for the atmosphere of the second opera.

Frank Wedekind, the author of the tragedies *Erdgeist (The Earth Spirit)* (1895) and *Die Büchse der Pandora (Pandora's Box)*, was born in Hanover in 1864. He traveled widely as a lecturer, actor, producer, and editor; he died in 1918. Wedekind was an implacable naturalist: "He threw himself on life," wrote Camille Poupeye,

. . . and forced it to give up its secret to him. And what he read in the deepest folds of the human soul were the carnivorous instinct, a tenacious will to live, and, beneath everything, those passions called bestial and unnatural, all the more hidden since they had been the object of the holy horror of genteel hypocrites. Wedekind said that he was studying and revealing to us the unleashed animal in man, the perpetually lustful beast tormented by its monstrous appetites and taking vagabond copulation as its natural right and irresistible need. It is hardly surprising that the writings of the cruel German dramatist were banned by a conventional (in appearance, at least) self-respecting society. Nor is it so astonishing that, after this society had crumbled, the democratic forces which provoked the collapse proclaimed Wedekind a precursor and prophet. . . . The avant-garde of German letters saw Wedekind as a master, and thought that what should above all be learned from this pitilessly questioning and cynical dramatist was the marvelously flexible and trenchant instrument with which he endowed poets and which constituted one of the most striking characteristics of expressionist theater: that expressive, hammering, articulate, and vibrantly dynamic style.

And here is how Poupeye sums up the two-play tragedy of *Lulu:*

In the prologue an animal trainer invites the public to follow the acts of the show. While most of the acts feature only domestic or tamed animals, he shows wild beasts and saves as the chief attraction of the show a terrible serpent, a marvelous beast created to drag man into sin, ensnare him, seduce, corrupt, poison, and murder him without arousing the slightest suspicion. . . . And Lulu, sweet and rosy, dressed as Pierrot, is carried onto the scene by a potbellied valet. In *The Earth Spirit,* Lulu, a little flower-girl of doubtful origin who at the age of twelve walked barefoot among the tables at the Alhambra Café and whose first protector, Schön, the editor of a large newspaper, had edu·

cated her and given her in marriage to an elderly doctor friend, appears before us in the fullness of her beauty and good fortune.

Lulu is a Circe by instinct, ambition, and above all whim. She causes the death of her first husband, who has a stroke when he finds her in the arms of Schwartz, her portrait painter. Poor Schwartz is horrified, and implores heaven for the strength and freedom of spirit "to be just a little happy. For her, only for her." As for Lulu, she doubtless feels a pang at the sight of the corpse, but the thought that follows immediately is that she is now rich. The painter, married now to Lulu and at the height of his talent, worries constantly that his happiness will crumble. But Lulu becomes an Eve and feels ridiculous at being only a wife to her husband. She is so restless that Schön, whom she has tried to tempt but who is on the defensive because of his forthcoming marriage, asks her if she is not worried about feeling the whip again. "Maybe I am!" she answers. When Schwartz learns of his wife's past, he goes mad and cuts his throat. The blood falls on Schön's hand; Lulu wipes it off with her perfumed handkerchief and tells him that not a spot will remain. And when Schön calls her a monster she answers with a diabolic smile: "You will marry me anyhow." Schön, drawn into the trap his young protégé has lured him toward from the outset, will be the third victim. Lulu is now dancing in a ballet written by Schön's son. Alva, who is secretly in love with Lulu, has been chiding his father for some time for not having formalized his relationship with his charge by marriage after the death of his first wife. Lulu is sought after by Prince Escerny who is enchanted by the physical and spiritual grace of her every movement; but Lulu will know no peace until she has forced Schön to break off his betrothal and capitulate totally to her charms. But hardly is she mistress of the household before she opens Schön's doors to a horde of parasites, one of whom is an old beggar who claims, rightly or wrongly, to be her father and who lusts after her. In this milieu we meet the young student Hugenberg, who is madly taken with the fiery Lulu, and Countess Geschwitz, a strange lesbian who is also in love with the sinful young woman. Alva, who is more and more bewitched, gives in to the brazen temptress, and when he finally tells her he has loved her always she replies, tenderly stroking his hair: "I poisoned your mother."

Schön finally discovers the perfidy of this angel of destruction. Disgusted with being dragged through the mud and ridiculed by this peculiar group, he decides to do away with the worthless creature; but she seizes on a moment of distraction caused by a call for help by the student hidden under the table and strikes down the only man she says she has ever loved. Then she throws herself, terrified, at Alva's feet and begs him not to let her fall into the hands of the police: "I am still young," she cries, "I will be faithful to you all my life. I will be yours, only yours."

In *Pandora's Box* Lulu disintegrates before our eyes. She escapes from prison, where she has been sentenced for a ten-year term, with the help of the ever-faithful Countess Geschwitz. This strange friend has taken advantage of a cholera epidemic and succeeded in passing her as a corpse under the noses of the guards. Everything is ready for her escape to Paris with the acrobat Rodrigo, who has agreed to marry her. Rodrigo knows how to break in animals as well—"I've ordered a whip made of hippopotamus hide, two inches thick," he says. "Female flesh doesn't care whether you make love to it or beat it. All it needs is a little distraction and it will stay firm and healthy."

Hugenberg, the student, who has escaped from the penitentiary, reads in the paper that Schön's murderer has died in prison and proclaims that her loss has destroyed all his interest in life. Alva, who is still entranced by her, after long hesitation crosses the border with the fugitive. The couple are next seen in Paris, still fairly prosperous; but disaster is imminent. The pretty Countess Adélaïde d'Oubra (alias Lulu) entertains an ambiguous crowd, and a doubtful marquis, Casti-Piani, who carries on a white slave trade, threatens to inform on her unless she agrees to enhance a house of prostitution in Cairo with her charms. Rodrigo, the rejected suitor, is no less hot in pursuit of the beauty and hardly less pressing in his blackmail than the disreputable Marquis. But his story will end tragically as well, for Lulu gives him over to her drunken father, who cures him forever of his taste for informing by entrusting him to the discreet waters of the Seine. Lulu escapes Casti-Piani's men disguised as a groom and turns up next in London, fallen to the lowest form of prostitution. A foul garret now shelters her activities as a decayed prostitute under the jealous eye of Alva, whom she has infected and exhausted, and the tender eye of her poor foster father who badgers her constantly for alcohol and love. When they are literally collapsing from hunger and cold, Lulu goes to wait in the street under the driving rain to lure rich clients; but she has too much character left to play the common streetwalker and cannot bring herself even to rob them properly. So, one after another, she brings on a sort of missionary, vowed to silence, who gives her money; a Negro prince, who kills Alva with a single stroke of his weighted stick; a Swiss student of philosophy, whose caressing glance she prefers to his small fee, but who takes flight on seeing the corpse; and finally Jack the Ripper, who is intrigued by her mouth, steals her money, and then mutilates her vilely. Nothing, not even the blackest scenes from

Gorky's *The Lower Depths,* equals the degradation pictured by Wedekind in the last act of this horrifying drama.

We have given this extensive résumé to show the atmosphere of expressionism at its apex. The crudeness of the drama is shocking, but it is difficult to take it seriously with its extremism and number of deaths. Tragedy here approaches caricature, as in George Grosz's drawings. Yet this double tragedy (Wedekind later condensed them into a single play) has extraordinary movement and incontestable dramatic power, moments of real beauty, and rich and subtle treatment of the polymorphous character of Lulu.

This character is decidedly what attracted Alban Berg. He alone was capable of composing a unified score and relegating to the background the mass of facts, events, and personages who clutter up the play. The music has the singular virtue of simplifying the play. Slower in developing and communicating ideas than are words, it leaves everything in shadow which is secondary in the play and expresses only the essential. Berg chose the leading scenes from Wedekind's drama and composed an opera in three acts around them. He places Alva on a plane with Lulu, balancing Lulu's seductiveness and irresponsibility with Alva's desire and fervor. Other personages are not sacrificed to Alva; the text has not been changed. But the music Berg created for the two protagonists is so suggestive and effective that it impregnates parts of the score where it seems to be absent. There is no one theme for Lulu or Alva; there is an ensemble of several themes, rhythms, and harmonies to characterize the two roles. The remarkable thing is that the music does not share the exaggeration of the text; it is not naturalistic and does not emphasize the intentional grossness and the often disgusting tone of the dialogue. Berg's expressionism is not carried to the extreme of ugliness, and as we have already pointed out, the composer has in a way salvaged the text and immersed it in his own sensitivity. He looked on the drama from above. He wrote *Lulu* as Baudelaire wrote *Les Fleurs du Mal*—his opera vibrates with evil passions, but their transformation in the spirit and beauty of the music makes it an inspiring work. Some time before composing *Lulu,* Berg had worked on poems from Baudelaire's *Le Vin,* adhering strictly to the twelve-tone system with the aim of avoiding their disorder of passions and imposing a formalized beauty on them. To write *Lulu* as he wanted to write it, this was the only solution possible.

The style of this work and the style of *Wozzeck* are quite different. Instead of a leading theme Berg uses such a number of themes that they are almost perfect melodies, as we can judge from those fragments on which the music for Lulu and Alva is based: *Example 39* arouses a feeling of restrained eroticism; the heroine's irresistible seductiveness is evoked in *Example 40.* The stagnant atmosphere of *Wozzeck* is in no way recalled. The friction of minor seconds has disappeared; on the contrary, everything points to continual movement. Harmony varies widely, from resolutions on the perfect chord to pure atonality, with the result that stresses draw on a large scale of intensity. Corresponding to a declared melodic curve are certain harmonies which themselves are dominant—a complex formed by diminished ninths and elevenths, and appoggiaturas not resolved by the dominant seventh, fleeting harmonies usually introduced by very plastic contrapuntal movements [*Example 41*]. The last chord of this example, with its A and D♭ in the upper register of the piano or vibraphone, plays an important part in the score: it is repeated each time Lulu calls on all her resources in a difficult situation. Certain particularly brutal passages by the piano, combined with the brasses, form agglomerations of sound like those shown in *Example 42.* The explosive peroration at the end of the second act [*Example 43*] is written in one of several main rhythmic schemes. The vocal music is very melodic. It has hardly any of the large leaps between intervals common in Schoenberg's and Webern's music and is often written in successive notes. In the dialogue, melody begun by one voice is taken up by the other with no interruption in the continuity of the music. The orchestra seems to incorporate the melodic flow [*Example 44*]. The unusual vocal sonority that marked each singing role in *Wozzeck* has entirely disappeared. In *Lulu,* the music comes in one swoop—the characters lose their individuality in a torrent of music that reveals the drama as a whole rather than in episodic detail. In addition, contrary to the muffled treatment required by the atmosphere in *Wozzeck,* the music in *Lulu* radiates color and the twelve-tone chords are luminous. The orchestra, moreover, is remarkably rich and powerful; the glow of Ravel's *Daphnis et Chloé* seems pale by comparison. Of all existing music, the symphonic suite Berg drew from *Lulu* is the work that has most enriched the orchestral palette. The gratifying, unremitting play of color brings the audience to recognize the seductive power of this monstrous woman.

We shall not go into a discussion of the symphonic construction of *Lulu;* its principle is the same as that in *Wozzeck,* but more generalized. The details of technique in *Lulu* insure clarity, transparency, and openness, and give the audience an impression of stylistic simplification. But actually *Lulu* is no less complex than *Wozzeck.*

Among the most beautiful passages of the work are the *Lied* in the second act which Lulu sings with disarming sincerity; the long duet sung by Lulu and Alva, also in the second act; and Alva's hymn to Lulu's beauty. There are also three magnificent interludes. The first, preceding the third scene in Act I, is filled with loving tenderness. The interlude entitled *Ostinato,* which plays during the second-act film showing a condensation of several scenes from the play, seems to be a disordered tumult, but is in fact carefully organized. In Act III the interlude between the two scenes, variations on a music-hall song composed by Wedekind himself, is played to evoke Lulu's progressive decline. The most beautiful music of the whole opera is the poignantly painful adagio in the last scene.

There is one theatrical fault in Lulu: there is too much text, the dialogue is too crowded. The thousand and one little details that are recited animate the naturalistic play but are incomprehensible in the opera. Since the music cannot follow this swarm of events, and its development and unity are therefore not influenced by them, there are certain moments of duality that divide the audience's attention disconcertingly.

Berg never heard his last opera. But he at least had the joy of hearing the *Symphony of Lulu,* a concert extract, which contains the musical substance of the work.

When he had finished *Lulu,* Berg was asked to write a violin concerto. He was about to refuse when he learned of the death of a young girl whom he was very fond of. The pain of loss gave him lyric incentive for a new work, which he wrote as a sort of instrumental requiem. It was to be his last composition. The concerto is dedicated "In Memory of an Angel." The music begins on the four open notes of the violin, which are repeated by the clarinets and harp. This idea is then developed in arpeggios, a scheme which the author must have liked, to judge by its importance in the double concerto, in *Lulu,* and in the fundamental element of the *Concerto for Violin.* This last composition is in two sections. The first begins with an andante, which is followed by an allegretto. In the second, an allegro concludes with an adagio. The work moves along a grade of expression, as does the *Lyrische Suite.* The serene initial andante leads into the tender liveliness of the allegretto. This scherzando, in 6-8 time, has a peaceful grace with no hint of agitation. The feeling it transmits makes the listener think of certain allegrettos in Mahler's works, especially in the *Fourth Symphony.* The allegretto passes imperceptibly into a moderate waltz movement, which in turn and with equal gentleness—it could be said with love—introduces an Austrian *Ländler* treated with pastoral freshness and simplicity. The movement dies away, like a sigh of regret, to conclude on a nostalgic minor seventh chord. This same chord marks the beginning of the impassioned, fiery allegro rubato, which is developed as a cadence whose rhythm seems inspired by the *Ländler.* But after its climax this vitality fades, seeming to obey the call of the violin, which slows the movement by announcing the melody of the final chorale. The concluding chorale is written around the verse: *"Es ist genug! so nimm, Herr, meinen Geist. . . . Mein Jesus kommt: Es ist genug! Herr, wenn es dir gefällt, so spanne mich doch aus. Nun gute Nacht, o Welt! Ich fahr ins Himmelshaus. . . . Ich fahre sicher hin mit Frieden. Mein grosser Jammer bleibt darnieder."* The chorale inspires an indescribable emotion. The violin states the melody, which is taken up by four clarinets in the harmonization Bach uses in the cantata *O Ewigkeit, du Donnerwort.* The music simplifies. The violin lays aside its solo role to join—or draw to itself—the violin section of the orchestra in a final and fervent commentary on the chorale. Distantly a last good-by sounds to the homeland, an echo of the *Ländler;* a last arpeggio wings upward and is dissolved on the heights; and then, the final *adieu* of the four open notes of the violin. Alban Berg leaves us; he sings his own requiem. Suddenly everything seems to be resolved. Pain, tension, desire, despair, everything which was his personality has gone. In the lucidity of the last days of his life, everything clarified and simplified.

What remains for us is this marvelous concerto, one of those works that dominate their period and are both its finest ornament and justification.

Schoenberg, Webern, and Berg form a homogeneous group. They created works that fall under the sign of expressionism, but which nonetheless did not reach the extreme of German pictorial expressionism. Their artistic aim is movement without pause or conclusion. Their language, born of the chromaticism of *Tristan und Isolde,* evolved toward a hyperchromaticism often called atonality. Actually, it always retains a discernible tonal effect, either because the tonalities change from chord to chord, or because one tone, while remaining latent, temporarily dominates. The word atonal is justified by what is heard in the first case, but not in the second. A given order of expression determines the language. Rhythm has lost some of its structural importance; the music is like a river, a flowing stream marked out with accents of expression. The twelve-tone system, which emerged from atonality to fulfill requirements of form, wards off anarchy and compensates for the loss of the tonal center of gravity as well as for the loss of articulated rhythm. When it is strictly applied, it leads to the most rigorous sort of formalism. Aside from such a severe style, it provides new and highly important means of constructing and developing which are applicable in disciplines other than atonal. The orchestra is still treated as a single instrument, a machine for generating timbres, used to create a sort of sonorous flow with a continuity which has a magic, spellbinding power.

Technically speaking, the movement Schoenberg began is the newest of all the movements that have developed in modern music. But from the point of view of expression and meaning, it is less up to date, since it is related to a conception of life that belongs to the end of the nineteenth century. Exception should be made for some of Webern's and Schoenberg's compositions which the writers kept free from any element of emotion and wrote with absolute adherence to form, analogous to Bach's *Art of the Fugue* or Frescobaldi's *Ricercari*.

The language created is a fixed system, and the works composed in it are equally fixed. The concept of atonality, which gave birth to works of merit, found itself in difficulty when faced with the problem of form. Since that day it has marked time. To continue bearing fruit it had to be less radically used. Alban Berg followed this line of thought and reintroduced a more durable and consequently a more constructive sense of traditional tonality into that absolute chromaticism which is, after all, atonality. Schoenberg, as well, chose this solution for works composed after 1938.

The history of atonality and serial composition does not end with the disappearance of its exponents. Dodecaphonism, to which the world of music paid relatively little heed before 1940, was adopted by numbers of European and South American musicians after 1945. The younger generation in a chaotic world, confused and shocked by the horror of the Second World War, needed to express its anguish and create some order in its music. Schoenberg's musical techniques seemed to offer it the only way to voice its despair. They felt that the somber fatalism and violent revolt expressed in *The Survivor of Warsaw* and *Wozzeck* were inextricably linked with dodecaphonism. The result has been a considerable number of compositions none of which reveal creative temperament, and all of which invariably give the impression of being students' exercises. Imagination is so lacking in these works, as much on reading as on hearing, that it is not hard to guess what will happen in the measures following those being heard. Dodecaphonism has become academic. There are, nonetheless, exceptions to this banal and impossible situation—the interpretation of dodecaphonism by the Italians, headed by Dallapiccola, and a few French musicians, the most significant of whom is Pierre Boulez.

3

IGOR STRAVINSKY

NO OTHER CONTEMPORARY work has caused the uproar that *Le Sacre du Printemps* did in 1913. While Schoenberg worked in silence and communicated his efforts and discoveries only to a small circle of devotees and interested parties, *The Firebird* and *Petrushka* revealed to the general public the existence of an extraordinarily powerful musician. The immense success of the Ballet Russe had helped spread the name of Stravinsky. *The Firebird* was an apotheosis, the final star-burst of the marvelous fireworks shot off by the impressionists and the Russian school of the Five; *Petrushka* had worked the magic of its pulsing life and the singular effect of its popular traits. *Le Sacre du Printemps* was like a sudden explosion which, without warning, crumbled the whole architecture of music as it had been conceived up to that time. General consternation followed the first performance of that choreographic symphony, and some time had to pass before the world understood that something had changed—that after *Le Sacre* music was to lose its traditional mode of being, and that not only impressionism but all nineteenth-century music was involved.

So violent and unexpected was the shock that for many years Stravinsky was known to the public and to most musicians only as "the composer of *Le Sacre du Printemps.*" His whole work was listened to and judged in relation to this composition, which is indeed a work of genius; but it is also true that it does not represent Stravinsky's complete personality, and that by itself it cannot explain the tenor of its author's art.

Schoenberg built a system. His construction took shape and then proceeded to perfect itself from one work to the next. Whatever its newness, whatever difficulties the listener had in accustoming himself to it, he could at least grasp immediately the sense of Schoenberg's revolution and understand his position in the face of the musical problem. Not so with Stravinsky. The world sought in vain to understand his development; no work resembled the work preceding it or following it. Stravinsky himself was sparing in his explanations, and what he did consent to say was so different from what musicians generally say about their art that his clarifications were often badly misinterpreted. Not until 1929 did some writers take the risk of attempting a detailed commentary on his work: Boris de Schlœzer, André Schæffner, Herbert Fleischer, and the present author wrote monographs between 1929 and 1931 on Stravinsky's work, and to these can be added the very elaborate *Souvenirs sur Igor Stravinsky*, by C. F. Ramuz. The perspective was still too narrow; each of these writers grasped but a part of the truth. Only today, nearly fifty years after the creation of *Le Sacre du Printemps*, does it seem possible to form an idea of the creative temperament of the composer and the significance of his works.

We have placed this study immediately after the one devoted to Schoenberg for two reasons. The first is chronological: in the history of modern music Schoenberg was the first to strike out, around 1910, toward a real reform. In 1911, Stravinsky broke with the immediate past in composing *Petrushka*. The two composers thus set out simultaneously. The second reason is, if I may use the expression, dialectical: since Schoenberg's art is viewed as a thesis, it is suitable to designate Stravinsky's as an antithesis. Stravinsky is in opposition to Schoenberg in the conception of his ideas as well as in their execution.

The two composers are the two poles between which all the music of our time gravitates. Whatever the differences and details that separate or ally other contemporary composers, whatever their greatness and sometimes their genius, they will all have an affinity for either the composer of *Pierrot Lunaire* or of *Oedipus Rex*—Schoenberg representing, in the words of Arthur Lourié, the "neo-Gothic" movement and Stravinsky the "neo-classic," the former concerned with expression as a point of departure, the latter with form. These two opposed directions, which can be found throughout the history of art, have been called in an earlier work (*Signification de la Musique*) "expressionism" and "formalism," the term expressionism extending to all periods, but formalism meaning not a type of academism but the art in all ages whose point of departure is form.

IGOR STRAVINSKY was born at Oranienbaum June 18, 1882.[11] His father held the position of vocal soloist to the emperor in the Russian court. From the age of nine on, Stravinsky displayed remarkable talent as a pianist. This fact persuaded his father to send him for regular lessons to a student of Anton Rubinstein's. The composer spent his youth partly in Oranienbaum and partly in St. Petersburg. A number of years passed uneventfully. The young student then entered the University of St. Petersburg, where he studied law and received his doctorate.

Still undecided about his artistic vocation, Stravinsky set out on a trip and visited the principal countries of Europe. In 1902 he met Rimsky-Korsakov in Heidelberg and developed a warm admiration for him.

This acquaintance decided Stravinsky on a musical career. He began by giving himself a solid intellectual foundation. He read extensively, visited museums, and attended as many concerts as possible. When he went back to Russia he showed his first attempts at composition to Rimsky-Korsakov, who agreed to oversee his musical studies. His first works were *Sonata for Piano* (1903); a suite of songs based on Pushkin's texts, *Le Faune et la Bergère* (1905); some melodies; *Scherzo Fantastique* based on Maeterlinck's *The Life of the Bee* (1908), and a *Pastorale* for voice and piano. It was also in 1908 that he wrote *Fireworks,* for the marriage of Maximilian Steinberg and Rimsky-Korsakov's daughter, the work which was to attract the attention of the musical world. He then wrote *Four Etudes for Piano* and began composing a lyric tale, *The Nightingale,* based on Andersen's story (1909).

While he was working on the first act of this composition, something occurred which decisively changed his life and career. At St. Petersburg, an organized group of highly cultured painters and writers fired by the ambition to forge ahead were publishing a review called *Mir Iskusstvo* (*World of Art*). Their leader was

11. That is, June 5 on the Russian calendar.

a young man who was not a writer or a painter or a musician, but who understood the life of art perfectly. He was gifted with exceptional insight, and dreamed of producing splendid spectacles with dancing and painting, harmoniously balanced. This young man was Sergei Diaghilev, and he had from the start recognized Stravinsky's remarkable talent. Diaghilev had decided to organize a great exposition of Russian art in Paris. Theatrical art in Russia was, and still is, of high quality. The theater was the spiritual center around which the best resources were grouped, and it was the object of the most detailed attention. Diaghilev decided to go to Paris with an operatic and ballet troupe to perform *Boris Godunov* and ballets by the best Russian composers. He formed a magnificent troupe of performers which included Chaliapin, Nijinsky, Pavlova, and Fokine. And he urged Stravinsky to compose a ballet, which was to be *The Firebird*. In 1909 dancers, singers, choreographers, painters, and musicians left for Paris. The Russian Festival of Châtelet was a complete and triumphal success. The scintillating art of the Russians captivated Paris and Western Europe with its colorful music and the almost musical harmony of its décors exhibited at the time when impressionism was on the wane and the *fauves* were coming to the fore.

From that moment until Diaghilev's death in 1929, the annual festival of the Ballet Russe was the crown jewel of every season, as much in London as in Paris. Diaghilev's intelligence and sensitivity, constantly on the alert, led him to sense where to find new creative forces and related talents, and in what direction lay their evolution. He knew how to choose and associate the choreographer, painter, and musician best suited to understand each other. His ballets created the tone and were the tangible result of the artistic climate. And not only of Russian art; from 1911 on, Diaghilev called on Western artists like Debussy, Ravel, Schmitt, Satie, Auric, Poulenc, Milhaud, Picasso, Braque, and Derain. The Russian ballet, outside of Russia, had rapidly become European.

The Firebird, first performed in 1910, found an enthusiastic reception. The ballet was not only of indisputable musical value, but also corresponded perfectly with the idea the Western world held of Russian music. *Schéhérazade* and the Polovtzian dances in *Prince Igor* had brought with them the fascination of their orientalism, and Western audiences willingly imagined that the Russian soul was impregnated with a voluptuous reflection of the Asiatic.

In 1912 Stravinsky was working on a *Konzertstück* in which the piano had the principal role:

In composing this music [wrote Stravinsky in his *Chronicle*], I had the clear image in my head of a puppet suddenly set free who, with his cascades of diabolic arpeggios, exhausts the patience of the orchestra which in turn responds with menacing fanfares. A terrific uproar follows which ends at its climax with the plaintive and painful collapse of the puppet. When I had finished the piece I walked along the banks of the Léman [Lake Geneva] for hours trying to find the title that would express in a single word the essence of my music and, consequently, the form of my personage. One day I started with joy—"Petrushka! the eternal and unhappy hero of all fairs of all countries!"

Diaghilev persuaded Stravinsky to develop his idea into a choreographic score. Thus, the *Konzertstück* became the famous ballet that brought its composer a fresh triumph, a work of strange newness and hitherto unknown audacity.

In the meantime, Stravinsky was composing a work whose theme he had come upon some time before. "When I was finishing the last pages of *The Firebird* in St. Petersburg, I had a sudden, absolutely unexpected vision . . . of the spectacle of a great pagan religious rite: old sages, seated in a circle and watching the death-dance of a young girl whom they were sacrificing to render homage to the god of spring. This was the theme of *Le Sacre du Printemps.*"

At this point, public feeling about his music began to go sour. The themes Stravinsky's imagination created for *Le Sacre du Printemps* were strong and brutal, even for those times. It generated a score of extreme tension, mercilessly pounded by an implacable, frightening rhythm and shored up with gigantic harmonic pillars which seemed to bear no resemblance to the harmonic language in use. Again, the conception of the work required a choreography which broke with traditions of plastic grace and charm. Something of the wild character of this music, which violated the expectations and tastes of the public, had been surmised from the long and frequent rehearsals.

The first performance, which took place at the Théâtre des Champs-Elysées on May 15, 1913, unleashed a scandal of such magnitude that not a note of music was heard, so to speak. Two parties formed; friends and enemies of this new art form shouted their wrath, challenged and hurled insults at each other. Catcalls and sarcasm from the opposition drew the fury of the defenders. This was the loudest uproar a work of art had caused since Victor Hugo's *Hernani*. *Le Sacre du Printemps* pulverized and scattered to the four winds all the ideas digested and passively followed in music, and abruptly established a new way of thinking. Some months later the work was played at a concert, after which it was more objectively judged. It was quickly understood that here was a true work of art and a new orientation.

Hardly had the waters calmed when, in 1914, the Ballet Russe presented a third important work by Stravinsky: *The Nightingale,* a lyric work based on Andersen's tale. It pleased the most perspicacious musicians, but left the majority of the public in a wholly understandable state of perplexity. Where was that terrible violence it had begun to accept, that primitive and elementary side to the music that it now expected? This *Nightingale* sang with a refined, delicate voice, and its unknown language was different from that of *Le Sacre du Printemps*. Decidedly, these successive works of Stravinsky were not alike. His personality was confusing. One thing at least seemed certain: Stravinsky was a revolutionary.

During the First World War the composer lived in Switzerland, where he made two close friends, the writer C. F. Ramuz and the conductor Ernest Ansermet. It was there that he composed *Noces, Renard, Pribautki, L'Histoire du Soldat* and *Four Russian Songs,* most of which were not publicly performed until after the war. Still at Morges, he wrote *Three Pieces for Solo Clarinet* and two "ragtimes" in 1918.

In the meantime, the Ballet Russe had been performing in Italy and, from contact with Italian musicians, Diaghilev had created two ballets in an unusual style which were destined to exercise a profound influence on Western music: *Les Femmes de Bonne Humeur,* based on a suite of sonatas by Scarlatti and handsomely orchestrated by Tommasini, and *La Boutique Fantasque,* based on instrumental pieces by Rossini and strikingly orchestrated by Respighi. Stravinsky had traveled from Rome, where he had met Pablo Picasso. Diaghilev had discovered unpublished pieces and sketches by Pergolesi, and Stravinsky, interpreting and rewriting them in his own style, had composed the ballet with chorus, *Pulcinella*. This new work was first performed publicly in Paris in 1920 with décor by Picasso and choreography by Massine. This performance, in quite a new spirit, had considerable success but gave rise to endless controversy: the savage Stravinsky, the composer of *Le Sacre du Printemps* and *Nightingale*, seemed to have become unrecognizable, to be heading toward classicism, to be treating the estimable music of Pergolesi without due respect. In 1920, the *Concertino for String Quartet* and the *Symphonies for Wind Instruments*, dedicated to the memory of Debussy, showed a new modification in the course of his evolution, a reversion to that complete liberty which had won grudging acceptance with *Le Sacre*. In 1922 *Mavra*, a comic opera based on a tale by Pushkin, appeared, revealing the influence of Tchaikovsky alongside an Italian influence.

Mavra perplexed a great number of listeners, as did the *Octet for Wind Instruments* (1923) and the *Concerto for Piano and Orchestra* (1924). What was the significance of this style—this meeting ground for Bach and a certain nineteenth-century quality in which Rossini and Liszt were brought together? The intentions of the composer were, to say the least, enigmatic. Henceforth, and until the performance of his most recent works, critics have not ceased to be confounded. Hardly had they assimilated one work than the next one threw them into further confusion. And so, from piece to piece, *Le Sacre du Printemps* was defended against *Mavra*, *Mavra* against the *Baiser de la Fée*, the *Baiser de la Fée* against *Jeu de Cartes*.

After the *Concerto for Piano*, among the works composed with regularity through the years are the oratorio *Oedipus Rex* (1927); the ballet *Apollon Musagètes*, and the allegoric ballet *Le Baiser de la Fée* (1928); *Capriccio for Piano and Orchestra* (1929); the *Symphony of Psalms* (1930); *Persephone*, a drama based on a text by André Gide (1934); the *Concerto for Two Solo Pianos* (1935); and the ballet *Jeu de Cartes* (1937). In 1938 Stravinsky began his American life. Settling in the United States, he wrote the *Dumbarton Oaks Concerto in Eb for Chamber Orchestra*. Since that date, his most significant works are the *Symphony in Three Movements* (1946); *Orpheus* and a *Mass* (1948); the opera *The Rake's Progress* (1951); and *Canticum Sacrum ad Honorem Sancti Marci Nominis* (1956).

Public and critical indecision about most of Stravinsky's new compositions, and the time it has taken for their significance to be understood and their value appreciated, show the climate in which has developed, with admirable sureness, the work of a man we feel justified in considering the greatest contemporary composer.

What generally allows the public to follow the production of a contemporary composer is that his works form a sort of suite, one after the other, and follow a continuous curve that traces a progressive evolution; each work announces, previews, and explains the following work. Such an evolution molds Schoenberg's production and facilitates an exchange of views on his work, despite his unusual concept and language.

But this is not true of Stravinsky. None of his works introduces the next one or prefigures it. *Le Sacre du Printemps* served no more as a point of departure than did *Oedipus Rex*. Each of his works stands alone and is governed by its own principles. Each incorporates a specific method (but does not utilize *all* the methods), the method being chosen in relation to the particular aim envisaged. "I live neither in the past nor in the future; I am in the present," writes Stravinsky. The dominant trait in his character is precisely that extraordinary concentration of his faculty of choice, critical sense, and inventiveness as a convergent cluster of powers focusing on a given point. A musical work is not to him a means of expressing his sentiments, or better, of expressing the *I*. The work is a thing to make, a certain material to govern, to which an appropriate form must be given. He stands before the material like a goldsmith facing the metal he must make into an ornament, like an architect confronting the space he must organize, holding in mind the materials which are put at his disposal. He works according to Goethe's reflection that architecture is petrified music, and says himself that his task is to organize time.

That objective and modest attitude in the face of the musical problem is the same as the Renaissance artist's, whether Donatello or Roland de Lassus; or of musicians like Schütz, Bach, and Mozart. It is opposed to the basic expressionist attitude of externalizing an interior climate, which Stravinsky mistrusts to the point of writing: "Music is in essence incapable of expressing whatever you will: a feeling, an attitude, a psychological state, a phenomenon of nature." What must be understood by this is that, according to him, music presents only relationships in height between sounds, creating melodic and harmonic tensions; relationships in duration, measured by meters; and relationships in volume, regulated by instrumentation, and that nothing except these qualities, which it really possesses, should be attributed to music.

What he proclaims in this much contested statement is the realistic point of view of a man who poses and superimposes sounds one after another. But of course, for Stravinsky as for most creative minds, the thought follows on certain perceptions, impressions produced by the outside world. And his words do not prejudice the attitude of the listener who, hearing the music and letting it act on him, discovers an expressive sense by associations of ideas and images. Stravinsky's dictum defines the area of his own concern, on which he concentrates the whole of his attention.

"Stravinsky is the most methodical man in the world," writes Roland-Manuel, "and the least systematic. Involved in the work to be done but not in the work done, nothing ties him to his successes. He deduces no system from them, for he never retraces his steps. This explains why none of his works resembles its neighbor, while he remains identified with himself, and it is generally imagined that he changes skins when what he does is to change tasks." Such a man should not be expected to create an invariable language to be used to solve all the problems that arise. He would not seek a single means of expression, but his personality would pierce through each work, and at every point in that work, in a discourse whose structure is a function of the object to be created. Roland-Manuel says further: "To construct his work with what M. Paul Valéry ingeniously calls the debris of the future, to profit from everything, be enslaved by nothing, agree firmly to accept the good where he finds it and not give in to the temptation to seek out the bad where he feels it—that realistic poetics defines the attitude of our musician and his obstinate course." This sort of artist will not make his task depend upon prior inspiration—he has expressed his opinion on this point clearly. Inspiration comes in working, says Stravinsky, as appetite comes in eating. But he knows that the creative process presupposes intuition of an unknown, possessed before it is discovered, which is to be elucidated and defined only by technique. The role of technique is specifically to impose an order upon the debris of the future, a real order without trickery or malice—*splendor ordinis, splendor veri.*

Stravinsky has his own interpretation of form. His primary concern is to arrange the time and be sure that something happens at each moment. While music like Wagner's annihilates time (*Parsifal* and the second act of *Tristan*), Stravinsky's gives a feeling of its flow because of the singular role played by the rhythm as pulsation, as the measure of time, and because the musical interest is continually renewed.

The notion of time is essential for a true understanding of Stravinsky's work. This requires some explanation, which Pierre Suvchinsky gives us:

The sensation of time is doubtless a quality accessible to all. Everybody knows that time passes in various ways, that the weight and intensity of the temporal process are always different and variable, and that man is even able to recognize himself simultaneously in totally different types of time currents. Expectation, anguish, pain, suffering, fright, contemplation and voluptuousness are above all categories of different times during which human life moves forward. Now, all this variety in types and modifications of *psychological time* would be incomprehensible if, at the basis of this whole complexity of experience, there were not the primary sensation—often subconscious—of the real time, of *ontological time.*

The peculiarity of the musical notion of time consists precisely in the fact that it is born and flows on either *outside* or *in the same time* as categories of psychological time, meaning that the musical experience can be considered as one of the purest forms of the ontological sense of time.

The art of music, which offers one of the most complete experiences of ontological time possible, is not limited only to reflecting that notion. It is indeed rare for psychological reflexes not to dominate the creative process; one could even say that their absence from the creative domain marks the presence of a special talent very rarely encountered in its pure state.

The experience of time, and thus the quality of the element of time in the work of different composers, is always distinct, but their model *par excellence*—ontologically or psychologically—can always be defined and, consequently, can lend itself to a typological classification.

There is in music a specific relationship, a type of counterpoint, between the flow of time, its own duration, and the material and technical means with whose aid that music has been expressed and scored. Either the musical material adequately fills the course of time, which so to speak *conducts* the music and determines its temporal form, or else it abandons this course of time, bridging or enlarging it, or convulsively transforming its normal course. In the first case, the music can be called *chronometric*, and in the second, *chrono-ametric.*

This discussion by Pierre Suvchinsky [12] leads us to place Bach (at least in his instrumental music) and Stravinsky in the chronometric category, and clearly demonstrates their profound relationship. What draws Stravinsky and Bach together is not works like the *Concerto for Piano,* which do show an occasional exterior resemblance, but compositions which do not on the surface justify such a comparison, like the *Symphonies for Wind Instruments,* the *Octet,* or *Jeu de Cartes.* Stravinsky's claim to living in the present is made much clearer by the comparison. His presence is manifested at every point in his work; his creative influence is disclosed in each moment during the flow of ontological time, and is always in harmony with it. Each musical moment thus acquires exceptional value because of its high potential; and his work, as a result, has incomparable power. This concern with the musical moment explains the determining quality of transitions and conclusions (we will return to this later) which also create the impression of being inevitably and necessarily what they are. It explains as well the particular value of silences in Stravinsky's music.

Such an art form is above all contrapuntal—a distinct movement of lines. The architecture of time is conceived in terms of the volume and weight of sound.

The idea we are forming in retrospect about Stravinsky's art, and which we think corresponds to the governing principles he

12. *"La Notion du Temps et de la Musique," Revue Musicale,* XX/191.

followed, still will not guide us through his early works. Such a work method is shaped slowly; this is understandable, since Stravinsky had to rediscover it after more than a century of psychologically based music, before the time of Karl Philipp Emanuel Bach. It took courage to resist the attraction of impressionism and turn away from Debussy, that popular genius for whom Stravinsky maintained a deep and affectionate admiration.

Convinced that musical values needed revision, Stravinsky shared his renunciation of established values with Erik Satie, whose *Parade* and *Socrates* he liked. Alfred Cortot describes that moment in history when the change of concept took place. We quote again, as it is interesting to group together the opinions on the life of music of several craftsmen:

It is an inclination natural to Stravinsky's genius, to conceive music first in the form of movement and volume. This is what caught Rimsky-Korsakov's attention when he looked over Stravinsky's early efforts. The vitality of his solidly buttressed melodies, the vigor of his counterpoint which sometimes seems to draw its bold *élan* from primitive descant, the splendor of orchestration that seems to our amazement to question the basic value of all timbres—none of these is as influential as that early conception whose effect on the trends in contemporary music is by no means weakening. One almost immediate consequence of his influence was a counterattack (I speak here of French thought at the beginning of the century) on the vague formulas of that decadent symbolism which the art of sound, negligent of its vitality if not of its nerve-stimulation, was adopting too readily for safety. It stopped a group of young composers short on the uncertain path of literary innuendoes and suggestive allusions. The deliberate accents of the implacable rhythm that he matched to the strong modalities of an uncomplicated melody stood in opposition to fainthearted, cautious musical poetics. For evasion, whatever its nature, has no place in Stravinsky's artistic methods. With this position, and maintaining proper proportions—replacing intentions with accomplishments—he espoused the aesthetic convictions of Satie. He emphasized the importance of their role, moreover, asserting that their example had opportunely contradicted the "looseness of decaying impressionism" by using "firm, clean" musical language "stripped of all ornamental imagery."

Thus, around 1910, Stravinsky was living in an atmosphere influenced on the one hand by Rimsky-Korsakov, Liadov, Liapunov, and Mussorgsky, and on the other by Debussy and Ravel. He had already composed the *Etudes, Fireworks,* and *Firebird.* With two giant steps he broke loose from that atmosphere. The first was the composition of *Petrushka,* in which he returned to a strongly stated diatonism, wrote passages in a counterpoint independent of academic rules, and laid the basis for an organic, directive rhythm. The second step was *Le Sacre du Printemps,* which destroyed all the accumulated theories of a century of romanticism and reached back beyond classicism, beyond the Middle Ages, to the primitive state of music. From the ruins he took the residue, the essentials, the elements of music—all that was most simple and most irreducible. He listened for direct, physiological sensations and measured the real degree of their effect: hence, the complete and ideal freedom of rhythmic pulsation and superimposition of melodies in the *Prelude,* and the superimposition of different rhythms in *Danse de la Terre.*

Reason and will alone cannot explain such an abrupt about-face from the height of refinement and subtlety, to humility in the presence of musical material. Intuition played a large part. C. F. Ramuz, who wrote the text of *L'Histoire du Soldat* and the French adaptation of *Noces* and *Renard,* gives us a picture of Stravinsky as he knew him in the canton of Vaud in 1915:

What I saw in you was a taste and sense of life and a love of everything living; and everything living was, potentially or actually, music to you. Your nourishment was mine. I am not quite sure why (for the analogy is not obvious), but I recalled that phrase of Nietzsche's: "I love the man who wants to create beyond his abilities and dies in the attempt." The man I loved in you (and whom I still love in you) is the one who, on the contrary, creates beneath his abilities and does *not* die. I mean (approximately) the man who first draws his convictions from beneath himself, makes sure of their soundness, and only then *climbs up on them,* if he can. To say it another way, a man must be a materialist (you were), then become spiritual, if he wants to or if he can (and I think that you could have), but not be idealistic in any way at any time. "The most mediocre German artists," to use Nietzsche's words again, "show genius in their faces, but have hands like everyone else's." And I do not mean to say that you have a face like everyone else's, but I like to forget your features and look elsewhere in you to find that mysterious creative power so often confused with thought—wrongly so, for it can be anywhere (that power, or those clues), in the walk, the size, the cut of the shoulders, the way a man holds himself, a way of moving, a way of resting. You are not very big, Stravinsky; you do not look very strong, at least from a distance. But you are very strong, secretly, because you will to be and need to be. You were soon going to begin forty-five minutes of the "Muller system" every morning. I looked hard at you on that terrace in Crochettaz and you were already what you still are for me, I mean that rarest of beings, a man, in the fullest sense of the word; not a social type, nor the simple product of a system of education, nor an "artist," nor a specialist or specialized in whatever you will. Quite the opposite of a specialist or specialized, you are a man, and a complete man, that is, a man cultured and primitive at the same time, one who is sensitive to complexities but to essentials as well, able to do the most complicated mental equations and simultaneously react directly and spontaneously—as it should be, because a man must be both savage and civilized. He cannot be only primitive, but must be *also* primitive.

As soon as Stravinsky had discovered the real, basic value of rhythms, intervals, and the timbres of instruments—that is, their real effect on hearing, nerves, and understanding, his only thought was to conceive music whose guiding principle in construction would be *economy*. He wanted to purify the language and throw out deadwood, like pruning a tree, cutting away dead or weakened branches and preserving only the wood with sap flowing through it, thus making the most effective use of his elements of construction. This attitude explains *Pulcinella* and *Oedipus Rex* as well as *L'Histoire du Soldat* and *Noces*.

Stravinsky likes to set himself, or be set, before a certain number of facts which define the boundaries of his field of activity, determine its meaning, and set the conditions for its form. Arthur Honegger tells a story that illustrates this spiritual disposition:

A personal experience gave me an idea of how completely Stravinsky saw everything from a craftsman's angle. I had met him at the Salle Gaveau—*King David* had been commissioned at that time—and I told him about the trouble I was having balancing a chorus of a hundred singers and an orchestra of seventeen musicians, the group imposed on me. "It's simple," he said, "think as if you had *wanted* that disposition and compose for a hundred voices and seventeen musicians."

This might seem oversimplified, but his reply gave me an excellent lesson in composition: to accept the thing given not as a thing imposed, but as a personal starting point and an inner necessity; hence, to begin with the sonorous material and to know what music and what technical combinations can be extracted from it. This point of view is often evident in Stravinsky's work, especially in pieces like the *Octet for Wind Instruments* and the *Concertino for String Quartet.* These works are not composed for a group of wind or string instruments; perfect music wells from the groups themselves. Many of the works of composers of this period are so indistinct, instrumentally speaking, that they can be played by interchangeable groups.

Here is what Stravinsky himself has to say: "What delighted me most when I was composing *Piano Rag Music* . . . was that different rhythmic episodes were dictated to me by my fingers. My hands took such pleasure in the piece that I set to work on it. Fingers should not be despised; they are sources of inspiration, and, in contact with sonorous material, often awaken subconscious ideas in you which would perhaps not otherwise be aroused." This objective and rationalist attitude is, in opposition to the emotional basis of romanticism, the mark of all classicism, and under the sign of classicism—in depth—stand all of Stravinsky's works after *Le Sacre du Printemps.* The *Schoenbergkreis,* instead, claims to believe that these works come under the sign of a type of academism which was a throwback to Bach, Handel, and Lully. This group, to which the notion of classicism was foreign and unknown, can be criticized for its somewhat disdainful and light treatment of the *Traditiönchen* of French composers, which is actually a permanent architectural principle supporting on its solid foundation a good many methods and transient or renascent ideas which are no more—and sometimes less—academic than the *Zwölftonreihe.* Dodecaphonism is a technique of construction, but classicism is a spiritual attitude which has guided the art of Racine, Mallarmé, and Valéry; Poussin and Cézanne; Lully, Bach, and Stravinsky. Classical thinking produces the perfect adaptation of form to matter.

Can we legitimately speak of principles and French art in connection with Stravinsky? The answer to that question will clarify the position of the composer of *Apollon Musagètes.* The fact that Stravinsky's outlook is generally held to be French in nature is explained by his having settled in France in 1920, after having spent the nine previous years in French-speaking Switzerland.

His natural inclination toward classicism could develop comfortably in a country where classicism is an accepted system. Stravinsky was no stranger in France.

Also, a Russian composer was thought of as an artist who derived from the Five, and who, like Rimsky-Korsakov, Borodin, and Balakirev, took inspiration mainly from oriental folklore. These modal or chromatic songs and melodies gave specifically Russian music an exotic, chatoyant quality. *Schéhérazade, In the Steppes of Central Asia,* and *Islamey* made listeners forget that Russians are Europeans, and that their culture has been opened to the trends which vitalize Western thought. Boris de Schlœzer describes the European aspect of Russian art:

> The case of Stravinsky seems to be incomprehensible. The composer of the *Symphonies for Wind Instruments* appears to have shucked off all vestiges of national character only in the eyes of those (but they make up the great majority) who hold to the old saying, "Scratch a Russian and you'll find a Tartar," and who think that Russian art is necessarily violent, wildly colorful and nostalgic. But anyone who knows that wonderful period of Russian history—its golden age—which encompassed the reign of Alexander I and the first years of Nicholas I's rule can readily trace Stravinsky's lineal descent. That age gave us Glinka, the first of the Russian composers, and Pushkin, the greatest Russian poet, whom Dostoevsky, in a famous discourse, proclaimed as the very incarnation of Russian genius. Pushkin, like Glinka, owes a good deal to his Western teachers. He was bred on foreign literature, especially English and French, and greatly influenced by André Chénier and Byron. I mention only Glinka and Pushkin, although I could name many others whose works are imbued with the taste, measure and balance which are the sign of the classical mind and which the West has a tendency to claim as its exclusive possession.

Glinka's operas do integrate Russian folklore with the Italian operatic style derived from Mozart. Tchaikovsky is Russian, but reflects German and Italian traditions. This interpenetration of a number of styles, melting down and amalgamating in the crucible of a powerful personality, is nothing new in Russian art; nor is there anything odd in Stravinsky's dedicating his comic opera *Mavra,* with its balanced Russian, gypsy and Italian components, to the memory of Pushkin, Glinka and Tchaikovsky.

Stravinsky's orientation toward a synthesis of Eastern and Western styles began with the composition of *Pulcinella* and *Mavra*. The direction of this orientation is corroborated by this important excerpt from Stravinsky's *Chronicles of My Life:*

[In 1921,] during that same stay in London, Diaghilev and I thought up another project that struck deep in my heart. What brought it to light was our infinite admiration and common love for the great poet Pushkin, who is, sadly enough, no more than a name to foreigners, but whose genius, in its diversity and universality, not only was particularly appealing and precious to us but marked out an entire program for us. In temperament, mentality and ideology, Pushkin represented the most perfect example of that extraordinary heritage which begins with Peter the Great—that happy alliance between what is specifically Russian and the spiritual riches of the Western world.

Diaghilev was incontestably an offspring of that lineage. His whole life-work confirmed the authenticity of his inheritance. I myself had always felt the germ of that same outlook, a germ that asked only to be developed, and I cultivated it henceforth most attentively.

There is a difference in this and the thinking of the Five, who did not take long to become academic and concentrate in the Belyaev group dominated by Rimsky-Korsakov and Glazunov. The difference did not lie in the fact that the one outlook claimed to be cosmopolitan while the other one was purely nationalistic. Nationalist traits are as important in Pushkin's work as in Glinka's and Tchaikovsky's. But these qualities flowed spontaneously from the very heart of Glinka and Tchaikovsky, while for the others, the nationalist tendency was a doctrinaire aesthetic which they were intent on imposing. This national-ethnographic aesthetic they insisted on cultivating is essentially not very far removed from the spirit of all those movies dealing with the old Russia of tsars and noblemen. What can be seen in these composers, as in modern Spanish folklorists, painters as well as musicians, is precisely that naïve but dangerous whim that brings them to rework an art instinctively created by the genius of the people. This is a rather sterile pastime, and an evil that afflicts a good many talented artists. Nonetheless, a Western influence came to bear on both of the two groups I am speaking of, although the origins were different. Tchaikovsky, as well as Dargomyzhski and others less well known, used folk melodies but did not hesitate to Gallicize or Italianize them as did Glinka. As for the nationalists, they also Europeanized their music, but took inspiration from quite different models—Wagner, Liszt, Berlioz, that is, from the descriptive and romantic spirit and from program music. Of course, a

Tchaikovsky could not escape Germanic influence. But if he echoed Schumann, and to the same extent as Gounod, for example, it did not prevent him from remaining Russian nor Gounod from remaining French. Both profited from the purely musical discoveries of the great German, eminently musical himself, and borrowed his phraseology and the peculiarities of his language without adopting his ideology.

The project I spoke of above ended in my composing the opera *Mavra,* based on a subject drawn from Pushkin's verse-tale, *The Little House of Kolomna.* This choice, in which I joined Diaghilev, confirmed my attitude toward the two currents of Russian thought I have just differentiated. On the musical plane, Pushkin's poem led me straight to Glinka and Tchaikovsky, and I put myself solidly in their camp. I crystallized my tastes and preferences accordingly, and my opposition to the contrary aesthetic, as I took up the good tradition established by these masters. This explains why I dedicated my work to the memory of Pushkin, Glinka, and Tchaikovsky.

It would be shortsighted to think that these Italian, German, or French aspects of Russian art are limited to an external influence. The impact went deep. Bach is frequently referred to in connection with the *Concerto for Piano,* and correctly so if only the principle of composition is considered. But when we listen attentively to each note, the movement of the parts and the harmonies, we must acknowledge that the music carries the imprint of a personality other than Bach's—Stravinsky's presence is felt throughout [*Example 45*]. Certain bathers or ballerinas in Picasso's work, also, were suggested by the work of some other painter; but in those paintings, the curves, proportions, and surface distribution—each detail and the whole composition as well—reveal Picasso's genius.

Stravinsky and Picasso have a good deal in common, moreover. They take what they need wherever they find it, considering that the art of their predecessors has become everyone's property, and they then use it as a basis for launching their own creation. Such was the procedure of Renaissance painters and musicians, Purcell, Bach, and Handel. The polymorphic quality of their art is a direct result of the economy and choice of their means, and is related to the point on the horizon they focused on. The so-called returns to Pergolesi, Bach, Handel, or Weber are not evidence of abdication or retrogression, but rather indicate the points of departure of a new art. Ingres or

Negro art has the same function in Picasso's work. And just as the painter did not evolve through his pink or blue period to integral cubism or a more recent phase but changed his pictorial concepts, so the composer did not evolve through the *Firebird* to *Le Sacre du Printemps* and *Oedipus Rex,* but changed his musical concepts.

They share a love of simple things and treat them with the same respect—a popular song or a banal theme has the same value for Stravinsky as the wires that Picasso, bending them in natural curves, uses in his works, or the bottles and boxes he transforms into good painting.

Stravinsky's technique cannot be properly discussed, since, far from being systematic, it varies in relation to the character of the work being created. We can at most indicate certain aspects of his language. Let us begin with rhythm.

Romanticism has impaired our sense of rhythm. Building on a literary or dramatic base engendered specifically arhythmic music. A leading theme or a leitmotiv with a well-defined rhythmic structure, which occasionally intervenes, does not ingrain the rhythm into the whole surrounding musical fabric, engulfed in a sort of orchestral stream almost devoid of articulation. On the other hand, we have seen that rhythm in the atonal system has the value of a figure which is subjected to modifications that distort it as soon as it appears. Perception of a rhythm presupposes its continuity, symmetrical repetition, or modification only within recognizable limits, just as tonality can exist only if it continues long enough to be heard.

Stravinsky restored rhythm to its original meaning. Heartbeats and breathing are the first meters of life. With their natural tempo, they are at the root of music. On this metric canvas, the periodic motion of work and dancing gave rise to musical rhythms. The body's vital pulsation in the complete regularity of heartbeat and breathing is used organically in musical construction, and sets the standard of measure that makes the flow of time perceptible. After the disorder created by romanticism, Stravinsky reinstated that primary function attributed to rhythm by Schütz, Bach, and Mozart, and made it the thread of his musical weave.

It has been said that the primary feature of Stravinsky's art is rhythm. This aspect does make a more immediate and striking impression than others. But the harmonic, contrapuntal, and melodic features are of no less importance in Stravinsky's work.

It might be useful here to review the factors relating to rhythm, since the secondary position it occupied in nineteenth-century music has caused some confusion. Briefly, the *metrical element* governs what derives from the difference between accented and unaccented notes, independent of the specific time value of the notes. The *rhythmic element,* properly speaking, refers to differences in time value (long and short notes), independent of the accentuation. The *measure* marks the distance which separates downbeats from each other. Finally, *tempo* insures uniformity in the speed at which ontological time flows. After the eighteenth century, but especially in the nineteenth, a piece of music was habitually composed of successive identical measures; the accent fell on the first beat of each measure and coincided with the long note. As a result, the potential of rhythm was markedly limited and its different qualities confused. Accelerandos, ritardandos, and rubatos were accumulated so that tempos followed in irrational succession with no common measure. These abuses may have been resorted to as a check on the weakening of rhythm. Re-established in its organic function of corresponding with our vital pulses, rhythm has once again become an irresistible force.

The passage *Augures Printaniers* in *Le Sacre du Printemps,* our *Example 46,* shows the constant repetition of the same rhythmic value in march tempo ($\rfloor$=112), a relentless beat serving as a springboard for a meter which does not coincide with the measure. Four different meters can be heard in the 2-4 time as a result of the placing of the accents. In the passage *Jeu du Rapt* of the same score [*Example 47*], meter and measure do coincide. The accents fall on the first eighth-note of the measure in 4-8 time and the measure in 5-8 time; the first, fourth, and seventh eighth-notes in the 9-8 time; and the first and fourth eighth-notes in the 6-8 time. Stravinsky's development of rhythm is perceptible here. Just as in harmony there are retards and advances or delays of accents, elisions, appoggiaturas, there are, in Stravinsky's rhythm, contractions and expansions to support the development of melodic motifs. The usual rhythm in *Jeu du Rapt* is in 9-8 time. In the measures cited above the accents of the motif change place, converting 9-8 time first into 4-8 time + 5-8 time, and then into 5-8 time + 4-8 time. The rhythm in the fourth measure is condensed simultaneously with the motif into measures in 6-8 time. Two measures after number 43, after a dynamic augmentation, there is a rhythmic climax based on a complex of 7-8 time + 3-4 time, and the theme is therefore played in 13-8 time. This diminishes into 6-8 time + 2-4 time, or 10-8 time, and is finally resolved into a regular 9-8 time. The rhythmic and thematic developments reinforce each other. In such a complex, the common measure is *one,* or here, an eighth-note, the smallest unit of the composition.

The *Danse Sacrale* which ends *Le Sacre du Printemps* should be fully examined as an example of Stravinsky's rhythmic development. A reading of the score will show that the first part of the *Danse* is built on the rhythm of *Example 48,* and then progresses by a process of condensation and enlargement analogous to the diminution and augmentation of the theme. At number 149, after a magnificent expansion, a fast rhythm based on the *one* simple unit sets in [*Example 50*]. The seeming irregularity in succession results from the silences, all of which equal the simple unit *one,* as do the sound portions. Negative measures—moments of silence—occur alongside positive measures, and acquire the same dynamic value, so that the performer who is familiar with the music marks these measures when his momentum meets no resistance with his whole body, as in a dive. It is the physiological effect that gives this passage such a painful throbbing quality—like the earth in labor.

After number 186 the first rhythm picks up again, this time without negative measures. Sounds follow on each other with the unalterable regularity common to machinery and the organisms of living beings.

The rhythm in the final *Danse* acts like a piston moving a heavy shaft that continues to turn by its own inertia.

Stravinsky often superimposes two different rhythms. By analogy with polyphony, such a superimposition is called polyrhythm. In the first scene of *Petrushka,* the fair, the binary rhythm of the song *Elle Avait une Jambe en Bois* is played by flutes and clarinets, while small bells and celesta play another song in ternary rhythm. The *Valse* in *Jeu de Cartes* is treated in the same way. Along with this proper polyrhythm, Stravinsky often uses another method of superimposition where rhythm is not really modified but the meter is variable within the measure. *Examples 49a* and *49b*, drawn from *Noces*, illustrate this rhythmic polymorphism. The rhythm is based on the *one* simple common unit, an eighth-note. The first and last of the six measures are marked by a regular eighth-note beat like the steady throb of a motor, which we have already felt in the ending of *Le Sacre du Printemps*. The second and fourth measures seem to lift the listener on a ground swell. He is overcome with a sort of dizziness, loses his footing, and is carried on the crest of a wave. The sixth measure gives him back his balance. What has happened? From the second to the fourth measures, we have the duration of twenty-two eighth-notes in all, on each staff. The diffused line throughout the two lower staves is regular. Those of the upper staves include five and seven eighth-notes respectively, and are repeated twice. The accent falls on odd eighth-notes, that is, the fifth and seventh of the regular line in the first rendition. In the second, contrary to all expectations, the accent is placed on the even eighth-notes (sixteenth and eighteenth) of the bass line. The tide has reversed and thwarts the usual flow of the rhythm, which does not return to normal until the sixth measure. If that period of four measures is considered, as it should be, as an indissoluble whole, the explanation of the work becomes plain.

Similar distortions in the relationship between meter and rhythm appear in the march from *L'Histoire du Soldat* and the overture to *Mavra*, among others. Stravinsky once said, "I race with my meter. My greatest joy is to feel myself master of my race. I run like a well-oiled machine."

The preceding examples show that the bar in this music is both an obstacle and a support. It affords resistance which the music then overcomes. Measures are rarely missing in Stravinsky's music. They are absent only in certain passages of a cadential nature, for example, in *Piano Rag Music*, in one of the *Four Russian Songs*, and in the *Capriccio*. The cadences are metric, and the rubato is excluded.

The independence of the metric and rhythmic systems provides wonderful motive power. It catches the listener off guard, because it contradicts his inner, bodily rhythm, and rushes him headlong into movement. It is not surprising to see that contradiction disappear in works like *Oedipus Rex* and the *Symphony of Psalms,* in which Stravinsky set out to create a static atmos· phere. Certain compositions are organized on a succession of varied meters within the melody with the polyphony submitted to that order. This is especially noticeable in the *Octet* and the *Dumbarton Oaks Concerto [Example 51]*.

Note as well the effect produced by successions of chords without accents, set down quietly and all the more clearly, in that they are separated by an obligatory breath. Movement seems to freeze or congeal, so to speak. The rhythm of the coda at the end of the *Octet* is braked by this device [*Example 52*].

Time plays a very important part in metric music, and, based on the speed of the value that serves as the common measure of the diversified rhythm system, this speed becomes uniform. The whole score of *Noces* is conditioned by the eighth-note whose uniform speed is 80 per minute. The music reaches a velocity that remains constant to the end. The mass put in motion cannot stop itself. This is so true that it is literally and physically impossible to cause an interruption between the parts—the continuity must proceed without pause.

Harmony and counterpoint are closely related. An examination of Stravinsky's work as a whole clearly shows that his system is contrapuntal. The composer has often spoken of how little he was interested in the study of harmony when he was young. Precepts of harmony were an obstacle for him, and he preferred to solve problems of this order in his own way. As we know, Schoenberg had already pointed out the shortcomings of the academic harmonic system, for all its freedom, relative to the present state of musical language. Stravinsky, on the contrary, stresses the joy he took in studying counterpoint, which stimulates ideas one on top of another, favoring creativity. In the majority of his works, the harmony comes from the encounter of voices.

Stravinsky's early works have a chromatic basis, not like Wagner's chromaticism but rather like Scriabin's, Debussy's, and

Dukas's. This is true of the *Scherzo Fantastique, Fireworks, Firebird,* and the first act of *The Nightingale.* In *Three Japanese Lyrics* the melody is occasionally atonal in the manner of Schoenberg.

The composer began his training in the atmosphere of chromatic oriental melodies of the Rimsky-Korsakov school. Russian folk melodies, on the other hand, are diatonic, and we know how important a role they play in Stravinsky's works after *Petrushka.*

The complex chords found in his scores are always conceivable in the framework of a given note, but they can be interpreted in many ways. Stravinsky's harmony is, moreover, essentially ambiguous. Like his themes and rhythms, it has considerable motive power. *Le Sacre du Printemps* contains one chord that directs the score and can be heard throughout the work in one form or another, and that gives the piece its harmonic basis. It opens the *Augures Printaniers.* This is the chord that struck Stravinsky's imagination at the outset and set in motion the creation of the score [*Example 46*]. The chord can be thought of as the superimposition of a perfect Fb major chord and the dominant seventh chord of Ab; or Fb major and Eb major (with inferior appoggiatura of the tonic); or finally, as the chord of Eb major with the appoggiatura Db in the upper part of the chord and, in the lower part, the three superior appoggiaturas Cb, Ab, and Fb. That basic chord, which André Schæffner in his excellent book traced throughout the score of *Le Sacre,* can therefore be explained (in the etymological sense of the word) in different ways within different episodes.

Similarly, in *Petrushka,* the chord based on C major plus F♯ major dominates the whole score. This is not a case of polytonality, which consists in an independent evolution of a number of melodic lines in different keys, as in Milhaud's music. Polytonality is contrapuntal. The proper term for this harmonic superimposition might be the one used by Émile Vuillermoz, *polyharmony,* meaning that the chord forms a whole, a unit, but that its sense is not polarized but multiple.

True bitonality occurs only rarely and is always resolved on the preponderant note. *Petrushka* offers numerous examples. On the harmonic plane also, the same chord may contain major

and minor thirds, and although only one tonal chord exists, the
two modes are involved [*Example 53*]. Superimpositions of tonic
and dominant chords also frequently occur, the effect being to
compound the functions of tonic and dominant into a single
note. Not only are these methods widely applied by Stravinsky
in his works, but they have become standard practice in almost
all contemporary tonal music.

Attribution of multiple functions to one chord or one note
has more value in counterpoint than in harmony. The note on
which different voices meet is thrown into sharp relief by the
importance given it at the moment of meeting, and it is often
the only contact point between melodic lines which could otherwise be totally divorced. Stravinsky calls it the "polar note." It is
not necessarily the tonic. The *Serenade for Piano* is in A—not
A major or A minor, and not even the key of A. But the whole
musical body converges on and revolves around that note, which
is necessary at every moment of the music, despite its frequent
change of meaning [*Example 54*]. Note also that in *Le Sacre du
Printemps* or *The Nightingale,* certain apparently inexplicable
chords become meaningful in their instrumentation, and seem
to melt into a single timbre or become more understandable in
the orchestra by the fact that certain notes acquire preponderant
sonorous weight [*Example 55*].

Stravinsky's harmony is no more systematic than his rhythm.
It is strictly dependent on themes, counterpoint, rhythm, and
orchestration. All these elements are subordinated to the absolute attitude taken at the outset by the composer, and are determined by his vision of the music to be made. Stravinsky's art
is above all realistic. Analysis, dissociating what is not made to
be dissociated, can therefore only give the listener or reader of
the score a few supports or signposts, and show him that each of
Stravinsky's works is a being ruled by its own laws.

There are no two works by Stravinsky which are conceived
for the same orchestra; and this is logical. In the nineteenth
century music which had been created for piano was often
orchestrated. Music was given instrumental clothing. The orchestra acquired a splendor so magnetic and spellbinding in its
particular charm that the musical material itself was often lost
from view or relegated to a secondary plane. Mahler had reacted

against the concept of the orchestra being focused on for itself alone, and used orchestration simply as a means of presenting his idea clearly.

Stravinsky invents according to each instrument. The musical phrase is a direct product of the natural and specific dispositions of the instruments in the orchestra. The concept of *orchestral continuum*, or *orchestra pedal*, is still strong in *Firebird*, but is not felt in subsequent works. Of course, the enormous orchestra in *Le Sacre du Printemps* contributes certain massive effects and mixtures of sounds to the magic feeling of the whole work. But there are numerous passages of music that seem to be shaped directly by the instrument—the opening, for example, written for solo wind instruments [*Example 58*]; the *Cercles Mystérieux des Adolescents*, which could not sound as it does if it had been conceived with another orchestral grouping in mind; or the prelude to the second part, built on the interplay of various homogeneous groups. This technique is also applied in *The Nightingale*.

In *Noces*, a percussion orchestra (four pianos used in a battery as percussion instruments) is set in opposition to the wind element, represented by human voices. *L'Histoire du Soldat* reduces the orchestra to the essential so that each group covers the entire reach of its sound scale: a clarinet and a bassoon, a cornet and a trombone, a violin and a double bass, and percussion. The "little concert" in this work combines the legato of the clarinet, staccato of the cornet, and the double strings of the bowed instruments [*Example 59*]. *Apollon Musagètes* is a string sextet. Each new idea, therefore, or each architectural plan, requires different orchestral arrangement.

André Schæffner makes the point that Stravinsky composes by sections, that the work unfolds like a fan, and that the various episodes take off from a common point to which he returns each time, giving an impression of unity. This impression is reinforced by the fact that the most concerted attention is given to transitions or junctures. The end of one section sometimes introduces the beginning of the next from some distance, as in *Noces*. In the *Symphony of Psalms*, the transition from the second to the third parts, by a mysterious affinity and by the chord progressions, seems like an obligatory passage which will not allow the two sections to be separated. The transitions in *Le Baiser de la*

Fée are probably the most carefully wrought in all of Stravinsky's compositions. Each part thrusts its roots as far as thirty measures back into the preceding part. Conclusions as well are always particularly beautiful. They are a sort of résumé, a condensation of the work, calling up its essence. First, the dramatic finale of *Petrushka,* remarkable for its expression of melancholy, is based on recalls of themes required by the dramatic action. Notice the end of the *Octet,* the *Symphony of Psalms,* the *Symphonies for Wind Instruments,* whose music seems to solidify in a suite of chords, petrify and become a sort of majestic colonnade. Listen to the ending of *Apollon Musagètes;* and, in another sense, the coda of the final fugue in the *Concerto for Two Pianos,* whose energy is so concentrated that it reaches the explosive force of *Le Sacre du Printemps.*

Stravinsky's themes are not important in their primary role of themes, but in the infinite number of combinations they are worked into. They are therefore generally very simple, but have a definite structural character.

With the exception of a few passages, the *Firebird* grows from a single cell [*Example 60*], and fluctuates around the major and minor thirds. The *Jeu de Cartes* is a really astonishing phantasmagoria on the three tones of the perfect chord.

A further word on the subject of vocal music. Stravinsky chooses his texts for their sonorous and rhythmic value. In *Noces* and *Renard,* as well as *Oedipus Rex,* the song is syllabic. As a result, articulation is clean and clear without the voice overriding the orchestra. The voices themselves are treated as integral parts of the orchestra, which is what gives *Noces* and *Symphony of Psalms* their cohesion.

Vitruvius's definition of symmetry, a much deeper definition than simple visual or auditory repetition and imitation, can be applied to Stravinsky's art. It is "the existence of a common measure between various parts, between the parts and the whole, and between the sum and its formal elements."

It is not within the scope of this book to discuss all of Stravinsky's works and their purpose. Almost all the music born of his genius is important and beautiful. We can only outline the character of some of the particularly significant compositions.

Firebird is a score whose bright colors wonderfully illustrate a fairy tale that might have come from *A Thousand and One Nights*. Its sensual, oriental melodies link with diatonic melodies of the Russian occidental type. The brilliant orchestration is reminiscent of Rimsky-Korsakov's best works.

Petrushka takes place at the St. Petersburg fair. It is the tale of three marionettes, Petrushka (the Russian Pierrot), the Ballerina, and the Moor, who are brought to life by a charlatan. The scenes of the play form the two central panels of a symphony. The outer wings are a sort of synthesis of the fair which repeat, with the insistence of a rondo's refrain, something like the music of an enormous accordion. *Petrushka* does not soothe the listener with a soft halo of sound or charm him with a play of lulling resonance. It is written in forthright, sharp language that gives the music the "close-woven" quality described by André Schæffner, who also speaks of "the mastery asserted in the fearless ubiquity of the polyphony and the unexpected abbreviations of rhythm or instrumentation; the willful but generous and concise character." Schæffner also quotes the opinion of Alain-Fournier, who calls the work "inescapable and precise like a dream." Jacques Rivière, in 1911, spoke of *Petrushka* in these words: "Stravinsky's audacity appears in his simplifications. He unhesitatingly uses a thousand delightful improprieties. He suppresses, he clarifies; and his touch is never anything but sure and brief. He takes a trumpet, and the beauty of it is that he takes only the trumpet. His innuendoes are powerful and his strength consists in what he learns to do without." These opinions from writers show that Stravinsky's art does not speak only to musicians. Stravinsky and Picasso are perhaps the two artists in the contemporary world who have awakened the greatest interest among all types of creative workers. For in approaching the most elemental materials of their art, and using them to build on a surface cleared of all inherited tradition, they allow the closest view of the phenomenon of creation. Basically there is often a special, distinct vision which conditions the least details of the work it inspires.

The germ of *Le Sacre du Printemps* (The Rite of Spring) was a daydream. Stravinsky had imagined a young girl dancing before an audience of men so incredibly old that they seemed petrified. The vision crystallized into a chord and a theme which formed the basis of the score. It was only later that the symbolism of the vision came clear—the opposition of that young, soft life to the mineral hardness of the old men, the bud breaking through the wood in springtime, growing and rejuvenating the old tree trunk. "Springtime, the Saint" should be the translation of the title. Stravinsky decided to incorporate the young girl's dance into a sort of ancient ritual. He approached the painter Nicholas Roerich, an authority on prehistoric Russia, and together they drew up the plan for the scenario of *Tableaux de la Russie Païenne*, the first part of which contains *Les Augures Printaniers*, the *Jeu du Rapt*, the *Cités Rivales, Cortège du Sage*, and the *Danse de la Terre*. The second part is called *Le Sacrifice*. The young girl is sacrificed to the earth so that Spring will return. The idea of sacrifice was what determined the definitive title, *Le Sacre du Printemps*. During the second part the young girl is immobile, surrounded by a mystic circle of adolescents. Then come the *Glorification de l'Élue, Évocation des Ancêtres, Action Rituelle des Ancêtres*, and finally the *Danse Sacrale de l'Élue*. Now surrounded by an attentive and motionless circle, she does the dance of death, offered as a holocaust to the forces of life.

Le Sacre du Printemps unquestionably ranks among the most overpowering works of music the world has ever heard. "The organ is of the earth," said Louis Laloy, "but a musician is at the keyboard." And Jean Cocteau called it "Georgics of prehistory."

Diaghilev never tired of saying that *Le Sacre du Printemps* was the Ninth Symphony of the twentieth century. It is certainly the most significant work of this century to date. It has re-established the natural and physiological values of the elements of music. Everything written since *Le Sacre du Printemps* has a mode of being and an attitude which would be impossible if *Le Sacre* had not been written. Others of Stravinsky's works may be as beautiful, or even more perfect, but none have been so laden with consequences. Listening to *Le Sacre du Printemps* negates all thought of aesthetic or technique. This is the work of a visionary and a genius, precipitous music of incomparable evocative power.

L'Histoire du Soldat was born from the desire to produce a small spectacle in poetry and music, a stage piece that could be mounted easily and well, even in villages. The outline of the story is borrowed from Russian folklore. Here is what Stravinsky says about it:

The subject of our play was furnished by the Russian tales in the famous Afanasiev collection, which at that time [1918] I was very much taken with. I showed them to Ramuz, who is very sensitive to the Russian muse, and he immediately responded to my enthusiasm. For the theatrical purpose we had in mind, our attention was especially drawn to the cycle of legends about the adventures of an army deserter and the devil who infallibly succeeds in capturing his soul with his devices. . . . Even though the atmosphere of these tales is specifically Russian in character, the situations they describe, the feelings they express, and the morals they draw are so human and general that they bear a relationship to all nations. It was precisely the essentially human side that tempted Ramuz and me in this tragic story of the soldier who falls mortal prey to the devil.

When he had chosen the seven concert instruments he would write his score for, Stravinsky decided to make the ensemble a visual part of the play.

If the movements [of the musicians] are solely the result of the requirements of the music and do not tend to distract the audience as extraneous flourishes, why not follow visually the motions which help your auditory perception, like the arms of the kettle-drummer, the violinist, or trombone-player? Frankly, the people who claim to enjoy music fully only when their eyes are closed hear no better than with their eyes open, but the absence of visual distractions makes it possible for them to give themselves over to reveries under the lulling influence of the sound, and this they love better than the music itself. These are the ideas which prompted me to put my little orchestra for *L'Histoire du Soldat* in clear sight on one side of the stage, with the other side occupied by a little stand for the reciter. This arrangement defined the hinging of the three essential elements in the piece which, in close liaison, should form a whole. In the center, the scene and actors, flanked by the music on one side and the reciter on the other. In our way of thinking these three elements alternately passed the word to each other and combined into an ensemble.

About the *Symphonies for Wind Instruments* (dedicated to Debussy), the composer says that "they contain none of those elements which the usual listener reacts to infallibly or is accustomed to hearing. It is useless to listen for a passionate *élan* or the dynamic explosion. This is an austere ceremony which develops through short litanies between different families of homogeneous instruments." The *Symphonies* evoke a touching, even poignant, feeling. They deserve to be considered as one of Stravinsky's most important works.

In this very rich and diversified body of work, with its sonorities so often renewed, *Noces* is the most striking score. It is suffused with joy from the first note to the last. Its music launches voices, pianos, and percussion instruments in a song of jubilation. Neither the orchestration nor the choice of melodies, only some of which are true folk songs, creates an atmosphere of folk festival. The rejoicing is an expression of pure happiness, and the joy sometimes sounds liturgical. Although it was composed with the stage in mind, this admirable cantata does very well without theatrical trappings.

For the opera-oratorio *Oedipus Rex*, Stravinsky asked Jean Cocteau for a text, and had Father Jean Daniélou translate it into Latin. He hoped to create a sense of tragedy by suppressing all action, keeping only the essential of the drama. He explains the choice of Latin thus:

By chance I found Jörgensen's book on St. Francis of Assisi, a book I had heard a good deal about. While reading it I was struck by a passage that confirmed a deeply rooted conviction of mine. We know that the usual language of the saint was Italian. But on solemn occasions, like times of prayer, he used French (Provençal?—his mother was Provençal). I have always thought that for things approaching the sublime a special language imposes itself, and not the language of everyday use. This is why I looked for the language most appropriate to the projected work and, finally, decided on Latin. My choice afforded an added advantage—I was having to do with material which was not dead but petrified, which had become monumental and immunized against trifling. . . . What a joy to compose the music around a fixed, almost ritualistic language, a high-toned language, and one that imposes itself. One no longer feels dominated by the phrase or the word in its proper meaning. They have settled into an unchangeable mold that guarantees proper expressive value, and they require no further commentary. The text then becomes a purely phonetic matter for the composer. He can break it down as he wishes and direct all his attention to the primitive structural element, that is, the syllable. Wasn't this the way the disciplined old masters treated texts? This was the Church's attitude toward music for centuries, and its means of preventing sentimentality and, consequently, individualism from pouring in.

These words show us how carefully Stravinsky weighs his judgments and elements before he begins composing his works. At each new beginning, everything is questioned anew. He starts from nothing and focuses the converging rays of his ideas.

Only once, I think, did Stravinsky make a mistake. In *Le Baiser de la Fée,* he is in a subordinate position to Tchaikovsky, whom he takes as his point of departure. We have seen that Stravinsky's short, simple themes, because of their often neutral nature, can be adapted to whatever combinations the composer forms them into. Tchaikovsky's melodies are true melodies. They contain their own harmony and are possessed of a complete meaning which nothing can modify. Stravinsky can underline them with magnificent counterpoints, create the most beautiful and perfect transitions, and the listener in spite of everything will still have the impression that he is hearing a work by Tchaikovsky. Stravinsky's personality is inoperative. *Le Baiser de la Fée* is quite the opposite of *Pulcinella,* in which Stravinsky has absorbed Pergolesi.

Apollon Musagètes, Stravinsky's gentlest, tenderest, and most intimate work, has a very interesting history.

When, in my admiration for the lineal beauty of classical dancing, I thought of doing a ballet in the same genre [says the composer], I thought in terms of what is called "white ballet," which to my eyes represents the essence of that art in all its purity. I found a marvelous freshness in it, due to the absence of polychrome embellishment or excess. These qualities prompted me to compose music with the same characteristics. Diatonic composition seemed to me to be the most appropriate means to this end, and the sobriety of its style decided my views on the instrumental group I would use. First I discarded the usual orchestra because of the heterogeneity of its construction—entire groups of strings, woods, brasses, and percussion instruments. I also discarded harmonic ensembles (woods and brasses) whose sonorous effects have really been exploited too often nowadays, and I chose strings. Orchestral use of these instruments has long suffered from a very unfortunate deviation. As often as they have been made to sustain dynamic effects, so often has their role been reduced to that of simple *colorists*. I confess I have myself done them this wrong.

The primordial role of bowed instruments, determined by their country of origin, Italy, consisting primarily in cultivating song and melody, has been abandoned, and with good reason. With these instruments, Stravinsky has created the supreme harmony of *Symphony of Psalms* and the lucid pleasure of the *Jeu de Cartes.*

Stravinsky went to live in California in 1938. There, free of irritations and removed from the polemics that have occupied too much of the European musical scene since 1945, he has been able to concentrate on his work in an atmosphere of peace. He has written some of his most perfect pieces in America: *Orpheus,* the *Mass,* and *The Rake's Progress.* Despite the clarity of his intentions and of his art, each new work still excites a controversy which ends, however, as soon as the world audience adopts the works.

If at one time Stravinsky restricted his work of assimilation and re-creation to eighteenth- and nineteenth-century styles, his field of activity has continually expanded in his most recent works. The Flemish Renaissance suggested elements of style to him for the *Mass* and *Cantata on Anonymous Elizabethan Songs.* He has amalgamated these elements with a melismatic song that appeared as early as *Oedipus Rex,* the source of which lies in Balkan and Caucasian folk music.

The opera *The Rake's Progress,* very rich musically, lyrically, and dramatically, is possibly the work which, of all his compositions, best exemplifies Stravinsky's personality. For this reason we will examine it closely.

To be understood, the norms prevalent in the eighteenth century must be renounced. In order to know the nature and purpose of the art of music and appreciate the value of its active elements, the phenomenon of music must be studied as a whole—from the mutterings of Australian aborigines to the abstractions of our youngest contemporary musicians. Unless the student is aware of measure and of the melodic succession of intervals of sound, or of the organization of time, and unless he realizes that the choice of intervals and rhythmic articulation constitute the essentials of music as do lines, angles, surfaces, and colors in painting, he will never see further than the surface of music; he will never be able to penetrate the interior of its being. On the other hand, music, like other manifestations of man's powers, can be thought to have nothing mysterious in its evolution. The creator works according to pre-existent models. These models, which he will modify and use as the basis of innovation, are chosen or imposed in relation to his own temperament and the trends of his time. If he is an artist, the creator mixes his models together, grinds them down and assimilates them—that is, he re-forms them into his own likeness and stamps them with his own genius.

This is a recognized process in the plastic arts, as Henry Focillon and André Malraux have amply demonstrated. El Greco is the heir of Tintoretto. It is neither the subject matter nor the composition of their canvases which distinguishes one from the other, but rather the economy of proportions, lines, surfaces, and range of colors which give each painter his own unique expression. Thirty years ago you could see Watteau's *Embarquement pour Cythère,* as repainted by Cézanne, hanging on a wall at the Jas de Bouffan. The subject and general plan had not been modified. But each Cézanne brush-stroke made the canvas an incontestable Cézanne painting. No one will dispute the power of Georges Rouault's personality, and the world cites the sources of his art like titles of nobility: early Egyptian paintings, mosaics from Ravenna, the stained-glass windows of Chartres.

But if a composer returns to sources which can stimulate his imagination, he is criticized—*The Rake's Progress* is put down as a simple pastiche of Mozart. Of course, it is easy to recognize certain Mozartian touches in the development of the music, but why was a similar accusation not made concerning *Noces,* which on the contrary was agreed to be authentic Stravinsky? The reason is that in this case the models were taken from Russian folk art, which is practically unknown in Western Europe. The same folk sources are fundamental to *Le Sacre du Printemps,* which explains precisely why the Russians attached little importance to this work and *Petrushka* when they were composed. Their judgment was dominated by the surface resemblance of the compositions to sources they knew well. But the external appearance and the inner being of a work must not be confused.

The act of artistic creation consists principally in carrying pre-existing language, not ideas, to a higher potential and greater power of action while correlating it to exigencies of the moment. From the resulting metamorphosis come the conceptions of the composer and of his era. Bach seized upon some of Vivaldi's concertos and Marcello's toccatas, and even some of Purcell's melodies, and transformed them from the inside—sometimes modifying the exterior appearance only slightly. So did Mozart handle the Italianism of the generation that preceded him. And so does Stravinsky transfigure his models. In the case of *The Rake's Progress,* it is easy to see the references to Mozart, Rossini, and Schubert as sources, but other contrapuntal models are not recognized because, by a stroke of fortune, they are much less well known by music lovers. Have audiences listened so poorly as not to notice the importance of polyphony in *The Rake's Progress* or to think of sources like Guillaume de Machaut, Dufay, Okeghem, and for that matter all of the forms of polyphony from the twelfth to the fifteenth centuries? Unquestionably, Slav epic songs are basic to Tom Rakewell's ballads in the third act.

Decidedly, listeners pay little attention to melody types, to those curves vibrating with truth and life because of the particular place reserved for the half-note, because of a tetrachordal relationship interfering with the function of the fifth, or an unexpected cadence—all resulting in an ending other than the classic major.

In details like these the spirit of the music is revealed and the talent of the creative genius can be appreciated. The same is true of the smallest details in accentuation and metric structure. Whoever uses the word *detail* is not speaking of *accessory;* he grasps the essential, the center and the heart of music.

Let us look at two chords [*Example 56*]. According to the eighteenth- and nineteenth-century concepts, they would be conceived as a seventh and one of its inversions. Present-day thinking would call the first a $\frac{4}{2}$ chord of D♯. It is dissonant. The second is a major seventh chord in E. It defines the key of E major with more precision and force than does the perfect chord. It is consonant in relation to the preceding chord. The linking of the two chords is a cadence whose expression and meaning are totally different from the classic cadence [*Example 57*].

Stravinsky is the modern world's greatest artisan of that natural, non-dogmatic harmony based on physical and physiological realities (see Hindemith's *The Craft of Musical Composition* and Kœchlin's *Traité de l'Harmonie*). To measure his importance, simply compare a recitative cadence from *The Rake's Progress* (piano and vocal score, page 2 [*Example 61*]) with what Mozart or Rossini might have written [*Example 62*]. The reader can feel the increase of power and drive that Stravinsky gives the beginning of the air following the recitative in carrying over the resolution on the perfect chord, which normally ends the recitative.

Following our examples of transfiguration on the harmonic plane, *Example 63* shows a polyphonic transformation. This is a piece of a ballad by Guillaume de Machaut that we place in contrast with a ritornelle from *The Rake's Progress* (piano and vocal score, page 60 [*Example 64*]).

People often seem to think that the works Stravinsky wrote after *The Rake's Progress* differ in essence from those that went before. There does not seem to be sufficient reason for drawing a line here delineating two different conceptions. If we look at the chronology of the composer's production after 1950, we see the following list: *Cantata* (1951-1952); *Septet* and *Three Songs of Shakespeare* (1953); *Dirge-Canons and Song in Memoriam Dylan Thomas* (1954); *Canticum Sacrum ad Honorem Sancti Marci Nominis* (1955); *Agon* (1957); *Threni* (1958); and *Elegy for Raoul Dufy, Movements for Piano and Orchestra,* and *Epitaphium für den Prinzen Max Egon zu Fürstenberg* (1959).

This listing exceeds the general historic period covered in this book by four years. This exception is justified because Stravinsky's art is characteristic of the first part of the century, and because the works written after 1950 do not break with those written before but are a continuation of them, and perhaps their fulfillment. The period 1951-1960, by general opinion, falls under the sign of Webern and Schoenberg because the principles of serial composition were adopted during that period. This does not alter the fact that it also falls under the sign of Bach and Gesualdo—Stravinsky wrote instrumentalizations of several of the works of these two masters.

If the principle of serial composition specifically evokes the thought of Webern, Stravinsky nonetheless adopts it only insofar as it is compatible with the tonal conception of music. If he orchestrates Bach's *Choral-Variationen über ein Weihnachtslied,* it is because he wants to immerse himself in the contrapuntal rigor he needs to pursue his path and achieve the aim he has set for himself, namely, the perfect integration of the musical composition. If he borrows from the madrigalist in his *Monumentum pro Gesualdo di Venosa* (1960), he does so in order to measure how far chromaticism and tonality are compatible and to evaluate the degree of freedom he confers.

The amalgam of tonality-modality, of chromaticism and serial composition conceived as an extension of the musical techniques of the fourteenth- and fifteenth-century polyphonists, defines the style of the works of the decade 1950-1960.

In the *Cantata,* written after *The Rake's Progress,* Stravinsky's concern with uniting the rhythms and sonorities of the English language takes a purely lyrical form. The piece is built on an alternation of a *Lyke-Wake Dirge* for voices and instruments in the key of D (the Phrygian modality of the Middle Ages), concluding in D major, with ricercari for solo voice and instruments. Like Willaert's and Frescobaldi's, these ricercari are canonical compositions offering extremely rich combinations of the subject in its four positions. The second ricercare is very developed and includes points of repose after each canon in the form of a ritornelle. Stripped of all dramatic intent, this long meditation is compensated by a duo for solo soprano and tenor. Its dynamism as much as the profane subject itself introduces the element of asymmetry into the symmetric structure that gives it movement.

The *Septet* marks a further step toward integration of the

sonorous material, drawn entirely from the theme of the first movement. This theme, which is diatonic, utilizes the entire scale, and is clearly written in A major. Its exposition and its combinations with its own augmentation introduce a fugato whose subject is established by the first six notes of the theme. The second movement, a passacaglia, is developed on a theme whose first five notes are a transposition of the first five notes of the theme of the first movement. It is treated in canons as a series not of twelve but of sixteen notes, only eight of which are different. The piece oscillates around two polar notes, E and A (the relationship of the fifth, the backbone of tonality). The final gigue is a succession of four fugues whose subject is the theme of the passacaglia. The composition is serial, but the series includes repetitions of notes resulting in more frequent use of certain intervals which then become predominant.

The delicately and sensitively lyric *Songs of Shakespeare* are similar in character to the *Septet*.

In Memoriam Dylan Thomas comprises a song for tenor solo and string quartet framed in the *Dirge-Canons* for four trombones and string quartet. The two groups are treated as two antiphonic instrumental choruses. The entire composition is strictly based on a series of five notes which are defined only in intervals of half-notes and a minor third. The axis of the whole work is the note E, which in the cadences appears sometimes as the third degree of C major and sometimes as the tonic of E major. The *In Memoriam* exhibits, as fully as does the *Cantata*, the composer's dual concern with form (unity of sonorous material, logic of the deduction) and with architecture (statement and proportion of various pieces, based on the symmetry of the whole and the asymmetry of certain details).

In the *Canticle of Saint Mark*, there is a sense of symbolism in addition to compositional concerns. Symbolism, a normal development in cultural groups which express thought by analogy, rules the arts in Asia and ruled them in Europe until the end of the Middle Ages. Was it his conception of the Byzantine character of Saint Mark in Venice which induced the composer to incorporate this element of symbolism, or did he include it from a feeling of greater general sympathy which is leading his thought closer and closer to that of the great fourteenth-century creators? Whatever the inspiration, the third or middle of the five parts that constitute the *Canticle* is the most important, just as the third cupola is the most imposing of the five that crown the Basilica of Saint Mark in the shape of a cross.

Architecturally, the first and fifth parts are balanced by their sonorous weight, and are registered by tonal basses. The second and fourth parts are built on a series of twelve notes which give no tonal indication except in the cadences. The third part, *Ad Tres Virtutes Hortationem,* is itself subdivided into three sections —*Caritas, Spes,* and *Fides.* The twelve-tone series demands the use of diatonic intervals, while the vertical sections of polyphony accent the fifths, fourths, and thirds, which, because of the frequency and the central position they occupy in the structure, form a sort of keystone that gives the music the solidity of a key tonal signature in a subtle but effective way. In this central portion the series acts as an instrumental *cantus firmus* supporting the polyphonic play of the voices.

The splendor of the *Canticle* makes it Stravinsky's masterwork of the years 1950-1960. Though the second part of the composition is reminiscent of Webern, the whole refers unmistakably, but in a modern fashion, to the musical thought of the end of the *ars nova* period, to that transition into the fifteenth century marked by Ciconia's elegant forcefulness and the rude vigor of Venetian compositions like Antonius Romanus's motet *Stirps Mocenigo-Ducalis Sedes.* This *Canticle* brings to full flower Stravinsky's concept of creating lavish music in austerity—the extremes touch in his interior life.

While the ballet *Agon* profits from the greater integration provided by serial composition, Stravinsky once again takes the opportunity to give free rein to his multifaceted imagination. But after this interlude he returns to the task of stripping his music, of weeding out everything that might be corrupting or superfluous.

Like the *Canticle,* the text of *Threni, Id Est Lamentationes Jeremiae Prophetae* is in Latin, taken from the Vulgate. The *Threni* differs from the *Canticum* in its spirit and consequently in arrangement.

Unlike the *Canticum,* the *Lamentations* is not a concert piece; it creates the feeling of a liturgical service. Basically a choral work, it is accompanied by an orchestra which is sparingly used in small, varied groups. More than in the *Canticle*, the polyphony here is concerned with the combination of the melodic lines on the serial foundation, apparently without disturbing the harmonic incidents. Given these conditions, for the sake of maintaining the tonal quality, the instrumental support takes the form of a double bourdon (tonic and fifth), the chorus periodically adopts a simple cadential function, and the series itself is submitted at times to modifications in the order of the notes. The *Threni* must be listened to in meditation "with the inner ear," that is, with the spirit and in meditation.

We might well ask why Stravinsky, having adopted serial composition, continues to abide by tonality. The answer is that he has always been convinced of the absolute necessity of this principle, considering it to be the backbone of all music. Though we might acknowledge the complete success of Webern's atonal works, we must not forget that his works were very short, never lasting more than a few minutes. This brevity allows the listener to grasp the piece as a whole, despite the absence of reference points. But the *Canticum* and the *Threni* are longer, lasting thirty to thirty-five minutes. As a result, the indications of tonality become indispensable to the perception of the statement and to the perspectives of the musical structure. Schoenberg himself claimed the right to refer to the perfect chord whenever he felt that it was needed.

In brief, Stravinsky's latest compositions make us think of Machaut, Ciconia, Schütz, Gesualdo, Bach, and Webern. Moreover, in these recent works the composer has preserved, above all, his total personality. These works constitute a whole, and one can freely say that through its integration into the whole, the potential of serial composition has become enlarged and its true significance has been found.

If we complete the list of the works we have been discussing with the last to appear at this writing, *Movements for Piano and Orchestra, Elegy for Raoul Dufy, Epitaphium für den Prinzen Max Egon zu Fürstenberg,* and *Monumentum,* we arrive at the conclusion that the works of the 1950-1960 period crown all the efforts and research of the first half of the century.

And these works may well represent for our time what Bach's *Musikalisches Opfer* was for the mid-eighteenth century.

Of all contemporary composers, Stravinsky, faithful always to the nature of music, has probably contributed the most that is really new. His personality as a composer is certainly the most sharply defined and the most amply developed of our time. After all is said and done, it is only the music he has composed that counts.

4

MUSIC IN FRANCE AFTER DEBUSSY

WHILE SCHOENBERG and Stravinsky both followed the plans they laid out, to reconstruct music from its elements, French music pursued an evolution whose point of departure would be useless to look for. Music in France seems to have evolved with no great conflicts or profound shocks, but with steady progression.

There is a French music, though not in the same sense as a Russian, Scandinavian, or Spanish music that people speak of to designate a heterogeneous union of works whose only common ground is their use of songs drawn from the folklore of the country. This classification unquestionably satisfied the nationalist preoccupations of the time, but artistically it was arbitrary, and related only to an external or even circumstantial aspect of music.

France is the archetype of the nation. Despite the diversity of its population and its climate, a nation is united by a common outlook and way of life—by long-held conceptions of the world, society, and the individual that are so widely accepted they are never questioned. Discussions and differences of opinion concern only manner, shades of interpretation, and details of that deep-seated and permanent understanding.

Just as a French nation exists, so is there a French art. Beneath the apparent diversity of innumerable personalities, certain constant characteristics manifest themselves which the French are the last to notice because these traits are so inherently their own and so integrally a part of the French tradition.

The contemporary Austrian composer Ernst Křenek defines the characteristics of French music by comparing them to the German conception of music. Křenek wrote a brief but very interesting article entitled *"Französisches und Deutsches Musik-empfinden,"* in which he gives a very good explanation of why the music of Gabriel Fauré is not widely played in Teutonic

countries, and why Brahms arouses only reluctant interest in the
French listener. He explains why the German adjective *musikal-
isch* does not have the same meaning as the French *musical*.

In the life of the Frenchman, take the average Frenchman, the interests and mental attitudes of artistic origin or order are always present,
even when they are unconscious. The German's relationship to art is
more interior, more *wesenhaft*, but he establishes this relationship
consciously, and breaks it just as consciously. The Frenchman's attitude
toward art is the same as his attitude toward his whole life: he is a
connoisseur in the strict sense of the word. The sum total of technical
knowledge an average Frenchman possesses when he talks about painting, for example—knowledge taken for granted and totally lacking in
snobbery—is astonishing. What he spontaneously offers you in the
course of a conversation on a musical work or its performance almost
always bears on its perfection or its artistic level—that is, on its work-
manship. His interest in its sentiment or the concept of life it interprets
is only incidental. This attitude is part of the eminently realistic sense
of the race, which is less impressed with an elemental reaction than
with the question of knowing "how that is done." The Frenchman is
a positivist by nature, and therefore art is for him less an emanation
of divine forces communicated mysteriously through the intercession of
a member of the elect than an object a man fashions with his own
hands under the control of his own intelligence. And that intelligence
is itself considered as the capacity for inventing interesting means of
production much more than any sort of reservoir of psychic forces. The
Frenchman will never forsake this way of thinking, and in this sense his
understanding of art is ever present and alert. This disposition has
always and rightly been admired as "taste."

The German has other needs. He wants his concept of life to be
touched, or moved, or shaken. He wants to be transformed in some
way by the work of art. The German cannot bear to think of himself
as a perfected, complete being, and consequently requires all his impressions to sustain him or put him in motion. Whatever does not
attract him, in the kinetic sense of the word, "says nothing to him,"
and this is the worst reproach he can level at a work of art. He would
like to see the world continually moving toward progress. All this is
foreign to the Frenchman, who has a static conception of life. He is not
interested in knowing what a thing will become, and the thing does
not interest him while it is in a state of becoming. The thing interests
him only when it is perfected or a reality. To cite just one example
of this, the French mistrust anything young, and respect whatever is
old and definitively fixed. (The form of friendly address used even

among young men is *mon vieux* [old man].) Conversely, the German puts all his hope in youth. It is of little importance to him that youth matures slowly, because whatever is done or completed seems empty to him and is no longer useful for that movement, that road to progress. "Mastery" has been a pejorative word in Germany for a long time. It is related to a static state, which is to the German synonymous with lifeless rigidity. The only thing expected of a master is his death. This is why Germany is so rich in artistic hopes that do not materialize, while for the Frenchman mastery is a state which must be attained as quickly as possible and is to be sustained as long as possible.

The complex the Germans find so interesting in music is meaningless to the French, and is in good part intolerable or even ridiculous to them. French music is essentially static, transparent, well organized on a solidly formed groundwork constructed entirely according to plan, in such a way that its structure can be perceived directly on hearing. Inner life is not wanting, but it is externalized in an entirely different way than in German music, (not as a disturbing force) but as a stable, fixed quality. It would be absurd to say, as it is often said, that French music has no soul. The only difference is that the Frenchman (prefers to express a psychic state) while the German prefers movements of the soul induced by the combined action of contrary force. The somewhat schematic quality of this comparison should not obscure the truth it contains.

The fixedness of French thought and its constancy throughout history is, moreover, a fact that needs no further demonstration. Regarding music and the arts in general, the basic tendency of the French was early recognized. Sainte-Beuve clarifies its meaning in his *Lundis:*

Charming and light Spirits who have been the grace and honor of the land of France from time immemorial; who began your life and pursuit of joy in the iron age, on emerging from savage horrors; who passed by the walls of cloisters and were sometimes gathered inside them; who were the happy soul of bourgeois evenings, and the refined entertainment of châteaux; who often flourished in the shadow of thrones; who lightened the boredom of ceremonies, gave style to victories, and learned to smile again quickly on the heels of defeat; who have appeared under many forms—playful, mocking, elegant, or tender, always graceful, and who have never failed to be born again at the moment you were said to have disappeared! Age is becoming hard on us; all leisure has fled; there is a desperation even in our pleasures that makes them seem like work; peace itself is no truce, so busy is it being useful; even on tranquil days, regrets and cares fill many a soul. Now is the time to awake, or never; now is the time to surprise the world again and infuse it with joy; you have always known the way, forever new: never abandon the land of France, charming and light Spirits.

Whereas the Frenchman knows what he means by *light,* the foreigner misunderstands and confuses it with frivolity. Everything can be said with lightness, even the most somber thoughts. Lightness is the quality opposed to clutter and redundancy, avoiding repetition and insistence and demanding simplicity and clarity. The qualities that Montaigne perceives in poetry, which are also the qualities of French music, are directly related to a lightness he understood thus: "From my earliest years, poetry has had the power to pierce me and transport me. But that quick response natural to me has been variously stimulated by a variety of forms, not so much higher and lower (for they were always the highest of each kind) as different in color. First of all, a gay and ingenious fluidity; then an acute, heightened subtlety; and finally a ripe, steady force." (*Essays,* 1, 38.)

And to call as witness one of the greatest composers France has ever had, here is an excerpt from a letter written by Claude Debussy to Paul Landormy in 1904: "The primary aim of French music is to give pleasure. Couperin, Rameau—there are real Frenchmen! That animal Gluck spoiled everything. Wasn't he boring, and pedantic, and overstuffed! . . . The musical genius of France is something like a dream in the senses. . . . Music must be freed of all scientific apparatus. Music must seek humbly to give pleasure; great beauty is perhaps possible within these limits." But Debussy does not say *to whom* music should give pleasure. He obviously implies the most exacting, subtle, and intelligent audience. Even when it adopts popular ways, French art is aristocratic. When it addresses the people it raises them to its level, refusing to lower its standards.

Returning to Montaigne, his definition of art is logical on every point. First, the fluidity of French music is due to a melodic gift without equal in other peoples. From the beginning of its existence, that is, around A.D. 800, to the present, French music has invariably been based on the invention and use of perfect melodies, melodies that are complete in themselves rhythmically, harmonically, and structurally. These melodies evolve in a temperate climate, without turbulence or paroxysm; they proceed by intervals of slight or moderate tension, avoiding wide leaps and consequently painful or frenetic strain. A fifteenth-century melody by Guillaume Dufay and one by Fauré in the twentieth century are equally supple, balanced, simple, and unadorned, and have the same clean, concise expression, so that the course of the melody is always smooth and swift, like clear, pure water. The theme or motif of three or four notes is simply material to be used in a more or less developed musical structure. But it has no life of its own, just as a brick is actually only the primary material of a house. The generative theme in Bach's fugues and the leading motif in Wagnerian dramas are little suited to the French temperament, for the French temperament begins with the individual or the particular. The melody must be well defined and specific from the outset. There is nothing cerebral or speculative in an art resting on such foundations; with the melody emphasizing the individualistic from the beginning, abstaining from immoderate formal development, maintaining the course of the music by using only elements with human meaning, it plunges us into a living, clear, and rapidly flowing river. And gaiety: we must not confuse gaiety with a superficial, fleeting enjoyment, momentary and unthinking. This is a profound and permanent gaiety. Listen to it in Guillaume de Machaut's *Mass*, in Claude Le Jeune's vocal fantasies, Lully's tragedies, *Faust, Carmen,* and I would even say in Fauré's *Requiem*. Here is a deep-rooted optimism and confidence in the future and the forces of life, a confidence that history has never betrayed. It is an act of faith which keeps thought from descending to weakness or discouragement and the spirit from capitulating under the weight of despair, even in tragedy.

This is the source of the sense of grandeur in the conception of tragedy—grandeur, and not sadness. We need only recall Berlioz's *Trojans at Carthage,* and the *Oresteia* as Milhaud interpreted it, or closer to us, the admirable *Médée*. Gaiety understood thus, as a deep interior joy, comes from contemplating a rich and beautiful land and the happy collaboration between men and a generous nature. Numbers of musical works stand in liberal evidence of such gaiety—Clément Janequin's *The Battle of Marignan,* Chabrier's *Joyeuse Marche,* and Francis Poulenc's *Chansons Gaillardes.*

Is this to say that a French composer is less capable than others of expressing pain? Not at all. But he expresses it in a very special way. Far from giving in to dejection, he takes a firm footing on his heritage of optimism, on that great, abiding *joie de vivre,* in order to react the moment he feels a blow. And his pain, instead of being passive and resigned, is instantly transformed into energy and response. French funeral marches resemble the spirit of Rude's "Marseillaise." Gaiety is not always opposed to and then ultimately merged with pain. More often, tenderness checks its momentum and turns it into humor. This amalgam gives rise to works like *L'Enfant et les Sortilèges* by Ravel, in which the feeling of gaiety predominates. If on the contrary the dominant element is tenderness, this complex produces a work like Henri Sauguet's *La Chartreuse de Parme.* Or again, the composer will contemplate his gift of glowing happiness in an atmosphere of perfect serenity, as does Gabriel Fauré.

This fluidity is ingenious in its perpetual effusion and resilience and in its ever alert curiosity, attributable again to individualism. Once the expressive power of an original theme is determined, it is useless and superfluous to repeat it even once. It would be hard to find in a non-French composer such fabulous diversity as we see in the innumerable pieces divided into twenty-seven *ordres* for harpsichord by Couperin, or such marked differences as those that distinguish Milhaud's many dramas. To take the two most similar modern French composers, Poulenc and Sauguet, the content of the works of one has nothing in common with the expression of the other. The reason for this is that a good French composer never creates according to formula. The work of meditation is very long, and the composer does not begin to write the work he has perhaps been thinking about for years until the day he has discovered or invented the specific and unique melodies suitable for what he will express only once.

Montaigne's second phrase tells us that he loves acute, heightened subtlety. Here we touch on the very essence of French art. Subtlety implies a particular type of relationship between man and the outside world. All the objects surrounding us partici-

pate in our lives. All witness and act in the human drama. Remember how Marcel Proust, stumbling over a stone, saw a whole
long-forgotten period of his life take form again, because that
period was linked to a similar incident, to a similar stumble
over the same stone. A traveler far from his country who receives
a trunk containing his own clothes he has not seen for years is
enveloped by the odor of his home when he opens the trunk,
and in a flash he again sees every rock, blade of grass, detail of
the faces of his parents, he hears once more a word they have
said at a moment long since past. Everything is interdependent;
we depend on the smallest grain of sand. But that grain will not
have the same significance tomorrow as it had yesterday. Other
people will see it or another light will shine on it, or the weather
will be different. The specific and momentary whole that existed
yesterday will never recur. Claudel defines co-birth in his *Art
Poétique:* "We are born at every instant, together with other
objects. At that moment we form with them a complex all of
whose members are interdependent and none of which is worth
more than another. How far this is from the conception that
puts man at the center of the world and tends to make him
superman!"

In French music, man is considered a function of his association with other beings, feeling their infinite and multiple radia-
tions, and sending his own out to them. His place in the universe
is modest, of course, but it is supremely beautiful, for it is illuminated by the flux of universal sympathy. In Debussy's *Pelléas
et Mélisande,* the mystery of the forest and the mystery of the
human soul merge. Ravel's *L'Enfant et les Sortilèges* sounds
the poetry of familiar things, the subtle communication between
a child and the features of his room. In Milhaud's and Claudel's
Christophe Colomb, the navigator's soul reflects all the seas of
the globe. And there is nothing more subtle than that marvelous
medieval music of Léonin and Pérotin who, in Paris, around
1180, composed with the finesse and evocative power of Debussy.
The Frenchman has never abandoned the earth. He is not an
artificial being; he is and remains a peasant. His rapport with
nature has never been broken. With only a few words or gestures
he brings nature to mind. An allusion, a light touch of color,
a chord, or a barely visible curve are enough to awaken a way

of feeling. Subtlety is acute in such works as Debussy's *Prélude à l'Après-midi d'un Faune,* Poulenc's *Bestiaire,* Roussel's *The Spider's Feast,* Fauré's *Bonne Chanson,* or Kœchlin's *Course de Printemps.* Verlaine says:

> *Car nous voulons la Nuance encor,*
> *Pas la Couleur, rien que la Nuance!*

And further on,

> *Que ton vers soit la bonne aventure*
> *Éparse au vent crispé du matin*
> *Qui va pleurant la menthe et le thym . . .*
> *Et tout le reste est littérature.*

Montaigne speaks finally of a "ripe, steady force."

And French music, so often criticized as frivolous, is strong. The secret of its strength lies in the precept of St. Thomas Aquinas, that art results from perfect correspondence between form and matter. All matter is molded by a form determined by the matter itself. A master form may well be convenient for manufacturing, but it would be inconceivable for creation. The French composer has never written repetitiously, except perhaps at the end of the eighteenth century, the weakest period in the history of French music. He writes only when he has something specific to say to us, when he has a message to transmit. Fixed patterns, therefore, are not in very good repute. The French are not composers of symphonies, like Haydn or Mozart. They may write one or two, but then they pass on to another exercise. In school we are taught that, aside from strictly fixed forms with contours and proportions defined without regard for content and material, there are free forms. And we are immediately— and wrongly—inclined to think of a sort of anarchy. The form in French music is not free, but it does change from one work to the next. It cannot take on a scholastic cast. And French music would not tolerate a Beckmesser.

Power of persuasion springs from the perfect adaptation of form to content. The works of Couperin, Satie, and Poulenc are models of an eminently effectual art, beneath their surface slenderness and despite their conspicuous conciseness. This is what we call force and not an impressive display of apparatus.

This conception of force has been handed down to us by the oldest Mediterranean civilizations, particularly the Greek, which developed it to such a high degree of perfection. The present-day French have received it as a direct legacy in an unbroken line of inheritance. That is why this force is characteristically so sure, natural, and mature. And it is constant. For St. Thomas's precept is such a simple and obvious truth to the mind of the French artist that it would not occur to him to turn away from it.

French music, like other French arts, is created on a human scale. It expresses and idealizes what is noblest in men—simplicity, clarity of judgment, warmth of feeling for other beings. French art is timeless. It does not consider the accidental, but only the constants of the human condition. And as a result, through its diversity, it escapes categorization. It is neither mechanistic nor experimental. It is always a rose, a nightingale, the sea, springtime, love.

Charles d'Orléans is a contemporary of Verlaine, Pérotin of Debussy, Couperin of Satie, Rameau of Sauguet, Machaut or Berlioz of Milhaud. And Fauré's last works reflect the clean lines of the Parthenon. There is no modern music in France. There is simply French music.

Since French art is a rational art, its technique is conceived in relation to its content. Technique is continuously changing, adapted by each author to his personal needs and the exigencies of his time. No trace of dogmatism can be found in it. A limiting system like Schoenberg's could not exist in France. Paul Dukas expresses the attitude of French musicians in these words: "One should know a great deal and make music with what one does not know."

French music, as we have pointed out, is primarily melodic, in the complete and real meaning of the word. It is this sense of melody, including in its definition the harmonic functions of its notes, that has protected music from the excesses of chromaticism. French harmony is still conceived according to the principle of tonality, which it has progressively enriched with chords of five, six, seven, or more notes. But even the most complicated dissonances are composed as appoggiaturas, suspensions, and passing tones; and when the relation of the dissonance to

the perfect chord becomes too uncertain or distant, an effort is
made to reaffirm the diatonic and make it stand out more clearly
through polytonality.

We explain this evolution in the following way. Impressionism in music is summed up in Debussy. Other composers took
delight in contemplating nature and, for our enjoyment, ably
translated the immediate and multiple impressions they drew
from contact with the outside world—Albert Roussel's *Rustiques,*
Kœchlin's *Paysages et Marines,* and the early works of Ravel,
Roland-Manuel, and Maurice Delage. They describe nothing,
tell no tale, and do not expose or impose the interior *I.* They
transmit that exquisite and peaceful joy, that delicate sensuality which comes from the communion a happy man has with
nature when he sees it as moving and fleeting beauty. André
Gide in *Les Nourritures Terrestres* says, "and put all your happiness in the moment." But Debussy's attitude toward impressionism was the purest and least distracted by other concerns.
Nuages and *La Mer* compare with the admirable passages
in which Proust describes his ever-fresh impressions of the sea
at Balbec. Along with Ravel's *Noctuelles* and *Vallée des Cloches,*
Debussy's *Prélude à l'Après-midi d'un Faune, Soirée dans Gre-
nade,* and *Jardins sous la Pluie* are impressionist masterpieces.
Just as Monet, painting his cathedrals and water lilies, translated the play of light on stones and water, ignoring the object
and keeping only its reflection and letting its lines and contours
disappear in the harmony of finely shaded colors, so the composer had a predilection for the play of harmonies, the light
of music. He cultivated harmonic thinking, conceiving music
vertically, and let a melody appear from time to time beneath
the vibration of the chords. That play of melody in harmonic
surroundings, as for example the song *"Nous n'irons plus au
Bois"* in the *Jardins sous la Pluie,* is a delight to hear.

Harmonies became more and more subtle, or more and more
rare. They separated further and further from the perfect chord
and resolved on it at infrequent intervals. The harmonic world
was enriched and enlarged by the introduction and acceptance
of exceptional resolutions, consecutive ninths and elevenths, sequences of fourths and fifths, unprepared dissonances, foreign
pedal notes, and unresolved appoggiaturas. This harmonic

evolution—from about 1880 to 1910—led from consecutive ninths in Chabrier's *Le Roi Malgré Lui* [*Example 65*] to the double and triple appoggiaturas in *Daphnis et Chloé* [*Example 66*]. Tact, balance, and infallible taste governed all these liberties. But when mediocre composers tried to exercise that harmonic freedom, the language became empty and senseless under their pens. Such second-rate and third-rate works were universally tabbed *Debussyism*—an incorrect label, for in no way did it reflect the genius of Debussy, who had a horror of superficial imitations. He himself was the first anti-Debussyite.

Debussy himself was not immune to the temptation to overuse harmonic language. *Images pour Piano* contains the selections *Reflets dans l'Eau, Cloches à travers le Feuillage,* and *Poissons d'Or,* in which the lack of melody deprives the harmonic play of support. The music is wasted in a search for resonances and colors, and settles in a sonorous dust lacking any form or cohesion. Debussy well understood that these pieces marked the end of impressionism. In subsequent works he stated the melody more clearly and concentrated on the problem of form. The composers of the postimpressionist phase then in progress wanted to reinforce the structural solidity that the composition was in danger of losing without sacrificing any of the new freedom in harmony. It goes without saying that there must be freedom of form to correspond with freedom of harmony. The sonata type, the "sonata form" D'Indy liked so well, was abandoned because it was too academic and cluttered with lengthy development sections to suit French thinking. French composers therefore rightly addressed themselves to the creation of free forms. For in France, where the sense of form and balance is innate, creating forms beyond ordinary canons is more in character than composing within the framework of a scheme foreign to the work in mind.

The postimpressionist period includes Debussy's *Préludes* and *Piano Etudes* along with his *Three Sonatas for Various Instruments, Le Martyre de St. Sébastien,* and *En Blanc et Noir;* Ravel's works, except for some early impressionist pieces; and the work of Roussel, Kœchlin, and Schmitt. The composers Roland-Manuel, Jacques Ibert, Claude Delvincourt, and Maurice Delage also belong to the movement. For Debussy, the period began in 1908 with the composition of *Trois Chansons de Charles d'Orléans,* for a mixed *a cappella* chorus. The songs are written in a style rather resembling Claude Le Jeune's. The composer is more concerned with the harmonic line than the contrapuntal. The songs have fairly ample melodic lines with little tonal characterization, and lend themselves to marvelous chromatic treatment skillfully handled so as not to upset the tonal scheme. Debussy also composed two collections of art songs: *Le Promenoir des Deux Amants,* set to poems by Tristan L'Hermite, and *Trois Ballades de François Villon.* The choice of poems is indicative of the composer's inclinations—subtlety in expression setting man in his modest place surrounded by sympathetic nature; conciseness and elegance of form. The melodies are quite distinct in design, and their tonality is often replaced by modal treatment. A deliberately modular style gives *Promenoir des Deux Amants* a particularly flexible character; the music has clarity and depth. The *Trois Ballades de François Villon* have a periodic structure—carried over from the form of the poems—which is unique in Debussy's work. A modal flavor, even more distinct than in the first collection, gives the work an archaic sound.

Modern French composers have adopted Gregorian modes, appreciating their particular expressiveness resulting from the placement of half-tones in the scale. The multiplicity of modes enriches the potential for expression and allows the composer to escape major-minor limitations without sacrificing the tonal foundation. Tonality thus becomes a specific case of the larger principle of modality. Fauré, Ravel, Kœchlin, Satie, Milhaud, and Poulenc have made the most natural and generous use of the modes.

Gigues Tristes and *Ibéria* from *Images pour Orchestre* still bear traces of impressionism. They appear as conflicts of multiple ideas and overwhelming orchestration and are as sensuously disturbing as tne wonderful central piece *Les Parfums de la Nuit* from *Ibéria.* The third *Image, Rondes de Printemps,* with its dancelike movement, belongs to the new period. The idea is developed more evenly, the structure is symmetrical, and the orchestration, using homogeneous groups of instruments, is less dispersed, so that the form and architecture of the *Rondes* are clearly audible. The *Rondes de Printemps* is much less often performed than the popular *Ibéria* because of the difficult orchestral requirements. It deserves to be better known; the piece has wonderful grace and freshness.

Debussy's *Preludes for Piano* are today as highly esteemed and as widely known as the *Preludes* of Chopin. The twenty-four pieces are almost all in ABA form. Although some are splendid, it is unfortunate that Debussy restricted himself to that type of symmetry. His temperament was better suited to creating completely free forms, as demonstrated by his twelve great *Etudes for Piano*. It is hard to know what to admire most in that magnificent monument of piano literature—the abundance of invention, solidity of form, or perfection of pianistic thought. No hint of impressionism remains. The music is a continuous, uninterrupted flow, as in the fiery pieces for two pianos, the suite *En Blanc et Noir*.

Debussy's last works are three sonatas, *Sonata No. 1 in D for Cello and Piano*, *Sonata No. 2 for Flute, Viola and Harp*, and *Sonata No. 3 in G for Violin and Piano*. Each sonata is comprised of three movements, but the plan of the movements is no longer related to nineteenth-century sonata form. While Schoenberg goes so far as to suppress the exposition of themes and attaches importance only to the *Durchführung*, Debussy, who hates developments, suppresses them and concentrates on expositions, which introduce themes directly, completely formed and expressed. The central movement keeps nothing of the scherzo except its humorous and capricious intent, and is based on strong contrast between two ideas. The great lines of the finale recall the rondo. This is the structural schema of the *Sonata No. 3 for Violin and Piano* and *Sonata No. 1 for Cello and Piano*. *Sonata No. 2 for Flute, Viola, and Harp* is more rhapsodic, and is, moreover, not so well achieved.

Le Martyre de St. Sébastien, one of Debussy's most important works, was composed in 1911 and was still impressionistic. The atmosphere of the Ballet Russe nonetheless gave the work a particularly plastic quality—broad patterns, each with its own color; large themes; and great chromatic melodies. Only the final chorus is diatonic, and it is perhaps a little too brief in comparison with the magnificence of other sections of that admirable score, which is said to be to *Pelléas* what *Parsifal* is to *Tristan.*

In 1913 Debussy gave *Jeux* to the Ballet Russe. This dance-poem, tremulous as the leaves at night in the park where the action takes place, is the final word of music before 1914, the last expression of that carefree happiness, that gentle life crowning a century of prosperity and social progress. The orchestra for *Jeux* is larger than any Debussy had ever used before. It consists of four sets of woods and brasses, and great breadth in the parts for strings (the first violins extend to a division into six parts, the second violins into four, the violas and cellos into three). Just as *Le Sacre du Printemps* announced the destruction of one of the most refined of all periods, *Jeux* bid it a tender good-by. Musical impressionism had never before achieved such a high degree of pulsing life and vibrancy.

Claude Debussy, *"musicien français,"* was one of the most radiant geniuses of the art of sound. The listener may prefer the purely impressionist period of his work, the period of *Prélude à l'Après-midi d'un Faune, Pelléas et Mélisande,* the *Nocturnes, Estampes,* and *La Mer.* And Debussy may well have said what was most essential in this period, and moved with greatest ease in this absolute freedom. The fact that his postimpressionist compositions are more set in form, more precise in thought, and slightly drier does not prevent them from being beautiful, too. A preference for one or the other period of the work of Debussy cannot be based on a value judgment, but only on the personal question of which manner best corresponds to one's own feelings.

GABRIEL FAURÉ's opera *Pénélope* appeared in 1913, along with *Le Sacre du Printemps* and *Jeux.* Almost the entire work of the highly original Gabriel Fauré consists of song cycles and piano pieces. In his youth he had written the graceful and appealing *Sonata for Piano and Violin,* two beautiful *Quartets for Piano and Strings,* preludes, waltzes, nocturnes, barcaroles, impromptus for piano, and numerous songs. His art might seem easy and superficial because Fauré had an unequaled gift for melodic invention. His melodies are decisive in all his compositions, and he did not bother to develop them through exceptional harmonies or studied counterpoint. Most of his songs and piano pieces are accompanied monodies for which he created a soft, brilliant flowering of pianistic embellishment. All this might seem to justify a reputation for frivolity and worldliness, but in fact his art has considerably more significance. The melodies have shapes of rare perfection, and the harmonies, simple as they are, were chosen with surprising discretion and aptitude. Under its seeming simplicity his art is governed by an impeccable taste that avoided affectation as much as it did banality.

After *Pénélope,* Fauré's art changed, not in its essential character, but in that it increased in weight, and thus grew in power. Debussy, in the same period, felt it necessary to establish a more substantial form. Fauré had no need to worry about such problems. Balance was the very foundation of his art, and its form had always been simple and fitting. He was to develop in the direction of greater concentration of means. His harmony, without becoming complex, increased in tension. He called on counterpoint to replace in his developments the appeal of pianistic embellishments. He progressively stripped down his art and gave up brilliant trappings, to attain the perfect cleanliness of the purest architecture in his last works, as in the *Second Quintet for Piano and Strings* and in the *String Quartet.* Fauré's last period includes *Pénélope* (1913); the *Sonata No. 2 for Violin and Piano;* two *Sonatas for Cello and Piano; Le Jardin Clos* (1915-1918), songs set to poems by Charles van Lerberghe; *L'Horizon Chimérique* (1922), set to poems by Jean de La Ville de Mirmont; *Mirages,* set to poems by the Baroness de Brimont; the *Second Quintet for Piano and Strings;* a *Trio for Piano, Violin, and Cello;* and the *String Quartet* (1924).

The harmony in his work is distinguished by innovations in chord successions, and not by the chords themselves. Fauré creates extreme tension with chords of sevenths which are simple but eloquent in their sequential progression; and moments of resolution are very graceful and supple [*Example 67*]. The same impression of originality is felt in the sequences found in his contrapuntal writing, for instance, the exchange of notes between parts [*Example 68*] in harmonies produced by imitation like the ending of the first act of *Pénélope,* where there also occurs one of those harmonic modulations which is an omission that greatly contributes to the concentration of language [*Example 69*]. The more Fauré advances in his work, the more he adheres to means of condensing the harmonic route, and gives only the points of departure and arrival, passing the intermediary stages in silence [*Example 70*]. His use of counterpoint also increases harmonic freedom [*Example 71*]. But his harmony is always kept within the limits of tonality. Frequent modal figures and passing modulations give flexibility to the tonal structure. The very diverse and subtle modulations are possibly what constitute the essence of Fauré's expression in his last works [*Example 72*].

From the point of view of architecture, we should point out that in the sonatas, trios, and quintet of his late period, Fauré deliberately develops his sonata movement on a single idea, doing away with the classic two themes or subjects. This peculiarity is due to the insistence on condensation that guides his harmony as well, and to his denial of color, which makes him avoid contrasts.

Starting with a more traditionalist conception than Debussy's, Fauré came closer in his later work to the new music than did Debussy—the architectural direction of his composition, his spirit of reduction, the conciseness of his harmonic language, the importance he gives counterpoint, and in the clarity of his melodic lines. His evolution, which began with gracious affability, ended in a serene grandeur like the grandeur that comes with knowledge. No drama or movement remains. The *Second Quintet* and the *String Quartet* attain the immobility of perfection.

Fauré was born in 1845. His students—Charles Kœchlin, born in 1867, Florent Schmitt in 1870, Roger-Ducasse in 1873, Maurice Ravel in 1875, and André Caplet in 1879—were to be the principal composers of the postimpressionist period, along with Albert Roussel, D'Indy's pupil, born in 1869.

MAURICE RAVEL composed some sixty works. We shall not discuss the first half of his work, written between 1893 and 1910, which includes the *Pavane pour une Infante Défunte, Jeux d'Eau*, the *Quartet in F, Schéhérazade, Miroirs, Histoires Naturelles*, the *Rapsodie Espagnole, L'Heure Espagnole, Ma Mère l'Oye*, and *Gaspard de la Nuit*—works that today are famous and even popular, but that are part of an artistic production that precedes the period we are interested in. Until around 1910 Ravel's music was erroneously thought to be following the same lines as Debussy's. The error is understandable. Ravel, like Debussy, sought out new harmonies, and an impressionist aesthetic underlay many works of that period.

The *Valses Nobles et Sentimentales,* composed in 1911, put Ravel on a path that separated him from Debussy. The *Sonatina for Piano* (1905) and *Ma Mère l'Oye* (1908) showed an inclination toward simplicity and clarity of form. The *Valses,* which cannot really be called simple, had nonetheless already discarded the brilliant arabesques that make the charm of *Jeux d'Eau, Miroirs,* and *Gaspard de la Nuit.* Melodic lines in the *Valses* are traced distinctly and without tonal ambiguity. Ravel believed it as necessary as Debussy did to confirm tonality through the melody, in order to avoid the danger music was exposed to by the harmonic embellishment for which they themselves were primarily responsible. Ravel's student Roland-Manuel correctly asserts that the *Valses* are the sum total of Ravel's harmonic experience. Further, Roland-Manuel clearly indicates what distinguishes Ravel from Debussy from the point of view of harmony. Debussy's harmony rests on the major ninth chord, while Ravel shows a marked preference for seventh and ninth chords of the second class [*Example 73*] derived from the modes on D and E. Ravel's melodic thought is also modal by nature, and these two modes are precisely the ones he takes up most often. The mode on E, the Dorian of antiquity, is also that of Andalusian chant [*Example 75*]. C major is just one key among others for Ravel, and Roland-Manuel could not find in Ravel's work a single example of the classic minor key. Ravel took acciaccaturas and single, double, triple, and unresolved appoggiaturas to an extreme. He was particularly interested in the superior unresolved appoggiatura of the diminished seventh [*Example 76*]. These dissonances, however, are always used in a way that does not threaten the tonal scheme. In *Le Gibet* from *Gaspard de la Nuit,* he introduces a pedal-note to confirm the tonal thread when harmonic complexity might lead to ambiguity. The *Valses Nobles et Sentimentales* sound with sharp, naked dissonances, incisive and clear and without need of support. The well-known augmented fifth, considered typical of impressionist music, was given free rein by Debussy and determined the use of whole-tone scales in his work. In Ravel's work its ambiguity disappears, for it is always a part of the natural eleventh chord. As a matter of fact, the whole-tone scale is never found in Ravel's music, and his language owes nothing to Debussy's. The two composers are independent of each other. But both owe a great deal to Chabrier and especially to Erik Satie, who will be discussed later.

Regarding the orchestra, as well, the composer of *Daphnis* diverges from the composer of *Pelléas*. Here is what Roland-Manuel has to say about this:

> [Debussy's] Verlainian orchestra is arranged so that
> > *. . . la nuance seul fiance*
> > *Le rêve au rêve et la flûte au cor.*

Curious to hear how it would sound to connect or juxtapose sonori ties that did not seem to go together, [Ravel,] with his Baudelairian orchestra, seems to imply that nuance generates expression rather than intensity, the latter depending only on the timbre, amplification, and number of instruments. This is obviously why Ravel, contrary to Debussy, requires more virtuosity from the performers than he does initiative from the conductor. Nuances in Ravel's work usually accord with the normal sound intensity of an instrument for a given tessitura. It is useless to force them. The musical lines, in return, take to extreme registers (Ravel likes his oboes and bassoons in high registers, and his clarinets low). This sometimes calls for perilous—if indispensable—acrobatics.

Daphnis et Chloé, begun in 1909 and finished in 1912, is a ballet-symphony commissioned by Diaghilev for the Ballet Russe. It is an enormous fresco, painted in large brush-strokes. Choruses without words combine with the orchestra (except for one interlude when they sing *a cappella*). The work is not very homogeneous. The best pages have been collected in two concert suites, and are admirable for their iridescent orchestration. The *Lever du Jour* is also Ravel's warmest composition. On the whole, *Daphnis et Chloé* is guilty of a somewhat academic development, which, fortunately for our pleasure, is compensated for by brilliant sonority.

Ravel may sometimes be guilty of academicism. Yet, it is an

academicism artfully enhanced by a virtuosity that makes people say that Ravel is to Debussy what Rimsky-Korsakov is to Mussorgsky. But what marvelous inventive freedom there is in works like *Ma Mère l'Oye*, admirably orchestrated in 1912, and the wonderful *Trois Poèmes de Stéphane Mallarmé*, composed in 1913. These songs, accompanied by a small chamber orchestra, are perhaps Ravel's most beautiful works.

Stravinsky at Clarens had composed *Three Japanese Lyrics* for voice and solo instruments. They were inspired by Schoenberg's *Pierrot Lunaire*, which pointed the way for music to escape the enormous workings of a full orchestra. Ravel visited near Clarens for two months to write a revision of Mussorgsky's *Khovantchina* at Diaghilev's request. Stravinsky played him his *Three Japanese Lyrics*. The two friends, united by musical interests which were closely related until the composition of *The Nightingale*, talked about Schoenberg, for whom Ravel never ceased to profess deep admiration. After the visit Ravel composed his *Trois Poèmes de Stéphane Mallarmé*, and his first student, Maurice Delage, conceived his delightful *Quatre Poèmes Hindous* in the same vein.

With the *Trois Poèmes*, Ravel unclutters the tools of sonority. Harmony is reduced to essentials. Melody becomes fuller and fuller, and the music takes on the transparency and purity Mallarmé's poetry requires. Ravel understood Schoenberg's lesson, but does not follow the composer of *Pierrot Lunaire* on the path of atonality. His French temperament deters him from destroying the melody and he cannot give up the charm and harmonious accord of sounds governed by a tonic of reference.

To the diminution of harmony corresponds a growing concern with counterpoint. This is a sign of the times, and Ravel, from 1920 on, follows an evolution similar to Fauré's and Stravinsky's. These three composers, each in his own way, incline toward a new classicism whose distinguishing features are its economy of means, the predominance of contrapuntal language, and an objective attitude toward the musical material. Ravel was to go the furthest in this direction, with his *Sonata for Violin and Cello* (1920-22) and the *Chansons Madécasses* (1925-26). Although Ravel, through *Daphnis et Chloé*, moved from sensation to a voluptuous intoxication with the beauty of sound, his character changed radically after 1920. He had always mistrusted emotion, fearful of the dramatic extreme to which it might lead him, and therefore he deliberately hid it behind a bantering, ironic air. His expression was reserved and distant, with glimpses of a delicate tenderness beneath his seeming detachment. Now, from 1920 on, he shows himself in an entirely different light. His reserve sometimes takes the form of excessive soberness, but since he can only tolerate it for a limited time, he bursts out in harsh, violent exclamations that give his music a totally unexpected tragic feeling. Between these extremes, the evidence of a tortured soul, calm returns and the tenderness so long constrained is sometimes freed and released in exquisite feeling.

La Valse, a poem-ballet for orchestra (1919-20), was commissioned by Diaghilev, who never used it. No one knows why the piece was abandoned. Musically speaking, the rejection is unexplainable. As was the case with most modern ballets, the work was a concert triumph. "I conceived the work," says the composer in a biographical sketch, "as a sort of apotheosis of the Viennese waltz, mixed in my mind with an impression of fantastic and fatal swirling. The waltz is danced in an imperial court around 1855."

In two great crescendos, the work unrolls a chain of waltzes that echo Schubert and, even more, Johann Strauss. From the beginning, the trembling of the orchestra in the low registers and the sounds of the bass clarinet create a raw, turbulent atmosphere which sustains the dizzying, menacing whirlwind of the waltz. "The second crescendo," writes Roland-Manuel, "shorter and much more vehement, gathers these multiformed melodies and their rhythms together, breaks them against each other, and opposes them or blends them together with violence. This is a brutal and skillful development which does not really begin until the stretto and combines with it to recall at the end the principal D major tonality." *La Valse* is not, as has been thought, a picture of post-1918 Vienna, but an interior drama, the struggle of a composer's soul between its two opposite poles —restraint and exuberance. The struggle ends in an explosion.

The *Sonata for Violin and Cello,* a tense, hard, unrelenting piece, has this same exasperated lyricism. The virtuosity of the two solo instruments sometimes creates the illusion that the piece is being played by a string quartet.

Amelette Ronsardelette is a work of utter simplicity. The music is stripped bare and only the spirit remains—a melody, a design on the piano composed of parallel fifths. For the first time, and fleetingly, Ravel frees himself and confesses an emotion. The feeling of tenderness it emits is to be fully expressed in *L'Enfant et les Sortilèges*.

Ravel had a predilection for the supernatural as expressed in fairy tales and in automatons. Their inner mystery entreated and invited him to quit the everyday world around him. He preferred fantastic imaginary creations to the unimaginative reality of everyday life. The souls of things, animals, and goblins beguiled him, and we get a clue to the secret of his own soul when we listen to the clock music in *L'Heure Espagnol*, to *Grillon*, *Martin-Pêcheur*, and *Scarbo*.

Ravel loved children and his own personality retained certain childlike characteristics. He tells us this in *L'Enfant et les Sortilèges,* a two-part lyric fantasy he composed on Colette's text. The idea of the piece is charming. A spoiled child who is bored vents his rage by attacking all the objects he finds in his room —the teapot, the curtains, the armchair. He stamps his feet, breaks and tears things up until he finally goes to sleep. And then the souls of all the inanimate objects he has betrayed speak to him and reproach him for his cruelty. He sees his garden at night. All the animals he has teased surround him and threaten to hurt him. But when the child falls and hurts himself, and cries bitterly, the animals take pity on him and recognize his basic kindness.

The quality of the score is at times uneven. There are pages in which the composer lets loose his penchant for everything comic, and there are others which sound like a Broadway musical. The verve of Ravel's orchestra serves him well, even though the orchestra is always kept in the background. There is a naive gaiety in these successive "numbers"—the fox-trot of the teapot and china cup; the arithmetic song; and the famous duet of the cats, which Honegger calls the most remarkable piece of the score. Naturally, Ravel doesn't simply imitate the meowing of cats; he uses the sound as inspiration for a melodic line. The

second part, which takes place in the garden, provides a strong
contrast to the first. Everything in it is delightfully poetic, and
the end of the piece, when the chorus sings of the child's inherent goodness, is moving. You would say that Ravel had laid
out everything he loved, and could not resist the temptation to
show us, just once, the very depths of his particularly delicate
feelings.

The *Chansons Madécasses* were composed in 1926 on poems
by Parny, for voice, flute, cello, and piano. The composer says:

> You must never be afraid to imitate. I myself followed Schoenberg's
> footsteps to write my *Poèmes de Mallarmé* and especially the *Chansons
> Madécasses,* which, like *Pierrot Lunaire,* have a very strict counterpoint
> underlying the atmosphere. If [the *Chansons*] are not totally Schoen-
> bergian, it's because in music I am not so afraid of the element of
> charm which he avoided to a point of asceticism, even martyrdom.
> Possibly just because he is Viennese, in reaction against the musical
> sensuality of his surroundings, which moreover does impregnate his
> early works.

Actually whenever Ravel has borrowed the technique of another composer the resulting composition bears no trace of that
other work. The *Chansons Madécasses* are no more like Schoenberg than the andante of the *Piano Concerto* is like the adagietto
of Mozart's *Quintet with Clarinet,* which was in fact its point
of departure. All he has in common with Schoenberg is the
independence of his parts. But again, in Ravel this development
of parts is carried out without destroying the principle of tonality. The sensual *Chansons Madécasses,* along with the *Concerto
in D for the Left Hand,* are the most beautiful music composed
by Ravel since the *Poèmes de Mallarmé.*

The sweeping success of *Bolero* (1928) surprised everyone, and
especially the composer. Ravel had no desire to compose when
he accepted Ida Rubinstein's commission for a ballet although
he did want to write orchestrations. He wrote a short bolero,
which actually has no musical interest. Then he came upon the
idea of repeating the piece a great number of times without even
modifying its harmony or even modulating, but instead varying
the orchestration in such a way as to increase the volume of
sound little by little until it reaches a climax at the end of the

piece. He brought to bear all the ingenuity and orchestral virtuosity he possessed. The effect is peculiar. The listener finds himself hearing music whose content he cannot approve of, but whose obstinate repetitions nonetheless force him to follow it. The single modulation preceding the coda is still irresistible after a hundred hearings. Ravel, probably unconsciously, has engaged the wheels of musical sorcery.

Of the two piano concertos written in 1931, the *Concerto in G Major* for two hands is brilliant but only slightly interesting except for the adagio assai, which develops in an atmosphere of radiant serenity. But the *Concerto in D for the Left Hand* is really remarkable with its compact form, its firmness of language and its feeling of tragedy, anguish, and revolt. The music is dark, rumbling, shaken with brutal and tearing beats, while its jazz syncopation creates astonishing effects.

Debussy was distinctly a pre-World War I musician, as was Fauré. The late works of these two composers of genius gave their successors no path to follow, but they did participate in the beginning of a general evolution in French music. The movement was characterized by a return to more marked melodic line, a style which gave more importance to counterpoint, more concise form, and more condensed language.

The second period of Ravel's work falls in the category of current developments. Of all French composers, it is undoubtedly the composer of *Valses Nobles et Sentimentales* who exploited harmonic discoveries to the greatest extent. With Charles Kœchlin and Darius Milhaud, he felt the importance of contrapuntal language in the new music, and in some passages achieved a bareness the equal of which can only be found in Satie. Lastly, he shared with Stravinsky and most of the more recent composers that objective, rational attitude with regard to musical material which leads to a new classicism. But these traits are not always present in the second half of Ravel's work. They alternate with earlier concerns with color, virtuosity, and the picturesque, which sometimes prevents his last works from having the homogeneity found in Satie's and Stravinsky's music. This duality should not be surprising in a composer who arrived at maturity in 1910 and who, from then on, was divided between the ideas of the turn of the century and those of the new era in which he lived and which he understood.

The question of polytonality in Ravel's music has been much discussed. It arises, actually, after the introduction of ninth, eleventh, and thirteenth chords in his harmony [*Example 74*]. The listener may be tempted to hear perfect tonic, dominant, and subdominant chords in a thirteenth chord; this would be a case of harmonic polytonality. Such an interpretation hardly seems valid. As a matter of fact, one of the three perfect chords which can be found in a thirteenth chord will always predominate by its position and sonorous weight, and will make a single tonic predominant to the ear. In the example given, the chord is distinctly in F.

Aside from this fact, it is remarkable that Ravel's most complex harmonies, which are always explicable in context, can be analyzed in appoggiaturas and passing tones that relate the chord to a single, well-defined tonality. If the existence of harmonic polytonality is contestable, especially in Ravel's music, his last works quite definitely furnish numerous instances of contrapuntal bitonality. Bitonality occurs whenever two superimposed lines follow different keys, even if the coincidences and vertical sections and their harmonic support create chords belonging to a single key. Examples of this can be found in the *Sonata for Violin and Piano* and *Chansons Madécasses*. The bitonality is limited, moreover, to the superimposition of neighboring tones which are quickly resolved into a single note.

FLORENT SCHMITT was five years Ravel's senior. He was born in Blamont, in Lorraine, in 1870. France has many faces, and you could almost say that each of her provinces has produced a composer to represent its character. Debussy sings of the sweetness of Ile-de-France; Ravel has the rather dry clarity of the southern mountaineer; Roussel represents the energetic exuberance of Flanders; and who could be more Provençal than Milhaud, more Tourainesque than Poulenc, or more Parisian than Auric?

Schmitt of Lorraine is positive, and his vision in his works is large. He has no fear of intensity and cares nothing for the metaphysics of the neighboring Germans. He loves the sting of battle and he has a boldness that does not hesitate before any obstacle. Perhaps his imagination lacks some of the inventiveness of other French composers of the same generation. On the other hand, the will to produce and to act on a grand scale is one of Schmitt's outstanding qualities. This characteristic was to influence Honegger, despite the great difference in sensibilities and concepts of form of the two composers.

Actually, Schmitt was largely a pre-1910 composer. His three principal works, those on which his reputation is based, are: the *Psalm 48 for Solo Soprano, Chorus, Organ, and Orchestra,* Op. 38 (1904); *Tragédie de Salomé,* drama without words for symphony orchestra, Op. 50 (1907-1911); and the *Quintet for Piano and String Instruments,* Op. 51 (1901-1908). *Psalm 48* is a work of such undeniable force and spiritual elevation that it should be ranked among the masterpieces of contemporary music. *Tragédie de Salomé,* with its heavy, voluptuous, oppressive atmosphere, continues to be one of the modern works most appreciated by concert societies. The *Quintet,* a soaring work of monumental proportions, is warm and poignant, but asks too much of the piano and strings, which are sometimes inadequate for the sonorous intensity demanded by the music. The form, as well, is outsized. Excessive development spoils somewhat an otherwise spontaneous, generous, and lofty art.

Florent Schmitt's compositions since 1918 include a number of important works: *Sonate Libre pour Violon et Piano,* Op. 68 (1918-1919); orchestration for Shakespeare's *Antony and Cleopatra,* Op. 69 (1919-1920); two lovely ballets, *Le Petit Elfe Ferme-L'Œil,* Op. 73 (1912-1923), and *Ariane la Sans-Égale* (1937); *Symphonie Concertante pour Piano et Orchestre;* and two chamber music works, the short, graceful *Sonate pour Flûte, Clarinette et Clavecin,* and *Suite en Rocaille pour Divers Instruments.*

CHARLES KŒCHLIN was born of Alsatian parents in Paris in 1867, and studied at the École Polytechnique from 1887 to 1889. He then went to the Paris Conservatory where he studied under Massenet, Gedalge, and then Fauré. Kœchlin was an exceptionally intelligent and extremely cultivated man whose scope of interest included all fields of human endeavor, no matter how diverse. Above everything else, he was profoundly rational, this quality stemming in part from his scientific training. Along with firm discipline Kœchlin developed a natural modesty which lent grace to his refusal of all compromise. Experimenters such as he are endowed with absolute purity of mind and complete detachment. These outstanding qualities of mind and will admirably assisted his delicate but powerful temperament and his essentially musical nature. But these same qualities are also responsible for the fact that Kœchlin's enormous body of work, as remarkable and original as it is, is little known and often misunderstood. He made few attempts to have his works performed, and was more willing to discuss his important theoretical writings than his compositions. He was a clear-sighted and enthusiastic defender of everything young and bold, provided it led to beauty; he devoted more effort to promoting the works of young composers than to spreading his own work. His most important compositions are still unpublished at present, and as a result his work is underestimated and has not been accorded the place of honor it deserves.

Kœchlin is a master, not only as a composer but also as a teacher. His teachings and his art testify to a great respect for tradition, but only when its precepts rest on a real and valid foundation. Tradition in music generally refers to the customs and requirements since the time of Bach, whereas Kœchlin was conversant with much older musical techniques—those of the Middle Ages and the Renaissance. He understood that these techniques, though lost from view during the periods of classicism and romanticism, are by no means outmoded. In fact, they correspond to any time when language is expanding and horizons extending.

Tradition according to Kœchlin means the spirit and techniques of the complete history of music from the time of Gregorian chant, and the application of that complete tradition to modern composition.

The freedom of Kœchlin's art is based precisely on that breadth of vision which formed his thinking on the language of music. Kœchlin was not bound to any formal system or any limiting concept of music. He did not concern himself with whether objectivity or subjectivity was the better route. He followed both. His music was born spontaneously as a manifestation of living forces. Modality, tonality, polytonality, and atonality were not different languages to him but aspects or different branches of a single language which were to his mind functions of different expressive needs. He accepted any imaginable chord and the most daring counterpoint as long as they could be justified by "musicality." He applied this attitude, which was natural to him and guided him in his own compositions, to the analysis of works of all composers and also to his teaching. His didactic writings are universally known: *La Théorie de la Musique, Étude sur l'Écriture de la Fugue d'École, Étude sur les Notes de Passage* (1922), *Précis des Règles du Contrepoint* (1927), *Traité de l'Harmonie* (1928), and lastly *Traité de l'Orchestration* (1944).

Kœchlin was able to retain all means of expression, no matter how old or new, without corrupting his language because as a true man of science he always sought the physical and organic causes of the phenomenon of music. Those fundamental causes do not belong to a time, a climate, or a system, but rely on the inherent qualities of sound as a physical phenomenon and the nature of the human ear which perceives the sound. The means used by the language of sound have relative, not absolute, value, and cannot therefore be molded by intangible dogmas. Especially for Kœchlin, whose point of departure was the desire for expression, the choice of means is conditioned by the character of the expression. He was astonished, for example, and rightly so, that today people do not understand that, along with a composer like Schoenberg for whom atonality is a necessity, one can also appreciate someone like Henri Sauguet, whose language is not only tonal but almost entirely consonant. Atonality, and dissonant language in general, do not mean progress at the expense of consonant expression. Consonant language preserves all its qualities and power if it is utilized by a composer to whom it comes naturally. Further, the same composer may in turn be atonal and tonal, dissonant and consonant, harmonic, contrapuntal, and monodic without being guilty of

eclecticism. Everything depends on perfect correspondence between the means and the end.

A specific example of this principle of relativity in music is
that in the realm of harmony the degree of dissonance is determined not only by the notes used in the chord. It will be related
to many other factors, such as the position of the chord, instrumentation, nuance, and context. The notion of consonance is
relative in the same way.

The breadth of Kœchlin's proposals derives from André
Gedalge's teaching. Instruction based on musicality, invention,
spontaneity, and consideration of the choice of technical means
in relation to the idea of the music runs no risk of turning
academic. On the contrary, it favors the development of personality. Almost all contemporary French composers of merit
were formed under the tutelege of Gedalge and Kœchlin.
Gedalge taught Ravel, Kœchlin, Milhaud, and Honegger, while
Kœchlin in turn guided the studies of Poulenc and Sauguet.

Kœchlin's mature compositions reflect a very marked personality. His counterpoint, unequaled in suppleness, gives the
impression of being totally free while it still follows the rules
of that technique in their most rigorous requirements. His many
fugues are remarkably varied and ingenious. The most complex ones are so clear and even the most unusual arrangement
is so apparent and natural that the compositions appear simple.
One must read his *Fugue en Fa pour Orchestre* or the finale of
his *Première Symphonie* to understand just how far the polyphonic cloth can be compressed and still retain the feeling of
spontaneity that safeguards it against sounding academic or
pedantic.

Kœchlin's harmony utilizes every conceivable tone combination, from the perfect chord to the chord of twelve tones, with
a unique sense of arrangement and a way of spacing and gradu-
ating tensions to avoid shock, abruptness, or harshness [*Example 77*]. Kœchlin is equally successful in passing from tonal
melody to modal chant. Actually, by using different modes inherited from Gregorian music and French folk music, he avoids
"the tyranny of the major" attacked by Maurice Emmanuel, and
progresses from simple tonality to polytonality. Kœchlin was the
first to realize this potential transition in counterpoint and har-

mony, and pointed the way for Darius Milhaud. Polytonality is not opposed to the principle of tonality, as has been incorrectly asserted. On the contrary, it is a result of this principle, and its utilization confirms the presence of a dominant and governing key. In order to create polytonality, each superimposed key must be established clearly. All the keys resolve sooner or later into the main key. The two leading threads of the polytonality, in Kœchlin's and Milhaud's meaning, are always distinctly audible, as is evident in *Example 78*, drawn from Kœchlin's *Heures Persanes*, in which D major and G major are superimposed on a pedal-note in E major.

The superimposition of chords in different keys requires that they be clearly separated in sonorous space because interweaving them would make a different harmony.

Besides harmonic polytonality, contrapuntal polytonality superimposes melodies in different keys. Here, too, care must be exercised that the voices meet in agreeable harmony. Kœchlin cites *Example 80* in his *Traité de l'Harmonie* and points out that "the melody for the right hand is not written with just any random relationship to the chromaticism of the left hand. Sometimes this chromaticism is expressed in passing notes, and sometimes it is related to the melody by the perception of certain chords thus created. In such unions the ear does not forget to hear vertically and would easily notice harmonic flatness, even momentary or formed by the movement of flexible and logical counterpoints." The author also sometimes conceives passages which in his opinion are atonal [*Example 81*]. If this selection were submitted to Schoenberg, he would certainly call it tonal. Actually, a definite key can be discovered in each eighth-note. The example shows that for Kœchlin tonality depends on a given key's being sustained for a certain time, and atonality is the state created by "an instantaneous tonality, as it were, which would change with a somewhat disconcerting speed."

The fact that Kœchlin accepts different states of the language (modal, tonal, polytonal, and atonal) as unified—the choice of which is determined by the expression—is confirmed in the following paragraph from his *Traité de l'Harmonie,* in which he comments on the example of atonality we have just given:

Could that impression of painful uncertainty and extreme remoteness be achieved with less dissonant combinations? Possibly. But the composer of this *Quintet* was forced to use them without intending to write anything other than neighboring tones and equally without wanting to write the same thing. I have spoken warmly of tonal clarity too often for the reader not to trust me when I now say: I know that at certain times it is useful to depart from the tonality or, at least, to affirm it so fleetingly and vaguely that it seems not to have been done. To evoke such feelings and express such passages, these new means are valuable. And by contrast, they prove the existence of the tonality, for if there were no tonality there would be no need to leave it to express musical ideas opposed to the impression of clarity created by tonal music (even Gregorian).

We are far from Schoenbergian, systematic, structural atonality. We are also far from the pure play of music which is Stravinsky's idea. We have here an art mainly concerned with expression, with different aspects of the language as a function of expression. In a way, Charles Kœchlin is to French music what Alban Berg is to the music of central Europe.

Kœchlin's ample work is not consistent in quality. But if there is some music of little weight, if the composer sometimes wanders into overly dense polyphonic brush, he has created other works of imposing and undeniable value. "Kœchlin has the wisdom of the old trees that surround him," Émile Vuillermoz said. And this knowledge of the world is indeed reflected in his works. Kœchlin seems always to look on the world from above. Its little accidents and moments of humor are not distinguishable from the vantage point he has chosen from which to contemplate the splendor of creation. He sees only its grandeur and beauty. His art includes neither tragedy nor comedy. It is a eulogy of life, a pantheistic hymn to nature. All his music is lyrical, by turns tender, thoughtful, contemplative, or wild, radiating like the midday sun.

No one can tell us better about the mystery of night, the mystery of those heavens where myriad stars trace their orbits, than can Kœchlin himself. He transports us into an immense and silent world. And no one has surpassed him in singing of apple trees in bloom or the freshness of youth.

Four collections of chamber music, mostly early compositions, deserve our attention. On the delightful *Sonatines pour Piano* (there are thirteen, written between 1918 and 1926), Émile Vuillermoz wrote: "Kœchlin has no hesitation, no doubt on what style to maintain. He has no interest in making a show of dignity and none of the coyness of an intellectual. His thought and expression are marvelously candid, a miracle of total rejuvenation worked by tenderness and memory. No work could more accurately paint that peculiar figure of the austere and affectionate scientist, the anchorite with the rough beard and tender eyes, the severe philosopher with the soft and well-modulated voice." We should also note *Paysages et Marines* and *Heures Persanes, pour Piano* (both works orchestrated); three String Quartets; the *Quintette avec Piano;* numerous *Sonatas for String and Wind Instruments,* especially those for cello, clarinet, flute or oboe; and the *Septet for Wind Instruments* (1937).

Beginning in 1899, Kœchlin worked on a large work for choruses, orchestra, and organ, *L'Abbaye,* a work evoking monastic life whose Christian inspiration contrasts with *La Forêt Païenne,* a ballet which is a kind of pantheistic invocation. *La Divine Vesprée, Chant Funèbre à la Mémoire des Jeunes Femmes Défuntes,* two Symphonies, and *Nuit de Walpurgis Classique* should not be overlooked.

Almost all these works have been performed with marked and even outstanding success, but it is true that they appear too seldom in the repertories of concert groups. This neglect can be attributed only to the composer's unbelievable modesty and to the fact that his orchestral works have not been published, except for *Cinq Chorals dans des Modes du Moyen Âge* and the *Fugue en Fa pour Orchestre.*

Among his most beautiful and important orchestral compositions is a cycle of works based on Kipling's *Jungle Book.* Their scope is very large and includes five separate compositions: *La Loi de la Jungle,* an orchestral monody acting as a prelude; *La Méditation de Purun Baghât,* a static, contemplative piece; *Les Bandar-Log,* a scherzo of the liveliest swarm of monkeys imaginable; *Trois Poèmes* for solo voices, choruses, and orchestra —*Berceuse Phoque, Chant de Nuit,* and *Chant de Kala-Nag,* which should be counted among the most beautiful songs with orchestra ever written; and *La Course de Printemps,* a prodigious fresco of animals racing feverishly through the jungle alternating with the impression of the weight of nocturnal skies. It is a poem of amazing musical imagination, daring, and mastery. This enormous symphony is one of the best works of contemporary art, and *La Course de Printemps* must be considered among the most admirable pieces of music composed in the twentieth century.

The beautiful *Symphonie d'Hymnes* (hymns to the sun, the day, night, youth, and life) was composed in 1938. The last of the hymns, sung by a chorus, moves a little slowly. But the other four are superb. The *Symphonie d'Hymnes*, like the *Septuor d'Instruments à Vent*, is composed of pieces written at different times. Neither hearing nor reading the score gives any evidence of this, for not a single page of Kœchlin is dated. His thought is timeless.

Kœchlin knew the secret of perpetual youth. In his late seventies he was still classed among the most advanced and inventive of modern artists. Movies interested him. He deplored their "agitation, the abrupt and often useless movements, comic grossness, melodramatic tragedy, and also certain suspect and shallow devices for duping the public, not to speak of the inferior quality of the screenplay and, more than that, of the music in films. But nevertheless the movies as they are sometimes give us snatches of beauty, not only in the frequently beautiful photography, but in the acting, some of which reconciles us with that art which, in most films, could stand improvement along many other lines."

With these sentiments Kœchlin wrote the *Seven Stars' Symphony* (1933) in homage to Charlie Chaplin, Douglas Fairbanks, Emil Jannings, Marlene Dietrich, Clara Bow, Lilian Harvey, and Greta Garbo. And in 1934 he wrote a suite for piano, flute, and woman's voice, the *Album de Lilian*, dedicated to Lilian Harvey.

"In this work, according to Kœchlin himself," says Jeanne Herscher-Clément, "the music makes no concessions, either in its presentation or its thought. It is faithful to the image of Lilian—light, lively, and elegant. This is a graceful resolution of the delicate problem presented by movie music, or rather, what the music should be."

There is much more that could be said about Kœchlin's art—the love of beauty reflected in everything he did (his books on Fauré and Debussy stand as evidence), his restless sensitivity to cosmic forces—but we must limit ourselves to the essential. We would hope that from now on musicians will pay more attention to Charles Kœchlin's work. There is no doubt that this eminent composer deserves to be ranked among the best composers of our time.

The gifted composer ANDRÉ CAPLET died very young. He was a member of a group of musicians, led by Gabriel Fauré, who founded the Société Musicale Indépendante (S.M.I.) in 1911, in opposition to the too-conservative Société Nationale. The original committee members were Florent Schmitt, Charles Kœchlin, Roger-Ducasse, Maurice Ravel, Louis Aubert, Émile Vuillermoz, and Caplet. These are the same musicians who were prominent during the postimpressionist period. Logically, only Albert Roussel (taught by D'Indy and the Schola Cantorum) and Erik Satie are absent. But Satie's time had not yet come, although in 1911, at Ravel's instigation, the S.M.I. had given an important festival of Satie's works.

André Caplet, a Norman who was born in Le Havre in 1879, gained public attention at a very young age as a conductor. After winning the Prix de Rome in 1901, he directed numerous concerts and, in 1912, conducted the first performance of Debussy's *Martyre de St. Sébastien*. Seriously afflicted with gas poisoning in World War I, he died of its effects in 1925. During the intervening years he almost completely abandoned his brilliant career as conductor in order to devote all his efforts to composing. Caplet was a warm admirer of Debussy, and could not free himself entirely from the influence of his chosen master. However, his point of departure was not based on Debussy's early impressionist period, but rather on that grander style introduced by *Le Martyre*.

Caplet dreamed of writing religious music which would be modern. His best works are the *Prières* (1917) for solo voice and piano, and *Le Miroir de Jésus* (1924), for which Henri Ghéon's beautiful poem helped create an atmosphere of intimate, clear, and fervent devotion. This work, his last, is written for soprano, women's chorus, string orchestra, and harps. The over-all effect is full and luminous, and the vocal parts have a rare fluency. His melodic line is ample and expressive, and in that part of *Le Miroir* known as *Mystères Douloureux* it attains exceptional tension with its leaps between large intervals and harmony that seems to tend toward atonality. In this moving part the intensity of expression approaches the caliber of the adagio in Alban Berg's *Lulu*. Outstanding among Caplet's secular compositions are *Adieu en Barque* and *Forêt*. His only significant instrumental work is a sort of concerto for cello and orchestra entitled *Épiphanie*.

MAURICE DELAGE was also born in 1879, in Paris. He was not quite twenty years old when he began to take an interest in music. Delage was instinctively musical; he never studied music. Ravel, who was only four years his senior, recognized Delage's delicate and profoundly intuitive musical talent, and worked with him and gave him advice. Delage had a marvelous understanding of music. He discussed music at length and meditated about it and then invented magnificent melodies which he wrote for the piano with infallible taste. In his remarkable piano compositions, he was guided by an exceptional ear and memory, which were backed by a very sharp critical faculty and an innate sense of balance. Unfortunately he had almost insurmountable difficulty writing down what he played, which explains why so few of his works have been published. Nonetheless he succeeded in writing the *Quatre Poèmes Hindous,* for soprano and ten instruments, in 1913, which excited Debussy's enthusiasm. The piece had great success, and today still preserves its freshness and beauty. The *Quatre Poèmes Hindous* were written after Stravinsky's *Three Japanese Lyrics* and Ravel's *Trois Poèmes de Stéphane Mallarmé*. These three splendid collections reflect the best influence of *Pierrot Lunaire* on French music in their time.

In a few pages Delage gives us a synthesis of a musical India which owes nothing to the picturesque and everything to the purest lyricism. The melody, embroidered on the chromatic scale, seems to unfold in the smallest intervals possible due to the succession of half-tones by conjunct degrees, thus recalling the subtlety of microtones in Hindu music.

This small masterpiece was followed by several less significant compositions. *Sept Haï-Kaï*, for voices and several instruments, published by Delage in 1924, is a piece of exquisite quality and captivating distinction of spirit.

Paul Landormy says, "Delage is both an inspired man who is never lacking in ideas, and a man whose cruelly critical mind destroys drafts of work in progress so rapidly that the work never gets completed."

Delage was the cause of the formation of the S.M.I. Ravel had presented one of Delage's works to the reading committee of the Société Nationale in 1910. D'Indy refused it, criticizing a note written for the horn, saying that the instrument could not sound it. That was the last straw, and the Independents severed their connections with D'Indy and the coterie of the Schola Cantorum. Admittedly, D'Indy's dogmatism fitted ill with the French temperament, which found a more favorable climate at the Conservatory with Gedalge and Fauré.

Given this dogmatism, which was only too real, we might well wonder how the Schola Cantorum could produce artists like ALBERT ROUSSEL and Déodat de Séverac. Séverac, who died in 1921, has had no influence on contemporary music. At the most, his animation and taste for the countryside can be likened to similar characteristics in Milhaud. Albert Roussel, on the contrary, did not reach maturity as a composer until after 1918. From childhood he had passionately loved the sea and music. He entered the École Navale and began a career in the navy which he left in 1894 at the age of twenty-five to devote himself exclusively to composing. But all his life he retained impressions of the sea, whose enchantment he had known. "There is nothing lovelier than the gentle, slow roll of a ship heeling slightly under the wind," he wrote, recalling a long cruise aboard a frigate. "There is nothing more delightful than to breathe the fresh salty air of the ocean while one is stretched out on the main deck under the magnificence of a full-blown sail."

Roussel is not an impressionist. He never wrote a symphony on the sea. But all his music is permeated with its rhythms. One day in 1915, while he was in the army (he had enlisted for the duration of the war), he wrote to his wife: "The sea, the sea! . . . There is nothing in the world more beautiful, is there; and we will go there to live out our days. And when we fall asleep we will hear its eternal murmur in the distance. I am sorry I left at home those admirable verses by Verhaeren which moved you so much. To say the same thing in music, succeed in suggesting the emotion, the sensation of power and infinity, of charm, anger, gentleness, everything that the sea is saying, that must be the greatest joy in the world an artist can receive from his art. . . ."

It was not by chance that Roussel found a model in Verhaeren. He felt strongly attached to the Flemish country, having been born in French Flanders. Like the Flemish people he had the gift of lively colors, controlled strength, constructive temperament, independent assurance, the need of space, and a desire to be more than individual.

Since we are talking about humanism, let me digress a moment. The evolution which has led from romanticism to the present state of music does not consist solely of a modification in language, which, whatever might be said, is but a tributary of a particular way of life, a particular conception of the world prior to all the niceties of artistic production. Romanticism put the individual in the center of the world, and the passions of the individual were reflected in a conception of nature which took whatever form that suited his psychological state. Nature stood as evidence of the individual's drama (as in *Harold in Italy* or *Symphonie Fantastique*). Impressionism also places the individual in the center of nature, but conceives of its force as centripetal rather than centrifugal. Nature is supreme, and the individual, perceiving the sensations he receives from it, becomes in turn the witness (*Nuages, Prélude à l'Après-midi d'un Faune, La Mer*).

For the postimpressionists, and particularly Kœchlin and Roussel, the individual cedes his place to mankind. The foundation of thought proceeds from individualism to humanism, as in Kœchlin's *Symphonie d'Hymnes* and Roussel's *Second Symphony in Bb*. This is the point at which artistic thinking returned to the classic humanist attitude. Later, nature in turn will be replaced by humanity, with man at the heart of humanity and music of the conscience with works like *Socrate, Orestie,* and *Antigone.*

Returning to Roussel, his thoughts were not bound up with the sea alone. The young midshipman had taken trips to India and to the Far East. Hindu thought and art had made a profound impression on the composer. In 1909 Roussel returned to India and Indochina to increase his knowledge of the Orient, whose cultures were to help free his artistic personality. After 1910 he dissociated himself from the influence of both the Schola Cantorum and Debussy, and a little later joined the Independents on the committee of the S.M.I.

Roussel's first works marked him as an individualistic artist. The *Sonatine pour Piano,* Op. 16 (1913), confirmed the authenticity and strength of his personality. The piece is imbued from the first to the last note with a well-defined rhythm that is at once supple and vigorous. The incisive vivacity of the scherzo gives way to the profound gravity of the slow movement. Its singular harmony based on chords of fourths, as far removed from banality as from excessive subtlety, forms this healthy, strong, and pure music [*Example 82*].

The *Sonatine* is, moreover, one of the best piano works in contemporary music. It is the last of a ravishing series which includes *Divertissement pour Instruments à Vent et Piano,* Op. 6; *Première Symphonie (Poème de la Forêt),* Op. 7; and *Deux Poèmes Chinois,* Op. 12, which contains the well-known *Ode à un Jeune Gentilhomme.*

The work preceding the *Sonatine, Evocations for Orchestra, Solo Voices, and Chorus,* Op. 15, was enthusiastically received on its first performance in 1912. It has been said that *Evocations* still shows an impressionist tendency and depends on the picturesque. Actually, this admirable triptych, inspired by the trip to India, is a very pure symphony. Impressions of India, far from being expressed in fleeting, momentary glimpses, are synthesized and stripped of accidental qualities. The first movement, disquieting and menacing, was thus inspired by the contemplation of the grottoes of Ellera: *Les Dieux dans l'Ombre des Cavernes.* A vision of Jaipur is carried in a luminous scherzo,

La Ville Rose. Lastly, Benares and the Ganges suggest the vast finale, *Aux Bords du Fleuve Sacré,* teeming with life, rising like a hymn to the sun and life, with voices and orchestra in perfect accord. Roussel has conceived India in his own way, and that conception is expressed in a language which is his own and owes nothing to Hindu music. There is no trace of local color. He has spiritually transposed the whole of the impressions he gathered. *Aux Bords du Fleuve Sacré* seems at first to be composed of a suite of fragments. Actually, these sections are musically linked. The end envisaged is not a development but a progression, a movement advancing like a procession of people climbing to meet the sun.

Evocations is a humanist, not an impressionist work, simple in architecture but sumptuous in its generous proportions and warm and brilliant in coloring. It has preserved the beauty it has been lauded for since its creation in 1912.

The exquisite *Spider's Feast* was written in 1913. The ballet was commissioned by Jacques Rouché, then director of the Théâtre des Arts, who had also just asked Ravel for *Ma Mère l'Oye.* The arrangement by Gilbert des Voisins is lovely. Arthur Hoérée gives a résumé of it in a book dedicated to Roussel:

In the manner of Fabre and Maeterlinck, Gilbert des Voisins presents us with a true little entomological drama in the form of a fantasy. The action centers around a spider web spun in the corner of a garden. Dame spider lies in wait for her prey while dung beetles and ants attend to their absorbing labors. It's herculean work to lift a rose petal! So the heavy music assures us. The butterfly comes along, dancing, carefree, and gets caught in the trap of the spider web. He thrashes about to the strident accents of the oboes and dies on a note of quiet lament. An apple falls with a crash and interrupts the ferocious dance of the spider in her savage joy. When all is calm again, two little fruit worms dig into the apple, despite the vigilance of two mantises, who scold each other for their plunder. Taking advantage of their argument, the spider captures them in her web and makes ready to begin her banquet. The two worms, gorged, come out of the apple groveling pitifully. But here comes a squad of dung beetles to the rescue. They free one of the mantises, who, choppers aloft, rushes on the spider and beats her to death.

The score is wonderfully light. It abounds with exquisite melodic gems, based on a harmony of successions of chords that transmit a sense of quivering. The sound of the small orchestra is like the rustling of insect wings. There is something metallic and crystalline about it that gives the music a unique quality of precision and transparency. The ballet seems to be enclosed by the prelude and conclusion in the lovely, mysterious atmosphere of a garden, that silent world in which a marvelous and secret life unfolds.

Roussel gives us the best of himself in the music of this graceful masterpiece—the love of life that fills him with tenderness for living things, the capacity to enjoy the happiness of being alive, a happiness that nothing can disturb. Roussel creates an aura of perfect joy—peaceful and intimate—which, like all perfection, has a shadow of melancholy.

After the decisive success of *The Spider's Feast*, Jacques Rouché, the newly appointed manager of the Paris Opera, commissioned Roussel to write another score. The composer chose to treat the legend of Padmâvati, which he had heard during his stay in India when he was visiting the ruins of Chittoor. He asked his friend Louis Laloy to write a libretto on the subject. Opera in France in 1914—outside common productions—was no longer concerned with literary development, and was concentrating on dramatic construction based only on the music itself. Vincent d'Indy had presented *Fervaal* in 1897 and *L'Étranger* in 1903, both musical plots inspired by Wagnerian formulae for lyric drama. But *L'Étranger* reflected a return to a more melodic form of opera. Debussy's *Pelléas et Mélisande* (1902) and Dukas's *Ariane et Barbe-Bleue* (1906) definitively broke with lyric drama. In opposition to the Wagnerian lyric theater, *Pelléas* established the ideal of the theater of atmosphere, and *Ariane* laid the foundation for symphonic drama. Ravel's *L'Heure Espagnole*, composed in 1907, infused new life into comic opera. From another source, the productions of the Ballet Russe after 1909 had shown that the plasticity of choreography went hand in glove with structural requirements in music, and *Petrushka, Le Sacre du Printemps,* and *Daphnis et Chloé* had shown what dramatic intensity ballet could achieve. Melodic drama and dramatic ballet could combine in ballet-opera. This is the form Laloy and Roussel chose by mutual agreement for *Padmâvati*. The stage of the Paris Opera could accommodate the large chorus, ballet company, orchestra, and sumptuous décor required. The work gave expression to the sentiment for a semi-plastic dramatic beauty toward which French music was then moving.

The story takes place in the thirteenth century. Ratan-Sen is the ruler of the rich city of Chittoor. His beautiful and virtuous wife, consecrated to the lotus flower, called *Padma,* is named Padmâvati. The government of Chittoor is just and good. A Brahman, expelled from the city, turns traitor and goes to the Mongol chief Alaouddin, who lays siege to the city and captures it by trickery, after demanding in vain that Padmâvati be given over to him. The second act takes place in the Temple of Siva, where Ratan-Sen and Padmâvati have taken refuge. In order to save the city, the king asks his wife to give herself up to Alaouddin. But this would be criminal, and Padmâvati, preferring death, stabs her husband and then herself mounts the pyre. This double sacrifice to fidelity and the gods takes place in an imposing funeral ceremony invoking the gods of evil. Alaouddin appears before the burning pyre to find nothing.

The action itself is slight. The opera is more a spectacle than a drama. The music is very beautiful, especially in the large ensembles. The music of the second act is particularly anguished. Roussel interprets the "sacred horror" of Shivaism and makes it live for us. The dance of the six goddesses is darkly splendid. The finale above all is remarkable. Arthur Hoérée describes it: "All the strength of the orchestra and the choral body is massed in a great, irresistible progression, which is cut into by mounting war cries. Deeply moving ritual lamentations then rise from a double chorus mixed with the voices of the priests. With the skillfully graduated polyphony, the timbres are arranged in tiers, rhythms are ordered, and the heart-rending lament ends in a dizzying melee of sound of rare power. This is the work of a master."

The music fills the listener with unrestrained joy. But the ballet-opera formula is not very satisfactory. The long dance passages obscure the drama, and when the voices of the singers are introduced again after the dances there is an inevitable hiatus —the audience is suddenly transported into another musical world. Despite this reservation concerning the form, *Padmâvati* is one of the best scores ever played in French theater. The frequency with which the Opera stages it attests to the public favor it continues to enjoy.

Because of World War I, *Padmâvati* could not be performed until 1923, but the work did not then seem dated. Since his brilliant *Evocations*, Roussel had taken a significant step forward. From the point of view of spirit, *Padmâvati* was indicative of a trend toward austerity. Technically, the language became more specialized with the use of altered scales and Hindu modes. This oriented the music toward a more contrapuntal form, and the harmony, often sharp or jarring, was created by the encounters of the voices. In 1914 this style of music was ahead of its time and therefore kept *Padmâvati* from seeming outmoded at its performance nine years later.

After 1916 Roussel worried about the change in thinking brought about by the war. He wrote: "All that [he was thinking of *Padmâvati*] will now be 'prewar,' that is, separated from us by a wall, a real wall. . . . We will have to begin living again with a new concept of life, which does not mean that everything done before the war will be forgotten, but that everything done after it must be done differently." In 1919 he composed two melodies: *Sarabande* and *Le Bachelier de Salamanque. Bachelier* resembles the *Sonatina* and the *Ode à un Jeune Gentilhomme. Sarabande* demonstrates a style of development in the slow movement to be used in such future works as the *Suite in F, Sonata for Violin, Third Symphony,* and *Fourth Symphony.* These are monothematic compositions, in which the melody is led toward a climax in intensity of expression and then brought back gradually to the tranquillity of the opening. The short symphonic poem *Pour une Fête de Printemps,* Op. 22, composed in 1920, marks a decisive change in Roussel's methods. The ideas are expressed with a vivacity and conciseness which are entirely new, and the slightly acid harmony and sonorousness of the orchestra underscore this liveliness and rhythmic clarity. The opening chord invites controversy. Roussel arrives at complex combinations that some attribute to polytonality and others explain as the interplay of appoggiaturas [*Example 79*].

In 1921 the *Second Symphony in B♭,* Op. 23, appeared, marking the end of Roussel's evolution. He had thrown off the last vestiges of the influence of impressionism, discarded poetic or dramatic incidentals, and grasped the essence of the problem of music structure as it was then being stated to the youngest composers. As he said himself in a note in the Concert Guide of October 12, 1928: "I resolved to enlarge the harmonic content of my style, and tried to approach the ideal of music intended and conceived for itself. My *Symphony in Bb*, I must admit, was not warmly received. The public and the critics were unhappy about its harshness. I know full well that it was a rather hermetic work and consequently rather unusually hard to understand. At the time when it was first performed, it could pass as an excessive composition."

The composer draws strong contrasts and modifies tempos continuously in the interests of dynamic development. Its content is progressively molded and defined so that its full significance is not revealed until the conclusion. Without owing anything to Stravinsky, the intention of the music bears analogy with the *Symphonies for Wind Instruments,* although the result and proportions are entirely different. Opinions of the work still vary. Some extoll it as one of the great monuments of contemporary music. Others admit its spirit of experiment, but think it failed to achieve its aims. Only further performances of the symphony—which is too rarely played—will end the perplexity in which it leaves the musical world.

The *Second Symphony* relieved Roussel of the need to experiment further. He had reached that state in which creation poses no more problems, because the creator has solved all the mysteries of the material and controls it from that moment on, to the point where he can do with it exactly what he wants, as he wants. From the *Second Symphony* until his last work (Op. 58, written in 1937), the composer was a classicist. Whether the work is large or small, the structure is transparent, the form rational, and the content devoid of individualism. Four purely symphonic works were created during this period of maturity: *Suite in F,* Op. 33 (1926); *Third Symphony in G Major,* Op. 42 (1930); *Sinfonietta for String Orchestra,* Op. 52 (1934); and *Fourth Symphony in A Major,* Op. 53 (1935). These four perfect works have a number of points in common. The rhythm is simple, deliberately binary, powerful and uncompromising, leading the composition with masterful constancy. The precise, impe-

rious allegros transmit the joy of their motion. Slow, sober movements based on long, tensely curved melodies mount in a great
orchestral crescendo and subside in a proportionate diminuendo.
And the scherzos are as typical in their impertinent lightness as
are similar pieces by Berlioz and Mendelssohn.

There is nothing superfluous in these admirable symphonies,
no padding or muddying, and no detail left in shadow. They
give the impression of marvelously controlled power used at full
force without draining its potential. Natural exuberance which
knows how to fall back for renewed attack never overflows into
grandiloquence. They reflect perfect balance of sensibility and
intelligence, interior ardor, and a touch of sportiveness, the
result of fine moral and corporeal health. Poetry and mathe-
matics, Roussel's two disciplines, unite and complement each
other. Necessarily, not all of the composer's works could be so
successful. Some, like the *Concerto for Piano,* Op. 36; *Concertino
for Cello,* Op. 57; and the *String Quartet,* Op. 45, have certain
flaws in balance, and the ideas are sometimes a little restricted.

On the other hand, the two ballets, *Bacchus et Ariane,* Op. 43
(1930), and *Aeneas,* Op. 54 (1935), are of the same caliber as the
four symphonies. The libretto of *Aeneas,* a ballet with choruses,
was written by Joseph Weterings. *Bacchus et Ariane,* with libretto
by Abel Hermant, perhaps marks the apex of Roussel's work.

To close our discussion of Roussel, I would like to draw
attention to *La Naissance de la Lyre,* Op. 24 (1924), based on a
lyric tale by Théodore Reinach drawn from Sophocles, which
contains some beautiful passages. *Psalm 80* for tenor solo, chorus
and orchestra, Op. 37 (1928), has a fine arrangement, but cannot
compare in brilliance or persuasiveness with Schmitt's *Psalm 48*
or the excellent choral compositions of Honegger and Milhaud.
Le Testament de Tante Caroline is a charming operetta composed in 1933 on a book by Nino. In chamber music, noteworthy
are the elegant *Joueurs de Flûte* for flute and piano, Op. 27
(1924); *Sonata No. 2 for Piano and Violin,* Op. 28 (1924), composed in the style of the third and fourth symphonies; a delightful *Serenade for Flute, Harp, Violin, Viola, and Cello,* Op. 30
(1925); and *Trio for Flute, Viola, and Cello,* Op. 40 (1929), which
is as lovely as the *Serenade.* Roussel also wrote numerous excellent art songs.

Albert Roussel's style is based on a number of technical details. The melody is generally long, sinuous, and rather ambiguous from a tonal point of view, and digresses into chromatics and modulations. As with Fauré, Ravel, and Kœchlin, the melody is often modal. It might be said that the postimpressionist period (a meaningless term used for lack of a better) is the period in which modality was rediscovered as a way to harmonic liberation. Roussel utilized not only the modes of the Middle Ages. When he was traveling in the Orient he lent an attentive ear to Hindu modes, and realized that they could enrich Western music, apart from any concern with the exotic. Our Western modes are all built on a scale including five wholetones and two half-tones. Oriental modes multiply the half-tones, and consequently imply intervals of augmented seconds. For the referent keys, Roussel considered the polar notes of each tetrachord as points of rest or centers of attraction, and the intermediary notes as points of tension or elements of movement. In harmony, Roussel went as far as major chords of elevenths and thirteenths. Thus the opening chord of *La Fête de Printemps,* which is often interpreted as being polytonal, is only the last inversion of a major eleventh chord with a minor ninth. Roussel's rhythms owe their suppleness to the effective arrangement of composed measures, which occur frequently, and involve the intervention of brief and incisive rhythmic accents [*Example 83*]. We have pointed out that in his later works continuous rhythms govern entire movements, as in Bach, and are thus a primary unifying factor.

We could not end our review of this postimpressionist period, so full of outstanding personalities and rich in numbers of masterworks, without citing some fine works by talented composers that reveal undeniable imaginativeness and good technique.

Such are *Orphée* (1913), a pantomime by Roger-Ducasse (1873-1954), a pupil of Fauré's, a work of lofty inspiration; his amusing comic-opera *Cantegril* (1931); and an important symphonic poem, *Au Jardin de Marguerite*. Roger-Ducasse's music is elegant, polished, precise, and sometimes very personal in these works, but in others he could not seem to throw off the academicism that stifles his very real gifts.

No one can say what capricious fate guided Henri Rabaud to write *Marouf, the Cobbler of Cairo,* the only twentieth-century comic-opera which has gained the popularity of *Faust, Carmen,* and *Manon.* Suddenly, in 1914, in the middle of a career of dull, uninteresting compositions appeared this light, fresh, full-bodied score, picturesque and colorful, in which dream and reality mix as in *A Thousand and One Nights.*

The young and prodigiously gifted Lili Boulanger, who won the Prix de Rome in 1913 at the age of nineteen and died in 1918 after devoting herself generously to the war effort, composed *Three Psalms* (1916), monumental works ardent in spirit, solemn, and sometimes violent in inspiration.

5

ERIK SATIE AND THE SIX

SINCE ABOUT 1880 France had been enjoying uncommon peace, stability, and prosperity. Rich and undisturbed, she basked in unconcerned and carefree happiness that nothing could trouble. The Frenchman's innate love of balance, beauty in itself, and purity in artistic expression harmonized perfectly with the atmosphere of euphoria he was living in. The art of that period is permeated with a serene outlook on a life which provided prosperity and contentment. The art of Verlaine and Mallarmé, Renoir, Monet, and Seurat, Chabrier, Debussy, Dukas, Fauré and Kœchlin, and the early works of Ravel and Roussel reflect those happy times. For them nature is a domain where all is good, gracious, and beautiful, and where contemplative life flows along, paradisiacal, in the current of the days and nights. Their art gives much importance to elegance and charm, for these are the marks of radiant sensitivity joyfully responding to all the signs of spring.

Their contemporaries Rimbaud, Cézanne, and Gauguin were not to find favor until an atmosphere of greater tension reminded Frenchmen of harder and more painful realities.

And then impressionism "shot off its last firecracker." The *fauves* began to speak their more turbulent and anguished language, and the thunderclap of *Le Sacre du Printemps* resounded. The world realized that a new era had begun in which moral values, and consequently artistic values, were undergoing a change.

It was at this moment that a young composer whom we have frequently mentioned began to attract attention. He was Erik Satie. In 1917 Satie's *Parade* was first performed. The work was a ballet based on a text by Jean Cocteau with décor by Pablo Picasso. It took the public by storm, and focused attention on a composer whose significance had heretofore been appreciated only by Debussy and Ravel.

Years had passed without anyone's paying heed to Satie or realizing the influence his personality and works exerted on Debussy and Ravel. Only after the appearance of *Parade* were any questions raised, retrospectively, about this strange man and his puzzling work. The misunderstanding surrounding his music and the jibes thrown by self-appointed eulogists of impressionism did not prevent musicians from gradually seeing the light and acknowledging Satie's importance in the history of contemporary music.

In accordance with the course of events, therefore, we turn to Satie as we reach the point when the world of music recognized his existence.

ALFRED ERIKIT LESLIE-SATIE was born at Honfleur, May 17, 1866, of a Norman father and a Scotch mother. He who was later to say, "I came into the world very young in a very old time," revealed an unusual personality from his early childhood. At the age of ten, he already had the rather veiled but piercing glance, the mouth with slightly turned down corners, the face hungry for knowledge of life and the somewhat distrustful expression he was to keep all his life. Candor and malice can be read in his features along with acute sensitivity which for his self-protection he later hid behind a mask of irony. It was a pose he was the first to suffer from, but unhappy the man who did not recognize the depth of hidden tenderness in his music, for the injury would unleash a torrent of abuse from him in language as scathing and vitriolic as it was imaginative, and which stung friends and foes alike. Mystical and ironic; fanciful, but severely austere in expressing this fantasy; supremely daring and clear-sighted, but so vulnerable that he took refuge in a secluded life; of rare goodness, equaled only by his diabolic spitefulness; brilliant, but wary of showing it—this was the composer of *Parade* and *Socrate*.

Satie left Honfleur when he was twelve, and moved to Paris with his family. He began to work with Guilmant. At the Conservatory he worked briefly under Descombes and Lavignac,

and next spent an equally short time in Taudou's harmony
classes. During his piano studies, the elderly Mathias encouraged
him to compose. Then suddenly in 1887, the unexpected fruit
of disorganized study came to life with three *Sarabandes for
Piano.* "I would like to emphasize," says Roland-Manuel, "that
the *Sarabandes* are a turning-point in the evolution of our music.
Here are three short pieces—composed in an unprecedented
harmonic technique springing from an entirely new aesthetic—
which create a unique atmosphere, a magic in sound which is
absolutely original. Claude Debussy was well aware of it. Four-
teen years later he composed a *Sarabande* that pays distinct
homage to Satie through charming effects of an influence deliberately sought after, and a relationship deliberately established."

There has been much discussion, and rightly so, of Satie's pre-
Debussy role. However, it would be a mistake to consider him
simply a precursor. We have only to examine the works Satie
wrote between 1887 and 1897 to see that the composer of
Socrate did not merely foreshadow the harmonic system and
sensibilities of the creator of *Pelléas.* In the *Sarabandes* the
composer links ninth chords by way of fifths, freely, without
preparation and without resolution [*Example 84*].

But little notice has been taken, it seems, of other germs of
contemporary feeling contained in this music. In the thirteenth
measure of the third *Sarabande* (less well known but no less
unusual than the second), a melody is born whose notes form
the basis of an arpeggio accompaniment which seems to emanate
from the melody itself. Schoenberg and Stravinsky were to
develop this same concern for the unity of the musical material.
The flexibility of his melodic line as well as the nature of his
harmony foreshadow the mature Fauré [*Example 85*].

In 1887 Satie was a frequent companion of Rodolphe Salis,
Alphonse Allais (who also came from Honfleur), Georges Auriol,
Maurice Donnay, Jouy, Rivière, and Tinchart. He took a job as
second pianist at the Chat Noir. In his spare time, he helped in
the production of Chabrier's *Roi Malgré Lui,* at the Opéra-
Comique, and enthusiastically endorsed that liberating work.
In 1888 he brought out the admirable *Gymnopédies.* The
sustained iambic rhythm, and the seventh chords gliding along
this persuasive rhythm in a very special way, underlie a melody

whose perfect curve is unique (that is, resembles no other). These three pieces were to excite Debussy, who orchestrated two of them, as well as Ravel, whose *La Belle et La Bête* in *Ma Mère L'Oye* is simply a fourth *gymnopédie* [*Example 86*].

The *Sarabandes, Gymnopédies,* and generally speaking Satie's compositions prior to 1900 are priestly or religious in character. There was a streak of mysticism in Satie's makeup; but it is an exaggeration to point to this, as Alfred Cortot does, as the explanation for his composing in threes, the mystic number. Why then three *Sarabandes,* three *Gymnopédies,* and three *Gnossiennes,* the three works of the series patterned on the same model, and strangely similar? Why that series of three in each of his collections of piano pieces written between 1911 and 1915? We asked Satie one day, and he answered that there was no mystery about it: "I invent an absolutely new form. The piece I write seems good to me. But might that not just be luck? If I compose a second and a third piece along the same lines but with different melodic ideas, and if these pieces are still good, then the form I have invented is good in itself." His words throw light on the thinking of a composer who did not aim at brilliance or power or dazzling effects, but who sought perfection for his own joy. Debussy understood this Gothic-architect outlook perfectly. In a copy of *Poèmes de Baudelaire,* he wrote the dedication: "For Erik Satie, a fine medieval musician who has wandered into this century, to the joy of his devoted Claude Debussy." In 1890 Satie presented the *Trois Gnossiennes,* in which Gregorian and exotic modes graphically illustrate the underlying perfect chords. (The exotic music heard at the Exposition of 1889 made a strong impression on the young composers at that time—Debussy, Ravel, Kœchlin and Roussel—and in part caused the return to modality.) Satie's mystic inclinations found satisfaction in the Rosicrucian Order which Joséphin Péladan involved him in around 1890. He wrote the *Sonneries pour la Rose-Croix* for brasses and harps and three preludes for *Le Fils des Étoiles,* Sar Péladan's Chaldean Wagnerism. In these pieces the six-note chords, constructed in fourths, prefigure a harmony which will later be heard in Schoenberg and Milhaud [*Example 87*].

Thus, in four years' time (1887-1891), Satie explored by him-

self a harmonic ground which would normally require a quarter
of a century to investigate thoroughly.

Satie soon broke with the Rosicrucians, for the atmosphere was
too dogmatic and tiresome for a man who so loved freedom and
fantasy. The mystical tendency still predominates in the *Danses
Gothiques pour Piano* (1893); the *Prélude à la Porte Héroïque
du Ciel,* based on the esoteric drama by Jules Bois (1894) and
orchestrated in 1912 by Roland-Manuel; the *Mass for the Poor,*
for organ (1895); and even in the *Pièces Froides,* for piano
(1897), despite their titles—*Pièces à Faire Fuire* and *Danses de
Travers*—that suggest the humor still to come. All of Satie's works
up to this time were exclusively harmonic in style. They gained
their composer limited recognition in circles influenced by Debussy and Ravel; but they saw in Satie only a brilliant precursor.
His importance would be slight if the works themselves lacked
inspiration or form. But this is not the case: *Sarabandes, Gymnopédies, Gnossiennes, Pièces Froides,* the first prelude of *Fils des
Étoiles,* and the *Prélude à la Porte Héroïque du Ciel* are much
more than just interesting documents. They are works of rare
beauty and reveal an emotion that is all the more powerful because it is expressed with the restraint and lucidity that mark
a great artist.

Satie met Debussy in 1891 in the Auberge du Clou, a place
both men frequented. Long after, the Master of Arcueil wrote:
"When I saw him for the first time I was drawn to him and
wanted to live uninterruptedly in his presence. I had the good
fortune to satisfy that wish for thirty years." Theirs was a marvelous friendship which suffered no blemish until shortly before
Debussy's death, when a painful misunderstanding arose.

Debussy himself never disguised the vital influence that Satie
had had on him. He repeated to Jean Cocteau Satie's remark
which had decided him on the aesthetic of *Pelléas:* "The orchestra should not grimace when someone comes on the scene.
Look. Do the trees in the décor grimace? A musical décor, a
musical climate should be created in which the characters move
and speak. No couplets, no leitmotivs—instead, it needs some of
the Puvis de Chavannes atmosphere."

Satie's works of the harmonic period should be performed and
listened to in exactly this spirit. The same holds true of his

masterpiece *Socrate,* in which, near the end of his life, he achieves that ideal of decorative, atmospheric music, opposed to the realism which he held in horror.

Why, as late as 1895, had Satie himself not developed an art based on the constructive principles he conceived so well? Obviously, no one understood him. Symbolism had unsettled poetry's dominion, and budding impressionism in music had begun to obscure precisely what Satie wanted to see clearly. He wanted force, and design as pure as Ingres's, when all the evidence pointed to a trend in the diametrically opposite direction. Satie must have known that he could not present his views fully at that point. Having discovered a harmonic language that others would use and abuse, he said no more. We are sure that the reason for this silence was the incompatibility of his inclinations and those of the times, and his conviction that he lacked the proper foundation. He held on to his feeling about atmosphere. But harmony alone was incapable of giving him that clean, continuous line he was seeking. This note, found in the margin of one of his notebooks, says it: "If I am loath to say right out what I think in a whisper, it is only because my voice is not strong enough."

In 1898 Satie withdrew, left Paris, and installed himself in an unattractive township in the suburbs, Arcueil. "In this spot," he said, "you can feel the mysterious presence of Notre-Dame Bassesse." He remained there until his death in 1925.

Very discouraged, leading a miserable existence, Satie shuttled back and forth between Arcueil and Montmartre, always clothed in gray velvet (his friends called him "the velvet gentleman"). Debussy alone stood by him and urged him to write. In 1899, he composed a delightful, lively suite of gigues, *Jack in the Box* (orchestrated by Milhaud in 1925). The harmonic conception of the pieces is echoed in Ravel's *Le Tombeau de Couperin.*

Then, unexpectedly, there appeared the famous *Three Pieces in the Form of a Pear (for Piano with Four Hands) with a Sort of a Beginning, a Continuation of the Same, and One More, Followed by a Repetition.* (That is the complete title of the work.) We know the origin of the title. Debussy had advised his friend to take pains with his form. Satie left, and several weeks later he presented Debussy with his pieces in the form of—a pear. For

Satie knew that form (and not construction) was a completely neglected notion at the time, and that its spirit had to be rediscovered by starting from scratch.

The *Three Pieces in the Form of a Pear* strikes a very new note with its resolute movement, its rhythmic breadth, and through the use in some passages of rather coarse music in reaction to the excessive elaborateness of the impressionists. The only thing humorous about the work is its title. It shows a development toward counterpoint—Satie was on the scent of what he lacked.

This composition, moreover, is one of the composer's most perfect, most beautiful, and most powerful works. Satie had at last set out on the right road. Apropos of *Pelléas,* he wrote to his brother: "Nothing further to do along those lines; I must look for something else, or I am lost." And in 1905 Satie went back to school, at the age of thirty-nine. He enrolled at the Schola Cantorum and studied counterpoint under Albert Roussel for three years. He applied himself to his work conscientiously. Debussy was crushed, fearful that his friend would lose his delightful intuitive sense. Nor could Roussel understand what had decided Satie to take his courses. "Satie had a calling," said Roussel. "His works already in print proved to me that he had nothing to learn. I could not see how he could benefit from theoretic and scholastic studies. Nonetheless, he kept at it. He was a tractable and assiduous student. He handed in his exercises punctually, well written and set off with notations in red ink. He was extraordinarily talented!"

Satie acquired a high degree of skill in counterpoint. But his object was not to produce a fine display or to busy himself with clever constructions. He used counterpoint to imbue his melodies with greater clarity than harmony could provide. He wanted to express only the essential and to condense his music to the utmost, so that the progression of parts would make the unusual harmonic columns more obvious and necessary. His language was to become more elliptical without losing its clarity. The first fruits of his studies were two suites for piano duet: *Aperçus Désagréables* (1908) and *En Habit de Cheval* (1911). The first is composed of a pastorale, chorale, and a fugue in which the composer waggishly introduces the response before the subject. At the entry of the subject he notes: "Smile." The second composition includes two chorales, *Fugue litanique* and *Fugue de papier*. The riding apparel is the shafts of a cart to which he is harnessed and which hamper his movement. But the humor in the title does not hold true for the music. The very compact chorales progress by striking harmonic short-cuts that give them strength marked with distinction, and reveal a new way of thinking. Satie had good reason to note "with breadth of vision" at the beginning of the chorale in *Aperçus Désagréables*. The *Fugue litanique* develops a Gregorian theme, and the *Fugue de papier* is exquisitely graceful.

The *Véritables Préludes Flasques (pour un chien)* was written in 1912. These are the *true* preludes because a first manuscript of the *Préludes Flasques* was refused by the editor. They are *flabby* only to mock Debussy's followers. The element of surprise is that the music is muscular and powerful. Finally, the dedication to a dog: the title is like a bone thrown to a dog to distract its attention. The titles and subtitles are there to amuse those who understand nothing of the music. *Sévère réprimande* is a short toccata; *Seul à la maison,* a creation for two voices, in which the ambiguous character of the melody [*Example 90*] is just the result of the progression of the other voice; *On joue* is a sort of *bourrée*.

After the *Préludes,* between 1913 and 1915, a whole series of compositions for piano appeared with amusing music as well as titles: *Descriptions Automatiques; Embryons Desséchés; Croquis et Agaceries d'un Gros Bonhomme en Bois; Chapitres Tournés en Tous Sens; Vieux Sequins, Vieilles Cuirasses; Heures Séculaires et Instantanées; Trois Valses Distinguées d'un Précieux Dégoûté; Sports et Divertissements;* and *Avant-dernières Pensées.*

People have long tended to be amused by the titles and the notations accompanying the music, and to treat the music itself with some disdain, failing to see that this is an absolutely new genre. Satie had invented comedy-music.

Do not confuse comedy-music with gay music. There had been comic situations in opera, and there had been comic songs. These were written with gay music, and the comic tone was primarily due to the text. By itself, the music could not convey a sense of comedy. We need only refer to Chabrier's *Le Roi*

Malgré Lui, Ballade des Gros Dindons, and *Villanelle des Petits Cochons,* and to Wagner's *Die Meistersinger von Nürnberg* and to Strauss's *Rosenkavalier* for examples of fresh, sprightly, gay music written to underline a comic text. In Dukas's *The Sorcerer's Apprentice* and Ravel's *L'Heure Espagnole* the feeling of comedy sometimes rises from the music itself, but almost uniquely from the instrumentation—the contrabassoon in *The Sorcerer's Apprentice* is famous for that reason.

Satie sets about making us laugh by using the piano alone. He presents brief sketches in which he generally uses a popular song or a hint of a well-known operatic melody to give them an expression or meaning they do not have. Similarly, Charlie Chaplin's gestures always end on a note of surprise which evokes laughter. But Chaplin's gift of poetry elevates his art to such a degree that we no longer think of his clownishness. He inspires dreams and thought. In the same way, Satie's little pieces drop the comic touch into an atmosphere of delicacy, balance, and charm which endows them with incontestable poetic value. The nocturne *Sur une Lanterne* (from *Descriptions Automatiques*) is limpid, mysterious, and smooth. The first notes of a hack tune are written into it, as though whistled by a happy-go-lucky fellow taking a solitary, lingering stroll. It is subtle comedy, not intended to arouse guffaws, but rather to bring out a smile. *Les Embryons Desséchés* are an open parody, with the untiring repetition of the perfect chord. The mockery is aimed at all the dry fustiness of academicism. And yet, what a beautiful movement is the *Embryon d'Holoturie!*

Each sketch has very specific characteristics which are so distinctive and formalized that they draw and hold attention and remain deep in the memory. They are set off with texts which are sometimes downright foolish. Why are they there, then, when they have absolutely nothing to do with the music? For comedy's sake. It is obvious that Satie wrote for his own pleasure, and not for the good of readers or audiences. If his little manuscripts, such as they are, please them, so much the better.

Above all, however, the music and text should not be confused. Satie gave the following instructions to his interpreters: "To whom it may concern: I forbid you to read program notes aloud while the music is being played. Any breach of this request will incur my righteous indignation. No exceptions will be allowed."

Here is one of these clownish notes, evoking the melancholy of the virgin forest:

VENOMOUS OBSTACLES

This vast region of the world is inhabited by one man: a Negro. . . . He is bored to death with laughing. . . . Millenarian trees cast a shadow showing 9:17 A.M. The toads call each other by name. To think better, the Negro holds his cerebellum in his right hand, his fingers spread. From a distance he looks like a distinguished physiologist. Four anonymous serpents charm him, hanging from the tails of his uniform, which is disheveled from trouble and solitude.

On the edge of the river, an old mangrove tree is slowly washing its roots, fouled with filth. . . . It is not the time for love's sweet surrender.

Other notations directly concern interpretation, humorous also, but very exact to anyone who knows how to read them. The pianist's every move is considered: "in the head"; "from the corner of the eyes and remembered in advance"; "a little bloodily"; "without reddening a finger"; "ignore your own presence"—many directions for touch, movement, sonorousness, and spirit.

Even the serious-minded Charles Kœchlin writes:

And why not think of these notations as necessary, especially in very short pieces in which the idea passes without restraint from one image to another? Why not allow this type of presentation? In itself, it is not at all illogical. This is something the bourgeois do not seem to understand—an artist acts, not in a *pose* or *according to type,* but for himself and because that is his pleasure. The bright red notations in the first edition of *Le Fils des Étoiles* and the careful writing with ornamented capitals written for the sake of *harmony* picture Satie to us as the last descendent of the good monks who copied their manuscripts with love. That shows character in these days when modern man subordinates everything to what is useful and (to do what else with it, dear Lord?) time-saving.

Parody, or nonsense, is only one aspect of Satie's comedy-music—there are others. In *Trois Valses Distinguées d'un Précieux Dégoûté,* the intentionally brisk short-cut in the music calls up an amusing image of the artificially ardent or too-tender waltzes our grandmothers adored. In the *Avant-dernières Pen-sées,* dedicated to Debussy, Dukas, and Roussel, sinuous lines caper around ostinati-pedal notes, then separate from them mischievously only to return and separate again. It makes the listener think of a kitten playing with a ball of wool.

But Satie displays a higher order of humor in *Sports et Diver-tissements* and in his melodies. Kœchlin again captures the essence:

There is no more illogicality. On the contrary, exact and scrupulous images (greatly condensed, moreover, restrained and striking) of the states of soul, landscapes, and actions give birth to the comic. It is an unencumbered comedy, faithful to the text which it describes with the precision of a painter of Japanese prints. I recall Chrysaline's astonishment in the face of Daphénéo's bewildering answer, but above all I think of the inimitable *Sports et Divertissements,* which deserves a special place in Satie's work. The uneasiness of the imprudent character who risks the "water-chute," the sticky blue-green octopus playing with a crab, and so many other passages in this suite of rapid pieces are to me netsukes of the best period. A few brief touches, nothing more is needed. Extra-condensed art—why not? To *develop* is not an end in itself, but a means, and is not suitable for all compositions. A small Japanese ivory is worth more, isn't it, than so many official statues that turn our public squares into cemeteries?

Alfred Cortot finds that *Sports et Divertissements* are real haikus in music, and best correspond "to the instantaneous nature of his singular genius. There is no better testimony to the descriptive power of all Satie's music—nor any which, in relation to the text, better justifies his ambition of the moment, as it traces for him the limit which it never should have exceeded."

The text and the music have the same exquisite and incisive quality, and are strangely extended into the ensuing silence. *Balançoire* is a good example.

Satie's songs are as original as his piano pieces. They also are humorous, but are shadowed with a hint of melancholy or resignation. The melodies of *Trois Poèmes d'Amour,* set to ironic poems, are permeated with sweetness and sadness, inspired, as Léon Guichard points out, by the Gregorian sequence *Victimae paschali laudes* and sustained on harmony of springlike freshness. There is nothing in all of music which is so tenderly disillusioned. *La Statue de Bronze, Daphénéo,* and *Le Chapelier* combine luminous poetry with avenging verve. The *Ludions,* set to poems by L. P. Fargue, tells of the love of humble things, of the refuge of those who are hurt by human society and of the disdain of grandiloquence. They communicate the intimate pleasure of true modesty. The music is intended to pass unnoticed. But it is too ingenious, too inventive, not to be noted.

After 1888 all Satie's creative activity was darkened with a shadow he did not try to dispel. His attentiveness had helped him to avoid both the transitory quality which, among Debussy's heirs, had led to the dispersion of music in a sort of inconsistent sonorous vapor, and excessive construction, which led to academic formalism. At heart, he had returned to the classic spirit which gave life to Couperin's work, the spirit of balance, vivacity, fitness, and simplicity which is the soul of all great French classics. It is not important that the works are short because nearly all of the harpsichord pieces we admire are that. As for the drollery of the titles, gaiety is an old Gallic virtue. The *Fastes de la Grande Menestrandise, Les Culbutes ou les x I . . .,* and *Les Calotins et les Calotines* did not serve to mask otherwise negligible music in Couperin's work. "There are works whose whole import is in depth—their *opening* is unimportant," says Jean Cocteau. "Satie's smallest work is small like a keyhole. Everything changes if you bring your eye close."

World War I hastened the evolution of ideas in music. The spirit of carefree well-being was replaced by a concern for basic necessities. The enjoyment of luxury gave place to basic minimum needs. The arts, reflecting social problems, adopted the way of economy. The need for reality, security, and certainty assigned to the arts the aim of painting the permanent characteristics of an object, and no longer the changing atmosphere surrounding it. Satie's hour had come.

At Ravel's instigation, the S.M.I. had already devoted two now historic concerts to Satie's work in 1911. But it was Diaghilev who put Satie in the limelight. In 1915, Jean Cocteau, enthusiastic about the *Three Pieces in the Form of a Pear,* sounded Satie out on a project for a ballet which was to revolutionize choreographic art. It was *Parade.*

French artists were infused with a new spirit that attracted them to certain guiding ideas: to express the enduring nature of things, as completely as possible; to reject useless ornamentation and formal development; to flee the premeditated sublime and choose the familiar, everyday world; to use a minimum of means, but with full consciousness of the value of materials; to avoid vagueness and reinstate the firm design; to stop using the work of art as a personal battleground, but to consider it objectively as having its own existence and detach it from the individual who has given it life.

In painting, this new spirit appeared in the canvases of Pablo Picasso and Georges Braque, and was called cubism. In literature, Guillaume Apollinaire and Jean Cocteau expressed it in their poetry. Satie fell in step with the movement naturally, and we must give credit to Cocteau's perceptiveness. In choosing Satie to compose the music for his ballet, and Picasso to create the décor and costumes, Cocteau made *Parade* a turning point not only in music, but in theater as well.

As for Diaghilev, we need to rectify the opinion, too often voiced, that the most significant years of the Ballet Russe were the first, from 1909 to 1914. The Ballet brought the sumptuousness of the Russian scene to the West, and reintroduced classic choreography and dance in France, which had lost these arts after the days of Petipa. Whatever the importance of *Le Sacre du Printemps* to music, Nijinsky's choreography for the ballet came at a bad time. It was premature, for it was based on traditional Slavic ritual dances, and could not have been understood by the public prior to 1952. We agree with Boris de Schlœzer that the outstanding and most influential period of Diaghilev's Ballet was 1917-1925. This was the period of growth when Diaghilev surrounded himself with painters like Picasso, Braque, and Marie Laurencin; composers like Satie, Stravinsky, Auric, and Poulenc; Cocteau, the genius of theater; and choreographers like Léonide Massine and Bronislava Nijinska, gifted with the understanding and imagination to collaborate fruitfully with the artists and composers. The art of ballet was rejuvenated and a new form of musical spectacle created.

Cocteau called *Parade* a realist ballet, "meaning by that: truer than the true, and counting only, to make my meaning clear, on the distance existing for the spectator between a ballet and this ballet, the realistic word and the unreal aspect of the spectacle." This is Cocteau's summary:

The décor represents houses in Paris on a Sunday. Road show. Three music-hall numbers serve as a Parade. Chinese magician. Acrobats. Young American girl. Three managers are organizing the publicity. They inform each other in their terrible language that the crowd thinks the parade is the whole show, and they try coarsely to make them understand. No one enters. At the end of the parade, the exhausted managers collapse one on top of the other. The Chinese magician, the acrobats and the young girl come out of the empty theater. Seeing the supreme effort and the collapse of the managers, they in turn try to explain that the show is inside.

In agreeing to paint for the theater, Picasso compromised himself with the purists of Montparnasse. But Picasso was not a man to "let himself get hooked." He thought there was a way not to paint *for* the theater, but to do *theater painting.* Braque, Derain, Dufy, Marie Laurencin, Matisse, Fernand Léger and a good many others were to follow his example and contribute their share to the new art of theatrical décor. Picasso left with Cocteau to join the Ballet in Rome, where it was then preparing *Les Femmes de Bonne Humeur,* based on Scarlatti sonatas, and, a little later, *Pulcinella.* During that time, Satie was composing in Paris. "Little by little," Cocteau writes, "a score was born in which it seemed that Satie had discovered an unknown dimension—you seem to hear the parade and the show inside simultaneously." Satie had agreed to write the score as a musical foundation for a symphony of suggestive sounds—sirens, typewriters, airplanes, dynamos. He was still concerned with making the music unobtrusive. The noises were to create an impression of ineffectual bustling, but they were not used. This did not diminish the impact of the spectacle—in fact, the score gained by the omission. The choreography discarded traditional steps and poses, and was patterned on movements drawn from real life.

Here is what Cocteau says, speaking of the directions he gave Satie:

These directions had nothing humorous about them. On the contrary, they insisted on the extension of the characters beyond the given scene.

where the Chinese magician was capable of torturing missionaries, the young girl of going down with the *Titanic,* the acrobat of consorting with angels. When Picasso showed us his sketches, we understood the importance of setting the three chromos off with non-human, superhuman, more seriously transformed characters who would actually become the false reality of the scene to the point of reducing real dancers to the dimension of puppets. So I conceived the managers as a savage, uncouth, vulgar, and noisy lot, who by their strange looks and behavior nullify their own efforts and—which they did—incite the crowd to react with hatred, ridicule, and shrugs.

It was decided to have the managers stamp their feet silently, which made them look particularly vicious.

Our boys looked like the insects whose brutal habits the film deplores. Their dance was an organized accident of false steps extended and alternating with the discipline of a fugue. The awkwardness of moving around in those trappings,[13] far from inhibiting the choreographer, required him to break with old formulas and seek inspiration not in what moves but in what is moved among, and in what stirred according to the rhythm of our march.

There was also a parade horse, made of cardboard and cloth and animated by two dancers inside it who stamped their feet in coordination with the managers. This is the only comic touch in the ballet, and it whipped the public into a frenzy.

There remain the characters in the parade:

Contrary to what the public thinks, these characters are closer to the cubist school than are our managers. The managers are part of the décor. They are Picasso portraits which move, and their very structure requires a particular type of choreography. For the four characters, we took a sequence of real gestures and transformed them into dance without losing their realist impact in the same way that modern painting takes inspiration from real objects and transforms them into pure painting without losing sight of the power of their dimensions, texture, colors, and shadows. For reality alone, even heavily disguised, has the power to excite. The Chinese magician draws an egg from his braid, eats it, digests it, and finds it at the toe of his sandal. He breathes fire, burns himself, hops around to put out the sparks, etc. The young girl comes on stage, rides a bicycle, imitates Charlie Chaplin, chases a thief with a revolver, boxes, dances to ragtime, falls asleep, is shipwrecked, rolls in the grass on an April morning, takes a picture, etc.

13. Picasso's costumes.

The acrobats [are] simple-minded, agile, and poor. We have tried to clothe them in that certain melancholy feeling of the circus, the Sunday evening, the last drum-roll, that moment when the children put on their coats and cast a longing final look at the ring.

Satie composed a smooth score, large but simple in design, which suggests a music hall elevated to a higher plane. The three numbers, with the ragtime piece in the middle, are enclosed in a double frame—an interior scene, consisting of the music for the managers before the first and after the third number, and an exterior scene (*Prélude au Rideau Rouge*), consisting at the beginning of the score of the exposition of a fugue, and at the end, of the conclusion of the fugue. The music is undramatic and entirely decorative, and its singular metronomic import insures metric unity. It unfolds smoothly and steadily, and yet is powerfully tragic. The rumble and shuffle of the crowd are not evoked. Satie has retained only the characteristic inflections of traveling-show music, the abrupt outbursts of the brasses, the muffled punctuation of the tuba, the piercing timbre of the clarinet in the high registers, and that certain way of expanding the nuance at the ends of phrases. He has eliminated all vulgarity. The waltz of the acrobats is particularly characteristic. *Parade* is not music-hall music, rather it sketches its portrait.

Through one of those mysteries properly attributed to genius, a sense of seriousness in the music conveys the underlying human drama.

The orchestration breaks all the rules. There is nothing brilliant in the music, nothing overpowering, no striving for color. There is something weary about it in its carnival-like crudity; the orchestra has no punch, but it evokes deep feeling in the audience.

Parade is a eulogy of poverty, and it is a true masterpiece.

Cocteau says, "No sorcery, no repetition, no ambiguous caresses, no fever, no miasma. Satie never muddies the waters. He speaks the poetry of childhood with the touch of a master." Kœchlin finds the best quality of *Parade* "in that sense of measure which the composer of *Socrate* never loses. It is hard to say just how, but his transpositions of folk art are never vulgar, and even his brutality (when he finds it necessary to be brutal) is held in remarkable control." And Stravinsky says: *"Parade* reconfirmed my belief in Satie's worth and the importance of his role in French music in countering the uncertainty of decaying impressionism with firm, clear language stripped of the embellishment of imagery." *The Soldier's Tale, Mavra,* and *Apollon Musagètes* would never have seen the light of day if *Parade* had not preceded them.

The first performance on May 18, 1917, at the Châtelet, created a terrible hubbub. The public and the critics understood nothing of the choreography, the décor, or the music. Provoked by an aggressive manifesto written by Guillaume Apollinaire, they roared their protest, thinking they were being mocked. Cocteau, Picasso, and Satie were called *"Boches."* The scandal became serious, for Paris was in a state of siege. Satie was overjoyed. He had his revenge. After thirty years of anonymity, he had taken the lead of a movement in music and had become the standard-bearer of youth.

The publicity surrounding *Parade* was really unbelievable. The press went so far as to accuse the authors of introducing German ideas into wartime France. Passions erupted. Satie sent insulting postcards to one of the more stupid critics, and was dragged to court and sentenced to eight days in prison for slander and libel. Officials did not hesitate to make political capital of the incident. For a short time, *Parade* was considered an act of high treason. Cocteau defended Satie with tongue and fist.

This was the memorable beginning of new French music. As with *Le Sacre du Printemps,* a concert performance of *Parade,* under the baton of Félix Delgrange, drew ecstatic praise of the score.

Debussy, very ill, bitter and defiant, was displeased at the movement forming around *Parade,* which placed his old friend in the center of public attention. Satie was hurt at not having received a word of approval from the man he was most eager to hear from. He wrote Debussy an offended letter. "Debussy received it in bed," Louis Laloy tells us, "to which he was confined for the several weeks preceding his death. His trembling hands crumpled the sheet and the paper, which was suddenly torn to pieces. *'Pardon,'* he murmured, like a child about to be scolded, with tears in his eyes. . . . By mutual fault, this was the unhappy end of their friendship."

Parade was the embodiment of the sentiments of some young composers who shied away from affectation, an overly aristocratic tone or a contemplative attitude, and who wanted active music which would be simple and direct without forfeiting any of its nobility. The poet Blaise Cendrars, who was then writing *La Fin du Monde,* conceived the idea of assembling these artists in a group. In June, 1917, a first concert was given, featuring works by Satie, Georges Auric, Louis Durey, and Arthur Honegger. After the concert Satie proposed the founding of a group exclusively composed of musicians. It became known as the *Nouveaux Jeunes.* Germaine Tailleferre joined Durey, Auric, and Honegger, and Honegger introduced his friend Darius Milhaud, who with Paul Claudel was on a diplomatic mission in Brazil. Jeanne Bathori, a remarkable singer and the first interpreter of Ravel's *Histoires Naturelles,* was devoted to the cause of the *Nouveaux Jeunes* and organized the group's concerts at the Théâtre du Vieux-Colombier. Jean Cocteau became a member, and crystallized the aspirations of his friends in his book *Le Coq et l'Arlequin—Notes Autour de la Musique,* published in 1918.

Cocteau was a poet who combined intensity with purity, a perceptive and original man of the theater, alert to all the signs of the times. He had written a strange book, *Le Potomak,* which treated the malaise of the transition period before World War I with great imagery and highly personal poetics. *Le Coq et l'Arlequin,* published in the form of a tract, is a manifesto of ideas concerning the state of music which he had gathered in conversations with Satie, Stravinsky, and Auric. On these grounds, the tract is a valuable document. Like all manifestos, being one-sided, it is not exempt from exaggeration. Revolutionary action consists precisely in taking a side or adhering to a given position, not verbally but through actions. And because this was an artistic revolution, the side taken was all the clearer since the spirit, much more than technique, was involved. Also, the war had produced a discipline of speed, effectiveness, and brevity, which explains the pace of this small book. The

cock of the title symbolizes the authenticity of an art based
solely on Gallic sources and traditions, while the harlequin
represents the confusion of an art which includes pedal-notes
(we will say, *constants*), basically belonging to other peoples
(German and Russian) which, when introduced into French art,
only distort and weaken its character. The book attacks Wagnerism most violently, and strongly warns against the Russian influence exercised by *Le Sacre du Printemps*. However, it is a
fair-minded warning because in no way does it detract from the
unreserved admiration Cocteau, Satie, and future members of
the Six had for Stravinsky's work.

Le Coq et l'Arlequin also contains pertinent comments on
the public, the theater, and the life of music in general.

Let us quote a few of the sparkling aphorisms strewn through
the book. "Art is science made flesh." That is, we want an
art based on the knowledge of means of action and their effects.
"Tact in daring is knowing just how much too far one may go."
In the course of a progressive evolution, when "one does not
skip steps," today's artists always go too far for yesterday's, that
is, they go farther than yesterday's. And in the unknown regions
an artist explores, the only control the imagination should admit is that of taste—an eminently French position. "Look out!
Be on your guard, for music alone among the arts can envelop
you. Musicians must rid music of tangles, deceits and sleight-of-
hand tricks, and force it to stay as close as possible to the
audience." *Pelléas, Le Sacre du Printemps,* and *Tristan* are spellbinding works. They enclose the listener in a world of sensations in which the individual feels captivated, drawn in, and
becomes passive. He submits to the music, and the music will
not let him go. The art should be clear and open, and should
leave the listener lucid and conscious. It should be an objective
art, detached from the individual.

Clarity, economy of means, and perfect effectiveness are qualities the young generation found in the music hall. It was
thought that in their "music-hall aesthetics" Cocteau and the Six
were extolling music-hall music, but this is a misunderstanding
of their point of view. What they admired was the absolute
economy of each gesture of the acrobat, the tight-rope walker,
and the magician. In the music hall there is no gesture or pose

extraneous to the construction of the "act." There is no unnecessary fantasy or superfluous ornament; music-hall art is objective, polished and pure. The music hall was therefore proposed as a model because of the purity and perfection of its work. It also offers an example of an art form which is based on coarse features, a summary and sometimes schematic expression contrary to the subtleties of symbolism and impressionism. Satie and the Six were attracted by that aspect. It furnished them with the means to free themselves from the voluptuous charm which permeated Debussy's and Ravel's music and which hampered them at a time when they needed to affirm their own personality. The circus, popular Parisian songs, and clowns were the order of the day. *Parade* had painted the portrait of the music hall. *L'Histoire du Soldat* was inspired by stage art. Poulenc wrote *Cocardes,* and Milhaud *Le Bœuf sur le Toit.* Jazz came to Paris. Here is the first contact, as reported in *Le Coq et l'Arlequin:*

What swept impressionist music aside was, for one thing, a certain American dance that I saw at the Casino de Paris. Here is what it was like. The American band played an accompaniment on banjos and big nickel pipes. To the right of the little band, and beneath a gilded pergola, stood a bartender dressed in evening clothes and loaded down with bells, rods, boards, and motorcycle horns. He made noise by mixing the instruments together in cocktails, sometimes adding a dash of cymbals, standing up, strutting, and smiling to the heavens. Mr. Pilser, in tails, thin, and made up with rouge, and Miss Gaby Deslys, a great ventriloquist's doll with a porcelain face, corn-colored hair, and ostrich-feather dress, danced to that hurricane of rhythm and drums a sort of domesticated catastrophe which left them drunk and blinking under a battery of six floodlights. The audience gave them a standing ovation, torn loose from its reserve by that extraordinary spectacle—which is to Offenbach's foolishness what a tank might be to a horse-drawn carriage, vintage 1870.

A healthy reaction to the sublime, the sort of music that is listened to while holding one's head. "Enough clouds, vapors, aquariums, water-sprites, and perfumes of the night; we want a music of the earth, an everyday music." What was needed was trenchant music, to clear away the confusion. "In the midst of the exoticism and disrupted tastes in France, the café concert had remained fairly intact in spite of Anglo-American influences. It represented a certain tradition which, for all its dissipation, is nonetheless a part of the race. Here, certainly, a young musician could pick up the thread lost in the German-Slav labyrinth." A feeling for coarseness marked the crisis. "We can hope soon to hear an orchestra without the soft touch of the strings—a rich choir of woods, brasses, and drums." The pursuit of reality was set over against confessions of the soul and the enchantment of sensations. "The artist who has a feeling for reality must never be afraid of being lyrical. The objective world preserves its power in his work, whatever metamorphoses his lyricism subjects it to."

This aesthetic of reaction also satisfied the need for gaiety and unbridled and violent joy to which poets and musicians gave expression at the victorious end of a long and painful war. It was to bear fruit until Satie's death in 1925. But it was not the only aesthetic of the time. Honegger, for his part, never subscribed to it. Auric wrote only one ragtime piece, and then entitled it *Adieu, New York;* and in Poulenc's and Milhaud's work the music-hall phase is represented by only a very few works, contemporaneous with many others which were totally different in style.

Still, the importance of this kind of music should not be minimized. It contributed a great deal to the simplification of language, and the clarity of presentation of ideas.

Satie himself was thinking about *Socrate,* which he composed in 1919, at the time when the music-hall aesthetic was at the peak of its influence. *Socrate* is a symphonic drama in three parts for female voice and chamber orchestra, and is based on sections of Plato's dialogues in Victor Cousin's translation. The three parts are *Le Banquet, Aux Bords de l'Ilissus,* and *Mort de Socrate.* The composition is a masterpiece and one of the most important works of contemporary music. The serenity and sustained emotion Satie expresses have no equal in either classic or modern music.

A *symphonic drama* is the opposite of a *dramatic symphony*. The drama, rather than impregnating the symphony and subordinating it to the dynamism of the play, is expressed according to laws of purely symphonic musical structure. No other work of music can help the listener to understand *Socrate*. But certain decorative paintings bear an indirect artistic relationship. Satie greatly admired Puvis de Chavannes, and his first works—*Gymnopédies, Sarabandes,* and *Gnossiennes*—reflect the painter's spirit. The language in *Socrate* is contrapuntal, and differs from that of *Gymnopédies*. But the spirit is the same.

Mural painting (like Fra Angelico's and Puvis de Chavannes's) promotes a feeling of calm, serenity, and peace, even if the subject treated is full of movement. This quality is peculiar to murals, and coincides with the aims of the decorative arts. It is achieved by observing certain principles.

A] *Absence of marked color contrasts.*

Think of the cloister of St. Mark's in Florence and the frescoes at the Sorbonne. The colors are delicately balanced in value, or blend with each other in gradations which erase contrasts. This rule applies not only to isolated panels but to groups of panels. In the same way, sonorous contrasts in *Socrate* are avoided, and the three pieces are of the same intensity. Harmonies and timbres all have the same degree of tension. Today we are eager for marked contrasts and sharp, well-defined harmonies. And they do have their beauty. But the absence of contrasts and brightness is beautiful in its own right.

B] *Schematic arrangement.*

Consider *Le Bois Sacré, Vision Antique,* and *Inspiration Chrétienne,* well-known works by Puvis de Chavannes. Parallel lines, almost equidistant, are deliberately repeated throughout. Moreover, a motif repeated in its unchanging form often alternates with another motif repeated in like manner. This is the principle of repetition, or alternation and interposition of repetitions constituting the background of the subject. The Japanese have made remarkable use of the principle, as have painters like Uccello and Botticelli. Botticelli's work influenced Satie in the bases he selected for the instrumental music for *Socrate*. The lines and motifs that accompany or support the song are cells of one or two measures, repeated a certain number of times. This scheme alternates with several others, each based on a different but rarely contrasting cell, contrasts being reserved for climaxes of greatest tension. The same principle of repetition gives rise to the use of a constant measure and an unalteringly moderate tempo for each piece.

c] *Arrangement of the subject against the background.*

A decorative panel includes a certain number of human figures, such as those in Fra Angelico's great *Assumption,* Botticelli's *Spring,* and Puvis de Chavannes's *Repos* and *Bois Sacré.* All the figures are of the same physical type. Yet they are not monotonous, because the poses, lines, and curves of each body are finished, perfect, and different. In opposition to the background of the picture, there is no repetition here. Each figure has the same amount of space, but as the focus of a play of new lines it becomes something finished in itself. The peaceful round of gestures and movements, unified by a constant intensity and rhythm which avoids dramatic impact, is arranged on the calm, smooth background.

Satie's songs correspond to the human figures in decorative painting. The terms *melody, melopoeia,* and *recitative* are inapplicable here, for Satie's song, although perfectly shaped, has neither the complete meaning of a melody nor the accentuation of a recitative. His song is divided into sections with similar durations, amplitudes, and intensities, each section defining a complete shape differing from its neighbor and corresponding to the expression of the moment. Also, all syllables have the same value, since their duration is standardized. Diphthongs which are too rapid are divided. In this way each cell of the song preserves the same value in time, as the harmonious curves of human figures of uniform proportions are arranged in equivalent portions of space [*Example 88*].

If we contemplate the fusion of these various elements, we touch on the secret of the emotion we experience on seeing or hearing decorative work. We are reminded of what in physics is called the interference of a number of series of vibrations. A single vibration forms which is slower and larger than each of the interfering vibrations. From this comes that feeling of gentle, serene, and warm gravity we have when we hear such music.

The first performance of *Socrate* took place in 1920 at the

Société Nationale. Such was the confusion in the minds of listeners that Satie was thought to be making fun of the world. Satie wrote us: "My music was rather badly received, and I am not surprised; but I was surprised to hear the audience laugh at the text of Plato. Yes. Strange, isn't it? They would almost seem to be saying that Socrates is a personage of my own invention . . . and that in Paris!"

Darius Milhaud had returned from Brazil, and a young pupil of Ricardo Viñes, Francis Poulenc, whose *Rapsodie Nègre* had just been performed with great success, joined the new group of composers. Henri Collet, analyzing the growing trend in the magazine *Comœdia*, entitled his article, "The Russian Five, the French Six, and Mr. Erik Satie." Thereafter Louis Durey, Germaine Tailleferre, Georges Auric, Arthur Honegger, Darius Milhaud, and Francis Poulenc were spoken of as the Six, and it was not long before a group aesthetic was attributed to them which actually did not exist. It was thought that the Six were a happy band of friends who aspired to no greater heights than music-hall art and devoted their talents to comedy and buffoonery. To dispel contempt, the group published the four issues of the magazine *Le Coq* in 1920, printed on handbill paper and set in handbill type. The magazine set forth the points of view of each group member and those of Satie, Cocteau, and Raymond Radiguet in an amusing and combative style. One of the issues contains a declaration by Satie, who was antagonized by the very idea of a Satie school. "Satieism could not exist," he says. "I would be hostile to it. There should be no slavery in art. With each new work I have always made an effort to throw off imitators of my style or material. This is the only way an artist can avoid becoming the leader of a school, that is, a *pawn*." Poulenc explained the current need for coarse music: "Vulgar melody is good in that it is *original*. I like Romeo, Faust, Manon, and even Mayol's songs. Refinement almost always obliterates the folk accent in your 'modern music.' When refinement and that folk accent combine in a nation (as in Russia), that nation has found its music."

At the same time, Milhaud went so far as to defend Ambroise Thomas. But *Le Coq* was less on the march against refinement—

a danger already past—than against its antidote, which in turn was becoming detrimental. "All the young men of one generation were poisoned by Oscar Wilde, as if by a Catherine de Médicis, with books, perfume, and gloves. Those were days of English dilettantism. Today dilettantism is American. The light bulb is the new orchid. The cult of the nut and bolt has replaced the cult of the jewel. We must be wary of it."

Cocteau and Radiguet suggested the founding of an "antimodern league" devoted to "a return to poetry, the disappearance of skyscrapers, and the reappearance of the rose." All the musicians agreed with the idea except Honegger, who had a passion for locomotives and claimed to have discovered a new source of lyricism in the play of their wheels and connecting rods.

The spiritual revolution was ended. The new path, freed of excessive refinement and the exotic, is described by Georges Auric:

Why should we be criticized for the circus, the music hall, the Montmartre fair? Our remedy made us realize more completely how serious the sickness had been. We had to create this coarse and loud commotion. Too bad if it was a little brutal in breaking the deep spell of Debussyism and discarding the attractive elegance of Mr. Ravel, which had bogged down tragically and in which the genius of the guilty was no longer in question. It was enough that we were awakened in time to discover the enormity of the danger. Ravel used a "wind machine" in *Daphnis et Chloé.* It is not surprising that we came one day to prefer a "wind-breaking machine." The jazz band astonishes us. To create such a counterpoint of noises and rhythms and shouts around a few dance tunes in such easy, ordinary music is indeed astonishing. The "sublime" has no degrees. There were so many evenings when I chose to listen to the banjo and saxophone at the Casino de Paris in preference even to Chevillard's orchestra. *Hindustan* and *Indianola* brought tears to my eyes.

Debussy, I know, reached the sublime in his throbbing chords. I find the sublime on every page and in every measure of Stravinsky's ballets. How could we forget *Le Sacre du Printemps,* that extraordinary tumult —an entire orchestra dominated by the genius of a man who for us was his whole race that day.

But today—and this so well expresses the weariness of the times— we have had to reinvent "nationalism." I want to think as I understand, now that I know where I stand. Jazz woke us up. Let us plug our ears to hear it no more.

Honegger did not repudiate modern mechanism. Milhaud kept himself open to the influence of certain types of American music, saturated as he was, on his return from Brazil, with the luxuriance of the virgin forest. But while Louis Durey left Paris and retired from the new musical movement, Poulenc and Auric turned to the Paris streets for inspiration. Poulenc's *Cocardes*, set to poems by Cocteau, describes the melancholy of the suburbs in music written for tenor voice accompanied by a violin, cornet, trombone, and bass drum—the little orchestra of street-singers. Auric composed a series of *Huit Poèmes de Jean Cocteau* for voice and piano, which graphically re-create the atmosphere of Paris. We can now understand what Auric meant when he said that the little orchestra of *Cocardes* was as entrancing to him as a page of Rameau.

The last act of the Six as a group was the production of a play by Jean Cocteau with music by the five composers—Durey had left for Provence. The play was *Les Mariés de la Tour Eiffel.* In *Parade,* Cocteau created a plastic expression based on ordinary gestures, not on classic dance positions. In *Le Bœuf sur le Toit* he used masks and combined agitated music and slow gesticulations to create the atmosphere of a performance by sleepwalkers. In *Les Mariés de la Tour Eiffel,* focusing his ideas about the theater, he created "theater poetry" as a counterbalance to "poetry in the theater." "In the theater," says Raymond Radiguet, "even the greatest poets have always made the mistake of ornamenting their text with poetic images which only curtail the interest of the action. Here, imagery is an integral part, not of the language, but of the play itself."

Modern elements—the Eiffel Tower, phonographs, cyclists—are so manipulated that they are stripped of their modernism and emerge suffused in the poetry of childhood memories and become more real than reality. Irène Lagut and Jean-Victor Hugo designed a décor, costumes, and masks which harmonized perfectly with Cocteau's text. The music composed by the Six was trenchant in style, savage, and Parisian to its core. Auric created a crackling overture, Poulenc the hilarious *Discours du Général,* Tailleferre a wonderful *Quadrille,* Milhaud the bantering *Marche Nuptiale,* and Honegger a joyful *Marche Funèbre.*

Satie and Honegger soon drifted apart because of irreconcilable differences of opinion. A little later Satie, whom age and illness had made more sensitive than ever, had a falling out with Auric and Poulenc for reasons unrelated to music. This difficult period is illustrated by numerous magazine articles in which Satie expressed his vengeful streak with biting vigor and furious humor. He handled a pen with amusing malice. He even wrote a short one-act comedy, *Le Piège de Méduse*, festooned with little pieces of music for a very small orchestra that are models of pithiness and effective instrumentation.

After *Socrate* Satie composed five *Piano Nocturnes*, wonderfully pure pieces echoing the serenity of his symphonic drama. In 1924 two important works appeared, *Mercure* and *Relâche*.

Mercure is a suite of flexible poses in which Picasso treats mythology in terms of stage art. He created scenery and costumes which are some of the best work he has ever done for the theater. Satie outdoes himself. This is not the music hall or a transformation or poetic rendering of the traveling show. He probes much deeper, and takes inspiration from the very technique of the stage. Never in all his works has his rhythm been so powerful, never has his music been so free or so persuasive. The orchestration has that very special and unmitigated rawness which pierces the clamor of the crowd, and is yet tempered with the muffled punctuations of the tuba. There is no hint of vulgarity. Quite to the contrary, *Mercure* is like a challenge. This art for the people is seized by a strong hand which, trembling with rage, lifts it to a level of incontestable nobility. Let there be no mistake. *Mercure*, far from being humorous, is endowed rather with sacred fury, and some of its passages sound with the measured violence of the voice of doom. They alternate with pits of silence that echo with serene tenderness. Satie has never been in such close communion with Picasso as in this beautiful score.

Relâche, the final work of the Master of Arcueil, intensifies the sense of vengeance felt in *Mercure*. Satie, whose last words were, "Ah . . . the bastards!" chose a collection of the most vulgar popular songs and threw it at the public like a slap in the face. The score was built around an idea of Francis Picabia's; it follows no apparent logic, and is interspersed with film clips. The main value of the work lies in its remarkable orchestration. For René Clair's pantomime film, which was shown between the two acts of the ballet, Satie composed beautifully appropriate music. The music had to be continuous. His composition is background music, with a number of decorative rhythmic cells repeated, but this time not used as support for singers or melodies. The characters are shining film figures, and the decorative music they move to is called background because it performs the same function as does a wallpaper frieze in a room. It is unobtrusive, but its absence would be noticed. It is music which does not have to be listened to, but which clothes the silence. This film music, which is not found at concerts, was a great success. The idea could well be examined and developed.

It was fashionable to consider Satie an amusing mischief-maker and to pay heed to nothing outside his writing. Indeed, his letters and reviews deserve to be collected in a volume of articles and letters. But Satie was much more than simply a humorist and precursor.

Although his luck was sometimes bad, although he was forced to maintain silence for a good many years because he was incapable of producing what he glimpsed, there is no denying that he was a creator of genius. His piano pieces form a rich collection which can be ranked after Couperin's *Ordres* and Rameau's *Suites*. *Parade, Mercure,* and *Socrate* are powerful works planned and orchestrated with assurance and a unique and inimitable style.

Satie's place in the history of contemporary music, in all justice, is among the greats. His work is touched with a certain mystery—the mystery of a great purity hidden behind an illusion of mockery, with an implication of tacit complicity between the composer and whoever is able to receive his message. Marcel Proust achieved comparable communication. A passage in *Guermantes Way* reads:

Who knows, perhaps as she was proffering her candies, the Goddess was saying in that ironic tone of voice (for I saw her smile): "Would you like some candy?" What did it matter to me? I would have found her deliberate dryness delightfully refined, Mérimée- or Meilhac-like those words addressed by a goddess to a demigod who knew what were the sublime thoughts they were both doubtless summarizing for the moment when they would go back to living their real lives, and who, playing along, replied with the same mysterious slyness: "Yes, thank you, a cherry." And I would have listened as avidly to that dialogue as to a scene from *Mari de la Débutante,* in which the absence of poetry and great thoughts, such familiar things for me and things I suppose Meilhac would have been able to infuse in it with perfect ease, seemed to me in her alone elegant, conventionally elegant, and therefore so much the more mysterious and instructive.

6

MILHAUD, HONEGGER, AURIC, POULENC:
AFTER THE SIX

THE ACTIVITY of the Six as a group was limited and transitory. A violent reaction against preciousness resulted in a degree of impertinence, a farcical aspect, and trenchant music. The consequences of that attitude were important. Musicians learned to approach composition with confidence, without that excess of scruples that paralyzed the drive of composers like Duparc, Dukas, and Delage. Composing became an everyday affair, a *métier*, as Charles Kœchlin proved. The word *métier*, used by the composers themselves to define the productive work by which they intended to make their living, scandalized those who thought of artistic creation as a luxury activity, an exceptional work undertaken only when inspiration struck. Around 1920 Stravinsky, Honegger, and Milhaud had to defend their point of view repeatedly. Stravinsky said, "Inspiration comes with working as appetite comes with eating." Honegger also asserted that composing was a legitimate profession. To wait for inspiration before taking up a pen means to an artist to waste time in sterile dreaming. It is invalid to assume that the fecundity of the young composers was the result of this attitude. Rather, their production was made possible because they were gifted with very great musical abilities. Composing or creating music has been as natural and indispensable to them as breathing, and the abundance of work produced, for which they were criticized at the outset, was as necessary to them as it was for Lully, Haydn, Mozart, Beethoven, Handel, and Bach.

The quality of such an abundant production, of course, could not be uniform. There are poor, indifferent, and good compositions. Posterity will retain only those of enduring worth and will forget mediocre works. It is shortsighted to think of the great classic composers as perfect beings who wrote only masterpieces. A casual glance at their complete works reveals that Haydn, Mozart, and Handel composed many insignificant pieces. And even in Bach's cantatas, there are pages which have disappeared into oblivion, and are neglected for good reason. The modern composers must be approached with the same attitude. We should not reproach them for having written uninteresting works. We should consider only the fine scores which, fortunately, are fairly numerous.

DARIUS MILHAUD.   To speak of Milhaud, Honegger, and Poulenc, we must forget the Six. In their work, which has developed over a period of close to forty years, the spirit of the Six died an early death. Milhaud's personality matured after 1913, and Honegger's after 1915. But since their names had become famous as a result of the activities of the Six, public opinion erred for a time, holding that those activities manifested an aesthetic common to the members of the group. The individual personalities of the composers were not distinguished at first, and the idea took hold that humor, mockery, and satire were to be the aim of any work their imaginations brought forth. At the dress rehearsal of Honegger's *Antigone,* someone asked us if it would be funny. At a performance of Milhaud's *Homme et Son Désir,* a spectator confessed to us that he did not find the work "as funny as all that." He was referring to the manner in which the audience laughed at *Socrate.* How true it is that those who really listen to music without preconceived or extramusical ideas are a small minority.

Today Honegger, Milhaud, and Poulenc are not only famous but popular. Their music is welcomed and played almost everywhere. Honegger was given recognition as a serious composer after 1920, but not so Milhaud. The enormous success of *Le Bœuf sur le Toit* established him in the eyes of the academic world as a gifted composer, but one who was too facile and too eager for the immediate effect, amusing himself by deliberately sounding a false note. He baffled public opinion by the number of trends his art seemed to follow, but this multipolarity was only an appearance, not real. The public found his venturesome language hard to grasp, and hesitated to acknowledge his lyricism at a time when the focus was on construction and objectivity exclusively.

This hesitancy and misunderstanding did not extend beyond Paris. Foreigners adopted Milhaud, and only later did Parisians bow to the evidence. Milhaud had become the greatest of contemporary French composers, and on the international level he was in the first rank.

It would be useless to try to compare Milhaud with other contemporary composers. Some found his temperament comparable to Mozart's, others spoke of him as a second Berlioz. Such a contradiction shows how difficult it is to classify the composer of *Christophe Colomb*. None of the modern characteristics seem to apply to his work. There is no question about objectivity. His music is subjective. Romantic? Possibly—but with a sense of balance that is properly classical. Expressionist? Sometimes—but not in the pessimistic sense of the word as it is applied to the Viennese composers. There is no trace of a system of his own, and yet his language is so personal that a single measure of his music can be identified with no possibility of error.

Milhaud, born in Aix-en-Provence in 1892, is Provençal. He is the most Mediterranean of all French composers. Everything related to the Latin sea, everything found between Constantinople and Cadiz and between Rio de Janeiro and the Antilles is present and fully expressed in Milhaud's music. He is far removed from the problems which central European artists seek to solve, far from that pursuit of a form which seems so hard to find. Milhaud has an innate sense of form and plastic beauty, but he does not make them his aim.

His ever alert sensitivity reacts to all the impressions he receives. Yet it is not impressions he transmits to us, but the deep, total expression of the world as he sees and feels it. He absorbs sensation completely, and it catalyzes the reaction of his whole personality, which sings as if it were endowed with all the knowledge and wisdom distilled and decanted by the ancient peoples of the South. Milhaud's lyricism is like that of Homer and the Bible. It is of the same order as is found in Jean Giono's *Serpent d'Étoiles, Naissance de l'Odyssée,* or *Colline,* or in Francis Jammes's *Géorgiques Chrétiennes,* and in Paul Claudel's *Cinq Grandes Odes.*

Can we still reasonably speak of subjective art in connection with such poetry? The subjectivity is in any case very broad. These poets and this composer do sing with all their hearts, but their hearts are so representative of an ensemble of things and events, and the fruit of such an old civilization, that the air is not that of an individual but the song of wisdom, knowledge, and perception. Such lyricism is the source of true grandeur and real powers. It feeds on age-old realities which are timeless and constant.

Attributing Milhaud's extreme sensitivity and lyric power to his Jewish origin explains nothing. Claudel, Giono, and Jammes are not Jewish, and their poetry engendered Milhaud's. Nor are Milhaud's qualities as an artist specifically Jewish in character. We must remember that the Jews came into Provence with the settlers of Marseilles.

Rather than try to overparticularize, we will simply point out that there is an intimate lyric relationship between Milhaud's best music and the Song of Songs, the Psalms, Greek epic tragedies and poetry, and the poems from the *Serpent d'Étoiles.* The lasting influence of Greek culture—or Mediterranean-oriental culture—in Provençal civilization is visible enough for the relationship between the works mentioned above to be considered quite natural.

Milhaud is open to stimuli from all directions. He is receptive to the whole range of emotions, and expresses tenderness, joy, pain, tragedy, or reverence with equal felicity. Skepticism and cynicism alone are repellent to him. Sustained by a prodigious capacity for work (at the age of sixty he had composed more than three hundred works), Milhaud has experimented with every genre—chamber music, songs, cantatas, ballets, operas, concertos, and symphonies.

Milhaud cannot be said to have undergone an evolution. From his earliest works, and through the inevitable influences exerted on him at the outset, his personality has continued to assert itself and his outlook has not varied. His language, as intriguing and personal as it is, has never been more than a tool of expression. And the nature of his expression is so specific that variations in language do not appreciably modify the essence of his music. A scene from the *Brebis Égarée,* written in 1910 in language deriving from Debussy's, strongly resembles any scene from *Médée,* written in 1938 in language free from all influence. The interior life of Milhaud's works is so sharply defined that youthful works like *Alissa* carry weight later, despite harmonic devices that recall *La Damoiselle Élue.* Inversely, the bold style that was so startling at first was no longer noticed after a few years, so apparent is its necessity to the expression which gave rise to it.

For Milhaud, the whole world is music. There is no subject, situation, state of soul or object he does not translate into sonorous discourse. The essence of that discourse is melody. In his creative act, the invention of the melody is the crucial, decisive point, and once the melody is discovered, the composition itself flows spontaneously from his gifted nature.

When he approaches a subject, Milhaud contemplates it for a long time. He roves, opens himself to the outside world and lets the atmosphere work on his senses until he grasps the melodic pattern that most completely expresses his vision, which is always original and personal but is based on wide human experience. During this long period of gestation, the architecture of the music is sketched and filled in, and the work seems to be almost entirely composed when he begins to write it. He puts it down on paper with surprising speed and assurance, and the finished work has remarkable unity.

Le Pauvre Matelot, a lament in three acts, was thus in formation for nearly two years and took only fifteen days to write. Critics, ignorant of this creative process, long accused Milhaud of composing too quickly and sloppily, and of being too easily satisfied—an unjust accusation, influenced by his exceptional speed in writing, and justifiable only in the case of defective works. What comes from the pen of this composer is either wholly magnificent or wholly negligible. There is never a middle ground.

Schoenberg's revolution destroyed tonal structure. It was a negative revolution, at the end of which new foundations were needed to fashion a new mode of being in music. The conservative revolutions of French composers, at least Milhaud's, Honegger's, and Poulenc's, do not eradicate the principle of tonality and do not require music to be other than what it has been since the Renaissance. Their upheavals are individual. Each works with experimental language formed by others, and selects those elements that suit his own strong personality and allow him to express himself freely.

Milhaud's language is essentially tonal, and even radically diatonic. Considering the melodic nature of his music, this is logical. As we have said before, melody is an organism complete in itself, whose significance is a function of the relationships of notes to a tonic. Milhaud willingly repeats the precept of his teacher André Gedalge, who required his students above all else to write melodies without accompaniment.

Milhaud's melodies are strongly characterized, both in shape and in rhythm. They are perfectly organized units, often somewhat popular in development, but always intensely individualistic. They attest to the composer's breadth of vision [*Examples 89 and 91*].

It goes without saying that the melodic material is not necessarily composed only of perfect melodies. Suiting the requirements of action or development, his songs often take on the appearance of melodic themes, which can be divided into different motifs. The well-defined melodic base attracts counterpoint. This is the method of development natural to Milhaud's thinking.

Born at a time when the complex chords of Debussy and Ravel were linked with tonal feeling by the ever-slackening line of unresolved double and triple appoggiaturas, Milhaud brought about a simplification. Chords of ninths, elevenths, and thirteenths can in fact be related to a given key, but can as easily be interpreted as being formed of simple chords belonging to different keys. A chord like the one in *Example 93* can be considered as unitonal, whether it is resolved or not, but each of the three perfect chords which compose it can also become independent and confirm the simultaneous occurrence of two or three perceptibly different keys [*Example 94*]. The result is harmonic bitonality or polytonality. For instance, we find chordal agglomerations like those in *Example 92* in which the two simultaneous keys are noticeably independent. Generally, these bitonal chords evolve into a cadence which makes them converge into a single key, and the temporary dissociation of keys only makes the domination of a preponderant key more striking. In bitonality or polytonality one key always dominates —the one that is the most intensely sonorous by its position. This property gives rise to pseudo-modulation, an effect which enriches the harmony [*Example 95*].

These two chords built of the same six notes, superimposing C and Bb major in both cases, have different significance. The first is dominated by Bb, and the second by C. The result is that there seems to be a modulation, although the tonal components have not been changed.

Besides these polytonal harmonies, there are chords which, through their movement, seem to indicate a bitonal sense. Actually, this is not so. They are like the unresolved appoggiaturas of ninths [*Example 96*] or the rows of fourths which leave some doubt for a time about their ultimate tonal position, so that when this position is stated it will achieve even stronger expression in proportion to the length of time it has been delayed [*Example 97*].

However, polytonality is best justified in polyphony, in that it can state and follow two or more different and independent ideas which are presented simultaneously. The excerpt in *Example 98* is clearly contrapuntal. On a pedal-note outside of the key, a melodic line is established in C major. The clarity of the key is accentuated by a sequence of chords of sixths. (The harmonies Milhaud superimposed in polytonality are always very simple, as is required for the chords to be perceived simultaneously.)

Creating polytonality requires great skill and active auditory imagination. In composing for piano, Milhaud did not venture beyond bitonality. When he wants to go farther, to superimpose a greater number of melodic lines, he utilizes an ensemble of solo instruments whose differing timbres sustain the clarity and transparency of his structure. *Example 100*, a passage from the *Third Chamber Symphony*, is wonderfully sonorous, and superimposes no less than five different keys. The ear hears the development of the six melodies perfectly, and is not tempted to re-examine them in vertical analysis. The counterpoint is no longer harmonic in the least, and the voices are kept independent without breaking the key of each melody.

This particular style of writing is necessary to his expression. Milhaud told us one day: "When I am in the country on a beautiful, calm night like this, I get the feeling that all points on the horizon, of the stars, and in the earth's core send me rays, silent signs. That feeling of the cosmos teeming with life around you, and the feeling that you are in the midst of it, is intoxicating. I have always tried to express these multiple lines of force, these multiple rays that permeate you in the heart of the nocturnal silence."

Polytonal language does not exclude unitonality. Often, and always according to the expression desired, polytonality is resolved on a single key. In other places, the composer leaves polytonality aside and holds himself to one key. Polytonality and unitonality are not partitioned off. The same relationships exist between them as between dissonance and consonance. Passing from one to the other engenders tension and release. Polytonality introduces harmonic developments into the field of counterpoint, and thus increases the range of expression and power of a language which has not been disordered, but whose limits have been extended. The finale of *Euménides* is an example of admirable use of polytonality. The scene is the march of the people toward the temple of Athena to celebrate the advent of the new law. The song of the enormous crowd, expressing long-awaited release from the heavy burden of the law of blood, resounds in the streets. The long processional is sung by the chorus and Athena, with an orchestral background of six actual voices whose structure resembles an ostinato and pedal-note by the use of short motifs that pass from voice to voice and undergo a certain number of modulations. Four major keys are superimposed at the beginning of this swelling, surging march: Db, E, G, and Bb. Tension mounts. Soon there are six superimposed keys, the motifs being heard in Db, Eb, E, Ab, A, and B. After a time, these are reduced to five: Db, Eb, Ab, A, and B. In progressive release, the music passes into four keys: Db, Eb, A, and B. Then into three: Db, Bb, and B, which clarify by resolution into two keys: C♯ (D♭) and B. These are resolved at the end of the single key of C major, in a sheer burst of light. Never has *ut* major known such imposing and inevitable triumph, and never has it had to overcome such strong and prolonged resistance to gain freedom. It shines out, at the end of the processional, with almost unbearable brilliance.

No law or system can indicate which keys can be superimposed. The compatibility of different keys depends on a number of factors: their separation in sonorous space, the timbre and intensity of the instruments they are assigned to, the character of the melodic line, and the expression desired. In its current state, musical language has no absolutely incompatible elements. Taste and musical sense guide the composer. General laws no longer exist. There are only special cases.

Rarely does Milhaud make use of other than major or minor keys. But these he combines in his polyphony to create a sort of intermediary state, a major-minor duality, an element of uncertainty which nonetheless holds fast to tonality.

In creating structures (improperly called *forms*), Milhaud is extremely inventive, and shows a preference for the fugue and the sonata. He uses the sonata structure in symphonies, string quartets, dozens of sonatas for various instruments, and concertos (for piano, violin, cello, violin and flute, and two pianos). To describe Milhaud's sonatas would require a volume of commentary, because no two follow the same pattern. They are as varied as Beethoven's, and for the same reasons. Although he always respects the general pattern of the classic sonata, his construction depends on and is secondary to how he wants to express himself. Usually the slow movement is the focal point of the work. Milhaud is the only contemporary composer who expresses himself most fully in an adagio. That peculiarity almost seems like an anachronism in a time when rhythmic dynamism and the most brilliant virtuosity are the dominant concerns. Ease and freedom in invention of forms are the mark of creative genius. The eighteen quartets Milhaud has composed make up a wonderfully varied series. They contain short, concise movements in which development is barred, and others which on the contrary are fully developed. Some are polyphonic, like the fifth; others, like the seventh, are written as almost unaccompanied monodies. Their mood is alternately ardent, tender, pastoral, sad, or grave. No one in contemporary times, except Béla Bartók, has composed string quartets so well planned and written as Milhaud. The fabric of his quartets is rich and transparent. They are luminously sonorous and totally absorbing. The instruments never rely on the effects of sonorities: harmonies, and playing directly on the bridge or on the frets, are rarely used. The music of these quartets is natural and spontaneous, reminiscent of the delightful lightness of Haydn's quartets or of the intensity of Mozart's, whereas Bartók's are more like Beethoven's in temperament.

What cannot be described in words is the great honesty of Milhaud's music. Except for a few unimportant works, he makes no concessions to passing fashions. What was new in the language might have attracted an audience's special attention and distracted it from the contents of the music twenty-five years ago. Today the situation is reversed. Audiences accustomed to language peculiarities and recognizing that they are dictated by the artist's sensitivity are discovering timeless art, great in its simplicity and lasting significance, and truly original.

Milhaud's vocal and dramatic music still surpasses his purely instrumental works in importance. He is above all a lyric composer: he has written more than a hundred and fifty songs, four series of vocal quartets, a dozen cantatas, fifteen operas, and ballets, as well as theater and film music.

Since 1910, lyric composition has been somewhat discredited. People have been exclusively concerned with form and construction. The supreme compliment an artist can be paid is to be called intelligent. Intelligence seems to be the primary requisite for the validity of any work, and no one realizes that there should be a corresponding lyricism. Without preliminary emotions, intelligence could not exist. In the final analysis, intelligence could act abstractly; but to allow the emotions which have given it life to function would in no way dectract from its luster or its lucidity.

Throughout periods of trouble and chaos, this thirst for intelligence to restore order is understandable and legitimate.

But the fever of the thirsty makes them see intelligence in too simple a light. Wanting it pure, and finding it hard to see in a complex of ideas and emotions, they require that intelligence operate on an elementary level so that an immediate appearance of order is given, which will satisfy them.

This urgent call to intelligence has led to a temporary taste for pure formalism. And we must be careful. Although cubist canvases and Picasso's compositions live and continue to attract us, all the intelligence of Albert Gleizes did not prevent him from painting pictures which have long since been forgotten.

Picasso's work is beautiful, not because he is intelligent, but because his intelligence communicates emotion to us. He transmits his perception of matter to us. When he fixes a shred of cloth, a scrap of paper, and a dried rose on a board, it is as though he is speaking to us. We feel the warmth of an interior life and hear the beating of a heart.

Pure intelligence in a work of art, separated from its function of transmitting emotion called up by the external world, leads to the dangerous route of analysis. If an artist studies himself, taking himself as the subject of his observations, he puts himself on the path of egocentricity and eccentricity. The content of the work, which should be first in importance, gives way to a manner which is ultimately damaging. Certain passages by Cocteau, Poulenc, and even Stravinsky are tainted with this extremism.

The exercise of pure intelligence in art, or adherence to intellectual values, makes the artist lose contact with real life. The interior void which results is masked by good taste. When an artist cuts himself off from the warm sources of life, he narrows his horizon. An intelligent artist may paint a lovely landscape whose balanced lines attract our eye. But a landscape by a great painter will be involved in a human action more complex than the description or the architectural scheme. "In Goya's pictures," says Eugenio d'Ors, "the background is as important as the figure. The cosmic element takes on an importance formerly reserved for anthropomorphism (as in Rembrandt's work), and is suggestive of the infinite."

This is the complexity of lyric artists. All the components of a composition, each selected by an act of the intelligence, are unified by a superior form of intelligence, that of the heart. Only then do we receive that sense of the infinite, and only then will it evoke that vibration, that particular sympathy which uplifts us. This is the power of true lyricism. Why should we distrust it? There is no danger of confusing it with sentimentality.

The foundation of lyricism is subjective, and subjectivity was thought for a time to be dangerous. Too individualistic an art was feared, because extreme individualism had previously led to anarchy. But individualism is not an inevitable consequence of subjectivity. Romantic individualism, like Schumann's, does not correspond to the current general trend. To make oneself the center of the world and reveal one's personal joys and sorrows is not the aim of spokesmen in a time when every vital concern involves the whole of humanity, and when a social revolution is taking place which is changing every life. Personal drama offers too limited a horizon in the face of tragedy that straddles entire continents. The individualism of a Debussy, that passive pleasure consisting of egoistic enjoyment of the echoes aroused in us by the spectacle of nature, belongs to a carefree time.

But the individualism of an artist like Beethoven is of a different order. Its aim is to merge with the emotions of all men, to be at one with the human race, not to consider oneself as an exceptional and isolated being, to sing of human emotions in the most universal sense, to be part of the sensitivity common to all, and to avoid eccentricity. Milhaud's lyricism resembles Beethoven's, as Stravinsky's art, in its second manner, is like Bach's. What we say here, of course, does not constitute a value judgment.

Milhaud's vocal works are of very different types. There are real melodies among them, for instance, *Trois Poèmes de Lucile de Châteaubriand* (1913), some of the *Quatre Poèmes de Léo Latil* (1914) such as *La Tourterelle,* and the *Petits Airs de Stéphane Mallarmé.* But these are exceptions. His scheme often extends beyond the scope of a melody, and is not expressible with strophic periodicity. It tends toward the continuity of a dramatic progression. His vocal works are deeply psychological, in the same way as Claudio Monteverdi's *Lettera amorosa in genere rappresentativo.* His point, in fact, is to represent states of emotion, and not to sing of himself. It is Milhaud's nature to portray states of soul, and not psychological movement. This trait is noticeable in his quartets and songs as well as in his dramas, and molds the character of his music to express duration, not the moment, and states rather than actions.

In *Existence Humaine et Transcendance,* Jean Wahl writes: "The human soul knows many countries as its own. This idea of regions through which the soul, the *I,* passes, is expressed by Blake. It is the theory of *states.* The *I* is not real; it is the states through which it passes that are real."

To this series of lyric or dramatic fragments (since they must be given a name, to distinguish them from the melody-type) belong, among others, *Le Rossignol,* a splendid composition based on a beautiful text by Léo Latil; *D'un Cahier d'Eugénie de Guérin,* and *Alissa,* composed on sections of André Gide's *Strait Is the Gate.* Alissa's long lament, in which she confesses a love hidden too long, found its perfect composer. Milhaud clothed it in infinitely sweet melodies, beautiful in their almost monastic simplicity and austerity. This poignant monologue, an early work, is one of the author's best works.

Sometimes Milhaud offers us short syntheses, portraits which condense a character or type into a few measures. Such are the *Chansons Bas* (Mallarmé) and *Soirées de Pétrograd* (René Chalupt).

Milhaud discovered in Paul Claudel's poetry the expression of his highest aspirations, treating states of consciousness behind drama. In his *Études,* he writes:

In 1908, the poems of Francis Jammes led me out of the mist of symbolist poetry and made me look at a whole new world which was as easy to grasp as simply opening the eyes. Poetry finally had returned to everyday life, the goodness of the countryside, the charm of humble beings and familiar objects. What a sudden splash of cold water on my face! I found myself on the threshold of a living, healthy art, disposed to receive the influence of that force which shakes the human heart, twists it, uplifts it, calms it, and transports it like an element of nature whose uncontrollable violence, harshness, poetry and gentleness you feel in turn—the art of Paul Claudel. Jammes gave me the

Connaissance de l'Est. I was immediately tempted to put to music some of those poems which are individual concentrated dramas, noble and powerful in form, and sustained by the interior rhythm of prose that grips you like a vise.

Claudel's poetic art is based on the primordial iamb, and its rhythm is measured by respiration, the respiration that divides discourse into successive waves of unequal duration, following interior rhythm and pulse. His poetry rises above individual sensibilities and is generalized to the point of becoming the song of the human mind. In the power of his imagination, the relationship he defines between the human and the divine, and his faculty for depicting states of consciousness, Milhaud is in perfect accord with Claudel. Collaboration between the two artists was particularly successful in the production of dramatic works.

Two works aroused public mirth in their time, *Catalogue de Fleurs* and *Machines Agricoles,* for voice and instruments. They were thought of as a bet or a joke, because Milhaud had taken his texts from farm catalogues. But the explanation of these two marvelous works is simple. The man who receives the spring catalogue from his seed store glances through it and makes his choice. The short descriptions create in his mind the image of the garden he is preparing to work in. He dreams of beautiful summer days, new greenery, and the bright, fresh colors splashed on it. This hope, this rebirth—*Catalogue de Fleurs* is a ray of sunshine through sparkling white clouds, the first sign of spring.

In the same way, *Machines Agricoles* is to be sung and played with thoughts of the magnificence of golden wheat on rolling plains, in the strong July sun. The big metallic insects which are the reaper, the binder, or the tedder are meaningful only in this setting. Giving the title *Rustiques* to this suite would be enough to make the world understand what the music means.

There is a series of eight songs that deserve particular mention for their expression of religious feeling, a rare thing in modern music. The *Poèmes Juifs* are famous. They express the most hidden corner of Milhaud's soul, and constitute a confession of faith in the strictest sense of the words. Despite the difficult times, here is confidence, hope, and faith that a better life will come at the proper time to recompense the just and the courageous. Milhaud's religiosity, free of pride and complexities, is simplicity itself. Human solidarity impregnates the songs, which are infused with the character of folk art. The *Liturgies Contadines* and *Prières Journalières* are the contrary of the trend that represents a peril to modern music: intellectualism. This cycle of religious songs is crowned with the superb *Service Sacré pour le Samedi,* for cantor, chorus, and organ or orchestra. Written in 1947, it defines to perfection the aesthetic position of the composer—faithfulness to the tonal principle, simplicity, social solidarity, and optimism.

After the song cycles, we should mention Milhaud's cantatas, works permeated with liveliness, freshness, and youth. Of special interest are the *Cantate de la Paix,* the *Cantate de l'Enfant et de la Mère,* the *Cantate Nuptiale,* and *Pan et Syrinx.*

Milhaud expresses himself most fully in his dramatic works. Between 1910 and 1915 he composed *La Brebis Égarée* on the play by Francis Jammes. Between 1913 and 1922, he conceived and wrote the music for the *Orestie,* Paul Claudel's adaptation of the Aeschylus trilogy, and for the satiric play *Protée* by Claudel, who also wrote the text for the ballet-poem *L'Homme et Son Désir.* Then in 1923 and 1924 came a series of ballets: *La Création du Monde,* on a theme by Blaise Cendrars; *Salade;* and *Le Train Bleu,* a ballet-operetta by Jean Cocteau. The opera *Les Malheurs d'Orphée,* with libretto by Armand Lunel, was composed in 1924; and the comic opera *Esther de Carpentras,* the libretto also by Lunel, in 1925. Cocteau wrote the libretto for the tragedy *Le Pauvre Matelot* (1926); and Henri Hoppenot wrote librettos for the three one-minute operas: *L'Enlèvement d'Europe, L'Abandon d'Ariane,* and *La Délivrance de Thésée* (1927). *Christophe Colomb* was written in 1928 in collaboration with Claudel. In 1930 a play by the Czech-born Viennese, Franz Werfel, in translation by Lunel, was set to music. The resulting opera was *Maximilien.* Again with Claudel, Milhaud composed a sort of scenic oratorio in 1935, *La Sagesse.* He then returned to Greek tragedy in 1938 with *Médée,* with a libretto by Madeleine Milhaud. In 1943 *Bolivar* appeared. *David,* an opera based on the play by Jules Supervielle, was written with Armand Lunel in 1952.

Short works, grand opera, tragic and satiric drama, ballets are all connected, despite their diversity, by a single dramatic concept. Divertissements are the exceptions—*Salade, Le Train Bleu,* and *Les Songes.*

We do not have the space even to describe in résumé the theatrical works whose titles are mentioned above, almost all of which are extremely important. The most perfect is possibly *Les Malheurs d'Orphée,* and the most imposing are the *Orestie* and *Christophe Colomb.* We are limited to an analysis of the characteristics of Milhaud's dramatic technique, without going into detail of his works.

All the objects around us participate in our lives. All witness and act in the human drama. Marcel Proust, stumbling over a stone, saw a long-forgotten period of his life take form again, events which were linked to a similar incident, to a similar slip of his foot. His dependence on that stone to tilt the rim of his memory was as real as a man's dependence on food as a source of energy, but with a qualitative difference: the stone would have another meaning to any other eye, or even to Proust's had a single component of the experience been missing.

The chair Pierre sits on in *La Brebis Égarée* is not the same as the father's chair in *Le Pauvre Matelot.* The sea in which Proteus and his seals frolic has nothing in common with the sea of Christopher Columbus's bitter strife, unless it is the sea's eternity and omnipresence. The farm machines are part of the broad serenity of Beauce, while they torment Paul's mind in *La Brebis Égarée* as a gadfly stings a horse.

Milhaud's art has no subjects or motifs, but only sums or indivisible wholes. Whether the chair is straw or leather is of no importance, for it does not exist as an object. It takes on existence only with the flux of forces that link it with other things and with the emotion of the moment.

The chair, a cup, flowers, people, in the process of that wonderful first scene in *La Brebis Égarée,* are co-born with us.[14] We become conscious of them. The poet and musicians thus fashion an art of consciousness, lifted above the art of sensibility.

14. See Paul Claudel's *Traité de la Co-naissance du Monde et de Soi-même.*

For sensibility here is only the source of the emotion conveyed to us by a vast synthesis.

The reader will pardon us for borrowing from Claudel's *Art Poétique* and speaking of Jammes while discussing Milhaud's music. For what applies to one applies to the others. There is such close correspondence between the music and the poetry that on hearing *La Brebis Égarée* we cannot distinguish the poet's role from the composer's. And it would be impossible to separate the poetry and the music of *Christophe Colomb*.

Milhaud's art is expressionist, but not in the central European meaning of the word. His expressionism focuses on the universality of life, distinct from the individual, who is considered as a contingent being in this world.

Whatever the subject, except in the divertissements, the substance is unique. It consists of a representation of the world in which all creatures are treated as equal and interdependent beings, situated in a single complex in the center of which occurs the only true drama: the drama of man fighting against all the forces that imprison him. The events occurring and the words spoken only lead the drama toward a climax ordained by an inner necessity, the *fatum,* the *ananké* of early times. The accomplishment of destiny, which is unmoving in relation to the flowing waters of life, is presided over by all the forces of the universe: the stars, fire, water, and wind, the forest and the animals, familiar and unknown objects. All these are oriented toward the purpose of the drama, toward man struggling in his difficulties, and are never used as a pretext for suggesting the picturesque or decorative. These forces are not additions, but are simultaneously actors and witnesses of the drama. Man feels them, approaches and observes them, and projects on them the fire of the inner life that shines from him in all directions. The cosmic preoccupation at the core of each drama reveals the general idea and unity of Milhaud's dramatic lyricism.

Milhaud first treats man's earliest age: the slow gestation period, the larva, the chrysalis that can hardly move in the night, crawling, bearing the memory of his origins, trying to find his place and meaning, moving toward a goal he does not consciously know. Destiny wraps him in its web before he has even seen light. This is *L'Homme et Son Désir*. Then he is being born along with the plants and animals, deep in the mystery of the forest, and receiving his mate. This is the moment when life, hardly awakened from its primordial immobility, begins to move, the moment when the tadpole, with a last shake, wriggles free of the egg and moves off in the fresh flowing water. This is springtime, the dawn of the *Création du Monde*.

In the course of life, man catches hold of the web around him. The threads strain under the prisoner's struggle, but do not give way or unravel. Man and woman, made to complement each other, move to join each other. Their paths cross, but their destiny is that they will not unite. Absence, void, interior wounds make a heavily sculptured mask for man—the lament of *Le Pauvre Matelot* whispers the tale, and *Les Malheurs d'Orphée* cry it out.

Man has had a revelation of his destiny. The unattainable goal has made him conscious of the role assigned to him, from which he cannot withdraw. Sometimes he tries to upset the imposed order, hoping to attain the fulfillment he aspires to. But the only relative peace he will find, as *La Brebis Egarée* shows, is in restoring the order he has disrupted. If he continues to revolt, he will end in the tragedy which is *Médée's*. But he will be greater if he follows the purpose he recognizes as his own. Shaken by a tempest of errors, he struggles to maintain his course, ties himself to his mast in order not to succumb to temptation. Through misery, failure, and crime, he does not lose sight of the goal to which his mind points. There he will be able to lay down his burden and be redeemed because he is saved by the Spirit.

Different facets of this greatest of dramas are treated in *Maximilien*, the *Orestie*, *Christophe Colomb*, *Bolivar*, and *David*. Finally *La Sagesse*, wisdom, dominating humanity, will force man to follow its precepts for better or worse.

This is the order of Milhaud's tragedies. Satire displaces drama. It is farcical and poetic in *Protée*, biting in *Le Bœuf sur le Toit*, its relentless dance written for emphasis into a Charlie Chaplin movie. In the *Opéras-Minute* the satire is sly, and joyful but sober in *Esther de Carpentras*, in which two worlds and two peoples cross each other's paths without uniting.

Milhaud preferred opera to lyric drama as his form. Lyric drama concentrates interest on the harmony of sounds and the text is treated as a sort of continual recitative, the musical value of which is generally less than that of the orchestral fabric.

Opera is bound to the beauty of the vocal line, an articulated structure including airs, ensembles, and choruses of purely musical architecture. While lyric drama subordinates the music to the text, opera maintains the primacy of the music. Poetry may have been undervalued in nineteenth-century opera, and librettos rudimentary with verse of little real worth, but the music was suited to the song. Do not forget that traditional opera mainly served as a decorative spectacle, whose function was to display the virtuosity of the vocal soloists, and was not intended to go very far in the realm of expression. Although certain passages in *Faust, La Traviata, Rigoletto,* and *Aïda* attained to great beauty of expression, operas generally had a rather superficial, albeit rich and captivating, charm. Their main aim was to entertain.

The import of Milhaud's operas, as we have seen, is quite different. He has selected plays of high poetic value for his librettos, and treated them with the love and respect poetry deserves. Just as a fine poem by Verlaine or Mallarmé loses nothing when set to a melody composed by Fauré or Debussy, so the poetry or prose of Jammes or Claudel finds appropriate musical expression in Milhaud's songs, which accord beautifully with the rhythm, sonorousness, and meaning of the text without inhibiting the composer's freedom of style. The orchestra as well is not limited to being a sustaining element or foundation of the song, but is intensely expressive, without, however, monopolizing the audience's attention. Milhaud's opera is actually as far removed from lyric drama as it is from nineteenth-century opera. It is directly descended from Berlioz's *Trojans,* and has a quality of balance and assurance in production, moreover, which Berlioz's work sometimes lacks.

The three-act opera *Les Malheurs d'Orphée* (1924) took many years of work before reaching fruition. In 1921 the composer wrote:

I am pursued by the idea of creating an Orpheus. This is such a magnificent subject. But I want to make it a *human* thing. Since nothing really works out in life, Orpheus must not find Eurydice. He must seek her without success, despite his lyric heart, and he must be made to understand that he must live with his animals like a good fellow and that he will find her only when he dies. . . . I would like a series of scenes in which greatness comes from the gravity of the dramatic action and from the purity of sound of the music. The choruses would all be replaced by a vocal quartet and the orchestra by a maximum of six or seven instruments.

How very much of a reality the old myths are for the Mediterranean races! There is no question of a theatrical Orpheus. He is not a hero; he is a "good guy" who lives very close to us. None of the pomp of mythological theater, no cynical interpretation of an old subject—we are far from all that.

By early 1924 the idea had ripened. When the music had been written, Milhaud drew up the scenic plans and gave the task of writing the text to his friend Armand Lunel. Lunel provided him with a perfect play.

Orpheus is the village bone-setter. His house, solitary and hidden, is at the edge of the village near the fields, beyond the shops of the wheelwright, the blacksmith, and the basketmaker. The artisans are shocked to see Orpheus waste his talents on wild animals. "You carry herb tea to the wolves and balm to the wild boars. One day they will tear you to pieces, Orpheus!" But Orpheus says good-by to the animals. He is waiting for "a bee he expects to come here on the chosen day." This bee, this woman, is a foreigner: "He would take a wife from outside our country? Horrors!" The woman, Eurydice, has come through here, "at this place, the most beautiful of four sisters, in a covered wagon. . . . Idiocy, to join that race of sneaks and scoundrels!"

Thus, he transgresses the law of the village, and she the law of the gypsies. Without the text's telling us, we understand that we are in the Camargue, feeling the sting of sun and salt. We know that Eurydice is a gypsy, and when she runs panting on the stage, she has escaped from a gypsy van coming back from Saintes-Maries-de-la-Mer. Eurydice is being pursued by her people. The chorus of artisans counsels the lovers to flee to the woods and join the beasts, who will defend them. "And tomorrow, we will reply to those filthy thieves who will demand

Eurydice by showing them the bone-setter's home, silent and shut."

Next we find the lovers in the shepherd's hut. The wolf, wild boar, fox, and bear mourn, for Eurydice is dying and Orpheus cannot save her. They speak the last words they will exchange, drinking in and breathing this short, heart-breaking, and so sweet conversation. Eurydice makes her farewells. She kneels and speaks to the animals as if she were a little girl. She entreats them to take care of Orpheus. And the animals, like good children, promise to do so. At the sight of this terrible scene, Orpheus cannot hold back his tears. He weeps, in a short, sad lament, while Eurydice dies in peace. The animals, crying a hoarse funeral chorus, carry off her body.

Orpheus, back at his village, sits, "his head in his hands before his large counter, between his pharmacopoeia and his scale," alone in the world with his pain. This evening his visitors will not be the animals. Eurydice's three sisters arrive in their stead. "What fury, what tenderness" in their voices. They hurl accusations at Orpheus, and demand retribution. He welcomes their frenzy, for they speak to him of his dead beloved, and he hopes only that they will kill him. They advance, armed with scissors, a gag and a whip, and fall on him. He offers no resistance, and dies, his arms extended toward his vision.

The three acts are each barely a quarter-hour long. The composer has included only what is strictly necessary, and has eliminated all elaboration. He aimed for quality in each detail and condensation rather than quantity and length. The quality of the music is such that it takes on the aspect of an offering, a prayer, a ritual act that brings consolation and repose to an overburdened soul.

Maurice Ravel considered *Les Malheurs d'Orphée* the most beautiful work to appear since *Pelléas*. The opera is undoubtedly a masterpiece of purity of form and power of expression.

The *Orestie* is Milhaud's most unusual work. He seems to have understood perfectly the Greek concept of tragedy that unites the human with the divine, simplicity of idea with richness of imagery, and the realities of Mediterranean life with supernatural law. This twentieth-century Phocian found himself at home in the ritual action of Greek tragedy; his song is neither anachronistic nor out of place. In his *Études,* Milhaud speaks of the *Orestie* in these words:

The language of Aeschylus in certain choruses and some dialogues suddenly takes on such marked meter and lyricism that the musical support seems to be born spontaneously. Claudel, starting with this viewpoint, arranges for a sudden interlude of music, which he has asked me to write. I wanted to avoid the ordinary "scene music," a form of expression I detest. There is nothing more fake than the intrusion of a musical phrase while the actors continue with their uninterrupted delivery of the text of the work. The words and melody move in two totally incompatible realms. To emphasize that excess of lyricism it was necessary to pass from speech to song. In *Agamemnon,* Clytemnestra does not sing until after she has committed her crime, at the moment when she comes from the palace brandishing her bloody hatchet. This is the very violent scene in which Clytemnestra hurls herself at the chorus of old people, and at the end of which a fanfare proclaims Aegisthus king. This storm past, the play resumes its normal course. The music is silenced and the actors take up the dialogue until the end of the play. . . . In 1915 I wrote the *Choéphores* on the same principles as the music in *Agamemnon,* but throughout the play there are a number of sung scenes: *Vociération Funèbre* on the entry of the Choephori; Electra's *Libation;* and the *Incantation* of the chorus, with Electra and Orestes standing over Agamemnon's tomb. Then two savage, cannibalistic scenes gave us one of our most complex problems. The lyric element was not musical. How were we to translate that hurricane and keep it in order? At this point I thought of having the dialogue spoken in measures, set to rhythm and conducted as if it were sung. I wrote spoken choruses on a background of an orchestra composed only of percussion instruments.

And for the conclusion, after Clytemnestra's murder, the music returns in its own right with the powerful *Hymne à la Justice,* which was written for choruses and orchestra. . . .

In 1916, Claudel sent me a translation of the *Euménides* he had just finished in Rome, and I made it into a three-act opera. Everything is sung. I know no more beautiful subject to work with. After horrors and crimes, after the first two somber and savage acts, comes the vote by the people of Athens, the acquittal of Orestes and the great scene of the appeasement of the Eumenides, and the growth of light and joy. Triple chorus of Athena, the pacified Eumenides, and the people of Athens. This Mediterranean people, this people so like the crowd that packs the port of Piraeus, fishmongers, vegetable sellers, merchants, adventurers, idlers, with all that immense Latin sky over their heads.

The score was begun in Rio de Janeiro in 1917, and the first act finished in Martinique in 1918. The second act was written in Paris in 1922, the third in Aix-en-Provence in 1923. The orchestration for the whole work was done in 1924. Therefore, I worked on the *Orestie* for twelve years.

The subject of the *Orestie* is the drama of divine law and the human destiny it ordains, and of a theomachy, one of those great mutations in the collective consciousness.

Personal drama is not in question here, nor human misery. The aim of the tragedy is to express a sum: knowledge. The musical language is entirely depersonalized, in the sense that it no longer bears the mark of an individual's experience. In the *Orestie*, the moral landscape itself, the relationship between man and the objects around him, disappears. The music is detached from all contingencies, as in a Mass, and consequently is often static in character. In no other score, except the *Euménides*, is there such wide use of polytonality, and with good reason. The interplay or interference of all those lines, those different keys, gives the impression of total participation, of a powerful sheaf of forces that dominates and directs human action. The *Orestie* transmits a feeling of severe grandeur and enormous dimensions, something superhuman that ends by being resolved in the blinding light of the processional of the Eumenides. The trilogy *Orestie* is a prodigious work which, except for its second section, the *Choéphores*, is almost unknown.

Christophe Colomb is now considered the culmination of Milhaud's work. When the Unter den Linden Opera was rehearsing its memorable production of this work, under the direction of Erich Kleiber, Paul Claudel discussed the drama in the journal *Anbruch* published in Vienna. We can do no better than to give a résumé of his article.

The poet did not intend to recount the details of the discovery of America. He made himself an interpreter of the world of ideas, questions, and feelings that four centuries of history have planted in the heart of the spectator. He conceived the idea of inviting the great Columbus, who had united the inhabited world, to speak in the name of all humanity. A great book is read to the people, who marvel at the prodigious adventure; they take the pro and con, applaud or accuse, or demand clarification of the navigator's acts.

And actually there are a reader and a chorus which listen to him. But each time the narrative approaches an action, the words stop and the action itself unfolds under our eyes, under the eyes of the chorus which takes part in it, and under the eyes of Columbus himself seated with the chorus. The chorus is not the same as in the dramas of antiquity, but rather resembles the choirs established in churches as intermediary between the celebrant and the people. A voice, an assistant charged with interpreting the thought of the authors, was needed between the anonymous mass of people and the drama.

Columbus dies in a tavern in Valladolid. At that moment, as he reviews his life, he becomes two people: he is the witness and the judge of his own acts.

The *colombe,* the dove, the symbol of the Holy Spirit, appears. It flies across the sea and leaves its message at Genoa in the hands of a dreaming child. There is the seaman in the Azores, where he gets word of flotsam from the beyond. Then, there is the hero in the clutches of creditors, courtiers, and skeptics; the captain, overcoming the mutiny; an hour of agony. Conceit and meanness of small minds. Then again there is the man who discovers the world, bound to the mast of his own ship, whipped by the wrath of men, prey to the fury of the elements. He suffers bitterly from the ingratitude shown him by the whole world, except for one woman: Isabella the Catholic. Death is close, and a dove brings a twig of peace as in the days of the flood.

All this does not happen in a void. Every voice, every word, and every gesture have an echo, a response, and demand and evoke immediately proclamation far and wide. The chorus plays the part of the press, from one end of the world to the other. It creates the same stir that the press creates whenever an important event takes place.

This intentional diversity brought out by the poet in the text is reflected by the music in the mixture, or rather the alternation, of narrative, rhythmic speech, and music and in the extraordinary changes in the atmosphere of the work.

The opera revitalized lyric theater in form and spirit. It is a combination of opera, oratorio, and film. Film was used to furnish not a landscape but a spiritual décor. It shows us the dove and the cross.

Drama has no limits. For man, it is a painful experience which goads him toward knowledge. The individual, society, and religion play their part in this tragedy of the conscious mind as they do in the *Orestie*. But while water, fire, vegetation, and the earth have disappeared in the *Orestie* and are plowed under and absorbed in the depths of consciousness, the material world is present from the beginning in *Christophe Colomb*. The facts are there, under our noses, brought to the stand as part of the evidence. Time itself is perceptible in the apparent chronological disorder. This material presence of facts and this irregularity in the flow of time, which is not disturbed in the *Orestie*, require a special style of composition to be expressed. Here Milhaud is again the architect of great, monumental structures. The *Orestie*, however, is a pyramid built block on block. Its lyricism develops, growing in intensity, and the insight into the conscious mind is steadily broadened until the end. *Christophe Colomb* is constructed differently. Starting from a central point, we are led successively in different directions in the drama. There is therefore no need for progressive increase in lyric intensity. The lyricism varies according to the scene shown, each scene being a dramatic moment determined by the interaction of characters and material objects. The sea, then, one of the dominant factors in the play, will in turn be that of *Protée* and that of *Le Pauvre Matelot*. All these single dramas, as different as they are, are integrated with the over-all scheme and form a whole.

Such unity in diversity results from the fact that only rarely does the music deploy all its resources at once. It is held ready at all times to aim at another point on the horizon. It constantly returns to the perfect chord to economize its forces. Each scene sets out again from a consonant point, develops its particular expression from that point, and is resolved in simple tonality.

In each scene the music sets out from new bases in a new direction.

Polytonal development, and utilization of the maximum capacities for sonority in the orchestra, from the highest to the lowest registers, are reserved for the dominant scenes: Isabella's and Santiago's scene, the churning of the sea, the typhoon, and finally Isabella's funeral.

Even in the final Alleluia, Milhaud abstrains from polytonality. Actually, the music does not mark the end of the drama. Rather, it is the expression of the judgment which we make on Columbus's life.

This splendid work should be considered as one of the most representative, not only of its composer but of the first half of the twentieth century. Like Berlioz, Milhaud was recognized and welcomed abroad before his own country accorded him the place of honor due him. While around 1920 performances of his works provoked such tumult in Paris that the police once had to empty the concert hall where his *Études pour Piano et Orchestre* were being played, by 1936 Frenchmen recognized Milhaud as the Mediterranean luminary who has helped to maintain contemporary music on a high level and who has enriched it with a personal gift of great value. Today it is clear that Milhaud is carrying on in the tradition of Berlioz and Bizet.

ARTHUR HONEGGER. The friendship of Milhaud and Honegger dates not from the time of the Six, but from several years earlier, when they were both students in Gedalge's classes. The independence of temperament and boldness of thought, and the ideal of greatness common to them both drew them together, and intense mutual admiration kept them close during their brilliant careers.

Arthur Honegger was born in Le Havre in 1892. His family came from Zurich, but Honegger has spent all his adult life in France. Trained at the Paris Conservatory under Gedalge and Widor, he took Vincent d'Indy's course on conducting, along with Milhaud. His first works were composed around 1916. Honegger belonged to the Nouveaux Jeunes and the Six. But he was not interested in the music-hall movement, and the joyful frolics of his friends gave him no pleasure. Moreover, his temperament clashed with Satie's. After contributing to the production of *Les Mariés de la Tour Eiffel,* he left this milieu, but continued on the best of terms with his friends.

Of the young composers in 1920, Honegger was the only one whose work was mainly symphonic. He devoted himself primarily to compositions for full symphony orchestra, and admired Richard Strauss and Florent Schmitt for their ability to express themselves in large orchestral compositions.

An important piece of stage music, written for *Le Dit des Jeux du Monde,* a play by Paul Méral, had drawn attention to this fiery, rhythmic new talent. A good deal of notice was also paid to *Le Chant de Nigamon,* a symphonic poem composed in 1917. In 1920 he composed the great symphony *Horace Victorieux,* originally intended to be a ballet, which fulfilled the hopes of the composer and those who had confidence in him. The indescribable beauty of the violent, even brutal, work won it favor. But the dramatic psalm, *King David,* written on a text by René Morax, was the work that captivated the public at large and brought Honegger popularity as well as academic acclaim.

His sudden rise to fame is easy to explain. The public was irritated by new composers whose works it did not understand. It could not follow Stravinsky, Satie, Milhaud, or Schoenberg, all of whom infused music with a new spirit of their own. Honegger said nothing new; he carried on the familiar tradition of Wagner, Strauss, and Florent Schmitt. His thinking was not original. Only the sonority of his music was new, and his innovations were solely of a harmonic order. The public is most offended when required to examine things in a new light. It is less disturbed if a picture is presented which is not strange, even if it is dressed in new colors.

Also, *King David,* which was to be performed in the Théâtre Populaire du Jorat in Mézières in the Juras, was composed of twenty-eight short pieces, mostly choruses, which had to be very simple in order to be sung by amateurs. The score is very variegated. Side by side with charming, light passages are sections that make the listener think of Handel and Schmitt. The work delighted the public, which had felt out of contact with contemporary music since the appearance of *Le Sacre du Printemps*. Here, finally, was a modern musician it could understand. In a perfectly natural reaction, there was a great deal of excitement over *King David*, which led enthusiasts, in all good faith, to put it at the head of the list of contemporary compositions. This created a misunderstanding which Honegger himself was to suffer from later on. The admirers of *King David* were disappointed that the composer did not adhere to the style of this work, and were hesitant to accept his more significant compositions. *Antigone*, his most beautiful score, written between 1924 and 1927, was first performed at the Théâtre Royal de la Monnaie in Brussels in 1927, but was not heard at the Paris Opera until 1942.

There was a fortunate side to the misunderstanding, however. While other young composers were still thought of as practical jokers, or their worth was underestimated, Honegger was considered a serious composer and a real musician. This created surroundings for him to work in which, if not always perceptive, were warmly receptive. Honegger was the only outstanding contemporary composer besides Paul Hindemith to enjoy this benefit.

Honegger's talent is characterized by his great ability to develop schemes. These are generally short. Unlike Milhaud, Poulenc, or Prokofiev, Honegger has no innate talent for melodic invention, nor does he have their ability to shape musical lines. With the exception of his composition based on six poems from Apollinaire's *Alcools* (1916), his melodies for voice and piano are not very interesting. In chamber music, the composer brought his efforts to bear on modernizing the structure of the various movements within the sonata form. The adagio of his *First String Quartet* (1917) is built on the scheme

a B C D E C D B a.

The first movement of the *Sonata for Viola and Piano*, which is Honegger's best chamber music composition, is peculiarly structured. Willy Tappolet analyzes it this way: "The andante and vivace alternate three times in the main movement, forming a skillful mixture of sonata form and *Lied* form in five parts.

If the *Lied* form is designated by A C A, the thematic part of the sonata by B, and the recapitulation by ᗺ, the scheme will be

ABCᗺA.

"The inversion of the letter B is not arbitrary. Despite the rule that the recapitulation of themes should occur in the order they do in the exposition, Honegger thinks otherwise, and inverts them for the re-exposition, beginning with the second theme. If we call the first theme A and the second B, the recapitulation of the exposition A B will be B A."

Such arrangements are indeed interesting, but Schoenberg's new developments in form, and those in Bartók's last quartets, show much more imagination and suggest more original and more intriguing structural possibilities.

The second and third quartets (1937) are noteworthy for their soundness, and in their time were lauded for the interesting devices they contain: double canons, canons played at three different speeds, and so forth. But at various points these quartets, like the composer's sonatas, suffer from weakness in the melodic line and lack of spontaneity and imagination.

Honegger needs a large orchestra to be completely at ease. Symphonic development suits his thinking best. Because he could not call on great, well-defined melodies to animate his music, Honegger sought to give it life with rhythmic and orchestral dynamism. He has a predilection for musical transcription of the sounds of struggle, racing, and combat, and in the expression of these actions he sometimes writes with real beauty.

In his *Mouvements Symphoniques,* the rhythm does not have the complexity it has in Stravinsky's works. It is much more simple, and sounds in a regular pulsation which has the character of an ostinato. This is particularly apparent in scores like *Pacific 231, Rugby,* and *Skating Rink.* All three compositions are descriptive in character, as is his overture for *La Tempête.* Many of these works, which were noted on their appearance for a modernistic outlook (they included locomotives, football, etc.), have today lost their attraction. The innovations in orchestral coloring are no longer interesting, and the music has been recognized as superficial.

One very fine score which has survived is *Horace Victorieux.*

in which all of Honegger's qualities as a composer can be found. His gifts as a builder are fully operative. *Horace* is the most compact work he has ever written. Its style is homogeneous and entirely personal, which is rare for Honegger. Also, the themes created are entirely sufficient for their task.

The symphony describes the battle between the Horatii and the Curiatii, Camilla's curse, and the murder of Camilla. Tappolet says:

There are no euphemisms to soften the brutality and barbarousness of the subject. The world of antiquity rises in the titanic battles, a world stripped of romantic sentimentality and the idealism of academic paintings with their soldiers in showy costumes. You think rather of Hodler's warriors in their primitive realism. The merciless fight between the two trios of athletes carries the listener from a subjective to an objective plane, into timelessness. This symphonic poem gives birth to an epic, the epic of action, of man acting, the glorification of the athleticism of our generation.

Horace Victorieux surpasses all of Honegger's symphonic works in its expressive power and the homogeneity of its structure.

Two other works deserve notice: the graceful *Pastorale,* whose delicacy has survived in all its freshness, and an equally lovely *Concertino for Piano and Orchestra.*

In 1930 Honegger composed the *Symphonie en Trois Mouvements,* in which he deliberately departed from classic and romantic symphony form. Moderate and concise, this concert music conveys a feeling of pure joy. The three movements have no connecting element, and each was written in a different style. The first is very chromatic and almost atonal, while the third is clearly diatonic. In 1943 his *Symphonie pour Orchestre à Cordes* appeared. The first movement is very successful. It is written in sustained polyphony with abundant feeling. The second does not come off so well. The composer has written it with the inflexible rhythmic pattern which makes some of his works monotonous and tiring.

Among Honegger's lyric works, which are more or less related to the oratorio, *King David* has been the most popular. *Judith* surpasses it in musical quality, and the battle scene is Honegger at his best. *Amphion* and *Sémiramis* were set to poetry by Paul

Valéry, and the *Danse des Morts* and *Jeanne d'Arc au Bûcher* to poems by Paul Claudel. There are two beautiful passages in *Jeanne d'Arc:* the song *Trimaso,* and the conclusion of the work, which show Honegger tender and poetic. Less popular than *Jeanne d'Arc, Antigone* is the composer's masterpiece, his most important and decisive work.

Milhaud adapted Aeschylus's *Oresteia* in collaboration with Paul Claudel, who did not abridge the trilogy. The poet respected its proportions and dimensions and preserved intact the prolific lyric development which is as important in Greek tragedy as are dramatic episodes. To compose the opera *Antigone,* Honegger used an adaptation by Jean Cocteau. In the preface to *Les Mariés de la Tour Eiffel,* Cocteau says: "I want to substitute a *theater poetry* for *poetry in the theater.* Poetry in the theater is delicate lace, impossible to see from a distance. Theater poetry is coarse lace, a lace of rope, a ship on the sea."

Cocteau condensed the Sophocles play. He compressed the lyricism of the choruses in order to preserve the high potency the play might lose in a literal translation. The dramatic factor, therefore, comes to the fore. In that concise and highly charged language characteristic of his talent, the poet says: "This is like trying to photograph Greece from a plane. You discover an entirely new aspect of it. This is how I wanted to translate *Antigone.* From a bird's-eye view some great points of beauty disappear, others rise. Unexpected perspectives, blocks, shadows, angles, and reliefs take form. My experiment is perhaps one means of making old masterpieces live. Out of habit, we look at them inattentively, but because I have flown over a famous text, everyone thinks he is hearing it for the first time."

Performed at the Théâtre de l'Atelier by Charles Dullin and his troupe, the adaptation was accompanied by several passages of music written by Honegger for harp and oboe. The day after the première, Raymond Radiguet wrote: "What a magnificent *exercise in style,* in the highest sense of the words, is that translation by Cocteau! We all know the chapter in *Secret Professionel* on style. I love to see an author's works silence debate on his convictions, which by themselves are debatable. In *Antigone,* Cocteau hits the bull's-eye at every turn without sacrificing either nobility or procedure to speed."

The light from the Greek classic comes to us refracted by the prism of a living personality close to us. We are all familiar with the subject of *Antigone,* the drama of sibling love. Outside its very special and preordained dramatic meaning, the tragedy is broader in scope. The hymn to Bacchus it contains reminds us of its ritual origin and purpose. It taught great moral laws to the Greek people.

Since the Milhaud-Claudel *Orestie* trilogy and the Honegger-Cocteau *Antigone* are outstanding works in contemporary music, it would help our understanding of them to reread the admirable words by Charles Péguy, whose comprehension of Greek tragedy is profound:

The man supplicated is a happy man. He is therefore, for the Greeks, a man to pity. In this dialogue of suppliant and supplicated, the supplicated can speak only in the name of his happiness, at the most in the name of happiness in general. This is not much. This is nothing. This is less than nothing. This is even contrary to any benefit. Happiness understood in this sense, like the success of the event, the slightly insolent and almost insulting success, is for the Greeks an infallible sign that a man is marked for Fate—by Fate. . . . The suppliant is a representative. He is no longer just himself. He is even no longer himself at all. He doesn't exist. It is no longer a question of himself. And for this reason the other must beware. Stripped of everything by that very same event which has caused the dangerous happiness of the supplicated, a man without goods, he no longer exists as himself. And from that moment on he will be formidable. He is a representative. . . .

This is why, in the supplications of antiquity, the suppliant holds the upper hand in the dialogue and in the situation. . . . He knows with a knowledge that the other will never possess. Unless he also passes through the same great and unavoidable trial.

By the same initiation.

. . . Tragedy is an immense operation of reversal in which he who was the suppliant at the beginning is no longer at the end, and he who was the supplicated, by the ministry of his great misfortune and destiny, is little by little, openly and officially, promoted to the rank and dignity of the suppliant. Antigone, little royal princess, little girl, the *dauphine,* little future woman of the gynaeceum. And after the catastrophe, Antigone, the eternal Antigone, Antigone who accompanied Oedipus, Antigone who buried Polynices.

And Creon, insolent in his happiness, criminal, supplicated at the beginning of the play, becomes the suppliant. Misfortune sanctifies him.

Milhaud composed the *Orestie* on Claudel's translation of Aeschylus between 1913 and 1924. In 1919, Satie wrote *Socrate,* based on the text by Plato. Stravinsky wrote music for Sophocles's *Oedipus Rex,* as adapted by Cocteau, between 1926 and 1927. Honegger worked on *Antigone* from 1924 to 1927. Four of the most renowned contemporary composers and two great French poets made an offering of the best of their talents to the genius of the Greeks.

The purity of their art is due to, and is a function of, their artistic integrity. By virtue of this fact, Honegger's most perfect creations are *Horace Victorieux* and *Antigone.* The composer is completely himself in these scores. He is true to himself from the first note to the last. He makes no concessions.

Since Honegger is essentially a dramatist by temperament, dynamic expression is particularly suited to his needs. Listening to his music, we get the impression that his sonorous inventions will materialize under our eyes and become living beings. His inspiration seems to take shape under the impetus of sight. He feels what exists around him, and transforms it into musical terms. Think of the march of the Philistines in *King David,* the wonderful battle and the moving murder scene in *Judith,* and the whole of *Pacific 231.* These are works by a composer born to write dramatic music.

His language matches his inner life. Choppy, roughly scanned themes are buttressed with chords of fourths and fifths, superimposed in all their coarseness, weaving an inflexible, strident polyphony unmitigated by any softening note. And yet, in this explosive mass of sound, this stormy, crushing atmosphere, there is always a ray of light. A long, seemingly frail melody infused with tenderness draws us by a charm it owes, not to its character, but to its contrast with the harsh and sometimes brutal context. It is the drop of water on the lips of the thirsty, the balm on the wound. Here Honegger gives us the secret of his heart. Here he is true, complete, and human; and this is why he is a great composer.

In the preface to the score of *Antigone*, he says:

These have been my aims in writing the music for *Antigone:*

1] To envelop the drama in compact symphonic structure without encumbering its movement.

2] To replace the recitative with a melodic vocal style that does not consist in holding the high notes (which always makes the words incomprehensible) or in purely instrumental lines; but, on the contrary, to write a melodic line created by the plasticity of the words themselves, in order to indicate contours and sharpen relief.

3] To find appropriate accentuation, primarily in the opening consonants, in opposition to conventional prosody which uses anacrusis; and in general, to do the honest work of an honest worker.

The narrative is begun almost immediately. There is hardly time for the music to be introduced to the voices. It reaches full stature in the symphonic drama developed parallel to the stage drama.

The elements of the symphony are the great themes supporting the personages Antigone [*Example 99*] and Ismene [*Example 101*]; the theme of the memory of the two brothers [*Example 102*]; and a rhythmic motif serving as a base for the bitter Creon [*Example 103*], for the cowardly and hesitant guard in charge of Antigone, and for the jeering people, savage music that ranges over the great themes of the suppliants.

These elements are not leitmotivs in the Wagnerian sense. Rather, they constitute an autonomous musical world, and do not condition every word and gesture. Commentary is larger and more independent here than in the work of a Wagnerian like Richard Strauss. The music really is a symphony, a continuous flow which does not hesitate at every obstacle in the text. Each scene is a movement of the symphony built on two or three themes.

All this expresses the drama properly speaking. The spirit of the ancient tragedy is present in the score as well, and the form of the tragedy is what ultimately determines the architecture of the music.

To all the themes we mentioned and others of the same kind, two elements are added which seem at first sight to be accidental. The first appears the moment the curtain lifts. It is composed of a cell in 3-4 time in which two melodic lines proceed in contrary motion [*Example 104*]. This contrary motion intensifies steadily to the point where it dominates the third act, the exodus of the tragedy [*Example 105*]. It intervenes indiscriminately in the actions of all the characters, and represents as much Creon's tyranny as it does anguish, misfortune, or death. It is the drama itself; it is Fate.

The second element appears suddenly at the first entrance of the chorus, that famous chorus in which Sophocles tells us that man is the cause of his own unhappiness, and that all tragedy pre-exists in him. The musical commentary here is summed up in a simple descending major third, with very pronounced rhythm, whose persistence and tense development attack the listener like a swarm of wasps [*Example 106*].

The themes for Creon, Eteocles, and Polynices are in substance elaborations of the cell which expresses man. This cell also reappears at the end of the tragedy, when Creon, the supplicated, will be promoted to the rank of suppliant [*Example 107*].

Everything disappears into the symphony, everything passes away, except this: man in the grip of the fate he has created; Creon falling into the trap he himself has set. In this, much more than in Antigone's fate, lies the meaning of the tragedy. Antigone is moving and pitiable. But Creon becomes lamentable and worthy of compassion. This the composer expresses beautifully. He realizes all the expressive means he has created.

If the recitation advances rapidly, the symphony moves like a tempest. The first chorus (the *Parodos* of antiquity), rendered by the man who ends the prologue, is incorporated into the drama and even becomes its human aspect. The last chorus, separating the *Episodes* from the *Exodus,* is the hymn to Bacchus, the ritual aspect of the tragedy. These two choruses, pivot-points of the structure, are sung in interludes while the scene is plunged into darkness. The central part, the *Episodes,* contains three plaintive choruses (the *Kommoi*). Here, the composer becomes subjective. Lyricism is substituted for drama. Listen closely to these choruses. Honegger withdraws into them to weep for Antigone. The orchestra disappears. The symphony

is quiet, allowing a melody haloed with goodness and com-
miseration to flower for a moment.

During recent years, Honegger's temperament has become
gloomy. He seems no longer to believe in the necessity for music
and to have been disappointed by the reservations of the public
concerning his art. He wrote about his disappointment in the
book *Je Suis Compositeur,* which appeared in 1951. Such pessimism is strange, coming from a modern composer who has enjoyed great popular success almost without opposition. His
discouragement finds expression in works like the *Symphonie
Liturgique* and the *Fifth Symphony (di tre re),* which reflect
the psychological state of Europe at the end of World War II.

GEORGES AURIC and FRANCIS POULENC. If two such different
personalities as Milhaud and Honegger can be compared, it is
due to their mutual liking for large construction and their talent
for singing of tragic and epic emotions. The temperaments of
Francis Poulenc and Georges Auric, their friends from the group
of the Six, made these two artists take another path. The works
of both composers have the lightness that comes from the expression of joy and happiness, or the vivacity due to a taste for
good-natured mockery, which breaks easily into satire directed
at falseness and absurdity.

This levity for which they are noted, and which characterizes
the younger composers Henri Sauguet and Jean Françaix, is by
no means a sign of superficiality. There is a tendency to think
that only painful and bitter emotions are noble and beautiful
and great. A light-hearted concept of life can be just as beautiful. The depth of an art is not determined by the feeling used
as its point of departure, but depends on the degree of perception and intensity with which the primary sentiment and the
basic idea, whatever they are, are expressed. Mozart's charm is
no less profound than Beethoven's pain.

Poulenc's affability and Auric's bantering should not lead us
to place them on a secondary level. Many of their compositions
which put us in gay spirits are equal in quality to many somber
works.

Auric and Poulenc are both Parisians. They both have the

quick mind and acute sensitivity which make them react immediately to the faintest impulses from without. They verbalize easily and have trained themselves to give an opinion or judgment on things without wasting much time in seeking a basis for the opinion or a motivation for the judgment. Their attitude is dictated by the moment, and their art does not take the future into account.

These ready qualities of vivacity and perceptiveness, supported by an innate sense of proportion and the talent for apt, rapid, trenchant expression, which is the charm of the Parisian temperament, are to be found in the works of these two composers.

Born in 1899, Francis Poulenc had his first work performed in 1918 during one of the concert series at the Théâtre du Vieux-Colombier. It was the *Rapsodie Nègre* for instruments and baritone voice. Ricardo Viñes immediately noticed the spontaneity and individuality which were to develop rapidly.

Today, Poulenc has composed some twenty works for piano, a dozen pieces of chamber music, two ballets, twenty-five collections of songs, an important series of choral works, a comic opera based on Guillaume Apollinaire's *Les Mamelles de Tirésias,* and some religious music.

For Poulenc, there was no problem of form to solve and no new language to discover. Gifted with an exceptionally rich melodic sense, Poulenc composes melodies as Monsieur Jourdain writes prose—without thinking. But his melody is always original, inventive, and particularly well conceived for voices. It is natural and fresh. Except for the human voice, the composer's favorite instrument is the piano. Poulenc's piano music is fluid and sparkling like Chopin's. His gifts are strengthened and exalted by his scrupulous care in putting his music on paper. His works have the unique charm and freedom of improvisation.

Great facility, and strength without ostentation; simple but strikingly apt expression; a taste for cleanly drawn lines; intense fervor that avoids emotional exaggeration—these are the artistic qualities of the Île-de-France. Poulenc's first works, *Mouvements Perpétuels* for piano (1918), the music for Apollinaire's *Le Bestiaire* (1919), and for Jean Cocteau's *Cocardes* (1919), are so solidly endowed with these qualities that they still retain their flavor and impact after many years.

Nothing seems so delicate as the *Mouvements Perpétuels*, which reposes peacefully on melodies that might have been taken directly from popular music. It is delightfully fresh. *Le Bestiaire* and *Cocardes* show how well Poulenc understood the poets of his time and environment, just as he grasped the spirit of the painters of the same generation and milieu. Poulenc has never taken up the great problems of style, as have Satie, Schoenberg, or Stravinsky; nor has he concerned himself with universal expression. His horizon is limited. He sings of the atmosphere of Paris, and captures every feature, to the slightest nuance. But he does not just give us fleeting impressions. He constructs a synthesis. He has greatest success in giving us this spiritual portrait of Paris in his songs and vocal works.

Poulenc is inspired less by models in the world of music than by those in the worlds of poetry and painting. Satie and Stravinsky were of great help to him, in the example of simplicity they provided him with and in the value they gave the commonplace as the point of departure for a work of art. But Poulenc found the motivating principles of his music in Picasso and Braque, not that his music is pictorial in the least, but because of a type of interior correspondence. The poets Max Jacob, Guillaume Apollinaire, and Paul Éluard also fired his imagination. With them, he moves in a range of emotions from childlike gaiety to Rabelaisian fierceness: his moods vary from slight melancholy to vengeful malice sometimes expressed as frantic and frightening hilarity in which buffoonery and tragedy are combined in bitter lyricism. Thus the terrible laughter of Alfred Jarry or Max Jacob can be heard in *Le Bal Masqué* and some of the *Chansons Villageoises*.

Jean Cocteau's *Cocardes* gave Poulenc the occasion to evoke the sadness of crowded suburbs, that Sabbath melancholy which seeks relief in artificial gaiety, the melancholy read on the faces of some of Picasso's clowns. To this "poetry in handbill type" Poulenc sets music for tenor voice and the anomalous ensemble of a violin, cornet, trombone, bass drum, and triangle, that poor little orchestra that plays with street singers in the courtyards of Paris apartment houses.

Of all the poets, Guillaume Apollinaire is most akin to Poulenc. Born after the decline of impressionism, the composer of *Les Biches* inclined toward the art of abridgment, corresponding to simultaneous perceptions of the surrealists, to attain full development in 1944–1945 in the spirit of revolt that inspired Resistance poets like Aragon and Éluard. Apollinaire provides the link that binds poetic symbolism to surrealism and, later, to the poets of the Resistance. Jacques de Lacretelle explains:

The poetic renaissance in France during the years of the occupation found support in the voice of Apollinaire, that voice which poses enigmas but is always simple. And what was actually the cause of this poetic renaissance? Possibly the constraint itself, that is, the need to speak with hidden words, by intimate communication or by allusion; and also the secret ardor that lived in oppressed souls, and the nostalgia that haunted the exiled. All these states and all these feelings found expression in Apollinaire's song, whether the poem took us through the streets of Paris or described a distant French field in autumn, blooming with meadow saffron. His images used passwords that recalled the odd and ingenious radio messages flung over our heads. Young men, fleeing the enemy and taking cover behind false names, discovered them easily or invented others just by looking at the stars in the heavens. Apollinaire was a friend to the hidden. . . . I want to make what I think is an essential distinction between the inspiration of the symbolists and that of the surrealists. The symbolist poet hears; the surrealist poet sees. The symbolist seeks an echo, and exposes himself to the influence of music; the surrealist works with memories which are almost always visual. This is so true that the symbolist school was closely related to the composers of its time (remember Dujardin and the *Wagnerian Review,* and Mallarmé and the concerts) while surrealism is entirely on the side of the painters. To understand it, you must be familiar with Braque's snapshots, Picasso's superimposition of planes and Dali's prophetic dreams. These sources have very different origins. And Apollinaire, straddling the two periods, draws on both.[15]

In his *Bestiaire,* Apollinaire compressed his poetic material and incorporated it in a series of quatrains. Poulenc set six of them to music. Just a few measures were enough for full and balanced expression. With no apparent effort, he achieved the level of the great French classics with his first attempt. *La Carpe* is as beautiful as Couperin's most graceful passages.

15. *New Statesman and Nation* (London), February 24, 1945.

He continued to compose for Apollinaire's work with the *Quatre Poèmes d'Apollinaire* (1932), *La Grenouillère* (1938), *Dans le Jardin d'Amour, Allons Plus Vite, Banalités* (1940), and, lastly, the comic opera based on *Les Mamelles de Tirésias* (1940).

Poulenc's buffoonery is based on recourse to vulgarity and even triviality. But he achieves such elevation and ferocious amplification that his creation is something electrifying and enormous. The words race along at a frenzied pace, but are always so controlled that every syllable is projected with vehement force and every accent falls exactly in place. Poulenc owes this style of delivery to popular Parisian singers. He never attempted to hide his admiration for artists like Maurice Chevalier, and used their craft as a springboard as he expanded its artistic potential. His greatest successes in this style, apart from *Les Mamelles de Tirésias,* are those in which buffoonery is elevated to true grandeur: *Le Bal Masqué,* a cantata (secular, of course) for baritone and chamber orchestra based on poems by Max Jacob, a convulsive work whose clownishness is sometimes mournful and vindictive in the style of certain sketches by Goya or Daumier; the cutting *Chansons Gaillardes,* based on sixteenth-century texts; and the disarmingly jovial *Chansons Villageoises,* based on poems by Maurice Fombeure. These works are a unique group in musical literature, as much in their significance as in the perfection of their composition. They show incomparable virtuosity in the intermingling of words and melodic line, very flexible and forceful rhythm that owes nothing to structural repetitions, and harmonic eloquence that transforms the most trivial melodic allusions into sources of energy and power. In this, Poulenc is the heir of Emmanuel Chabrier.

Poulenc's collaboration with Paul Éluard possibly surpasses his work with Apollinaire's poetry in importance.

Surrealist poets suppressed comparisons. Two images are no longer linked by the preposition *like.* The images overlap and fuse into a single impression. Such poetry, and above all that of Éluard, whose imagination is particularly rich and alert to nuances, suited the composer's needs and gave him a foundation for the development of a sober and pure lyricism. His collaboration with Éluard produced first the collection *Cinq Poèmes* (1935); *Tel Jour, Telle Nuit* (1937); *Miroirs Brûlants* (1938);

then *Figure Humaine* (1945). In *Tel Jour, Telle Nuit,* Poulenc reaches the apex of his talent and fully expresses his personality.

André Schæffner does not exaggerate when he says that "Francis Poulenc adds to French music a little of what Schubert and Mussorgsky added to theirs." A composer so sensitive to the climate in which he lived was needed to become the voice of occupied Paris, to sing of France forsaken.

In 1943 Poulenc wrote *Le Pont de Cé* and *Fêtes Galantes* on two poems by Aragon, portraying the spirit of Paris during the German occupation. But it was above all in a choral work that this spirit was to find expression, the musical setting of the poems published and distributed secretly under the title *Figure Humaine.*

Poulenc's choral works express his personality in the same way as do his melodies. In 1937 he wrote the *Mass in G Major,* for *a cappella* chorus, and in 1939 *Quatre Motets pour un Temps de Pénitence* appeared. *Sécheresses,* for chorus and orchestra, based on poems by Edward James, was also published in 1937. Then followed various *a cappella* choruses based on Éluard's poetry, and in 1945 *Figure Humaine.*

All these works are remarkable. Some were written for a simple chorus, others for a double chorus. The parts are always divided, and the style is reminiscent of Claude Le Jeune; that is, there is no real polyphony, but the harmony is written with a dominant melodic voice and the syllabic character of the song allows the text to be heard clearly because of careful prosody.

These choral works have a full and rich sonority. Their play of colors is due to Poulenc's talent for superimposing major and minor modes, a language peculiarity which came into wide use after Stravinsky.

Figure Humaine, a work of considerable dimension, is written for a double chorus, and contains divisions which sometimes run to an ensemble of sixteen voices. The work expresses to perfection the nostalgia of an oppressed people and their cry for liberation. The tension of the last poem, *Liberté,* makes a forceful impression. Conceived as a sort of litany, it becomes more and more impatient as the measures progress.

Of the two ballets Poulenc wrote, the first, *Les Biches,* is the better. Incorporating beautiful French songs, it was one of the greatest successes of Sergei Diaghilev's Ballet Russe. Bronislava Nijinska created its excellent choreography, and Marie Laurencin's blue and rose décor was wonderfully suited to the tender, waggish, mischievous music.

Poulenc has sometimes been accused of playing the easy game of pastiche. This is a somewhat superficial view of a trait rooted deep in the composer's nature. For many composers, the source of inspiration is a visual impression, an odor, or a story. Poulenc is often inspired by an impression already in musical form: a harmony, an accent, the timbre of a voice, a fragment of melody. As a result, the last measures of Stravinsky's *Apollon Musagètes* inspired and influenced Poulenc's *Aubade*. Some of Maurice Chevalier's popular tunes stimulated the composition of *Gars qui s'en vont à la fête* in *Chansons Villageoises*. The spirit of Chopin suddenly appears in *Les Soirées de Nazelles*. None of these works are imitations, but reflect and comment on bygone times which are loved and missed.

Poulenc, a true child of Paris, discovered the antidote to neutralize sentimentality in sarcasm and banter. And this is the spirit which, with the immoderation of Guillaume Apollinaire's text, provokes the enormous jest which is the comic opera *Les Mamelles de Tirésias*.

In 1957 he completed the *Dialogues des Carmélites,* an opera based on the play by Georges Bernanos. Produced by La Scala in Milan in 1957, it is unquestionably his most important work. It was performed that same year by the Paris Opera Company, and later in San Francisco, and was enthusiastically acclaimed by a wide and diverse audience. In the *Dialogues des Carmélites* the composer has combined his great melodic abilities with his profound but unostentatious religious sense.

In 1920 no one could speak of Poulenc without thinking of Georges Auric. Also born in 1899, Auric began to compose in 1914. In that year he published *Interludes,* a remarkable collection of songs set to poetry by René Chalupt, written with nervous wit, and revealing the composer's penetrating intelligence.

Auric was Erik Satie's favorite among the Six. Much was expected of him, especially after he published his *Huit Poèmes de Jean Cocteau* in 1918, which remains today his most remarkable

work. Paul Landormy says: "These pieces, as the composer himself intended, have an air of Paris about them, comedy without
bitterness, very distinctive melodic lines and the daring use,
where necessary, of language which could be criticized as vulgar
because it is so close to popular inspiration, but which is always
artistically motivated."

This collection, whose subjects are Le Douanier Rousseau,
Marie Laurencin, Satie, barracks at dawn, and country fairs, is a
marvelous picture of artistic milieus in Paris of the time, written
with great wit and subtle irony.

At about the same time, Auric composed a score of incisive,
stinging music for Molière's *Les Fâcheux*. The biting orchestration reveals the fretful side of Auric's temperament. This very
fine score was expanded with a few other pieces of lesser quality
to serve as a ballet for Diaghilev. Auric's best ballet is *Les
Matelots,* in which a feeling of agitation is sustained throughout the score.

Several good compositions for the stage, among others one for
Marcel Achard's *Malbrough s'en va-t-en guerre,* and excellent
film pieces are equally noteworthy.

7

FRENCH MUSIC AFTER THE SIX

WHILE THE talents of several members of the Six matured under Erik Satie's paternal eye, a younger generation paid homage to the composer of *Socrate* by founding a new group— the so-called Arcueil School. Henri Sauguet, Roger Désormière, Henri Cliquet-Pleyel, and Maxime Jacob were not really Satie's pupils and there was really no school. But they were inspired by the Master of Arcueil's example, by his honesty, his modesty, the freedom of his music. Désormière became an outstanding conductor, putting his talent in the service of his contemporaries. Jacob entered the priesthood. Sauguet alone found himself sufficiently gifted to build a work meriting lasting attention.

HENRI SAUGUET, born in Bordeaux in 1901, arrived on the scene after the period of rhythmic and harmonic discoveries. He is not an innovator. His melodic invention moves in a temperate climate. His acute sensitivity is warm and sometimes profound, and he has no fear of impassioned outbursts which, handled with a sense of measure and taste, elevate his best compositions to true greatness. There is nothing spasmodic or fitful in his expression of feeling, even in the most dramatic moments. As with Poulenc, his instrumental compositions are less forceful than his vocal works. Sauguet is a lyricist: he needs a poetic text to guide his muse. His melodies unroll in long curves, original and perfect in design, and carry almost all of the expression. Simple harmony is all that they need for support. Any emphasis or commentary would be superfluous. But simplicity is difficult to achieve. It is only beautiful—and this Satie understood so well—if it is pure. It must be free of triteness. Sauguet does not always avoid that triteness, which today threatens all resolutely consonant music. Still, in the major portion of his work, there is such delicacy in the ordering of his thirds and sixths that the play of these intervals has never seemed so smooth and sweet. A convincing example is the conclusion of his ballet *La Chatte* (1927), which was one of the most enduring successes of the Ballet Russe. Schoenberg was right when he said that "there are still a good many things to be said in C major."

Among song cycles, we must place beyond comparison the *Sonnets de Louise Labé*, written in a well-sustained mood of meditation; the *Visions Infernales* and *Les Pénitents en Maillots Roses*, two cycles set to poems of Max Jacob, and a cycle set to symbolist poetry.

Sauguet's dramatic work includes two comic operas, *Le Plumet du Colonel* (1924) and *La Contrebasse* (1930), based on Chekhov's work; a grand opera, *La Chartreuse de Parme* (1927-1936), based on Stendhal's novel, with libretto by Armand Lunel; a comic opera based on Sedaine's *La Gageure Imprévue* (1942); and *Les Caprices de Marianne* (1951), based on the work by Musset.

His talent is at its most brilliant in these works. His ironic zest is not the same sort as Poulenc's; in Sauguet, an indulgent smile replaces the tart satire. The composer's sympathies are with the puppets in *Le Plumet du Colonel,* and he looks with affection, as on the play-acting of children tenderly loved, on the gestures of the characters in the droll tale told us in *La Contrebasse.* These two comic operas, the second a perfect gem, are treated as sketches of society as it existed in the latter half of the nineteenth century. We find in them, as in certain Poulenc pieces, nostalgia for a charming and refined period whose peaceful happiness contrasts oddly with the present world's harshness and anguish.

La Chartreuse de Parme, in four acts and eleven scenes, is an opera in the nineteenth-century sense of the word. Vocal art reigns supreme and the orchestra takes second honors. Actually, a better choice of title would have been *Fabrice et Clélia,* for the character of Sanseverina does not have the importance in this work it has in Stendhal's novel.

Sauguet's opera opens on a rather playful note, and consequently the scene of the conspirators at Milan's La Scala is a perfect touch. Here again is a poetical recall of that beloved nineteenth century, crowned with a splendid sextet whose eloquence equals that of the quartet in *Rigoletto*. The opera becomes increasingly serious and intense, and in places attains unquestionable grandeur. Three long, poignant duets of Clélia and Fabrice, masterfully developed, are incomparable. They are so perfect that it would be impossible to find other fragments of purely vocal operas—except the duet in the first act of Verdi's *Otello*—which have such nobility or sustained musical value.

Written in the middle of a period when artists were devoting all their energy to "being different," and deliberate experimentation was apparent in the most outstanding works, *La Chartreuse de Parme* brought nothing new. It fitted perfectly into long-accepted conventions and was expressed in long-familiar language. And yet everything it says, the entire content of this work, is new. Scenes such as the ones in Fabrice's cell, and the scene of the sermon on light, combining spontaneity with beauty of presentation, are among the most moving. It is noteworthy that *La Chartreuse de Parme* was the first grand opera to be composed and produced after the reign of lyric drama. Other subsequent works, especially the production of Benjamin Britten's *Peter Grimes* in 1945, would seem to indicate that a return to vocal opera is a real possibility.

Sauguet's exceptional dramatic gifts have been confirmed by the complete success of his most recent vocal work, the irresistible *Gageure Imprévue,* first performed at the Paris Opéra-Comique in 1944. The opera unseated whatever prejudices the public still had against an art whose interior calm is so removed from the major preoccupations of our times that it could seem anachronistic and even incomprehensible to an observer caught up in vital current problems. In 1946 Sauguet completed the moving *Symphonie Expiatoire,* dedicated to the memory of innocent war victims. It echoes the sincere accent of the most lyric moments of *La Chartreuse de Parme.*

The talent of JEAN FRANÇAIX (born on May 23, 1912, in Le Mans) has evolved along lines parallel to Henri Sauguet's. His work has a more superficial character than that of Poulenc's or Sauguet's. It lacks inner life, and owes its easy charm to great dexterity in the handling of orchestral timbres. His most profound piece is a lively fantasy for two voices and small orchestra based on Lesage's *Le Diable Boiteux.*

A survey of French postimpressionist music would not be complete without mention of some isolated works of high quality: the very amusing comic operas *Angélique,* by Jacques Ibert, and *Isabelle et Pantalon,* by Roland-Manuel; a lovely *Concerto pour Piano* by Henri Barraud, and his *Mystère des Saints Innocents,* based on texts by Péguy; and Jean Cartan's moving *Pater.*

We have now reached the end of an evolution which, begun by Debussy, reaffirmed the primacy of melody and the solidity of the principle of tonality. These two characteristics seem necessary to the very existence of French music, which generally connotes clarity and transparency, and whose expressive domain is the reflection of a generous and attractive nature, the gift of a balanced and deeply happy people.

Most French composers are firmly opposed to all propositions tending to displace the tonal system—and among the most strongly opposed are Schoenberg's. Recent statements bear witness to the violence of that opposition and to the conservative attitude (not to be confused with a retrogressive position) of French composers. Georges Auric wrote in *Les Lettres Françaises* of April 21, 1945: "In 1918, Darius Milhaud, Poulenc, Honegger, Germaine Tailleferre, and I wrote a cordial message to the author of *Pierrot Lunaire:* 'Arnold Schoenberg, the young musicians salute you!' At that time, this was not without some meaning. But in 1945, we can smell the odor of corpse given off by an impostor art by which we are not duped." In the same journal (May 5, 1945) Francis Poulenc writes from another angle: "The Schoenberg question is pigeonholed. Let us once and for all speak of it as in the past. Or otherwise, I am quite ready to write about him, as much and wherever I can, using Père Ubu's word to his wife—with or without the double *r.*" [16]

These stinging ripostes gave answer to the very young French musicians René Leibowitz and Sergei Nigg, already forgotten moreover, who, perhaps following Olivier Messiaen's example,

---

16. Père Ubu's *mot* throughout Alfred Jarry's series of plays is the rolling *merdre* (with two *r*'s), which Ubu uses with gusto by itself or in word plays like *armerdre* and *mer decin* (see *Ubu Roi, Ubu Enchaîné, Ubu sur la Butte*).

were drawing away from the path laid down by Satie and the Six, finding guideposts in Schoenberg's theory that better served their purposes. It is possible that personalities like Poulenc's, Auric's, or Sauguet's are more offended by Schoenberg's painful, brusque temperament and his spasmodic expressionism than by his views on structure. Or they may not distinguish clearly enough between Schoenberg's temperament and his technical innovations to discover what might be extracted from those innovations for a different kind of expression. This last supposition seems close to the truth, since Poulenc gives homage in the same article to the "striking beauty" of the works of Alban Berg, who himself adapted Schoenberg's views for his own needs.

This interesting dispute, which is indicative of the thinking of the post-liberation Paris music world,[17] began in the movement that sprang up on the appearance—or rather, the growth in prominence—of Olivier Messiaen.

At a time when all the signs pointed to increased stability and the birth of a general style (implying the danger of a new academicism), everything was again called into question.[18] OLIVIER MESSIAEN, half-Flemish and half-Provençal, was born December 10, 1908, in Avignon. His expression is very remote from objec-

17. This dispute also includes the defense of Stravinsky's recent works, attacked as *retrogressive* by Messiaen's students, an opinion also voiced by so respected a master as Charles Kœchlin. So is the defense of Darius Milhaud, to whom Paris has never given the eminent position he deserves. Georges Auric wrote: "We must take a unanimous position on a man like Darius Milhaud" (*Lettres Françaises,* November 4, 1944).

18. Since 1936, a number of young Frenchmen have expressed dissatisfaction with the neoclassical pursuit of balance. They have been disappointed by the objectivity of Stravinsky's recent works, and declare the need for certain considerations of a spiritual order as preliminary to the conception and execution of a work of art. Yves Baudrier (born in 1906), Daniel Lesur (born in 1908), André Jolivet (born in 1905), and Olivier Messiaen (born in 1908) form a group called *Jeune France.*
For Baudrier, "the only justification for a creative artist is his selective love, which alone can create an aesthetic emotional climate. Contemplating sometimes violent but always harmonious beauty necessarily engenders the most effective ethos and pathos. This means to what degree the artist thinks that art, to achieve transcendence, has the duty to be human, to quit its ivory towers and the sterile contemplation of its perfection."
Jolivet tries "to give back to music its original character of the early time when it was the magical and ritual expression of human clans. Music must be a sonorous manifestation in direct relation to the universal cosmic system."

tivity, simplicity of style, or economy of means. Messiaen is a mystic. Paul Landormy accurately describes him in these terms:

Olivier Messiaen is an innovator in his own way, but he is not a revolutionary. He would not think of improvising a new musical technique without taking tradition into account. Much to the contrary, he bases his innovations on intensive and meticulous study of the past. He has explored all of ancient, classic and modern music. He has devoted particular study to Gregorian chant and Hindu rhythm. He was instructed on quarter-tones by Vyshnegradski, and on the ondes Martenot by Martenot himself. He has listened with deep attention—and, where possible, carefully noted down—the songs of birds. His technique has been enriched by valuable discoveries in all these broad and very different domains.

The moderns have taught him a great deal: Debussy and his *Pelléas,* Jean and Noël Gallon and their theories on "the true harmony" borne in the melody, Marcel Dupré and his taste for counterpoint, Maurice Emmanuel and his lectures on the variations of musical language, Paul Dukas, Stravinsky, Alban Berg, his friend André Jolivet, Mussorgsky, and Rimsky-Korsakov (he named these influences off to me at random, without trying to list them in order). . . . A predilection for airy sumptuousness in harmony, habitual inclusion of the organ [19] and frequent use of the prismatic orchestration of Paul Dukas led him toward "those swords of fire, those streams of blue-orange lava, those starbursts, those spinning sounds and jumbled, spiraling rainbows" he speaks of lovingly in the preface of his *Quatuor pour la Fin du Temps.*

But then these are only means. This is his purpose: Olivier Messiaen is first and foremost a Catholic composer. All his works, religious or not, carry the mark of the Christian faith. His only aim is to *sing of God and the mystery of Christ.*

Messiaen gained renown after 1930 with his orchestral tone poem *Les Offrandes Oubliées,* followed in 1935 by a great polyptych for organ, *La Nativité du Seigneur.* In 1936 he composed *Poèmes pour Mi,* for soprano and orchestra, in which his personality is more strongly expressed. The delivery of the poems resembles Milhaud's style in *Cinq Grandes Odes* and the *Orestie.* The harmony is an extension of Dukas's in *La Péri,* and the complex rhythmic scheme is freed from the restrictions of tempo and the bar-measure system. The melody tends to be continuous and is built on modal or defective scales. Above and

19. Messiaen is the organist at the Église de la Trinité, Paris.

beyond this, the music does not seem to be conceived as an organic whole, an architecture, a division of time. All evidence indicates an intention to destroy time, discard the idea of duration, and convey an impression that the music has neither beginning nor end. The listener is oblivious of time, and is drawn toward contemplation and religious ecstasy.

Let us say in passing that examples of abolition of the concept of duration can be found in much of the religious music of the Middle Ages and in the melodic development of Hindu ragas.

These practices are even more marked in the *Quatuor pour la Fin du Temps,* for piano, violin, clarinet, and cello, which Messiaen wrote in captivity in Germany in 1941, based on a passage in the Apocalypse of St. John. A few measures from the first movement, *Liturgie de Cristal,* will serve to show the independence he acquired [*Example 110*]: chords of seven notes, agglomerations of small intervals; a sort of harmonic mist on the piano, reflecting the influence of Scriabin's synthetic chord; melody with a fleeting tonality, or even an atonal character in the clarinet; varying sonorities on the cello providing a persistent pedal of timbres; bird-chirping on the violin. The many semi-independent elements, occurring simultaneously, create a sensation of infinite space and constant vibration, causing continually shifting coloring, but without displacement, without movement. Two sections, one for cello and piano, the other for violin and piano, contain long melodies of inhuman slowness (that is, slower than the slowest vital movements of our bodies) that induce ecstasy. Listening to such music has the effect of contemplating a stained-glass window, and Poulenc justly compares Messiaen's spirit and art with Georges Rouault's. Messiaen opens perspectives on a mysterious space, reaching into obscure regions of the subconscious. His music is music from the soul, which subjugates as it frees.

Messiaen himself defined his concepts in the treatise *Technique de Mon Langage Musical* (1944), in which he says:

We are trying to create chatoyant music to give the auditory sense voluptuous and delicate pleasure. At the same time, this music must be able to express noble sentiments, and especially the noblest of all: the religious sentiments exalted by the theology and verities of our Catholic faith. This charm, simultaneously voluptuous and contemplative, resides especially in certain mathematical impossibilities in scales and rhythm. Modes cannot be carried beyond a certain number of transpositions, because the same notes always recur; rhythms cannot retrogress, because then the same order of values recurs. These are two absolute impossibilities.

We can immediately see the analogy of the two impossibilities and how they complement each other, rhythm accomplishing on the horizontal plane (retrogression) what the modes accomplish on the vertical (transposition). After this first relationship, there is another between the values added to the rhythm and the notes added to the chords. Finally, we superimpose our rhythms (polyrhythm and rhythmic pedals) as well as our modes (polymodality).

Not everything concerning rhythm in this technique is new. Added values and polyrhythm have had wide application since the appearance of *Le Sacre du Printemps*. Messiaen's music is distinctive rather in his particular application of these principles, not to motifs and themes, but to whole melodies. The added values increase or decrease the tensions and rhythmic waves, according to whether they are shorter or longer than the primary rhythmic values [*Example 108*].

This motor element is opposed by another, which tends to neutralize it: isorhythm, or fixed rhythm [*Example 109*]. The same in melody: the added notes constitute the factor of movement, and the use of modes with limited transpositions lead to immobility. Take, for example, the following mode, composed of similar trichords (a half-tone followed by a whole tone— *Example 111*). The fourth transposition already leads back, enharmonically, to the same notes as in the first form of the mode. It is therefore impossible to transpose the mode more than three times [*Examples 112, 113, 114*].

Superimposing transpositions cannot, as we know, lead to polytonality. We remain within the scope of several simultaneous tonalities without their becoming formalized. Messiaen says further:

Think of the man listening to our modal and rhythmic music. He will not have time during the performance to verify non-transpositions and non-retrogressions, and during that time these questions will no longer interest him. He will want only to be engrossed. And this is precisely what will happen. In spite of himself, he will be captivated by the strange charm of the impossibles: a sensation of tonal ubiquity in the non-transposition and the unity of movement in the non-retro-gression (with beginning and end interwoven because they are identical) will lead him by stages to that sort of theological rainbow which musical language, the theory and structure of which we are looking for, should be.

It is not surprising that today, after a time of torment when the soul of France was almost annihilated, young artists are flocking enthusiastically around a composer who offers them a means of escape, who shows them the existence of a spiritual life apart from the temporal. It is not surprising that to this young group, which seeks new reasons to live and hope and finds in Messiaen's music a language fulfilling its mystical aspirations, the sharply defined art of Stravinsky seems to be too narrow and his thought too concrete. Their eyes naturally turn to Schoenberg once again in the hope of finding their freedom in his teaching as did Messiaen.

There is no doubt that a new period of experimentation has begun in French music. Here again is the simmer of ferment. But this time the aim is not to enlarge the musical language. The search is spiritual.

The *Visions de l'Amen* for two pianos (1942) had already received universal acclaim. The *Vingt Regards sur l'Enfant Jésus* (1944), a huge suite for piano lasting over two hours, threw such a spell over its listeners that they lost all notion of time. The magic power of the music pleased those who were disposed to accept it, but irritated the rationalists.

In *Les Lettres Françaises* of April 2, 1945, Roland-Manuel wrote about *Petites Liturgies:*

Under the equally modest and intimidating title of *Trois Petites Liturgies de la Présence Divine,* Messiaen offers us three mystical poems for nine women's voices in unison, celesta, piano, vibraphone, ondes Martenot, maracas, gong, tam-tam, and string orchestra: *Antienne de la Conversation Intérieure; Séquence du Verbe, Cantique Divin; Psalmodie de l'Ubiquité par Amour.* The words are the composer's. Why not say it? This mystagogic literature, this Balinese orchestra, and the program notes comprise a suspect mixture at first, calculated to antagonize the best-willed listener. Music has been too hard put to rid itself of the obscure nonsense of art-religion and the contrivance of the exotically picturesque for us to wax enthusiastic over finding these elements re-united in the work of a composer who has such a large and devoted band of disciples.

This music, which I think is the clearest and most direct Olivier Messiaen has ever composed, converts us instantly to his views because it bears the irresistible mark of truthfulness. The surprising language appears natural and necessary to us. From that moment on, it is un-important to us that Messiaen borrows from the Balinese the system and devices of an instrumentation which he makes his own and which delivers us a message as personal as it is new and deeply moving. It does not matter that in the final *Psalmodie* certain percussion effects recall the sonority and particular rhythm pattern of Stravinsky's *Noces.* The spirit that animates each of the two works is entirely different. But the enchantment and power of the work are shown with the most striking purity and clarity, I think, in the second part, *Séquences du Verbe, Cantique Divin.* This is the most simple and marvelous song of triumph.

Messiaen here reveals the secret of his power, the power that his taste for the worst literature and mystagogic picturesqueness are incapable of destroying. His secret is that of a born melodist who knows through instinct and experience that rhythm and tonality are connected by deep roots, that consonance is the basis of harmony. But an ear whose acuteness has no equal—an acoustician's ear—channels it into the art of catching and fixing the caprice of partial sounds and orienting them toward their poles of attraction. For despite appearances, Olivier Messiaen is much more the master of harmony than the slave of counterpoint.

Messiaen's intriguing ideas, which he proves in the *Petites Liturgies,* nonetheless seem hard to extend to further develop-ment and application. The symphony *Turangalila,* which con-tains moments of real beauty, gives the impression that the composer's expressive means are limited, and especially that he is prisoner of the language he has created. It would be good to see him break out of the framework that inhibits his freedom of movement. In other respects, Messiaen's influence on young musicians is beneficial. He encourages them to seek out new means of expression and constantly draws their attention to the possibilities offered by forming scales using microtones, as is the practice in Asiatic cultures. Messiaen is the only European composer who thus far has emphasized the need to study Asiatic and African music, the artistic meaning of which is obviously conditioned by the melodic and rhythmic media chosen. Such study is doubtless an excellent way to develop the imagination. In this connection, we might point out Yvette Grimaud's lovely *Chants d'Espace,* in which quarter-tones are effectively used, being introduced only in the melodic order and not in the harmonic order, where they are not suitable. Two recent works, *Livre d'Orgue* and *Oiseaux Exotiques,* have caused considerable comment.

André Jolivet, originating from the same group as Messiaen, is gifted with a warm and forceful temperament. One of his first works, the *Poèmes Intimes,* reveals his very real qualities. Drawn by the purity, evocative strength and magic power of primitive pure rhythms and sounds, and investigating the nature of Polynesian chants, he conceived the remarkable piano études *Mana.* Then, aligning himself with the efforts made by Edgar Varèse in the same direction, he composed the *Concerto pour Piano et Orchestre,* whose too calculated violence set off an uproar at its first performance at Strasbourg, with public opinion divided into two contradictory and equally heated camps.

At the Paris Conservatory, the two theories professed by Milhaud and Messiaen respectively have nurtured the most free and diverse talents. Messiaen's tendency toward seeming unreality is counterbalanced by Milhaud's solid good sense. It is not surprising that artists of all nationalities have attested to the benefit of this education. The only limitation on the free development of initiative is that imposed by the natural exigencies of the sonant world. This atmosphere is responsible for the fluency of composition and freedom of thought of such different spirits as, for example, Louis Saguer, whose *Musique d'Eté* and *Musique d'Après-Midi* give promise of an interesting personality, and Pierre Boulez, who has already put his manifest gifts to remarkable use in his *Polyphonies.* Besides these reputedly progressive musicians, others, perhaps more traditional, are important: Jean-Louis Martinet, whose *Orphée* and *Trilogie des Prométhées* have a sense of grandeur; Maurice Le Roux, for the expressive subtlety and mobility forecast by his *Deux Mimes.* One other composer who is developing well is Henri Dutilleux. whose *Symphony* (1951) is an established success.

8

MUSIC IN SOVIET RUSSIA

AFTER STUDYING under Rimsky-Korsakov in St. Petersburg, and immediately following the composition of the *Firebird*, Stravinsky left Russia for France, where he lived, except for occasional periods in Switzerland, until he went to America in 1939.

As he became more and more convinced that sounds act according to their own nature, or their sonorous weight, he progressively cut away all descriptive or picturesque elements so as to emerge with music that was absolute. His genius gave birth to bodies of sound infused with their own life, independent of any subject matter and expressing nothing, but reaching us in the manner dictated by their essential character. Stravinsky's awareness of the reality of the phenomenon of sound led him to nonacademic composition conditioned directly by the real impression of sounds on the listener.

The final stage in the evolution of the St. Petersburg school is Stravinsky's *Jeu des Cartes* and a series of works he composed in America after 1940, which fulfill the ideal of the pure play of sound.

The Moscow school professed contrary ideas. The musicians teaching and studying there espoused a subjective point of view. What was most important to them was to express emotion through music. They believed in the principle of a preconceived plan for expression and in the psychological development of the musical work. The musical problem was subordinated to extra-musical philosophic concerns.

The master who formed the contemporary generation of exponents of the Moscow school was Sergei Ivanovich Taneev (1856-1915). His most important students were Alexander Scriabin (1872-1915), Sergei Rachmaninoff (1873-1943), Nikolai Medtner (1879-1951), Reinhold Glière (1875-1956), and Serge

Prokofiev (1891-1953). Prokofiev also studied under Rimsky-Korsakov and Liadov in St. Petersburg, and Glière in turn taught Nikolai Miaskovsky (1881-1950).

In general, the production of the Moscow school did not arouse the same interest in the West as did the brilliant works by students of the St. Petersburg school. They were steeped in a literary and philosophic atmosphere that did not attract Western audiences, and the music did not stand up well under transplantation. Taneev, Rachmaninoff, Medtner, and Glière were pictured in the West as latter-day romantics.

By far the most interesting member of that generation was Alexander Scriabin. He was the most vital representative of the trends of the Moscow school. He thought that music should be used as a means to propagate theosophic ideas, and pictured it incorporated in a new religion. He became entangled in metaphysical considerations which were really rather heady. But he was right in thinking that the magic power of music is not an illusion, and that this power belongs to the very nature of music. This conviction stimulated him to intensive experimentation in harmony, which in a way prefigured some of Schoenberg's discoveries.

Scriabin's point of departure, like Schoenberg's, is the harmony in *Tristan*. He relies on the dominant ninth chord. In his obsession for movement and his desire to give the thought no rest, he avoids using the perfect chord. With the role of primary importance passing to the dominant, on which he builds dissonant chords by superimposing thirds, his music always remains tonal, but allows no resolution.

After the *Sonata No. 5,* Op. 52, the perfect chord disappears entirely from Scriabin's compositions. His last works (*Sonata No. 6* through *Sonata No. 10*) and his *Preludes,* Op. 74, engender even greater tensions, the basis now enlarged to dominant eleventh and finally the dominant thirteenth (B♭, D, F, A♭, C, E♭, G), a chord of seven notes which completes the cycle of thirds without destroying the tonal sense.

Scriabin gives varying degrees of tension to these chords by changing their positions. Further, he insures the unity of the composition by not limiting himself to vertical superimposition of the notes of the chord chosen. He uses them, to the exclusion of other notes, to trace melodies, or rather themes and motifs, a method which suggests Schoenberg's "twelve-tone" technique. His generating chord, from which all the elements of the composition emanate and which he calls the synthetic chord, is a "row" in Schoenberg's meaning of the word. The difference is that all the notes in Scriabin's compositions are still always referred to a privileged note—the dominant.

Miaskovsky followed Scriabin's ideas for a time in some of his symphonies, as did other Russian composers. But an event of supreme importance was to change the course of destiny. The Revolution of 1917, barely two years after Scriabin's death, put a stop to experimentation in harmony.

As soon as the Soviet regime was established, life in Russia was reorganized along new lines. The rupture with middle-class ways, customs, and tastes meant also that bourgeois music was no longer acceptable. Music had to be written for the proletariat. Rather than a refined art which would please only an elite, composers had to address themselves to the people, conform with the people's aspirations, and express themselves in a way that all could understand.

Such a reversal cannot be effected without mistakes and setbacks, and several years passed before the world began to take notice of the new music of Soviet countries. Composers themselves were not quite sure what to hold to, and had trouble distinguishing what was allowed from what should be avoided. Even if freedom to express what individual imagination suggested—without taking the audience into consideration—were tolerated at all, the resulting work had little chance of being heeded. The expectations of the consumer of music had to be satisfied, and creators were made aware of this requirement by music critics.

Such a conception of the life of music unnerved Russian composers for a time. André Gide brought back notes on his trip to the U.S.S.R., summing up the situation in a critical time when the last breath of an individualism which tended to cut itself off from the general moral climate had been stifled. Gide discusses the performance of the Shostakovich opera, *Lady Macbeth of Mzensk (Katerina Ismailova)*.

"You understand," X explained to me, "the public no longer asks for anything like this; we no longer want anything like this. His last work was a very notable and noted ballet." (*He* was Shostakovich, whom people had talked to me about in that awe-inspired tone reserved for genius.) "But what do you expect the people to do with an opera when they can't hum a single tune after they have left?" (Heavens, they have come to this! And yet X, an artist himself and a highly cultured man, had made nothing but intelligent remarks to me up to that point.) "What we need today are works that the whole world can understand, and understand instantly. If Shostakovich doesn't feel this himself, they will make him feel it acutely by not even listening to him any more. You see," he continued, "an artist in our country must first fall in line. Otherwise, the most wonderful gifts will be thought of as formalistic. Yes, this is the word we have found to designate everything we don't want to see or hear. We want to create a new art, worthy of the great people we are. Art today must be popular or else not exist."

So an opera whose melodies could be hummed was revolutionary. And what we call nonconformism was called formalism. The very meaning of the words has changed. But rather than stop at the impression of a French critic, let us consult the statements of revolutionary Russian composers. We should remember that the cultured elite was dispersed after the Revolution, and the problem was to create a sensitivity to music in the working masses who had never had the benefit of an artistic education. The course laid out for musical culture, therefore, was to start at the beginning.

In 1931, Paul Weiss published a manifesto in the name of the Association of Proletarian Musicians, a group whose duty was to organize musical activities within the framework of the Five Year Plan. An extract of the most striking passages will give us a picture of the attitudes prevalent at that time:

The principle of our program is Marxism-Leninism, or, in other words, dialectical materialism. If we apply that concept to the arts, it is evident that in a class-structured society, all art is class art. Consciously or not, each artist is the ideologist, the spokesman, of a given economic class. He interprets the realities around him from the point of view of the class to which he belongs. His works propagate the attitudes of that class, and reinforce its self-confidence and its will to fight. Those attitudes are opposed to the interests of the enemy-class, and must weaken that class's combative faculties.

For the two classes of modern society, this means that it is to the interest of the dominant bourgeoisie to maintain the existing political and economic order. This is why its art depicts present conditions as stable, just and unchangeable. It passes over the crisis—the bankruptcy of capitalism—in silence, and describes the condition of the oppressed class in as rosy terms as possible, and the domination of the bourgeoisie as optimistically as decency will allow. The art of the decadent modern bourgeois class is therefore false. It not only deludes its enemy, but it leads the bourgeoisie itself into error.

The art of the revolutionary proletariat, on the contrary, fully exposes the evil consequences of the bourgeois system. It shows the forces inherent in the old order that can contribute to the preparation of the revolution. . . . This is why proletarian art must not be *above the fray*, but must participate in it. It must be realistic.

Realism is not the best word to define the attitude of proletarian art. Actually, this art is not intended to copy or photograph reality as faithfully as possible. To the contrary, it must illustrate the active principles of reality more clearly and more really than life itself does. It must show the generality represented by each concrete fact, and explain it to those who are unable to untangle the complexity and diversity of daily life. In this way, art must arm and inspire the listener, reader, and spectator for the socialist struggle. This is what the creative method of a dialectical materialist must be.

How can these principles be effected in the realm of music? Can music express ideas? Not only can it, but it does, and always has.

Through music, the proletariat presents the major aims of its struggle: to bring about revolution in capitalist states, to build a socialist state in the Soviet Union. For this reason, proletarian art, far from wanting in freedom, is a pioneer in the struggle for complete liberty in a society where there are no more class differences.

That Soviet Russia has chosen a certain type of music for its use and rejects others which it finds unsuitable is understandable and even normal. The Chinese and Greeks both subordinated music to political purposes and made it serve to maintain collective discipline. This has been the case in many societies in the process of organization, and the same is true for the establishment of ritual in all religions.

But in trying to rationalize the choice made, Russia has, in the opinion of the West, confused an issue which is really simple and clear. It would have been better to say: As a result of the suppression of class distinctions, music must be created whose meaning can be grasped immediately by the uncultured citizen, and that music must be clear and positive in character. We will avoid all music which is morbid, pessimistic, or too difficult to understand. The manifesto also defines the line to be followed. Included as acceptable are:

1] The music called folk, insofar as it manifests solid support of the exploited peasant class, or reflects the movement to liberate an oppressed nation.

2] Bourgeois music, if it dates from the revolutionary period of the bourgeoisie when, as the third estate, it constituted the majority of the people, represented the oppressed, supported them against the oppressors, and worked for the interests of the whole of humanity. The two composers whom proletarian musicians consider as their masters *par excellence* are Mussorgsky and Beethoven.

Such regimentation in music may well have been salutary for Russia at a time when her workers were being delivered from not only material but moral oppression. Let us not forget that workers and peasants had been left in a state of almost total ignorance. It is obviously unthinkable to expect such a people to absorb all the aspects of a culture overnight. It took the West three thousand years to establish that culture and give it flexibility, so that by the twentieth century members of society achieved complete individual cultural freedom and responsibility and a state of awareness which would allow consideration of the most diverse forms of thought as well as submission of these forms to a highly developed critical sense.

If we can admit that all areas of a society in formation must submit to certain more or less imperious directives in order to avoid chaos and anarchy, and if we keep ourselves from comparing the state of Russia's new society to our Western democratic societies and trying to apply our norms and criteria to it, we will come much closer to understanding the cultural efforts that have been carried out in the Soviet Union.

What we must first realize is that under the old regime the cultural life of that enormous country was concentrated in a few large cities, principally St. Petersburg and Moscow, and the population as a whole was neglected. One of the first Soviet accomplishments was cultural decentralization. The reader of all the reports on this subject is struck by the importance given statistics—the number of instruments manufactured, the number of music schools opened, the number of theaters operating, the number of organizations devoted to stimulating interest in music.

Truly, everything remained to be done, and everything had to begin at zero. Today, there are concert societies, opera and ballet troupes, conservatories in Azerbaijan, Armenia, and Georgia, as well as in the Ukraine and White Russia. There is musical activity at Baku and Tbilisi, as there is at Kiev, Leningrad, and Moscow.

We must also take into account the differences between the republics of the immense Soviet territory, each with its distinct character. To engender music and stimulate musical creation, what would be more natural than to use native folk song as a base? A young composer from the shores of the Caspian Sea, sprung from the people, has not inherited the great European tradition. His education and background are necessarily rooted in elements of folklore, the authentic expression of the spirit of his native land. This need was felt in the nineteenth century in countries like Bohemia, Hungary, and Spain, and is inescapable in countries where European culture has not penetrated.

The Russians talk a great deal about new composers whose talent affords them independence and respect in the cities where they practice their art. Most of these composers are of little interest to a Western audience. Their innumerable compositions are generally orchestral fantasies, songs for voice and orchestra, choruses, and sometimes operas, the main value of which lies in the use of folk songs. But for the most part their music lacks individuality and creative worth. Almost all these composers are in the first phase of the development of music: the production of folk material without the transformation a creative act assures.

Anyone straying from the established order is called a formalist. No exact meaning of this worrisome term can be found, though some circles have tried to pin it down. L. Kullakovsky's investigation ended by attaching the word to a good number of theoreticians. According to him, Riemann, Kurth, Javorski, and Konus "show the same tendency to underestimate the expressive richness and ideological scope of music. All their idealistic theories share the common trait of denying that music has a message." Hanslick and Glebov, says the critic, are even more blameworthy, because they claim that music acts only according to the rhythms, intervals, and harmonies which produce greater or lesser tensions in the nervous system. Consequently, if we are to believe Kullakovsky, the accusation of formalism can be directed at any composition which claims to act by virtue only of its notes, this being the ideal goal for us. Pure music, or absolute music, is subject to his suspicion.

Although they sometimes seem to belong to the past, these ideological discussions are always current because they are periodically revived.

The transition from the old to the new regime was effected by musicians like Glazunov, Steinberg, Ippolitov-Ivanov, Miaskovsky, and Glière, all of whom, with the exception of Glière, were trained in the school of Rimsky-Korsakov. Serge Prokofiev was in Russia at the time, but was not teaching. He soon left his country to live an international life for many years. The works by this first rank of Revolution composers are of limited value, except for Miaskovsky's. He composed grandiloquent symphonies, and by 1941 was writing his twenty-first.

The music which should be remembered as characteristic of that period includes Steinberg's fourth symphony, *Turksib*, and Glière's ballet, *The Red Poppy*. The two composers were the masters of a new generation, whose most significant representatives are Dmitri Shostakovich and Yuri Shaporin, students of Steinberg; Aram Khachaturian, Vissarion Shebalin, and Dmitri Kabalevsky, students of Miaskovsky; Lev Knipper, and Ivan Dzerzhinsky. These, along with the older Serge Prokofiev, illustrate what Russian music has been since 1920, granting that Stravinsky has played no active part in the life of music in the Soviet Union, and that his influence is nil.

There are two distinct periods in the work of these composers. The first lasted until 1929, and coincided with Lenin's New Economic Policy. During the time of the N.E.P., every extreme of musical language was allowed. The point was to see who could be the most modern, and there was nothing more modern in Russia than industrialization and mechanization. The symphony *Turksib* glorified the building of the Turkestan-Siberia Railway. Mossolov's *Iron Foundry* (1928) imitates whistling steam and flowing molten metal. It is written with a rhythmic ostinato technique reminiscent of Honegger's *Pacific 231*, and has an orchestra as overpowering as the one in *Le Sacre du Printemps*. Prokofiev's ballet *Le Pas d'Acier* (1925) was produced by Diaghilev in Paris. Meituss based *Dnieprostroi*, a new symphony on great public works, on imitative harmony. Except for *Le Pas d'Acier*, these works are known only by name. A few records still exist to preserve for posterity examples of that slightly childish admiration for the new toy—the machine. This admiration, which had as a corollary a satiric and sarcastic attitude toward the old regime, is manifested in some of Shostakovich's work, like the polka in the ballet *The Golden Age*.

In 1929 the first Five Year Plan was begun. All writers and artists were invited to contribute to the success of the Plan. Art was to be the incentive and reward for the worker, of whom, it was said, enormous effort was required. Governmental control of artistic production became more severe and persistent, and the gospel of Soviet realism, the dogmas of which we discussed at the beginning of this chapter, came out in 1932. There were to be no more machines, no more sarcasm, and no more formalism. Folk art and lyric symphony were to lead the program of glorifying the Revolution which, due to World War II and in a rush of national pride, was to broaden steadily into a glorification of the whole of Russian history.

Prokofiev and Shostakovich are unquestionably the most representative Soviet musicians in the eyes of foreigners.

SERGE PROKOFIEV was born in 1891 in the Ekaterinoslav region. He went to the St. Petersburg Conservatory where he worked under the direction of Rimsky-Korsakov and Liadov. In Moscow he worked with Taneev. In 1918 he left Russia and went to America. From 1922 to 1935 he lived in Germany and France, and around 1935 returned to settle in Russia. Prokofiev pursued the double career of pianist and composer. His precise, elegant technique with its inexorable rhythm, devoid of bombast, corre-sponds closely with the character he reveals in his compositions. Like many modern composers, Prokofiev was very prolific. Our contemporaries do not wait for inspiration to begin writing. They believe that the act of writing, composing regularly every day, is a stimulus for the imagination. Writing a great deal makes for increased flexibility in the act of writing and greater ease of expression. Hindemith and Milhaud wrote any time and anywhere—on a boat, on a train, or during a conversation around their work table. Satie wrote on the corner of a café table. And at the end of *Chroniques de Ma Vie,* Stravinsky says:

Just as an organ will atrophy if it is not engaged in continual ac-tivity, a composer's faculties will weaken and die when they are not sustained by exercise and training. The layman thinks that one must wait for inspiration to write. This is a mistake. I am far from denying the value of inspiration; much to the contrary. It is a motor force found in any human activity and is in no wise the monopoly of artists. But that force is only called on when it is activated by an effort, and that effort is work. As appetite comes with eating, it is just as true that work brings inspiration if inspiration is not present at first.

Prokofiev spent his first years composing mainly for the piano. Among his best works are the *Visions Fugitives,* Op. 22, and eight sonatas, several of which were revised and corrected some years after the first versions were published. *Sonata No. 3,* Op. 28, composed in 1917, had been written in its original form years earlier; *Sonata No. 4,* also composed in 1917, comes from a 1908 work. These sonatas *d'après de vieux cahiers* show the constancy of the composer's temperament. Most composers say that they are incapable of taking up an old work for correction because their feelings, tastes, and ideas have changed. Not so for Pro-kofiev. As he was at the beginning, so he has remained, and that lack of evolution explains a remarkable fact. When he re-turned to the Soviet Union and bowed to the restrictions re-quired by the party line, after living and working in America and Western Europe, his art hardly reflected this great change at all. A very slight unsteadiness due to adjustment was noticeable for a short time, but he quickly regained his balance, and his later works can be related to those of his youth with no difficulty.

The real Prokofiev is easily recognized by certain very specific characteristics which are found throughout the first and third periods of his creative activity: the binary cut of his melodies, with the simple rhythm (quarter- and eighth-notes) and a predilection for abrupt modulation [*Example 115*]. He was also particularly fond of plagal cadence, which is popular with a good many other Russian composers. Prokofiev handled the cadence (and its derivatives) with lively imagination, which allowed him to vary its appearance continually.

His violent allegiance to tonality and diatonism is expressed in a marked preference for the ninth major chord [*Example 116*], endowing his music with a biting quality, a sort of cold-bloodedness in its movement which is the personal mark of the composer. Prokofiev's music, neither polytonal nor atonal, still avoids the scholastic shackles of tonality. His harmony willingly does without overly leading notes (notes which hold the discourse too long within a given key). The composer can therefore make use of the rapid modulations toward all keys that so enrich his musical palette.

The best known of his piano works is the magnificent *Concerto No. 3 for Piano,* in which all the characteristics we have just discussed are united. Prokofiev's mastery of pianistic writing in this work is unique in contemporary history. It is a work of great virtuosity and, at the same time, a veritable symphony, as are all beautiful concertos. The variations are magical, and the carefully controlled ecstasy in the finale, a poem of swiftness, is overpowering. If this concerto, among all similar modern works, has become the most popular, it is due to its perfect achievement, of course, but also to the freshness and gaiety which are comparable (the question of style apart) in charm only to Mendelssohn's *Violin Concerto.*

The indifference of pianists to Prokofiev's eight sonatas is hard to understand. They are almost all excellent. Their style and thought are sometimes very reminiscent of Medtner's sonatas, but with more dash, imagination, and freedom. The melodic ideas in them are clearly contrasted, and their development is based, for the most part, on rich invention of piano ornamentation and figurations. Prokofiev shows no inclination toward thematic development. His melody by itself is eloquent, often elegant and sometimes intense, but without emotional exaggeration.

Balance, simplicity, and natural grace constitute the art of these sonatas. By avoiding both excessive formal work and sloppiness, and by keeping the melody always in the foreground, Prokofiev has given them a charm that is also found in a series of later works like the *Concerto No. 3 for Piano*, the *Concerto No. 1 for Violin*, and the delightful *The Ugly Duckling*, for voice and piano, based on the tale by Andersen. Such youthfulness and good humor are very attractive. The listener is put in direct contact with a lucid idea and a feeling of vigor and freshness. This ease of communication is undoubtedly what put Prokofiev in such a favorable position in the Soviet Union after he began to participate in Russian musical life.

When Prokofiev put aside his confident attitude toward life which made his expression happy and peaceful, he became sarcastic, passing without transition into scathing irony. Works like the ballet *The Buffoon* suffer from this state of mind, which is translated into an accumulation of dissonances and a brittle thematic quality, the caricatural import of which is not motivated by musical exigencies. This "grotesque" genre, intentional and rather artificial, was fashionable in Russia at the beginning of the Revolution. But the satire and gaiety are much more natural and spontaneous in operas such as *Love for Three Oranges*, based on a comedy by Gozzi, the March of which rapidly became very popular; and in *The Gambler*, based on Dostoevsky's story.

Love for Three Oranges contains delightful clownish inventions. An important role is given the chorus of commentators, who are, moreover, very active: the Tragedians, Comedians, Lyricists, and Emptyheads. The laborious birth of the laugh that will save the Prince from hypochondria makes some of the best comedy in music. The magic scenes unfortunately are too dry and lacking in life, which detracts somewhat from an otherwise sprightly play.

The Gambler is one of Prokofiev's most well-constructed and interesting works. The libretto has little in common with Dostoevsky's novelette, but this is unimportant. An opera is an autonomous work. It exists in itself, and the libretto may as well be an original creation by the composer as inspired by a book. In the latter case, the opera need not carry the book over in exact detail; it may take a different direction. *The Gambler* was begun in 1915, later completely rewritten, and orchestrated in 1928. This Opus 24 forms a group with the *Scythian Suite,* Op. 20; *The Buffoon,* Op. 21; *Visions Fugitives,* Op. 22; and the *Concerto No. 3 for Piano,* Op. 26. It was composed in the middle of a particularly fine creative period. The outstanding quality of *The Gambler* is that it is alive from beginning to end. To be alive, a thing cannot mark time: it must grow. And this *The Buffoon* does not do. In *The Gambler,* the growth of intensity is remarkably well handled. In the first two acts, the elements of melody, clearly defined, appear fleetingly. They are continuously reiterated; hardly is one rhythmic or harmonic combination heard before another succeeds it. The flight of the music is kept firmly in hand. A thousand delightful details attract our ears, while our eyes follow the comings and goings of the many characters who people the scene. In the third act, tension mounts. Thematic elaborations are more sustained and focus our attention on the impending drama. The fourth act is the culminating point. All through its three scenes the music is sustained on an elevated plane. Melodies soar on great wing strokes, and the structure is splendid. The scene of the gambling room is a masterpiece. The noise of the crowd, the gambler's folly, and the evident disorder of the dialogue that fuses and crisscrosses are held in a strict form, a sort of deafening rondo whose vivacity, now harsh and strident, can only be ended in the sad peroration of a thought that began in an atmosphere of charming gaiety. The opera *Semyon Kotko* is also successful, while *War and Peace* sins by excessiveness; it is too long. The *Flaming Angel* appears to be Prokofiev's best opera.

Prokofiev also composed works of an epic character which have great value, like the *Scythian Suite* (1914), and the cantata *Seven, They are Seven* (1917), the action of which has considerable power.

The massive *Russian Overture* of 1936, the music for the

movie *Lieutenant Kije,* and the choral cantata extracted from the music for the movie *Alexander Nevsky* (1939) are written in the same vein. These works, the last of which sometimes attains great beauty, make use of folk song in a zealous spirit that makes the listener think of *Boris Godunov.* Prokofiev is most faithful to his own gift when he sings with Russian peasants and exalts the soul of the people. His art then abounds with an enthusiasm that infuses it with warm life.

Prokofiev's return to his mother country did not prove damaging to his work, and the restrictions brought to bear on artistic expression in the Soviet Union do not seem in any wise to have hampered the talent of a composer whose natural boundaries coincided with those established in the society to which he belonged. The composer's *Fifth* and *Seventh Symphonies* attest to this fact.

DMITRI SHOSTAKOVICH belongs to the new generation that came of age after the Revolution of 1917. Born in 1906 in St. Petersburg, he hardly knew the old order. In a short autobiography published in 1936, he states:

My penchant for music came to light in 1915, the year I began my musical studies. In 1919, I enrolled at the Leningrad Conservatory, where I finished in 1925. There I worked under the direction of L. Nikolaiev (piano and theory of composition), Professor Nikolai Sokolov (counterpoint and fugue), and Professor Maximilian Steinberg (harmony, fugue, orchestration, and advanced composition). After I had finished my studies at the Conservatory, I remained as a junior assistant in the composition course taught by Professor Steinberg. I began to compose while I was still studying at the Conservatory. My *Symphony* (the first), for example, which has been performed by almost all the symphony orchestras of the world, was my thesis composition at the Conservatory.

I soaked myself enthusiastically and uncritically in all the knowledge and skills taught me. But once my studies were finished, I had to make over a large part of the musical baggage I had acquired. I came to understand that music is not only a combination of sounds disposed in such and such an order, but is an art capable of expressing the most diverse ideas or feelings in its particular way. I did not arrive at this conviction painlessly. It is enough to say that, during all of 1926, I did not write a single note. But from 1927 on, I never stopped composing. During that period I wrote two operas: *The Nose* (based on Gogol) and *Lady Macbeth of Mzensk* (based on Leskov's book); three ballets, *The Golden Age* and *Button* among them; three symphonies, two of which were *Ode to October* and *May 1st Symphony;* twenty-four piano preludes; a *Concerto for Piano and Orchestra;* movie music, etc. . . .

In that interval of time, my technique took on form and substance. Working constantly to master my art, I applied myself to creating my own musical style, which I wanted to be simple and expressive.

I do not conceive of my future progress outside our socialist structure. And the aim I assign to my work is that it help build our remarkable country in every respect. There is no greater joy for a composer than to be conscious of contributing by his creation to the scope of Soviet musical culture, which has been called upon to play a role of prime importance in the reconstruction of the human spirit.

This profession of faith describes Shostakovich's position. While those around him speak of objectivism, of absolute music, he has taken a resolute stand against that concept. He is as opposed to the Stravinsky of the *Octet* as to the Schoenberg of *Variations for Orchestra*. He clings to viewpoints we are tempted to call romantic. Our designation would be wrong, moreover, for a good many earlier masters; for example, Monteverdi and Schütz, who cannot be charged with romanticism, were equally of the opinion that music is made to express emotions.

Music existing on its own behalf, or sounds determining emotions; or again, the sonorous world on the one hand, expressive content on the other: it would be useless to discuss, and more so to take sides with, one or the other thesis. The most detailed analyses always balk this side of a certain point, precisely that point beyond which lie the secrets of the gestation and significance of music. It is nonetheless certain that two types of music do exist: the music whose beauty we admire, and in which we are not tempted to look for anything other than splendor; and the music that suggests an expressive text or an explanatory note. Mozart is on one side, Beethoven on the other. Stravinsky's thinking is the same as Mozart's. Shostakovich is allied with Beethoven, by way of Gustav Mahler.

Actually, Stravinsky's position in Russian music is exceptional (that is, Stravinsky post-*Pulcinella*). Russian music almost always includes visual elements, or preconceived emotional motivation. The existence of visual sensitivity is as evident in Mussorgsky's *Enfantines* as in Rimsky-Korsakov's *Schéhérazade,* and the aim of expression guides the development of Tchaikovsky's symphonies as well as Scriabin's sonatas.

Shostakovich was doing the most natural thing in the world, in his statement, in assigning to music the role of translating the most diverse ideas and emotions. This conception is as natural in Russia as abstraction is in Western Europe. And when he says that he wants his style to be simple and expressive, it would be wrong to think that he meant to make a deliberate change as a result of the criticism directed at *Lady Macbeth of Mzensk.* The import of these critiques seems to have been somewhat misunderstood in the West. The performances of *Lady Macbeth* took place during the transition from the N.E.P. period to the period of the first Five Year Plan. At the beginning, *Lady Macbeth* was an enormous success. It was not until some time later that a campaign was launched against certain tendencies particularly highlighted by this remarkable opera.

The attack on *Lady Macbeth* was directed against a whole order of events and circumstances. It was the occasion and pretext for a revision of artistic thinking in the U.S.S.R. Because of the importance of this case, before commenting on Shostakovich's music itself, it is worthwhile to cast an eye here on how theatrical life developed after the Revolution.

The Russians dearly love the theater in any form: drama, opera, or ballet. Under the tsars, the theater was the object of particular attention. Russian producers and choreographers had bolder, larger, and more advanced ideas than their confreres in the West. They devoted the necessary time and care to producing polished spectacles. Elsewhere, we have seen that credit for the renaissance in contemporary ballet is due to Russian choreographers like Fokine, Nijinska, Massine, and Balanchine, and to the existence of an imperial dancing academy.

The Revolution, far from suppressing interest in the stage, encouraged it. For the stage was a powerful vehicle for use as a means to spread the new ideology.

Until around 1930, every liberty was allowed in the matter of dramatic aesthetics. The life of the theater until that time had no real importance outside the great metropolitan centers. In the case of opera, the repertory did not as yet include any new works. Operas by Glinka, Tchaikovsky, Rimsky-Korsakov, Borodin, and Mussorgsky were standard. *Carmen, La Bohème,* and *Die Meistersinger von Nürnberg* were often performed. But in a good many works the texts were adapted to Soviet ideology. The speech of Hans Sachs in the last scene of *Die Meistersinger,* for example, was made to extol the relationship between art and the workers. The libretto of *Carmen,* as well, was heavily reworked and adapted for propaganda purposes.

Every liberty was allowed, but composing new works was sacrificed to experimentation in production. A dramatic work became merely a pretext for scenic construction.

A number of new trends appeared in this connection. On the one hand, realism as formulated by Stanislavski had operas and operettas played as dramas and comedies, the singers directing their movements, gestures, and expressions in a realistic way, according to the text, without heeding the requirements of the music. Opposed to Stanislavski was Tairov, who rejected naturalism to concentrate the substance of the drama in a few schematized gestures. He did away with the human aspect of drama to bring out certain abstract formulas and an architectural scenic construction. The result was a "liberated theater" which caused a rift between drama and spectacle, and made the spectacle the essence of the production. This concept was unfortunate at a time when efforts were being bent to impress the masses with ideas exposed in the theater. Tairov's experiments put critics on the alert, and persuaded some that creative freedom should be curtailed.

A third trend was Meyerhold's "biomechanism." All the mechanism of the theater—scene changes, placing and working of lights—was made visible and actively participated in the play. Architectural experimentation was carried to extremes, but all the elements, actors and objects, moved and were directed in reference to the human significance of the play.

The care exercised in production was equally great under each of these three methods, whose originators were directors of genius. Nonetheless, Meyerhold and especially Tairov can be criticized for having relegated the content of the works they staged to the background. The instructive potential of the theater, on which the Revolution had placed enormous importance, was neglected, and more and more pressure was applied to bring scenic art closer to the requirements of popular education.

During that period of complete liberty when a bold imagination was considered revolutionary (as in the West), the latest works from Europe were well received. Křenek's *Johnny Strikes Up* and Alban Berg's *Wozzeck* were performed. The latter work made a strong impression in Russian artistic circles. The somber pessimism of Viennese expressionism found an echo in the Russian soul, whose agonies Dostoevsky described with such genius. It was under the impact of *Wozzeck* that Shostakovich composed his extraordinary *Lady Macbeth*. It was an admirable work, to which the whole world rendered homage. But critics thought that, with *Lady Macbeth*, the trends in theater, which important producers had already carried to alarming lengths, were taking a turn they considered unhealthy and, in any event, incompatible with the effort to be required of the workers. To effect the Five Year Plan, the mood of the laboring class had to be joyous and courageous. The artists were given the task of contributing to the success of the Five Year Plan by watching over the moral health of the worker.

Lady Macbeth, written between 1930 and 1932, was first produced in 1934 in Leningrad by Smolich and staged at Nemirovich Dantshenko's Little Theater in Moscow. The libretto had been taken from a short story by Leskov. It tells the tale of a woman whose lover kills her husband and who is deported to Siberia with him. The lover neglects his mistress and leaves her for another woman. The woman tries to push her rival overboard during a river crossing. Both women drown.

Shostakovich had chosen this subject because of its rich dramatic situations and its social significance. He considered it an exposé of the position of Russian women under the old regime, and thought that this lamentable picture was especially suitable to the new type of dramatic art. He strove to portray the drama in simple and expressive language.

Lady Macbeth was the first notable opera written after the Revolution. The composer distinguished his characters clearly in order to create strong contrasts between personalities. He found that sharpening his means of expression provided dramatic power, as Alban Berg had done in *Wozzeck*.

Everyone realized the exceptional value of the score. It was not until 1936 that critics began to voice objections, and even then not of its worth but of the trend it followed. In a series of articles, *Pravda* asserted that Shostakovich would have to orient himself toward greater realism. This new regard for realism grew in opposition to dramatic concepts which had prevailed until the writing of *Lady Macbeth*. The term meant not a type of naturalism, but the need to situate the work of art in current circumstances, in the realities of the current life of the Russian people. The individual was no longer interesting. Evoking conditions of a time past had no meaning for the people of the present.

The attack on *Lady Macbeth* was not caused by a misunderstanding on the part of the critics. It was not a violent and impulsive reaction against music which was not liked. It was a reflective act in which the personal tastes of the judges were not taken into account. The sole criterion was the greater interest of the country under exceptional circumstances.

The result of this judgment was that the score was withdrawn from circulation, and the course of that beautiful work was interrupted. Thus, on the appearance of the first Soviet opera, the lines which dramatic music would have to follow in the future were laid down.

Western critics have said that after this misfortune Shostakovich's wings, if not broken, were at least somewhat clipped. This is not the impression that a study of the composer's works gives. He himself has always insisted on the expressive and human side he wants to give his music. Between *Lady Macbeth* and works like the *Seventh Symphony* or *Eighth Symphony* there is no essential difference. There is only a difference of attitude, and consequently accentuation of certain details in the writing of the music. In the ballet *The Golden Age* and in *Lady Macbeth*, there is still a good deal of banter in the air, burlesquing old-regime characters and sentiments still fashionable shortly after the Revolution. The spirit of caricature called for a special orchestral arrangement that cannot be considered characteristic of the composer. Further, the dramatic situation as Shostakovich saw it led to the expression of extreme emotions. There is no evidence that this convulsive style was to be definitive—earlier works do not at all prepare the way for the opera. And since there is a real relationship between the *First Symphony* and the symphonies following *Lady Macbeth,* it seems logical to conclude that the style in *Lady Macbeth* is rather the exception in Shostakovich's work, and that it was required by the nature of the drama.

It is noteworthy that the polemic it provoked did not involve the composer's temperament. The dispute should not be interpreted as an attempt to level or standardize the art of music. Egor Boelza remarks that "realism in art admits of a wide variety of forms of expression and styles, right as well as left, but it must avoid taking root in false ground. Innovations in art must be warranted by the introduction of a new element intrinsic in the artistic creation, and must not serve simply to make a purely formal invention predominate." Perhaps if we relate this thought to what we said on the subject of the situation in theater, and especially Tairov's methods, we will have the key to the fear of formalism so often expressed in Soviet Russia.

After writing *Lady Macbeth,* Op. 29, Shostakovich drew a fresh, rejuvenating breath, and wrote the enchanting *Concerto for Piano, Trumpet, and Strings;* the absolutely simple and unusually graceful *String Quartet,* Op. 49; and the *Quintet,* Op. 57. The absence of pretention in these works mirrors the temperament of their composer.

But Shostakovich's most noteworthy compositions are a series of symphonies, varying in quality but most important in their dimension and spirit. The basis of these symphonies is original melodic invention. The composer is gifted with exceptional virtuosity in orchestration, which he does not call on for the sheer pleasure of impressive display, but to state the melody clearly. Shostakovich is less guilty than Mahler of the fault of drawing out a work excessively, and the character of his compositions is more pronounced and more independent of outside influences than the Austrian composer's.

The *First Symphony,* Op. 10 (1926), already shows incontestable mastery. Shostakovich composed it in his youth. The *Second*

Symphony, Op. 14, celebrates the tenth anniversary of the October Revolution. The *Third Symphony*, Op. 20, is entitled *May 1st*. These are patriotic compositions, as was Berlioz's *Symphonie Funèbre* in its time. In 1936 appeared the *Fourth Symphony*, Op. 43, followed in 1937 by the *Fifth*, Op. 47. The central figure is man in the fullness of his sentient life. The finale brings the resolution of tension and tragedy, which are dissolved in the sunlight of hope and joy.

Characteristics appear in the *Fifth Symphony* that are more sharply defined in the *Seventh* and *Eighth Symphonies*: very important slow movements that are developed in a single stroke, so to speak, under the pressure of an inner drive, and that, as a result, successfully retain the listener's attention despite their length; a penchant for march movements in the allegros; scherzos replaced by popular dance movements (as Mahler's scherzos often take the form of *Ländler*); and slow, unbroken ascents toward climaxes of expression which seem all the more exalted because they have been long in coming.

The *Fifth Symphony* is a culminating point for Shostakovich. It shows great unity, remarkable continuity, and partial success in adapting homogeneous sound structure to aims of expression.

The *Sixth Symphony*, Op. 54, was written in 1939. The drama of man is forgotten. The music is a light-hearted invitation to youth and joy.

Then came the War, the great trial over which the new Russia was to triumph and which would justify in the eyes of the world the hard life this great country had had the courage to impose on itself for so many years. Shostakovich was in Leningrad. He shared the fate of his fellow citizens, bore with them the siege of the city, and rejoiced in the liberation and victory. From the trial emerged the *Seventh Symphony*, Op. 60, written in the teeth of the battle. It is a work of enormous proportions (it lasts an hour and a quarter), in which a second choir of brasses is added to the usual symphony orchestra. Two worlds meet in this monumental composition: that of the most noble human aspirations, love, joy, creative work; and that of destruction, mechanized barbarity, and death. The first part of the symphony includes a great march, occurring between two andantes, which symbolizes the growing strength of the Russian army after the

German attack. This march has been criticized as being modeled on the development technique of Ravel's *Bolero*. The criticism seems sound at first sight. There is, in fact, a theme that insistently recurs and undergoes a variety of orchestral presentations. But there is no question here of virtuosity or color. The theme is deliberately poor, stripped of all allure, and the development is progressively enriched with counterpoint calling for the addition of more and more numerous masses, while the force of the music remains interior. The scherzo is built on folk dance themes and rhythms, without pomp or flourish. The character of the music resides in its spirit of abnegation, in the concentration of emotion. Each measure is lighted from within. The slow movement best displays Shostakovich's more recent stylistic leanings. Melodies which are simple in appearance actually introduce inflections and modulations at every turn marked with the stamp of a distinctive personality. Contrapuntal lines, as well, avoid conventional phrasing and academic superimpositions. The music seems to give birth to an art which has been unostentatiously freed of the commonplace.

The work ends with a moderate movement of increasing exultation, but not in a burst of glory; rather, it leaves an impression of heaviness and fatigue, like the feeling of having thrown off a crushing weight—a more impressive and true conclusion than a spectacular song of triumph.

The *Eighth Symphony* (1943) is the most complete and accomplished composition its author has written to date. Like the *Seventh*, it is a work of immense proportions. Its performance lasts about sixty-five minutes. There is no subject, and yet the meaning of the symphony is clear. It is not yet a portrayal of joy, but after the tension of the *Seventh Symphony*, the music affords release and meditation. It is certainly no coincidence that the first theme of the opening movement begins with a tempered reiteration of the march theme of the preceding symphony. Calm returns, and after stress come withdrawal and recollection. More than ever Shostakovich rejects exterior display and clings to inner life. The music is beyond pain, and achieves a state of serenity. Never has Shostakovich's art been more firm and masterful than in the great initial adagio. The whole movement, which lasts half an hour, is woven from two melodic themes, without the development being overburdened or academic at any point. A short march movement, an active element, follows it. Some clarinet, bass clarinet, and piccolo passages have little character, but are nonetheless interesting. The work is enlivened with unusual color produced by the use of the overshrill registers of the flutes and clarinets. However, the piercing quality of the very high registers, instead of producing a coloristic effect, confers a certain degree of intensity on the idea. The orchestration of the symphony utilizes only the most simple means. There are few divisions of the strings, and the wind instruments are given long solo passages, always clearly placed in the foreground due to the prudent scoring of the background.

The orchestration is frequently built on the techniques of grouping and doubling, but all the dangers accompanying this method are avoided. The tutti passages, despite the importance of the orchestral body, are never weighty but retain their lightness as a result of judicious apportionment of intervals and registers.

The pivot of the last movement is a splendid passacaglia, in which the composer disdains exterior effect and infuses his music with inner truth. As a coda to this new meditation, there is a sweet, tender conclusion expressing increasing calm and the slow return of hope.

The *Eighth Symphony* is very comforting. It proves that regardless of watchwords, prohibitions, and more or less strict directives, true originality can develop and find the freedom necessary for expression. We must admit that after the *Eighth Symphony,* the gay and carefree *Ninth* was not favorably received by Russian authorities, because its tenor of entertainment was considered too inconsequential in relation to the great social problems Soviet Russia must face. The *Tenth Symphony,* which is nearly as important as the *Eighth,* was well received.

Lady Macbeth of Mzensk was the first Soviet opera. After its first performance, Russia began to develop her regional artistic centers. If we examine the whole of musical production since 1930 (which we cannot do in detail, since as yet scores are not easily obtained in the West), the most interesting works seem to be in the field of opera. There exist a good many symphonies, and concertos as well; dozens of odes to Stalin have been composed. But the works are generally not remarkable. Even the best of them, like Khachaturian's concertos, lack real individuality.

If we abstract from the work of the two most important artists, Prokofiev and Shostakovich, the most striking elements that emerge are the utilization of folk songs, and the creation of operas dealing with life in Soviet Russia and, more recently, with glorious episodes from the whole history of Russia.

Among these operas there are a number which have acquired some fame: Ivan Dzerzhinsky's *Quiet Flows the Don,* and his *Storm,* based on Ostrovski's work; Dmitri Kabalevsky's *Colas Breugnon,* based on Romain Rolland's *Le Maître de Clamecy;* Lev Knipper's *Vent du Nord;* Alexander Krein's *Zagmuk;* Prokofiev's last two operas, *Semyon Kotko,* Op. 81, and *War and Peace,* Op. 91 (1941) based on Tolstoi's novel; and Yuri Shaporin's *The Decembrists,* with libretto by Aleksei Tolstoi. Prokofiev's *Flaming Angel* was played at the Venice Festival in 1955 and was unanimously acclaimed by musicians and the general public.

Of all these works, one has been cited as a model opera. It is *Quiet Flows the Don,* composed from 1930 to 1932, and widely performed with great success. Dzerzhinsky's opera, contemporaneous with *Lady Macbeth of Mzensk,* has the advantage over the latter of being based on a realistic libretto. The subject is life during the Revolution. It has the added advantage of a steady use of peasant folk songs.

9

GERMAN MUSIC AFTER RICHARD STRAUSS

IN A LETTER dated May 12, 1919, from Zurich, Ferruccio Busoni
wrote:

I long lived in a world of music which was under the spiritual tyranny
of Beethoven and, for all practical purposes, Wagner. Other than these
two personalities, great in spirit and power, Chopin alone was still
tolerated. The rest (among them Brahms and Bruckner, who also
dreamed of writing a ninth symphony) were only composers who tagged
along in the footsteps of the two masters. Bach's place in music was
comparable to the place that the Catholic Church has in society. As
for Mozart, he was really relegated to the background. Every time he
was mentioned in the same breath as the masters, he was considered a
child at whom one smiles without really understanding him. The whole
development of music in the nineteenth century was distorted by this
error.

If we had been raised with Mozart's music, and if we had understood
Berlioz better, we would be more advanced and our paths would be
surer. But we turned away from Mozart's purity and neglected Berlioz's
innumerable suggestions. Unwittingly, we moved out of the domain
of music little by little to enter that of philosophy. We lost the sense
of pure expression. We were saturated with great thoughts. We made efforts to accept the burden. We prolonged Wagner's very difficult victory
beyond its time; hence our present backwardness. Everyone had been
raised on Liszt (in France, César Franck and Saint-Saëns; in Russia, all
the composers of renown and, last but not least, Richard Wagner)—
and then were free to go on and (which costs little) to make fun of his
weaknesses, point a finger at his warts and slight the nobility of his
features.

Now the point is not to discredit, but to create constant values. We
must erect a new classic art. All the experiments at the beginning of
the twentieth century should be re-examined and incorporated into the
definitive style now being formed.

The age of instrumental virtuosity seems to me to be past. We should admit this fact and deduce the necessary conclusions, that the piano is an instrument to be used as an intermediary, and that the violin is an orchestral instrument of the first order. As for song, the importance of words should be diminished and its true nature revived. Opera should again become a scheme in which the text is only a reason for the music. The whole must be concise and interesting, a very free ensemble with many resting points. Let us open the windows. Let us have no more worry-lines on the listener's face, but a smile and tears instead!

This great pianist, a famous interpreter of Bach, Chopin, and Liszt, Italian by birth and German by training, had left Germany at the outbreak of World War I and spent the last years of his life in Switzerland. It was not generally known that he had composed a great deal and that among his writings were remarkable works.

His blazing career as a piano virtuoso had obscured his activity as a composer, as well as the ideas he professed, from the eyes of the public. However, after 1913, his surprising *Indianisches Tagebuch* and some of his *Elegies for Piano* had attracted the attention of some of the most advanced thinkers, and the staging of his *Arlecchino* at the Zürich Opera House in 1917 earned Busoni his proper place. He introduced a radical reform in German music, then still under the dominion of romanticism. It was a spiritual reform followed by rejuvenation of language.

Busoni's relationship to German music is analogous to Satie's to French music. Both were precursors. Both produced certain types of new music, and both acted as an influence which will continue to have salutary effects for some time.

In 1907 Busoni published the essay *Entwurf einer neuen Aesthetik der Tonkunst*. In it he expounds his ideas on the future of music and proposes methods to bring it new life. Music in Germany was hampered by an exaggerated respect for established tradition. Against these the Latin Busoni took up the sword. He demands liberty of movement for music, believing that when music is freed of the forms imposed prior to its creation, it will be absolute music. Originality is required, and yet composers are forbidden to create new forms. Busoni then shows that if we are loyal to Mozart, it is because of his human grandeur and not because of his tonic-dominant system and its elaborations. This is an obvious truism to Latins, but it was as difficult to make Germanic peoples understand it in 1910 as in 1940. We must admit a fundamental difference between the German concept of music and the concept natural to both Latins and Russians. For the German, music is born of a formal design around a theme, or a certain number of motifs. Music is primarily a building whose construction poses problems. For the Latin and the Russian, music is born of an expressive melody, and although technique plays an important role because of its obvious necessity to the materialization of the work, it nonetheless remains secondary. It is not used for the pleasure of setting up numbers of combinations. For the Latin, who has an innate sense of balance, the creation of a work of art is not a problem to solve. Further, he does not devote himself to experimentation—experimental music has existed only in Germany. Given these facts, it is logical that the German clings to methods of development or patterns of manufacture, and that he finds it hard to understand that the system of composition he has learned is neither universal nor eternal.

Busoni stands at the opposite pole, and maintains that a few composers have glimpsed what absolute music could be, when they were able to give up symmetrical relationships. Beethoven did this in the introduction to the fugue of the *Sonata für Hammerklavier,* Op. 106; Schumann in the transition to the last movement of the *Symphony in D Minor;* Brahms in the introduction to the finale of the *First Symphony;* Bach in his *Organ Fantasias* (not in the fugues) or in certain recitatives in the *Passions.*

Busoni urges the Germans to create music of the emotions, and discard structural forms and schemes and program music (à la Wagner and Strauss). German musical theater suffered from the artists' misconception concerning the nature and potential of music. Music was used to establish scenic action, instead of being limited to expressing psychological states.

"The creator," Busoni says, "must not accept a traditional law. He must consider his creative work as something exceptional, to be opposed to everything that already exists. He must invent a law to satisfy his own needs, and as soon as he has made one perfect application of it, he must destroy it, in order not to fall into repetition in the course of new works. To create is to make something spring from nothing [*Schaffen heisst: aus Nichts erzeugen*]."

With these words, Busoni was portraying all the great creators of our time. But how can one create something new if he respects stereotyped language? Busoni notes the exhaustion of the harmonic-polyphonic system. He says that inventive efforts must be bent on creating abstract sound and a technique which knows no tonal limitations. He sanctions the multiplication of modes by changing the intervals in our accepted scale. He is thinking of the superimposition of several modes, or polymodality, and of making these modes govern harmony as well as melody.

Some of Busoni's ideas were to be taken up by Schoenberg, and some by Hindemith. But his thinking was too Latin to be fully understood in Germany, and there is no doubt that on the whole the work of men like Stravinsky, Bartók, and Milhaud corresponds more completely to Busoni's ideal than does the work of Hindemith and Schoenberg.

Satie had had the courage and strength to break with tradition entirely and build a totally new work. In composing, Busoni was not so radical as the composer of *Parade*. Aside from audacious fragments in which he puts his views on polymodality into practice, all his works contain passages which are still firmly tied to the romantic traditions he wanted to throw off. As a result, his compositions, which at moments open interesting perspectives, are hybrid in character. But rarely do we find a homogeneous piece written with assurance. Thus, the four pieces of *Indianisches Tagebuch,* which appeared in 1915, would be very convincing if they were not sometimes injured by banal conclusions. The *Sonatinas for Piano,* in which the composer achieves complete freedom, are beautiful. *Sonatina No. III ad Usum Infantis* is particularly captivating in its fresh simplicity.

Busoni's ideal for the theater was Mozart's opera. He wrote two works under the inspiration of the *commedia dell' arte: Arlecchino,* for which he himself wrote the libretto, and *Turandot,* based on the work by Carlo Gozzi (1917). *Arlecchino* is a lively satire from which the composer excerpted the very fine *Rondo Arlecchinesco* for orchestra.

This comedy contains excellent pages, but there are others in which the character of the music is not sufficiently defined. *Turandot,* on the contrary, is an exquisite and very homogeneous score. Nearly all of its episodes have a winning charm.

Doktor Faust, one of Busoni's last works, was too ambitious for the composer's creative ability.

The new classicism which the composer of *Turandot* dreamed of was not brought into being by him. We have also seen that Schoenberg, Berg, and Webern, far from breaking with Wagner and romanticism, were to continue in, and even develop beyond, the tradition of *Tristan.* It was left to Paul Hindemith to make the definitive break with romanticism and establish the bases for a nonindividualistic German art.

This is what the critic Heinrich Strobel says about Hindemith:

He came from a family of Silesian artisans. He grew up away from those bourgeois milieux which alone, at the beginning of the century, possessed a musical culture. He did not receive a bourgeois education, and he was responsible for his own development through the unaided drive of his essentially musical nature. Long before he entered the Conservatory, he played in movie houses, operetta theaters, jazz groups, and later in the symphony orchestra. He grew up playing the violin, and was a virtuoso at the age of thirteen. At twenty he was the *Konzertmeister* of the Frankfurt opera. His first childhood impressions were received in circles where music was practiced as a profession. And when he began to compose, he did it quite naturally with an eye to practical execution. He wrote music destined for immediate use, for friends, for himself, for small groups, for music festivals. Indeed, he was surprisingly productive, and yet no work appeared which had not been asked for or commissioned.

This method of working was opposed to that of romanticism. The resulting music was composed for a given purpose, instead of being a subjective confession. And this music "for use" (*Gebrauchsmusik*) presupposes musical craftsmanship. The joy of expression involved the joy of technical mastery. Henceforth only strict construction could be allowed, determined by the elements or the materials used. And quite naturally, Hindemith turned to the style that provides the richest development of the potentialities of musical craftsmanship—polyphony.

PAUL HINDEMITH's fecundity is equaled at present only by Darius Milhaud. By 1940 he had written about a hundred works. His production, like Milhaud's, is torrential, and his intelligent curiosity has led him to examine all genres. But while the French composer's gift is lyrical, the German's interest lies in the constructive element. And while Milhaud was individualistic from the outset, Hindemith found it more difficult to be so, enmeshed as he was in the heavy tradition of the nineteenth century.

Wanting to break with the chromaticism of Wagner and Strauss and rediscover pure music, Hindemith took as his remote point of departure Brahms, with whom he is connected by the intermediate link of Reger.

The period of liberation encompasses his first twenty-five works (from about 1915 to 1923), most of which are heavy and complex. *Kleine Kammermusik,* for wind instruments, Op. 24, No. 2, was his first really personal composition. It was followed in 1923 by *Das Marienleben,* a song-cycle based on poems by Rainer Maria Rilke, which is one of his most beautiful works. From 1924 on, Hindemith displayed full technical mastery. The joy of craftsmanship inspired him to compose a series of brilliant works, written with remarkable skill but rather often lacking in interior life, a fact that does not seem to disturb the author.

This is the period of the *Kammermusik,* Op. 36, the opera *Cardillac,* Op. 39, and music for mechanical instruments. In the music of this period, intelligence predominated and the concept of *musical play* triumphed, sometimes drawing the composer into polyphonic excess. Logically, the attention Hindemith gave to questions concerning the execution of music led him to write exercises. He began to take an interest in amateurs, in musical circles, in that German people who love music not only to listen to but also to play and sing. Hindemith undertook an enormous enterprise for popular culture. His Opuses 43, 44, and 45 (1926–1928) are evidence of his concern. He wrote instrumental and vocal music for amateurs. This work had important and fortunate consequences, for it led him to more simple writing and oriented him toward a more melodic and open art. His contact with the people developed his sensitivity, and made him understand that music is a play of forms only from one point of view, and that it must also have an inner spirit.

Hindemith rounded out his artistic viewpoint, and began to write his most significant works: the *Concerto for Piano, Brass, and Two Harps*, Op. 49; the comic opera *Neues vom Tage* (1929); the *Lehrstück* (1929); the *Choruses for Men's Voices* (1930); the *Mathis der Maler* (1934); *Der Schwanendreher*, for viola and chamber orchestra (1935); and the ballet symphony *St. Francis* (1938).

The first works are still offshoots of the chromaticism of *Tristan*. Hindemith realized that if he went beyond *Tristan* and discarded the dominant cadence, he would suppress the action of the leading tone (*Leitton*) and would free the forces which were polarized by the tonal principle. Two ways were open to him: that of adopting atonality, a choice Hindemith did not follow, or that of establishing a chain of chords not directed by the attraction of a leading tone. The latter offered the possibility of giving music a new harmonic meaning. With *Marienleben*, Hindemith set up a harmonic system based on the acoustic properties of complex chords (chords of five, six, seven, or more sounds), and on the degree of tension a chord possesses, not in relation to a tonic but in itself, and tending to create progressive harmonic tensions and releases in the succession of chords of greater and greater or less and less tension in themselves. Presently we will see what this harmonic system consists of. It is already apparent that this harmony, freed from the restriction of tonal relationships, allows the melody to develop in the scale of twelve tones. In this harmony, the activating principle is the gradation of internal tensions; likewise, Hindemith gives the twelve-note melody motor force (which diatonic melody has in the tonal relations of its elements) by infusing it with rhythmic energy.

Two consequences derive from these two bases. The inner tension of the chords varies according to the intensity given each note. To achieve a specific tension, the intensity of each note must be carefully measured. This explains Hindemith's preference for a chamber orchestra with solo instruments as opposed to the massive effects of a grand orchestra. Stravinsky, Milhaud, Bartók, and Schoenberg draw the same conclusion: the more complex the harmony, the clearer it must be, and the sonorous weight must be such that it is regulated automatically by instrumental arrangement. The second consequence is that in his need for rhythmic energy in the melody, Hindemith was to turn away from dramatic recitative, inherited from German lyric drama, and turn toward rhythmic articulation of popular songs. The rhythmic arrangement of the song, moreover, is similar to that of the dances to which Stravinsky returns [*Example 117*].

To insure clarity, further, and to justify the juxtaposition of chords which are sometimes very remote on the tonal level, vertical superimpositions of notes often appear as melodically required. To say it in another way, they are induced by the counterpoint. Lastly, deciding that the ear can only clearly distinguish two or three melodic lines simultaneously, Hindemith, like Bach, gives preference to counterpoint with two real parts and to a canonic liaison of the two lines.

All the opacity of the massive effects of romantic music disappears, and a transparency, a limpidity prevails that allows the ear to grasp the inner relations of the chords immediately and to hear their succession.

With *Marienleben*, Hindemith had thrown off all trace of romantic influence. He began to write purely polyphonic music. He wrote *Marienleben* in three voices. In the melody he discarded chromaticism in order to orient it, instead, toward a modal diatonism. *Marienleben* shows the determining role of intervals of seconds and fourths [*Example 118*], by which tonal determinations are avoided. Another marked trait of Hindemith's style appears in this composition: his melodic curves are not pure melodies. They have a thematic function. Although they are strongly defined, they gain full stature only through polyphonic or harmonic commentary, and the discourse unfolds through the work of motifs which constitute the themes. This recalls baroque technique, modernized by the emancipation of tonality [*Example 119*].

Polyphony, thematicism, and the use of motifs—hereafter,

Hindemith makes use of old forms: variations, passacaglias, bassi ostinati.

If the worth of *Marienleben* lay only in its splendid style and the unity of its conception and form, this cycle would be an impressive work. But along with these exceptional qualities, it is remarkable for great richness of invention, nobility of sentiment, and delicacy of taste. The music represents a peak not only in Hindemith's work but in all contemporary art as well. While many of the composer's works are dynamic, this one is contemplative, and shows concentration of thought and emotion in a calm, recollected atmosphere the equal of which it would be impossible to find. In 1948 he published a definitive version of *Marienleben* in which certain complications, which had weighed down the polyphony or obscured its clarity, have been eliminated.

After *Marienleben,* Hindemith spent some time working with instrumental music, especially in the form of the concerto, with or without solo instruments.

In his study devoted to Hindemith, Heinrich Strobel expresses some sound opinions concerning the concerto type as the composer sees it. In substance, he says:

The concerto has become the type of composition through which Hindemith best expresses his dual ideal of polyphony and dynamic force. It is at the opposite extreme from the sonata. The latter is based on the duality of two themes that provoke thematic conflicts and consequently create tensions in the development of the music. The concerto calls for unopposed allocation of the elements of the musical play—no conflict, no tension. A single theme is needed to unify the material. And if there are several themes, they are chosen from the same schematic type, and have the same import. The nineteenth century erred, according to Hindemith, in degrading the concerto by reducing it to an exercise in uncontrolled virtuosity, and by disfiguring it with the introduction of symphonic tensions.

Hindemith utilizes all the possibilities of solo playing for his concertos. But even where figuration is richest and most detailed, it is always incorporated in the thematic organism and is always part of the polyphonic play.

The concertos for piano and cello in the *Kammermusik* series, Op. 36, must be considered as preparatory works. The violin and viola concertos are more mature. In this series, all the instruments of the orchestra are soloists, and the music is truly in *stilo concertante* for all the parts. This conception is most beautifully applied in the *Concerto for Piano, Brass, and Two Harps,* Op. 49, and *Der Schwanendreher,* written in 1935.

The *Concerto for Orchestra,* Op. 38, does not follow suit. This piece, as well as compositions like *Concerto for Strings and Brass,* Op. 50, or the *Philharmonic Concerto (Variations for Orchestras),* written in 1932, allow some groups to play in concert, thus taking the role of the concertino in the old concerto grosso; but the orchestra as a whole is limited to filling the needs of the movement while avoiding symphonic tension. This arrangement of the orchestra and the spirit which it reflects suit the requirements of opera as Hindemith conceives it. His idea of musical theater is like Busoni's, in that it is opposed to Wagnerian musical drama and the subordination of musical construction to the phrase-by-phrase development of the text. Music must have an autonomous structure. Richard Strauss felt that need in *Der Rosenkavalier,* and partially fulfilled it in *Ariadne auf Naxos.* Busoni had been more radical, in a Mozartian sense, in his *Arlecchino.* Nonetheless, although he was successful in that light comedy, he failed in the task of expressing the dramatic power of his *Doktor Faust.*

Hindemith's first opera was *Cardillac,* a very lively play, whose drama is actually rather superficial. He takes Handelian opera as his model because of its solid architecture, and because each scene is a musical body of homogeneous structure. His second model is Verdi, who adds to this organic quality the feeling for broadly conceived melody. The abduction scene in *Rigoletto* is an example of dramatic action through the contrast of the sonorous material of successive scenes, each scene being treated, moreover, as an autonomous and cohesive unit. We might also recall the scene of the council chamber in *Simone Boccanegra,* and certainly that conclusive demonstration which is *Falstaff.*

Hindemith now had at his command the orchestral strength and substance of his concertos to approach opera music, and he applied the principles of his compositional methods to *Cardillac.* He was not completely successful. Actually, the music is too dense for the theater. Polyphonic style, excellent for a concert, is too rich for an opera which lasts a whole evening. The listener tires under the strain of so much spiritual tension.

The lesson did not go unheeded. *Cardillac,* written in 1926, was followed in 1929 by *Neues vom Tage,* that marvelous vaudeville which provided many an entertaining evening at the Kroll Oper in Berlin. This great musical comedy, written on a libretto by Marcellus Schiffer, full of fancy and unbelievable buffoonery, amused the Germans enormously, and the memory of its success is interwoven with the memory of those few peaceful years Germany had before the advent of the Third Reich. This work translates somewhat feverishly the desire for unfettered gaiety and the need for carefree laughter of a people whose life rarely provided time for entertainment. The performances of *Neues vom Tage* marked a fleeting moment of respite for the intellectual world of Berlin.

Hindemith's score is perfect. The music relinquishes none of its rights, but is exquisitely transparent. All excesses are avoided with grace, and the voices stand out easily above a polyphony that develops with a filmy lightness achieved without sacrificing the solidity of the whole cloth. The music is an uninterrupted flow, like clear running water. The fantasia is lively and varied, but never overdone. It is channeled into such a precise ensemble of forms that it can be reduced to a schema. As an example, here is the musical outline of the first act:

SCENE 1: A B A form.
Interludes on A and B motifs.
SCENE 2: Scherzo; trio ending on a pedal.
Interlude on the trio.
SCENE 3: A B A form.
Interlude, divertissement on A of Scene 3.
SCENE 4: A B C D A: introduction, air, duo, air, re-exposition of the introduction.

After this luminous fantasia, it remained for Hindemith to adapt this free and supple language to a serious dramatic piece. The result was *Mathis der Maler* (1934). The opera, for which Hindemith himself wrote the text, was produced at the Zurich Stadttheater, in 1938. The idea for the opera came to Hindemith from Matthias Grünewald's work, the Colmar altarpiece. It is a musical commentary on both the famous triptych and the drama of the relationship between the artist and the people in the religious struggle which set Lutherans and Catholics in opposite camps in the period of the Peasants' War.

Hindemith's artistic expression in this score attains radiant beauty. Everything learned from previous works is utilized here. Just as *Christophe Colomb* represents the sum of Milhaud's art, so *Mathis der Maler* contains the most precious stones that Hindemith has mined, one by one.

Hindemith had now taken the final step. He had converted the melodic themes of *Marienleben* into true melodies, which made the curve of the lines more powerful and intensified the inner life of his ideas. This last achievement was not effected in a single stroke. It was the result of the extensive labor Hindemith devoted to the relationship between the public and music. He had gained true melodic feeling in writing *Frau Musika* and *Ein Reiter aus Kurpfaltz* and in probing the real sources of old German folk airs in the aim of re-educating the people. His research, moreover, provided the inspiration for simple and vigorous works like *Lehrstück* and *Plöner Musiktag*.

In rediscovering the spirit and secret of German Renaissance and baroque art and adapting them to current trends, Hindemith should be considered the most thoroughly and authentically German artist of all. If there is a modern artist in harmony with the genius of his people, it is indeed the composer of *Mathis der Maler*. The whole of the opera is as yet little known. But the symphony Hindemith drew from it includes many of the most beautiful passages of that admirable score: the *Concert of the Angels* and the *Death of Mathis* are unquestionably summits of contemporary art.

Not satisfied with having written so many remarkable works and having given so much of himself to popular musical culture, Hindemith took the trouble to set down his views on music in the two-volume work *Unterweisung im Tonsatz (The Craft of Musical Composition)*, published in 1937 and 1939. The essential section of the book is an exposition of his concept of harmony. His is probably the only explanation which today has a solid scientific and objective basis, and it is applicable to almost all music—that of the Middle Ages as well as Schoenberg's, modal music as well as tonal or the music called atonal.

Hindemith sets forth what in his opinion are the fundamental characteristics of composition as they are determined by the nature and constitution of sounds. Consequently, they are universally valid because they are free of all considerations foreign to the nature of sound and the physiological conditions of its reception by the ear. This precise definition is, moreover, the only one we need retain if we want to know what was meant by *neue Sachlichkeit* in German music of the period 1920-1934.

The author's point of departure is natural resonance. Natural overtones through the sixth constitute the perfect chord, which is in a state of physiological balance. Let us note in passing that the ear is the only sensory organ which perceives quantitatively. It measures precisely the relations of wave-lengths. The seventh overtone (B♭, starting from C) is not included in this chord. The placement of that note in our musical scale is higher than that of the natural overtone. This explains why the dominant seventh chord is not consonant.

To obtain a physically pure scale, the chromatic scale must be built from the first six overtones alone. If this is done, only one flaw will be found in that ultratempered scale—the F♯ and G♭ will still have a difference of one vibration per second. There is no need to make a study of divisions smaller than the half-tone. The chromatic scale is natural because it only includes natural overtones.

The harmonic system of the eighteenth and nineteenth centuries derives from the use of the major scale and its relative minor. The actual state of harmony today can no longer be explained by this system. On the contrary, the adoption of the chromatic scale is sufficient to explain all types of chordal agglomerations.

Tones are always related to a fundamental, or root, and it is impossible to conceive of sonorous aggregates which do not take the degree of relationship of the sounds into consideration. (Here Hindemith's viewpoint is contrary to Schoenberg's.) These degrees of relationship are in the very order in which the series of twelve tones rises from natural resonance. It would be helpful to refer to the order in which they appear at the bottom of the table on page 64 of *Unterweisung*, the degrees of relationship being more and more remote the farther the sounds are to the right in this list which the author calls *Series 1 [Example 120]*.

Aside from these degrees of relationship, there is another phenomenon we should take into account—the *combination tones* which occur spontaneously when two tones are sounded simultaneously. For example, if a fifth is played (C-G), the C does not, according to natural resonance, produce the G immediately above it. But the G does produce the C as a lower harmonic, which doubles the C actually sounded. This C thus acquires a sonorous weight physically superior to that of the G. It will predominate, and will be the root of the fifth.

In the same way, it can be shown that in a fourth, the higher note acquires greater weight by doubling, and will be the root. (These acoustic observations, by the way, explain the *invertibility of intervals*.)

The octave has no dominant note, the resonance of one doubling the other. Since the two notes are the same, there is therefore no need to choose a root. Finally, the tritone has no root because neither of the two tones is reinforced by natural resonance. This gives rise to *Series 2*, as it is shown in *Example 121*. (The arrows indicate the notes which are reinforced, and which are thus the roots.)

Let us also say that in each pair of intervals the first is more sonorous, because it benefits from being doubled by the most intense combination tone, the intensity being the function of the remoteness from the natural overtone which doubles the note actually sounded.

This explanation is scientifically exact for all pairs of intervals except the combination minor third-major sixth, treated by analogy.

The result is that of all chords the perfect major chord is the most sonorous, because it is the most strongly doubled by combination tones. We can see the importance of these observations. If a chord of more than four notes contains the notes of a perfect chord, the latter will predominate physically and will be more acutely perceived physiologically. As a result, it will determine the tonality of the chord, the root to which it is referred.

Tritones, with their combination tones, always give rise to sevenths. This is why they have a dominant effect.

Examining *Series 2* will not allow us to establish a natural distinction between consonance and dissonance. We pass from the octave, the perfect interval, to the major seventh, the least satisfying interval to the ear, by way of a progressive series. The notion of consonance and dissonance must thus be accepted as a relative value; one interval will be more or less consonant or dissonant than another. This is all we can say. As for the tritone, it is neither dissonant nor consonant. It falls outside the series of intervals by reason of its neutrality.

The facts established by *Series 1* and *2* provide a basis for propositions regarding a new harmonic system. The accepted concept of harmony is too narrow because:

1] The principle of the superimposition of thirds is inadequate. It does not furnish an explanation for chords composed of other intervals. To speak of unresolved appoggiaturas does not make sense; for an appoggiatura to exist, it must be resolved, and if it is not resolved, the chords are consistent in themselves.

2] The principle of the invertibility of chords is no longer admissible, without speaking of more complex chords. Most chords, and above all those which are not produced by superimposing thirds, are really not invertible.

3] In the old system, harmony could be enriched by the alteration of diatonic intervals. Now, all chords based on alterations can be found in all keys. The explanation by alterations marks the end of diatonism, and is actually already in the chromatic domain.

4] The significance of augmented or diminished chords is ambiguous. These chords are defined only in relation to those which precede or follow. If a justly tempered scale were used, these chords would disappear, and only major and minor chords would remain. All chords must be interpreted as the ear perceives them, hence, independently of the artifices of notation.

The bankruptcy of the old harmonic system thus had to be remedied by formulating new propositions for the definition of chords: the superimposition of thirds should no longer be considered as the point of departure; the principle of the invertibility of chords should be replaced by a broader principle; and what until now has been the ambiguous significance of certain chords should be done away with.

Hindemith made a concrete proposal: to create a hierarchy of chords based on the value of intervals (as established by *Series 2*) and measured by degrees of relationship to *Series 1,* thus holding in mind that the more to the right in *Series 1* a note occurs, the more remote it is from its root, and that the most determining intervals fall to the left in *Series 2,* and the least, to the right.

Thus, to find the root of a chord, the chord must be broken down into all the intervals it includes. The lower sound of the most determining interval is the root, in the case of a fifth, a third, or a seventh; if the most determining interval contained in the chord is a fourth, sixth, or second, the upper note of that interval is the root of the chord. And if the chord contains the same interval repeated several times, the lowest, therefore the one most doubled by lower overtones, becomes the most determining.

Every chord has a fundamental note and is subsidiary to a given key. The more or less exactly determined the key, the more or less power it has. All chords with a single root are therefore subject to a real hierarchy according to their own value. We will not show the author's elaboration of that hierarchy in detail here, but will only say that it can be divided into two large groups of chords: Group A, which contains no tritones; and Group B, which does, the first group being more determined than the second. Each group can be subdivided into three sections: 1] chords without seconds or sevenths; 2] chords with seconds and sevenths; and 3] chords whose significance is undetermined, resulting from superimpositions of the same interval or predominance of the tritone. In the six groups thus defined, the determination decreases in the order A_1, B_1, A_2, B_2, A_3, B_3.

This system has the advantage of including all chords without exception. There are therefore no chords foreign to the key, no appoggiaturas, and no suspensions. Hence, the art of chordal agglomerations in a given key consists of making the chords follow each other in a progressive augmentation or diminution of sonorous power, which is evoked by the greater or lesser tonal determination of each chord. This is the principle of *harmonisches Gefälle,* a difficult term to translate, "harmonic slope" or "harmonic efficacy" being only approximate renderings.

To summarize: "While the values of the whole of sonorous material (in the usual concept of harmony) are definable only in relation to a pre-established tonal framework, and harmony as a result has only relative values, we are building a system of absolute values. Between maximal and minimal sonorous values of intervals and chords, we recognize a great number of intermediary degrees, each unit of which preserves the same value under all circumstances." [20] Thus, the *harmonisches Gefälle* differs from traditional harmonic progression because only the absolute value of chords is taken into consideration, and not the relative values the classic concept of tonality attributes to them.

The *harmonisches Gefälle* takes into account the play of tensions, but does not show the direction the harmonic progression will take. The chord roots must be followed to find the direction of that progression. (As we have seen, the root is not always the lowest note of the chord; we are therefore not dealing with the principle of the figured bass.)

Logically, the passage from one root to another should follow the degrees of relationship to *Series 1.* Hindemith calls this progression by degrees *Stufengang. Harmonisches Gefälle* and *Stufengang* therefore become the guiding principles of the harmonic scheme of a composition. The decisions to be made in this domain are guided by the melodic order and by the two-voice counterpoint, the *übergeordnete Zweistimmigkeit,* the primary basis for musical composition. A harmonic architecture such as this can understandably be used for extensive elaborations, thanks to the clarity of its articulations. The tonic issuing from a composition, finally, is the *Grundton,* the most forceful fundamental and the most often repeated.

The concept of tonality is singularly broadened in this way, and it is clear that Hindemith's tonal determinations make the concepts of atonality and polytonality impossible.

20. *Unterweisung im Tonsatz* (Mainz: Schott, 1937), I, 129.

It is remarkable that if works so disparate as medieval compositions, music from the classic period, and Schoenberg's works are analyzed according to Hindemith's method, modal, tonal, and so-called atonal compositions are all subject to the rules set forth by this method, which highlights the unity of musical thought regardless of age and aesthetics.

Series 1 and *2,* set forth by Hindemith as the basis of his harmonic structures, are in substance instruments for measuring tensions and weight. This brings us close to Stravinsky's sonorous weights and polar notes.

The new principle of tonality corresponds to facts which are largely true in music. But it calls forth certain reservations.

It seems to us that the *harmonisches Gefälle* and *Stufengang* are laws generally observed in *thematic* music. In such music, the themes do not exist independently. Polyphony and harmony carry the energy of the composition. In this case, scrupulous attention must be paid to harmonic development for it to be logical, and for the music to be understandable.

But there is another type of music, a type which is favored by modern Latin composers: *melodic* music, whose eloquence is almost exclusively the property of the melody. Harmony is subordinated to melody and is even often indefinite. This type of music does not always follow Hindemith's principles, and it need not do so, for the sturdiness of its structure is insured by the precision of the melodic curve.

Also, it is imprecise to say that polytonality cannot exist because the vertical cut in the musical cloth can be referred to a root. This may be true in harmonic polytonality, but certainly not in contrapuntal polytonality. When two melodies in different keys are superimposed, the ear can perceive the simultaneous occurrence of these two keys perfectly, if they are well defined and if the melodies are sufficiently diatonic.

As for atonality,[21] because each aggregation can be referred to a root by analysis, this is not sufficient reason to deny the existence of atonality. The tonal base must still be perceptible to the ear. This is not always possible, especially in the case of

21. In 1940 Hindemith wrote: "He who, in singing, above all with others or in a quartet, has tasted the subtle charm of harmonies purer than those allowed by the tempered scale will be convinced that atonal music, music which contradicts the principle of natural resonance, cannot exist."

rapid succession of very complex tonal combinations, for the ear will receive a clearly atonal auditory impression even if roots can be determined when analyzed on paper or when the piece is played slowly. Furthermore, good composers who write atonal or polytonal music always observe the order of natural resonance.

Taken in its entirety, *The Craft of Musical Composition* contains the most widely applicable propositions formulated in many years. It clarifies the meaning and exact place of its author's music. The collection of twelve fugues and twelve piano interludes published by Hindemith under the title *Ludus Tonalis* in 1944 illustrated his conception of harmony. Each fugue is in a specific key, but the notion of a major and minor has disappeared. The keys of the fugues follow each other according to the order of their relationship.[22] A number of symphonies and concertos mark Hindemith's sojourn in America. They add nothing to the glory of the composer, and are cast somewhat academically. His best works since 1940 are *The Four Temperaments,* an attractive suite for piano and string orchestra; a beautiful *Requiem* based on a text by Walt Whitman; and the symphony *Harmonie der Welt.*

Germany correctly recognized Paul Hindemith as its most authentic composer, and the Nazi Reich's repudiation of the composer was absurd. But before we discuss that event, we should turn our attention to other musicians who lived in Germany between 1920 and 1934.

Before the National Socialist Party came into power, Germany was a country in which theatrical activities had developed on a large scale. The multiplicity of lyric theaters and their degree of regional interdependence made it possible to stage new works—which were more warmly welcomed the more experimental they were—as much from the point of view of the play itself as from the point of view of its production.

This intense theatrical life gave renown to a number of composers whose success was rather widespread but ephemeral. Among them are two whose talent is worthy of discussion.

---

22. On the subject of acoustics and the physiology of hearing, see G. Van Esbroeck and Fr. Monfort, *Qu'est-ce que jouer juste?* (Brussels, 1946), and Stevens and Davis, *Hearing* (New York, 1943).

ERNST KŘENEK, the Austrian composer, produced his work in
Germany. An intelligent, cultivated, and sensitive artist, he was
interested in the Schoenbergian movement. He had great dramatic talent, and was perfectly schooled in musicianship. The
author of several operas, his general theme was the conflict of
two forces, the more tenacious of which would be victorious. His
first opera, *Die Zwingburg*, produced in 1923, drew wide notice.
It was followed by *Orphée* and *Vie d'Oreste*, in which mythology
is transposed into a modern world. But these transpositions have
something artificial and superficial about them which makes the
works rather unpalatable. The most considerable success Křenek
had was that of his jazz-opera, *Johnny Strikes Up*, in which the
world of mechanism and jazz is set against the world of Viennese
sentimentality. Its success in Germany was enormous, but in
foreign countries it failed completely. Even in Germany, when
its novelty had faded, the work was forgotten, because people
soon realized its mediocrity. In 1933, Křenek produced *Karl V*,
a severe and not uninteresting work but one which used the
language of Alban Berg rather less than well. Nothing has
survived of Křenek's numerous orchestral works and chamber
music, except perhaps the agreeable *Concertino for Flute,
Harpsichord, and Orchestra* and a collection of pretty songs,
Reisebuch aus den Oesterreichischen Alpen. These two works
show a tendency Křenek should have pursued, namely, a continuation of the paths Schubert had followed. The memory of his
Johnny alone remains, an example of the hubbub that could
be made in Germany over a theatrical event which, although of
no interest in itself, might provoke endless controversy because
of its pseudo-modernist tendencies. In 1946, Křenek composed
the beautiful *Symphonic Elegy* in memory of Anton Webern.
This piece gives us hope that this curious and sometimes contradictory talent will produce other interesting works.

The success of KURT WEILL, composer of *The Threepenny Opera*
and *Mahagonny*, had more meaningful causes.
   There was enough material in Germany to satisfy enthusiasts
of serious music: they had Hindemith on the one hand and
Schoenberg on the other. But neither of these touched the masses

of the people. The German people are music-minded. In Germany, Beethoven and Wagner are played in restaurants and bars. The moderns had no contact with the people. Hindemith was concerned about this state of affairs, and took a decisive step. He wrote music of quality which could be easily understood and performed. In so doing, he reached, influenced, and was responsible for the formation of numerous groups of amateurs. But unfortunately, this *Gebrauchsmusik* was too lofty for the general public. Kurt Weill, treating subjects less elevated than *Frau Musika,* was able to attract large circles of listeners. He wrote skillfully, but he wrote in a way that appealed to the most uninformed tastes. His music is vulgar, but because of certain details of composition, lively orchestration and proper accentuation, it elevates otherwise rather disagreeable musical material.

In choosing John Gay's famous *Beggar's Opera* as the subject for a modernized version entitled *The Threepenny Opera,* the librettist Bertolt Brecht (who also wrote the text for Hindemith's *Lehrstück*) sought to democratize the theater. Opera was stereotyped: the subjects treated in this art form were far removed from the interests of the people. What was needed was a proletarian theater. The magnificent *Beggar's Opera* was excellent material for an effort of this sort. This violent play, crude, bitter, powerful and splendid, dealing with thieves and the underworld, was very successfully produced at the Kroll Oper. Kurt Weill wrote a series of fiery and nostalgic songs for the opera which suited the atmosphere of the play to perfection and which gained immediate popularity. The dramatic impact of the organ-player's lament, *Mack the Knife,* or the *Kanonengesang* cannot be denied. But the music must be viewed in the framework of the performances for which it was intended. Taken alone, its poverty puts it on a level with the hackneyed music of café concerts. Aside from this reservation about the intrinsic value of the music in *The Threepenny Opera,* the staging of this epic play, its production, and the suitableness of the music to the setting make the work a stunning spectacle.

Aufstieg und Fall der Stadt Mahagonny by the same authors (1930) was an interesting production, but it did not have the power of *The Threepenny Opera.* The form adopted for it is that of the chronicle, schematically illustrating the mores and social drama of the twentieth century. The music is not in the vein of *The Threepenny Opera*. Nonetheless, *Mahagonny* was taken very seriously, because at that time everything that had to do with social questions caught the public's ear in Germany. Anything that sang of despair, anything bitter or disenchanted gratified the taste of a people who at the limit of their strength would soon submit passively to tyranny.

Things had reached the point where public opinion no longer judged a work of art by estimating its real value. It was concerned only with intention and trend, and sensitive only to what stated—badly or well—its fatigue and disgust. In *Johnny Strikes Up* and Weill's music there was a sort of lethargy (not just a *likeness* of lethargy) that partially explains certain reactions whose effects would be felt with the advent of Nazi dictatorship.

The Moravian ALOIS HÁBA (born in 1893) also participated in the musical life of Germany. His ideas and works drew considerable public attention between 1920 and 1930. Hába advocated a reasonable use of the quarter-tone and also thought of the third and sixth of a tone as usable intervals. He claimed that certain complex chords are clearer and more sonorous with the use of these small intervals, which is justified in part since natural harmonics, from the seventh on, no longer coincide with the notes of the tempered scale. It is also true that quarter-tones introduced into music for string instruments, as well as in vocal music, produce delicate and often agreeable effects. Hába wrote his first quartet in the system of quarter-tones in 1921. He not only dreamed of achieving a harmony more truly in conformity with natural resonance, but he went further. In opposition to the existence of a harmony based on degrees of relationship between notes, he established the possibility of a harmony based on the absence of relationship between notes, thus thinking in terms of an absolutely new world of sound.

Unfortunately, his works themselves, although intelligently constructed, did not contain sufficient—or, above all, sufficiently specific—inner life to prove the need for this new world of sound. But it would be incorrect to conclude that Hába's ideas should be passed over. Certain passages in his more recent compositions, and notably his opera *Die Mutter* in 1931, unveil perspectives which indicate that Hába's theories might be fertile. Hába not only introduces intervals smaller than the semitone (which is a normal practice in oriental music), but has also set himself to writing athematic music. The Dutch, he maintains, formed our musical world. After Dunstable were Dufay, Okeghem, and Josquin des Prés, who outlined and circumscribed our sonorous domain in creating polyphony based on imitation. From the standpoint of form, after Josquin des Prés everything had been said and done, and music from that time until and including Schoenberg has been an outgrowth and development of the Dutch polyphonists—Schoenberg crowning the monumental edifice of our Western art by achieving absolute mastery in working with the twelve semitones. To go further, aside from mastering smaller intervals, one would have to create music which no longer proceeded by imitation. An art form has been established in which invention is reduced to the creation of a thematic cell. Development is entirely arithmetical and technical. A type of music was needed in which melodic invention would be sustained from the first to the last note, and in which polyphony would be engendered not by an idea and its imitation but by the superimposition of radically different ideas.

The problem is whether this creative flow is really possible and, if so, whether a listener would be able to follow and grasp the movement.

These are difficult questions, and these theories which in themselves are not lacking in logic or truth need to be organized and illustrated in convincing works. To quote Hába:

Compared with the thematic method, which offers the composer numerous technical devices (repetitions, transpositions, inversions, variations) for economizing on invention, and which puts the elements of construction to work and thus makes the composition of great musical forms possible, the athematic method is the most difficult imaginable, lacking as it is in all these auxiliary techniques. In using this method, invention is needed as much as is music. Or, conversely, music appears only where there is invention, and there is no technique of composition except where there are musical ideas. On the contrary, in the thematic method, creation plays a minimal role, while illustration of an idea with technical devices is developed to the maximum. This has been the state of music in Europe since the fourteenth century. Anyone can test this fundamental difference between these two methods. He need simply think up a single-measure motif and repeat or transpose it six times; and then try to find six different single-measure motifs which can be so arranged as to form a melodic whole. The first method is a good deal easier than the second. In a polyphonic piece, the differences are much more apparent.[23]

Until now, only certain passages of the opera *Die Mutter* give any proof that Hába's ideal is not an impossible dream and that the perpetual exercise of invention, freed from the play of forms, might be the point of departure for a deeply expressive art form. The theory of making asymmetry and non-imitation predominate is, moreover, not new. It carries on in the line of Busoni's reflections on the absolute creative spirit.

For general interest, the orchestra ensemble for *Die Mutter* includes a double string quartet, a double-bass, two clarinets in quarter-tone, two trumpets in quarter-tone (equipped with a fourth valve), two slide trombones, a piano in quarter-tone (two keyboards, one of which is tuned a quarter-tone higher than the other), a harmonium in quarter-tone, two harps (one of which is tuned a quarter-tone higher than the other), and percussion.

There was once a Piscator theater in Berlin, the Kroll Oper, where *Neues vom Tage, The Threepenny Opera,* or Leoš Janáček's last opera were performed; there was a time when the Unter den Linden Opera House produced Milhaud's *Christophe Colomb,* when Hába's *Die Mutter* was staged in Munich, and when all the theaters in Germany played Alban Berg's *Wozzeck.*

23. "*Im Vergleich mit dem thematischen Musikstil, der den Komponisten viele technische Hilfsmittel (Wiederholung, Transposition, Umkehrung, Variation) zur Schonung der Erfindungs—und Gestaltungskräfte bietet und das Schaffen grosser Musikformen dadurch fordert, ist der unthematische Musikstil der denkbar unbequemste Stil, ohne alle technischen Förderungsmittel. Es muss in diesem Stil soviel primäre Erfindung da sein, wieviel Musik man haben will, oder umgekehrt, es ist nur soviel Musik da, wieviel primäre Erfindung da ist: Und es ist nur soviel Kompositionstechnik da, wieviel musikalische Gedanken da sind. Dagegen repräsentieren die musikalischen Gedanken im thematischen Stil das Minimum und ihre technische Verwertung das Maximum. Das Intellektuelle hat Oberhand über das Erfinderische. Es ist in der europäischen Musik seit dem 14. Jahrhundert so. Diese grundsätzlichen Stilunterschiede kann jeder selbst erproben, wenn er z. B. ein eintaktiges Motiv erfindet und es sechsmal wiederholt, oder transponiert und dagegen dann versucht, sechs neue eintaktige Motive nacheinander so zu erfinden, dass sie eine sechstaktige melodische Einheit bilden. Der erste Vorgang ist bedeutend leichter als der zweite unthematische. Im polyphonen Satz sind die Unterschiede noch grösser.*" (Anbruch, XIII/4.)

In 1934, the intellectual life and the corresponding intense musical vitality were swept away by National Socialist dictatorship. Overnight, modern art lost its freedom. Stravinsky, Hindemith, Schoenberg, Milhaud, Berg, and Bartók were banished or silenced, some because they were Jewish, others because their art "did not suit the German people" and reflected a "*kulturbolschewistisch*" aesthetic.

Actually, the people did not take part in aesthetic quarrels. The moralists and art theorists of the new Reich camouflaged an offensive, led by a mass of mediocre musicians, against men of value, with high-sounding objective phrases. Under the wing of Nazism, mediocre artists campaigned to win stature and obtain positions in conservatories, theaters, and concert societies. The most purely German of the composers, Paul Hindemith, was accused of Bolshevism and left Germany.

A torrent of absurdities was spouted by newspapers and the radio. The tritest slogans and the most obvious errors were broadcast with a voice of categoric authority that brooked no retort under pain of a sojourn in a concentration camp. Without describing in detail the campaign of false propaganda which was to reach a climax during World War II, we will set down a number of catchwords as they were hawked by one of the spokesmen authorized by the Hitler regime. In an exposition on "The Current Situation of German Music," Fritz Stege wrote in 1938:

The life of music in Germany today is difficult to understand unless it is considered from the viewpoint formed by combining and unifying the three concepts *people, State, art.* For a State without its people or a people without their art are as inconceivable as an art existing for itself alone and unable to rise to expressing the thought of the people. For is not the State, which incorporates the will of a people, their emotions and interests, an organism whose harmonious composition unites with the work of art? . . .

This State which incorporates the will of a people, by cremation and vivisection, by extermination of all opposition—this state-work-of-art—we will not dignify with a discussion of its empty phraseology. Instead, let us continue with this edifying lecture:

An intellectual and spiritual reaction necessarily followed the postwar period in the domain of art, for all exaggeration leads inevitably to an aesthetic reaction. It would be entirely false to say that this reaction was brought about by violence [!]; no, it was enough to open the eyes of the people, it was enough to point out the errors that had enslaved them. If Negro jazz is defended, if the enemies of the people compose intellectual music devoid of soul and heart, without finding an audience in Germany, these decisions are not arbitrary. . . . What would have happened if the aesthetic evolution of German music had continued in the direction of the postwar years? The people would have lost all contact with art. They would have become spiritually rootless, the more so as they found less and less satisfaction in a degenerate and intellectual music better for reading than for listening. The abyss between the people and art was becoming unbridgeable. The theaters and concert halls would have remained empty, and the composers, who were working in a direction opposed to the soul of the people, would have ended with only themselves for an audience, provided, of course, that they were still able to understand their own lucubrations. . . .

Finally, a little sincerity shines through:

Germany can take pride in the fact that she stands among the most musical nations. The number of harmonica and accordion players, harmonica ensembles, groups of guitar players, amateurs and enthusiasts of orchestral and especially choral music can be counted in the hundreds of thousands.

This is true. In this the restrictions placed on musical activity under the Nazi regime are exactly like those imposed in Soviet Russia. And here we find the accordion as the symbol of musical taste of the high priests presiding over the artistic destiny of great peoples.

Obviously, to force music to stoop to the level of the accordion, one must have "an organization that guides the movement with a sure hand." This was the Reichsmusikkammer, to which all musicians, including amateurs, belonged. This music council, under the direction of Professor Doktor Peter Raabe, had the cultural responsibility of "official music," which was the only music left, of course. Finally, let us turn admiring eyes on this masterpiece of insidious perfidy:

Let us not compare this council with a judicial authority which would dictate to art with prohibitions and condemnations. It gives art free rein, but supervises the way in which artistic production is handled.

We will pass over the horrors these honeyed words cover—they are only too well known—and see the results.

After Hindemith's departure, and after silence had been imposed on modern art, new composers sprang up to whom the Reich gave complete freedom in execution, state publicity, and public honors.

WERNER EGK became in a way the official musician of the Third Reich. In 1935 *Die Zaubergeige* appeared, an opera conceived in exemplary bad taste. A series of Tyrolean airs and rosalias lead music that caters to the lowest public desires—platitude and vulgarity. Egk was not, however, totally lacking in talent. *Natur, Liebe und Tod* (1937), a cantata for bass voice and solo instruments, has a true lyric value similar to that which characterizes the music of the Frenchman Henri Sauguet. It can be said that since 1944 Egk has found in freedom sincere and undeniable qualities.

The opera *Peer Gynt* of 1938 is superior to *Die Zaubergeige*. But the listener feels neither the dramatist's nor the musician's touch. The opera is simply a good libretto with facile music adapted to it. It is totally undemanding. Everything in this score is superficial. The harmonic language is French, but heterogeneous, and ends in cadences of wearisome banality. Imagine a compromise between Massenet and the music of a Bavarian tavern, and you will have an idea of the atmosphere of *Peer Gynt*.

In 1940, Egk wrote a ballet with choruses, *Johann von Zarissa*, with which the Germans hoped to delight Parisians. The performances at the Paris Opera were a failure because of the indifference of the public. Compared with previous scores, the ballet had greater distinction. It was graced with a rhythmic clarity that seemed French and prestos which (I shudder to say) were thought to reflect Auric or Milhaud. But the melodic inventions were indeed feeble, as was the harmony which, hesitantly, followed Poulenc's from afar.

Here, then, was the official German composer, completely dependent on French music. This was what was called "being in harmony with the soul of the German people."

Other young composers, like Cesar Bresgen, turned their attention to old German songs and treated them as did Hindemith, but in a naive and rudimentary way. The master exiled, the apprentice is welcomed.

Despite everything, there were musicians who, although not officially protegés, were nonetheless not "cast out of the heart of the country," and who had more talent and taste than did Werner Egk.

HERMANN REUTTER attracted notice around 1933 with an oratorio for solo voices, choruses, children's choruses, orchestra and organ, *Der grosse Kalender.* The composer had thrown off all the pretentiousness of romanticism. He was more interested in melody than theme, and seemed to have rediscovered folk feeling, in the best sense of the words. The oratorio has passages of lovely freshness. Unfortunately, with the change of regime came the pursuit of mediocrity. Reutter's *Doktor Johannes Faust,* written in 1936, had not even the honest simplicity of *Der grosse Kalender,* and rivaled Werner Egk's operas for honors in vulgarity. The *Odysseus* of 1942 is more serious. But as with all German music since 1934, it has absolutely no individual character. Fear of individuality was so intense that composers did not dare modulate, for passing from one key to another would lead to chromaticism and personal expression. This was the extreme to which the servile attitude of composers who had adopted the Nazi regime had led. The true decadent music of the twentieth century is of their making.

The only interesting figure among young German musicians who continued to work under the Nazi regime is CARL ORFF. This intelligent artist holds a place apart. He owes nothing to either romanticism or Hindemith. In his three remarkable scenic works, *Carmina Burana* (1936), *Der Mond* (1939), and *Catulli Carmina* (1943), Orff utilizes the primary active forces of the world of sound. He uses musical elements in their virgin state, calling on their physiological and magical effect, and not allowing a preoccupation with construction to come between the music and the receiving ear. Here is a language incorporating persistent rhythms, pure sonorities, untiring repetitions, and rhythmic psalmody. Orff works with pure melody, melody existing with its own life independently of harmonic support, and consequently seeks diversity in his use of keys and choice of scales. Like Stravinsky, he limits tonality to the attraction toward a polar note.

Each of Carl Orff's works was brought into being with special regard for style in the choice of melodies. The ballet-opera *Carmina Burana* is a tableau of the Middle Ages based on poems discovered in the Abbey of Beuron. The rhythmic strength and choral power of the score are incontestable. The work can be criticized for the obvious influence of Stravinsky. *Der Mond* is likewise a work for voices, a sort of small *Welttheater* with charming text. The score reflects German folk and peasant art, but it is less eloquent than *Carmina Burana*.

Orff's most unusual work is *Catulli Carmina,* a ballet with music based on love poems by Catullus, sung in Latin. The exterior wings, where the chorus is supported by four pianos and percussion as in Stravinsky's *Noces,* frame a series of scenes sung *a cappella* in modal style, sometimes in unison and sometimes in a succession of perfect chords which fill the ear with consonant sound in a steady but pulsing rhythm. From time to time a dissonance is struck which, because it appears so suddenly and unexpectedly, causes a moment of violent tension. In the progression of the bass voices, Milhaud's influence is noticeable. *Catulli Carmina* is in the trend toward contact with the people, and is an exaggeratedly sensual work.

The musical politics of the Third Reich ended by distinctly lowering the quality of works produced. This was foreseeable, for art demands absolute freedom of movement. The Reich authorized the publication of music of secondary importance, whose origins can be found in Stravinsky, Hindemith, and Milhaud. All the ideas on which Nazi politics of music were based proved unworkable.

It should be noted that during the Nazi dictatorship young independent German composers probably worked in silence.

One of them had already come into prominence: Karl Amadeus Hartmann, whose symphony *Miserae* drew notice in 1935. This composer was especially intent on writing of the sufferings of the German soul under the oppression of the dictatorial will that suppressed self-expression. Hartmann depicted this drama in his remarkable chamber-opera, *Des Simplicius Simplicissimus Jugend* (1935), a work which could not be performed until 1945. A severe and proud musician, he has composed six important symphonies since the end of the war. They are somewhat heavy but infused with a moving dramatic spirit.

Following in the tradition of Reger and Hindemith, and showing Schoenberg's influence to a greater or lesser degree, are the young Germans Bernd Alois Zimmermann and Hans Werner Henze. Two works by Henze have drawn public notice: *Boulevard Solitude* and *König Hirsch*.

Since 1948, the life of music in West Germany has taken on new vigor, thanks to the energetic activities of radio stations, which reserve an important part of their programing for current international works.

10

NATIONALISM AND ECLECTICISM

WE HAVE reviewed the outstanding events in contemporary music in Germany, Austria, France, and Russia. We have tried to throw light on the talent and work of some of the great composers. Generally speaking, these composers have followed traditions and developed or restated techniques established through the centuries. They have gone beyond individualism and particularism. We can no longer say that Schoenberg's music is German, Stravinsky's is Russian, or Milhaud's is French. Their music is the expression of various aspects of European thought. Nationalist feeling has disappeared.

There are other eminent composers in whom the nationalist outlook is still predominant. Some are citizens of countries in which musical culture has long been under the influence of neighboring cultures, while others come from countries where musical culture is still in formation.

Thus the Czechs, wanting to throw off Germanic tutelage, have given us, after Smetana and Dvořák, a composer like Leoš Janáček. The Hungarians, sandwiched between Germanic and Slavic peoples, are creating their own culture as well, with Béla Bartók and Zoltán Kodály forging that country's liberation. Spain, long dominated by Italian traditions, became progressively independent. Manuel de Falla is the successor of Felipe Pedrell and Isaac Albéniz.

In the Americas, composers expressed the need to throw off the traditions imported from Europe. Among them are William Grant Still in the United States, Heitor Villa-Lobos in Brazil, and Carlos Chávez in Mexico.

This movement toward independence is based on the study and application of folklore and the observation of indigenous music. This method was advocated in Europe in the nineteenth century, and is still applied by composers in Russia today. But there is a great difference in the way the nineteenth century regarded folklore and the way it is used by contemporary composers such as those we have just mentioned.

During the romantic period, folk songs were considered elements of local color. They were used as points of reference, but were deprived of organic function. In *Má Vlast*, Smetana bends popular songs to the rhythmic requirements of a music which, in itself, is not unusual in character, and resembles in structure numerous symphonic poems composed in other countries. Dvořák's *New World Symphony*, which draws on American folk songs, is in no way specifically American.

The generations following the pioneers of national independence have a different concept of folk music. They attempt to pick out what is authentic, what has remained pure. Their first task is to organize the body of folklore of their country in order to unveil the secrets of the specific sensitivity and expression of their race. They then set out to study melodic and rhythmic structures, accents and modes, and the peculiarities of a polyphony which, although often rudimentary, has nonetheless a marked character.

This absorption has often been confirmed by the composers themselves. When he was organizing the *cante jondo* competition in Granada in 1922, Manuel de Falla wrote:

Our aim has been not only to stimulate a renaissance of these admirable songs, but to purify them musically and elevate them morally. . . .

The song of the past, solemn and religious in nature, has degenerated into that ridiculous flamencoism of today in which the essential elements, those that comprise its glory and justify its claim to nobility, have been adulterated and modernized. Sober vocal modulation—the natural inflections of song developed by the division and subdivision of the notes of the scale—has been transformed into an ornamental and artificial motif, closer to the decadence of the bad period of Italian art than to the primitive oriental songs, which ours can be compared with only if they are pure. The limits of the reduced melodic intervals in which these songs unfold have been ineptly extended. The modal wealth of their ancient scales has been replaced by the tonal poverty that comes from preponderant use of the two unique modern scales, those scales which have monopolized European music for more than two centuries. Lastly, the phrasing, in an ungraceful meter, has lost the rhythmic flexibility that was one of its most beautiful traits.

Again, Felipe Pedrell writes in his *Cancionero Musical Español:* "The musical orientalism that persists in various Spanish folk songs is deeply rooted in our nation because of the influence of the ancient Byzantine civilization. This is reflected in the formulae of the rites used by the Spanish church from the conversion of our country to Christianity until the eleventh century, after which Roman liturgy properly speaking was introduced." The goal, then, was to rediscover ethnic characteristics in their pure state as means of natural expression, and to restore to music the richness and freedom that were lost as a result of the restrictions imposed by classical art. The latter is an aim common to all twentieth-century creative musicians, however different they may be in other respects.

In Spain, Pedrell was the precursor of the nationalist movement. Albéniz and De Falla were its most important agents. In Central Europe, the Czech Leoš Janáček was the first to test with exactness the scope of an extensive tapping of folk-art sources. He also found in folk music the means of freeing himself from major-minor duality, of escaping from tonality to regain modal and rhythmic suppleness. But the Hungarians Zoltán Kodály and Béla Bartók were the ones who refined the methods of investigating folk song, and Bartók was to pursue these investigations to their ultimate conclusions. De Falla's observations on the *cante jondo* are echoed in comments by Bartók on Balkan songs, Villa-Lobos on the songs of Brazilian Indians, and Chávez on Mexican song. The aim is the same everywhere: to establish characteristic expression, and to free musical language through the use of an ethnically pure inheritance.

Of all the precursors, LEOŠ JANÁČEK is the only one who was composing during the period we are interested in (Janáček died in 1928). His first important work, the opera *Jenufa,* was completed in 1903. The opera was a great and durable success in all the countries of Central Europe, but strangely enough, it is almost completely unknown in Western Europe. The music is both gracefully and vigorously animated. Melodies unroll rapidly with continuous movement. The music flows like water, avoids tonal certainty and leading notes which might determine it, and repeatedly takes flight in modal changes, in sudden and unprepared modulations. The progression of chords is perfectly free, and recognizes only laws of natural resonance as valid guides for directing interchordal relationships. There is just enough counterpoint in the music to create movement. But there is no elaboration at all. Janáček captured what was most valuable in folk song—its compactness, its spontaneity, its perpetual flow. *Katya Kabanova* (1921), less well known than *Jenufa*, has similar qualities. In 1923 Janáček finished *The Alert Fox*, a very peculiar piece, part fairy tale, part comedy, which abounds with rhythmic and orchestral gems, but whose too-complicated general plan destroys the unity of the music. In 1927 he wrote his last dramatic work, *The House of the Dead*, based on Dostoevsky's novel.

As he grew older, Janáček became more and more original and individualistic. *The House of the Dead* is more narrative than dramatic in character. It is a powerful, brutal work. The orchestra concentrates on the bass and high registers, leaving a kind of void in the middle section, a device which sometimes produces impressive effects. One of the works in which Janáček expresses himself the most fully is a great song-cycle, *Diary of One Who Vanished* (1916), based on a poem by an unknown author. It is the story of a young peasant who abandons all he holds dear—his parents, his farm, his country—to follow a gypsy who has captivated him. Written for tenor, three contraltos, and piano, it is very rich in invention, and transposes folk song to an idealized plane.

We should also mention the lovely, childlike songs, *Rikadla;* a remarkable series of choral works; and a fine quintet for wind instruments. The music of these pieces is strange and persuasive, and totally free. Its simplicity is the result of the deliberate and progressive discarding of inessentials. Equally personal and remote from stereotypes, and owing nothing to outside influence, is the *Sinfonietta*, for full orchestra (1926), which requires no less than twelve trumpets. Each of the five movements of this work is written with different orchestration. The work is clear, light, and joyful. It is impossible to describe this music. Its thought and style carry us into an entirely new and different world. It is luminous music, strange without being hostile, and as fresh as a story told by a child. A child's words only suggest the marvelous things he sees in his story. They are simple and inadequate words, but the way the child says them tells us more than if he were to state his thought more precisely. There is something analogous in this exceptional *Sinfonietta* [*Example 122*].

Progressively, instinctively, and without design, Janáček frees himself from everything that could be learned. His *Sinfonietta* evolves in an atmosphere freed of all influences, and his imagination moves in a zone which other musicians have not penetrated.

Janáček's last work is the very important *Glagolitic Mass*, for mixed chorus, soloists, orchestra, and organ (1928). "Clearing the slate," says Daniel Muller, "of all known traditions about masses, and reaching back beyond the classic period, the Renaissance, and the Middle Ages to early Slavonic liturgy, he has written a mass which is a mass in name only, which we can already see is pagan by the pure joy it expresses, and in which an almost completely secular mood dominates throughout. . . . He has dared to sing of a humanity which will have broken all its chains, which will have become ideally free, to extol in equally free music the dawn of a society transformed." Beginning with folk song as a source of new spirit, Janáček goes beyond the nationalism in his last works and achieves complete originality.

In Hungary, the transition from the romantic concept of nationalism and the modern concept was brought about by Ernö Dohnányi, born in Pozsony in 1877. This composer sought the secret of form in the works of Brahms. His construction, however, is somewhat unsure, and his works lack conciseness. Dohnányi is more at ease in composing pieces in rhapsodic form, like *Ruralia Hungarica* for violin and orchestra, one of his most typical works. The structure comes from the very nature of popular songs, which no longer seem like picturesque descriptions. In addition, the violin composition is directly inspired by traditional Hungarian technique and the sense of color for which extemporaneous Hungarian virtuosos have a gift.

Around 1910, BÉLA BARTÓK (born in Nagyszentmiklós in 1881) and ZOLTÁN KODÁLY (born in Kecskemet in 1882) undertook to advance the evolution of Hungarian music in the direction indicated by Dohnányi. They took a more radical stand in order to arrive at the very roots of folk inspiration.

Actually, what was known by the name *Hungarian music* was for the most part the art of the gypsy. The gypsies had absorbed the authentic peasant music of Hungary and the Balkan countries, had transformed it, and above all had degraded it by standardizing the modes and destroying rhythmic accentuations. The result was the famous so-called Hungarian key (A, B, C, D#, E, F, G#, A), the melodic framework lacking up-beat, and an unvaried tonality in binary rhythm alternating with imperfect cadences. Authentic peasant music had to be found beneath this mutilation. This was a long work, and one of scientific nature. Bartók and Kodály therefore visited the peoples of the Balkans—Hungarians, Slovaks, Bulgarians, Romanians, Ukrainians—armed with good recording instruments. They took down thousands of songs, which they classified in logical order. They were ultimately able to discern the specific characteristics in the music of each people and to isolate typical melodic patterns. They came to understand the play of various modes and rhythms and their expressive and architectural roles.

Having analyzed the complex of Balkan music into its distinct elements, the two composers took these elements as the foundation for the construction of a musical language entirely free of foreign traits. The first attempt they made in the direction of a thoroughly Hungarian art was to create harmony for folk melodies in conformity with the spirit of the melodies, that is, in drawing from the melodies the harmonic and rhythmic material suitable to them. Two important collections grew from this effort: Kodály's *Zongora Musika* and Bartók's *Ten Easy Pieces for Piano* (1908). The two collections can be considered as the starting point of Hungarian music liberated from outside influences. Sustained and encouraged by Debussy's example, the young Hungarians were not afraid to break with the practices and rules of traditional counterpoint and harmony and to take their inspiration from indigenous folk usages. In Kodály's *Zongora Musika* progressions which are parallel at the fourth can be heard, while in Bartók there appears a harmony taken from the modes in which the melody moves [*Example 123*].

Thenceforth, the characteristic qualities of new Hungarian music were established and the independence of its development was assured. The personalities of the two composers would hereafter evolve according to the temperament of each.

Kodály, inclined to sweetness, gentleness, and joy, was to write music for Hungary comparable to the art which Debussy and Ravel practiced in the framework of French music—a balanced, sensuous, happy expression, avoiding drama to engage in the play of light and shadow. His brilliant and captivating works, orchestrated with cultivated taste, quickly became popular. Outstanding are two dance suites, *Galánta Dances* and *Marosszék Dances*, and a very important stage work (later developed into an opera) on a play by Béla Paulini and Zsolt Harsányi tracing the adventures of *Háry János*, Op. 15. This is a large score with lovely songs, choruses of folk music, and orchestral passages enlivened with joyful and delightful fantasy. In the same period, Kodály presented his beautiful *Psalmus Hungaricus* for orchestra, chorus, and tenor solo, Op. 13, a magnificent work which is considered to be his masterpiece. The opera *Szekler Spinnstube* followed later. It is a work more noted for its surge of folk lyricism than for its dramatic qualities, which are not remarkable.

A clearly defined message comes across in Kodály's three main works, *Háry János, Psalmus Hungaricus,* and *Szekler Spinnstube. Háry János* portrays the adventures of a poor, ridiculous braggart whose lies are constantly exposed by reality. Nonetheless, he is a hero in his own way. Háry János is a poet. He invents his exploits because this affords him the means to escape the mediocrity of his daily life. He, a common man, aspires to something noble and great. Unable to achieve his aspirations, he dreams. *Szekler Spinnstube* describes the miserable existence of the peasant and his desire for a fuller and broader life. In the end, the walls of the room disappear, and the song of the people rises in the heart of all nature.

Starting with either comedy or tragedy, Kodály develops, amplifies, enlarges the subject to the point where he moves into the realm of luminous poetry, freed from material bonds. *Psalmus Hungaricus,* the song of anguish of a people who have suffered terribly in the apocalyptic march of history across Europe, is as well a cry for grandeur, for the light of human truth and beauty. As his point of departure, Kodály chose the heart of the Hungarian peasant, and has magnified it to universal proportions.

Béla Bartók's approach is different. Bartók also started with the particular sensitivity of the folk idiom and ended by achieving universality, but he used individual expression as his means. This is one reason why he is frequently compared with Beethoven, a comparison which, moreover, is justified by the power of some of his compositions.

From Bartók's many works, we should single out his piano compositions, harmonized folk tunes, and chamber and concert works. Most of the songs and piano compositions are treated with a technique adapted to the spirit of folk song.

Like his friend Kodály, Bartók was guided by Debussy's attitudes in the field of harmony. Bartók, however, led by an expressionistic instinct which Kodály did not have, sought out the elements of language which were the most detached from the hold of tonality, and a rhythmic method which would free his music from the bar-measure system. This is why he was interested in Stravinsky, whose rich metric system he adapted for his own use. For the same reasons, he studied Schoenberg's polyphony closely. What attracted his interest was the contrapuntal progression which is not concerned with harmony.

But Bartók adopted neither atonality nor the twelve-tone system. From Schoenberg he took the suppleness of thematic inversions and reversals (the cancrizans technique) and the motif work, adapting this technique to the use of modal scales. All Bartók's originality in technique originates in these specific elements, which have been discussed previously and need not be taken up again. It suffices to remark that although Bartók does not follow Schoenberg's twelve-tone technique, he nonetheless achieves the liberal spirit of the twelve tones by using various ancient modes simultaneously, either by superimposition in bimodality or by fusion or interpenetration of different modes.

In this way, the twelve tones are always verified, but the clear impression of the presence of modes prevents the disappearance of the notion of tonality. Tonality is broadened, relationships become more free, but the backbone of the tonal principle is retained—the tonic-dominant relationship, including the cadential function of the dominant. Here is another point, for those who want to view Bartók's work more closely. Before 1926, his language was mostly homophonic, with interest centered on harmony. Later, it became more and more polyphonic. A sort of analytic panorama of Bartók's technique of composition can be found in the important didactic work he wrote between 1926 and 1937, *Mikrokosmos,* which includes a hundred and fifty-three piano pieces in six books. The pieces are written to be increasingly difficult instrumentally, and are very useful in accustoming a young pianist to all the intricacies and techniques of the composer's writing and style. In this large work there are some beautiful pieces, like *Ostinato, Diary of a Fly,* and *Six Dances on Bulgarian Rhythms.*

Among his other piano works, the most noteworthy are the *Sonata* (1926) which has a certain intensity, but whose three movements are somewhat weakly connected; and the suite *Out of Doors,* which contains a flaw often encountered in Bartók's work: abuse of the play of sonorities, which sometimes reduces his music to a shower of sound, something he is even more guilty of than the impressionists.

Foremost among the numerous collections of folk songs are the *Twenty Hungarian Folk Songs,* written in 1929, for solo voice and piano; and *Village Scenes,* written in 1924, for female voices and chamber orchestra.

Of Bartók's orchestral works, the pantomime *The Miraculous Mandarin* stands out. It is a dazzling piece, but its rhythm is sometimes too close to Stravinsky for the work to be entirely original. The best orchestral works are unquestionably the *Concerto No. 2 for Piano and Orchestra* and the *Concerto for Violin and Orchestra.* The latter work especially, written in 1937-1938, has the unity Bartók strived for over many years and which he rarely achieved. The concerto is really a symphony in which the violin is simply one of the necessary components. The part of the violin is treated in the spirit of Hungarian virtuosity, and at the same time Bartók avoids extraneous effects. The orchestra, arranged with balance, leaves to the violin the responsibility of exposing the ideas, which are captivating and illuminated with inner life. This moving concerto, with Berg's the most beautiful written since Beethoven and Brahms, crowns Bartók's achievements. It incorporates all the composer could express in the field of chamber music—a field in which Bartók reached the height of his genius. The brilliant *Concerto for Orchestra* was written in 1943. Its qualities have won it well-deserved international acclaim. The *Cantata Profana* (1930) merits attention. It is one of his best compositions and particularly significant because the material treats of ancient myths: subject matter, poetry, and music form a homogeneous entity.

Bartók's chamber music consists of a monumental collection of works which should be placed among the most splendid of this century. It includes two *Sonatas for Violin and Piano* (1921 and 1922); six *String Quartets* (1908, 1915-1917, 1927, 1928, 1934, 1939); *Music for Strings, Percussion, and Celesta* (1936); a *Sonata for Two Pianos and Percussion* (1937); the suite *Contrasts for Piano, Violin, and Clarinet* (1938); *Sonata for Unaccompanied Violin* (1944); and *44 Duos for Two Violins*.

All the piano works and harmonizations of folk songs would seem to have been preparatory exercises for the composition of chamber music. Only in the latter does Bartók trust himself to us entirely and tell us what he has to disclose. For there is a disclosure. He reveals something of the human soul, as does Beethoven in his sonatas and quartets.

Bartók's expressionism, as shown in his quartets, has been carefully studied by Denijs Dille. Among other things, this commentator says:

The expressionist is usually a man of impulse or a thinker, often possessing these two characteristics simultaneously. The impressionist is a sensitive dreamer. His sensitivity is passive and receptive. It records sensations. The expressionist's sensitivity is active. It organizes and creates. The expressionist chooses as his subject a fact, a cause, a situation, an impression, and communicates the effect it has had on his own soul. For him, everything is a psychological question in which the will-factor is determinative—the will to express, the will to communicate. While impressionism faithfully respects the sensation and is concerned with individual particularity, expressionism tends to re-create situations and insights according to the order of intensity; it runs the gamut between individualism and impersonalism, and moves between the opposite poles of the fantastic and the catastrophic. Impressionism remains faithful to sonorous beauty, the ideal of romanticism, and to sensual enchantment. Expressionism uses sound brutally, and violates it. Here again are the two opposed positions: extreme tension is as often sought in a kind of explosion of the sonorous structure as in an elliptical impoverishment and seemingly impassive linear construction.

From the fantastic to the catastrophic, from explosion to ellipsis—I could not describe Bartók's feelings and technique better. Where the individual element prevails, we find the disconcerted attitude of an unconsolable soul and exasperated sensitivity. We stare into an abyss of desolation, but we also find moments of serene contemplation, and are stirred by the breath of idealism. How fully and with what self-mastery this is expressed! There is so little—besides the nervous writing —to show what is happening behind the notes. And it is this that sometimes creates a misconception about the breadth of his art. I believe I have found the thinker intervening here who weighs and seeks the balance of everything—a habit which I think is part of the character of the peasant, who suffers in silence. There is no instance of grandiloquence in Bartók's music. In the period in which his expressionism seemed to be sharpest, the expression of emotions did not become more grandiloquent. Much to the contrary, it seemed to be clothed in a lyricism that threatened to become too abstract, too pure—this is the case in many passages of his *Sonata No. 2 for Piano and Violin*. Too often has this phenomenon been called an aberration, a mistake. Actually it was only a logical consequence of the situations created by the composer's general line of development. Things problematical are so often hidden from public view in a man whose life is so interior and to whom expressionism is never pure enough in its manifestations.

From the moment Bartók's impersonal side appears, the atmosphere of country dances emerges and makes the sonorous structure whirl with a gaiety as naive as it is uninhibited. It would be a mistake to look for a Freudian or psychoanalytic aspect in this art. The vital and healthy peasant nature Bartók has retained is opposed to such an interpretation. Moreover, even slight familiarity with his music is enough to show how impossible such an attitude would be.

The *String Quartet No. 1*, written in 1908, demonstrated both the power of Bartók's conceptions and the mastery of his writing. It would be useless to try to separate the form from the expressive content in the work; the one is a function of the other, as in Beethoven. The music becomes more animated as the three movements proceed—lento, allegretto, allegro vivace. The first two parts are expressive, and the introductory lento produces a good deal of tension. The allegretto marks a release and a transition into the concluding allegro, which is pure motion. The last movement most clearly reflects Bartók's personality in the period when he composed this work. The first two movements still show some postromantic influences.

The *String Quartet No. 2* was written between 1915 and 1917. The composer's personality shows a maturity it did not have before the war. The harmony has become more free. The melodic line is permeated with the spirit of folk songs. At this point appears that alternation of true rhythm and complicated meter which would long be a dominant trait of the composer's expression, as well as the extreme variability of tempo which would give the movement of his music a bizarre and capricious character.

All these techniques were used to the fullest extent in the two sonatas for violin. The general scheme of this second quartet includes an expressive first part, the material of which is extraordinarily condensed, and which is dominated by strong tensions that transmit a feeling of pain. The second part is an absolute contrast to the first: it is totally unexpressive, and serves only to unbridle rhythmic force. The third part reintroduces the expressive intention. Tensions are relaxed little by little, and the work ends on a contemplative note.

After this powerful work, Bartók wrote his two sonatas for violin and piano. The *Sonata No. 1* (published in 1922) is in three distinct parts. The first part is intensely expressionistic, and is written with large leaps of intervals and violent rhythmic accents [*Example 124*]. The peaceful lyricism of the adagio brings a release. The finale is rhythmic.

The *Sonata No. 2* (appeared 1923) is one of Bartók's most perfect and most characteristic works. Of the two movements, which are played without a break, the first is treated as an introduction to a rhapsodic sequence, due to the caprice of a totally irregular tempo [*Example 127*]. But the movement only resembles a rhapsody; its structure is too well-ordered by the alternative play of two ideas. Furthermore, it only appears introductory because the piece has a complete meaning in itself. The second movement is rhythmic, but not purely dynamic. It contains expressive ideas which, as they are introduced, create increasing tensions that break into new rhythmic storms at their climaxes.

With these two sonatas, Bartók reaches his ultimate power as an expressionist. With the *Third Quartet* (1927), his form becomes noticeably more solid. Actually, as with Beethoven, the drama of Bartók's music lies in the struggle between his desire for freedom of expression and the necessity of fitting the expression into the framework of a form. As with Beethoven, and contrary to what has happened to Stravinsky since 1920, there in no "spirit of form" in Bartók. The expression always guides the discourse, and the role of form (or rather, of structure) is restricted to making the discourse coherent. In an understandable reaction to the completely free development he achieved in the first movement of his *Sonata No. 2*, Bartók devises a very compact structure for his *Third Quartet*. The first, moderate movement is followed by a rhythmic second movement. The third movement is a recapitulation of the first. A coda drawn from the second movement ends the work.

The *Third Quartet* is more contrapuntal than the two preceding it. Hereafter, counterpoint and the principle of variation (inherited from Beethoven and Brahms) govern the form, which becomes clear and easily perceptible. It is built with such harmonious proportions that the question of form will seem as important as the question of expression. The *Fourth String Quartet* (1928) has the symmetrical architecture of the *Third,* but on a large scale. It has five movements. The first and fifth movements are composed on the same thematic material, the fourth is a variation of the second, while the third forms the central pivot of the composition. Bartók achieves the supreme goal in this work. The features of folk song are assimilated and put to use in melodic ideas in which no trace of folk music remains. An autonomous style is established: the fusion of the chosen expression, the carefully wrought form, and the folk-music source is complete. These components are amalgamated in the crucible of Bartók's powerful imagination.

In 1934, Bartók wrote his *Fifth Quartet,* the structure of which resembles that of the *Fourth*. However, the composition shows a simplification, a starkness that is more and more pronounced in subsequent works. Without achieving calm and serenity, this *Fifth Quartet* nonetheless does not display the degree of tension found in parts of the *Fourth*.

Two years later, in 1936, Bartók composed *Music for Strings, Percussion and Celesta,* which is his most finished, most powerful and moving work. It is conceived for a double string orchestra, piano, harp, drums, cymbals, kettledrum, and celesta. It is hard to know what to admire most: the distinctiveness of the form, the thematic richness, or the imaginative use of sonorities. The most commonly used forms undergo a mutation here that gives them new life. The opening movement is a sort of fugue which, by entries made at the fifth, above or below, runs the complete cycle of tones to return at the end to the original note This sonorous architecture is based on a chromatic phrase, tender, subtle, and troubled in expression. It moves with a complex and supple rhythm that gives astonishing diversity of accent and articulation to the superimposition of voices [*Example 125*].

This expressive fugue is followed by a passage in sonata form which has enormous rhythmic power and extraordinary elasticity, and in which the music is passed from one group of strings to the other in a play of sonorous contrasts which has no musical equal. A third passage, in "bridge" form (A-B-C-B-A), is very mysterious in expression. The finale reintroduces, before the stretto which serves as its conclusion, the theme of the introductory fugue in diatonic form in an enthralling abbreviation, which is resolved in the most moving way possible [*Example 126*].

Music for Strings, Percussion and Celesta, in its perfection, in the fullness and nobility of its song, is a great masterwork, one of the most outstanding compositions of the twentieth century. The splendid *Sonata for Two Pianos and Percussion,* composed in 1937, is also remarkable.

After the massive and poignant works of the years 1934–1937, Bartók finally entered a period of beneficial repose. From this new-found serenity came his last quartet, the *Sixth,* composed in 1939, a work of moving simplicity. The benevolence and graciousness of this admirable man, the tenderness of his generous and loving heart are expressed here as the last testament of a composer who was one of the creative geniuses of our time.

The *Cantata Profana* for double chorus, soloists, and orchestra should also be included among Bartók's most important works. It is strange and captivating music, very difficult to perform from a choral point of view. As yet, it has not been sufficiently well produced for us to make a true estimate of its value. The text for the *Cantata* is taken from the cycle of legends *The Enchanted Deer*, widely known among the Hungarian people and the peoples who have a close affinity to them, such as the Finns. Bartók discovered the idea for his poem in a Romanian version, the plot of which, as in the legend, is symbolic. It is especially characteristic of peoples who live on the border between the occidental and oriental worlds, and have known from the beginning of their history the pain of migration.

An old man had nine sons. He had taught them no manual work, neither ploughing, nor horse breeding, nor animal husbandry. He had taught them only how to hunt on the mountain.

The nine sons were hunting on the mountain. They followed the trail of a large deer and crossed a bridge. Then, they lost their way and were transformed into stags.

The old man worried when his sons did not return. He took his gun, went to the mountain and discovered the bridge. But he only found the trail of the herd of deer. Following the trail he overtook the herd near a stream. He knelt down to take careful aim, and just as he was about to pull the trigger, the largest stag, his oldest son, said to him: "Dear Father, do not shoot at us, for if you do we will impale you on our antlers and will drag you from peak to peak and will break your body against a boulder. We will reduce you to pulp."

The father replied: "My dear sons, come back to the house, come to your beloved mother who is waiting for you in the torchlight. She has set the table for you, and has filled your cups. Your cups are filled with wine, and her eyes are filled with tears." But the oldest son replied: "Dearest Father, go back home. We cannot follow you. For our antlers are too wide for us to pass through a door. We can move only on the mountain. Our bodies can no longer wear clothes. They will only wear green leaves. And our mouths can no longer drink from cups; only streams will satisfy them."

The legends of *The Enchanted Deer* are the song of peoples who, to escape bondage, emigrate to free countries. The choice of such a subject in 1938 was prophetic. The drama was soon to take place. Bartók, who had analyzed the songs of his country into their distinct elements in order to compose a genuine musical creation which would magnify the spirit of his land, had to abandon his mother country when tyranny cast its shadow over that land. In 1938, the *Cantata Profana* was the twilight song of Europe. For this work, Bartók created the simplest, most naked language, and with it he ended his long exploratory voyage in the domain of the Hungarian folk song. He transfigured it, and made of it the most universally human song. He reached this ultimate point at the moment when everything collapsed, when the life of Europe seemed to be irrevocably destroyed. The *Cantata Profana* is thus a song of separation, a song of farewell. Contrary to its title, it is expressed in the form of an incantation, its melodies impregnated with religious feeling.

Bartók admitted that he had a marked preference for the *Cantata Profana*. It is indeed one of his most moving and perfect works.

In America, where he went in 1938 and died in 1945 without seeing his native land again, Bartók wrote the *Third Piano Concerto* and *Concerto for Orchestra*, the latter a rather extended divertissement whose objectivity reminds the listener of Stravinsky's later works. His last work, *Sonata for Unaccompanied Violin* (1944), is so austere that one is reminded of similar works by Bach. In his lifetime he re-established the place of perfect melody in a music in which all the elements had undergone a complete reformation.

To extract the essential from folk songs to rediscover the true soul of the people, and then to use the melodic curves and the specific rhythmic and harmonic textures which have thus been isolated (to speak in chemical terms) to build a national art from within—such is the aim of the contemporary musicians who have felt the need to return to what is most fundamental in the folk inspiration of their countries. Janáček and Bartók thought of their music in this light, and traveled farther and farther from the picturesque art of the romantics.

Music in Spain evolved in exactly the same way. After the glorious period of the fifteenth and sixteenth centuries with

Juan del Encina, Luis Milán, Cabezón, and Victoria, Spanish music was dominated by Italian influences. Its specific character, composed of an opposition or capricious alternation of religious gravity, spiritual austerity, and mysticism on the one hand and the joyous spirit of the people on the other, had completely disappeared and only reappeared in the eighteenth century, thanks to the Neapolitan Domenico Scarlatti. Scarlatti took Spanish dances, and particularly the *seguidillas,* as the basis of his artistic expression. His writing was inspired by the guitar, with its brusque virtuosity and its practice of acciacatura, which consists of sounding a given note of a chord and its appoggiatura simultaneously, providing the harmony with a very special mordent. Following Scarlatti, the true essence of Spanish music was again forgotten; in the nineteenth century, Italian opera almost monopolized the public interest. Toward the end of the century, Felipe Pedrell laid the foundation for a renaissance of national art, but his works (*Pirineos* and *La Celestina*) were only imperfect attempts at realizing an ideal which, at that time, still had to struggle against an overpowering foreign and cosmopolitan tradition. Manuel de Falla, born at Cadiz in 1876, understood Pedrell's intentions and became his pupil. Roland-Manuel discussed Pedrell's beneficial influence on De Falla:

It was Pedrell who first showed the future composer of *Master Peter's Puppet Show* and *Harpsichord Concerto* the need to purify writing in order to express only the essential. It was Pedrell who helped him at the beginning to discover the uselessness of fixed forms, aside from those "which a fatal, unconscious power created to suit the genius of the race, its temperament and its mores" (Felipe Pedrell, *Para Nuestra Música*). Pedrell did not convert him to the religion of authentic folk data—the disciple was to split from the master on this point—but he did essentially enlighten him on the meaning and spirit of the lasting traditions of the national genius, against which individual whim could never prevail, since there is nothing really original outside of the original, in the apt words of Miguel de Unamuno. Such was and is Pedrell's lesson. It is the laborer's lesson to his children. It would soon allow Manuel de Falla to "till his field."

MANUEL DE FALLA lived in Granada, and it was Andalusia that first attracted him. From 1902 to 1905 he wrote *La Vida Breve,* a lyric drama in two acts, with passages in which passionate and very personal music breaks through a lyricism still somewhat cosmopolitan. This early, the composer has already endowed folk music with affective nobility and very broad expressive potential, especially in the magnificent interlude that paints Granada at sunset and in some of the songs in the second act in which the *cante jondo* style is re-established in its original purity. In 1907, De Falla went to Paris, where he lived until 1914. He became friendly with Claude Debussy, whose music attracted him.

As was the case with Albéniz, the discovery of Debussy's language was decisive. De Falla found in the freedom Debussy had recently won for harmony the example of a rational artistic attitude toward the material treated, the example of the invented technique which breaks with academic traditions and yet is capable of achieving unity and cohesion.

Spanish art won its liberty and self-knowledge through Debussy. And it was also through Debussy that Bartók and Kodály found their way to independence. If we think of the importance of Debussy's attitude in the formation of other foreign artists, like Stravinsky, Schoenberg, and Alban Berg, we come to realize that the music of no country would have reached its present stage without the composer of *Pelléas et Mélisande*. This score is the real point of departure of all contemporary art.

De Falla showed Debussy's influence early. In 1916 the *Nights in the Gardens of Spain* was finished. It is an intensely poetic symphonic impression for piano and orchestra in which all the sorcery of subtle orchestration is brought into play. In it we rediscover that abandonment and nostalgia which are the charm of Debussy and Chopin as well as a voluptuous tenderness for all of nature. Debussy's *Iberia* was not an impressionist sketch but a synthesis. The *Nights in the Gardens of Spain*, also, is the crystallization of an aggregation of images, expressing all at once everything the composer feels and thinks about that Andalusian land to which he is tied with all the fibers of his being. This work is a love song, and ranks among the most beautiful ever written. While he was composing *Nights*, De Falla brought out his famous *Seven Popular Spanish Songs*. The work is a favorite with many audiences and serves as a model of what a re-created folk song can be. The composer achieves a really extraordinary concentration of thought. The songs are more true than true. Following this collection appeared *El Amor Brujo* (1915), a ballet with vocal part in which the ardor and rhythm of the gypsies are exalted. The substance of folk art is extracted and concentrated. The melodies are supported with chords and have no polyphonic commentary, with which they would be incompatible by nature. Movement is stirred by whirlwind treatment, so to speak, which keeps the music in one place and prevents its development. But it communicates a spiral movement which at times is dizzying, as in the *Danse de la Frayeur* and the *Danse Rituelle du Feu*. Magical vertigo, whipped by crisp, abrupt orchestration, contrasts with the voluptuous involvement of *Nights in the Gardens of Spain*.

But gypsy sorcery is only one aspect of Andalusia. Peasant life furnishes another feature, one which De Falla pinpoints in his second ballet, *The Three-Cornered Hat* (1919). Concerning this work, Roland-Manuel very appropriately quotes the words of Don Quixote: "But what is it, dear Lord, when these poets lower themselves to composing a type of poetry, so popular in Candaya, and then called *seguidillas?* For this was the dance of souls, shaking of bodies, bursts of laughter, and finally the ravishing of all the senses." (Part II, Chapter 38.) These few words describe to perfection the scintillating score written on the book by Pedro de Alarcón, in which the life of an Andalusian miller and his wife is portrayed in gay and lively episodes. The rhythm is wild, the melodies are written with fine wit, and the dances are inspired by traditional folk dances—the *farruca, jota, fandango,* and *zapateado*. The texture of the music is more complex than in *El Amor Brujo*. Here are the same rapid and fleeting contrapuntal lines that are found in literature for the guitar. The orchestra as well recalls the guitar with its embellishments and short imitations, and the transposition of the *rasgado* technique, which makes the chords seem so agitated. This last point is especially noticeable in the *Miller's Dance*.

But there is something else in *The Three-Cornered Hat*. Having given expression to the Andalusian folk spirit, De Falla began seek a form of thought which would set him apart from overspecialized nationalism. He thought of Scarlatti. As a result the entire score of *The Three-Cornered Hat* is endowed with that unity of organization and internal rhythm found in the sonatas of the great Domenico. To understand this evolution, it is enough to listen to the introduction to the second scene, *The Neighbors*. The melody unfolds spiritedly in the very fluid key of G (transposed into D), and the whole passage has a lightness and grace of form drawn directly from the art of the eighteenth century, while it conserves its Iberian color and modern accent. The elegant precision of Scarlatti can be heard here [*Example 128*].

The Three-Cornered Hat, first performed in Madrid in 1917 in an arrangement for small orchestra, was produced by Sergei Diaghilev's Ballet Russe in 1919 with marvelous décor by Pablo Picasso and choreography by Léonide Massine.

A new period opens with the composition of *Master Peter's Puppet Show* (1922), which is based on an episode from Chapters 25 and 26 of Part II of Cervantes's *Don Quixote*.

Master Peter's puppets present the adventures of Don Gaïferos, who frees his wife Melisendra from captivity by the Moors. A little boy, the spokesman, armed with a pointer, explains the spectacle to the audience which includes Don Quixote. The story ends in the punishment of the Moor and the routing of his troops. Don Quixote interrupts, taking the puppets for real people, and slashes the little theater of Master Peter to pieces with his sword.

De Falla felt himself drawn to Castile. His thought became more austere. The point of departure for his inspiration was the Romanesque music of the Middle Ages, the large style of the vihuelists, like Luis Milán, and the simple and supple declamation of liturgical music. The score has something rough and bare about it. It discards the accidental and becomes interior. Manuel de Falla's Hispanic music has become European. The quality of the score, moreover, is splendid; it is one of the most beautiful contemporary creations. The Castilian spirit finds total expression in this succession of scenes. There are nobility, pride, that passionate contemplation not found elsewhere; cutting mockery, and that breadth of vision which characterizes men who love life in all its manifestations, on the condition that it carry the stamp of nobility. Possibly the most beautiful passage is the tender music we hear when Melisendra is on her balcony. The orchestration is delightful. The chamber orchestra is led by two oboes and an English horn, instruments which, along with the bassoon, mix very well with the harpsichord and harp-lute which hold the place of honor. Several string instruments supply the exact flexibility necessary, and their introduction is always written with an extremely fine touch. Two horns, a trumpet, and the percussion section give the proper lift to the ensemble.

After this admirable work, from 1923 to 1926 De Falla wrote the *Concerto for Harpsichord and Five Instruments* (flute, oboe, clarinet, violin, and cello). The simplification witnessed in the *Puppet Show* did not end De Falla's evolution. He traversed the stage of austerity and began a period of asceticism, as so many Spanish artists, notably Zurbarán, have done. The art of this short instrumental composition is stark. Spiritual passion has burned everything perishable; there is hardly a skeleton of music left. One would say that the composer was no longer even interested in the external, auditory effect. His eyes are turned inward, toward the soul, toward the spirit. The first two parts of the *Concerto* have something absolute about them, like an echo, rhythms that arise from folk airs.

After 1927, De Falla worked on a great composition for solo voices, choruses, and orchestra, *La Atlántida,* based on a poem by Verdaguer. He died without being able to complete the orchestration, and the work has not yet been published.

Manuel de Falla was not so prolific as was Béla Bartók. But each of his works marks a very distinct stage in an evolution which is parallel to that of the great Hungarian composer. This evolution is typical of our time. Nationalism is no longer the goal: it is the point of departure for the creation of a language. In the measure that the language becomes more characterized and precise, it becomes universal. The same process is noticeable, moreover, in Stravinsky.[24]

Young Spanish musicians, following in Manuel de Falla's footsteps, seem to want to head in the direction of an art which,

24. Oscar Esplá, a contemporary of Manuel de Falla, shows rather the same development that led to *Master Peter's Puppet Show.* The *Veillée d'Armes de Don Quichotte* and the *Sonate du Sud pour Piano et Orchestre* can be counted as some of the best music to come out of Spain.

having gained autonomy, will free itself of nationalism. Joaquín Rodrigo has composed an interesting *Guitar Concerto* in this vein, taking inspiration from the style of the vihuelists. *Sinfonietta* by Ernesto Halffter is characterized by its marked humanistic tendency. It has brought the composer to the attention of the general public. During the Civil War, the Republicans produced phonograph records of marching songs harmonized by Pittaluga, Rodolfo Halffter, and others. This was the last word from Spain. These harmonizations, as well as their orchestration, were remarkable. One could hear in them a style in which the various European influences, especially De Falla's and Stravinsky's, were mingled. Pittaluga went to live in Mexico, where other Republican composers, like Rodolfo Halffter and Adolfo Salazar, had been welcomed.

The place of nationalism in contemporary art led Eugenio d'Ors to draw the following conclusions:

We would have gained nothing in the attempt to make room for foreign elements if their presence had been judged as merely the result of multiple influences and their interplay. You are perhaps familiar with a paper which I read in Seville on "The Humanities and Comparative Literature." The internationalist criterion was as strongly opposed as nationalist prejudice. The internationalists were described as searching for extrinsic relationships between local artistic or spiritual creations, and as accepting the hypothesis of essential diversity between these creations. Thus, "comparative literature" bogs down in explanations of this order. It becomes involved in the mechanics of precedents, influences, and reminiscences. The concept of "humanists," on the contrary, is a living, synthesizing concept, which supposes the organic unity of the object and talks not about "relationships" but about *communion.* In the same guise, on the political plane, what the synthesis "empire" means is rather different from a great League of Nations or any "international" organism whatever. Now, Victoria's work belongs specifically to the "musical humanities." What a marvelous moment, what a point of destiny in the year 1583 that brought the Fleming Roland de Lassus and the Spaniard Victoria together in Rome to study under the Roman Palestrina! Our Avilan priest, an ardent Castilian soul, learned from Roman classicism the strict geometric meaning of form. This is why his songs accord so perfectly with the powerful, clear line of our Escorial.

Among the artists of the generation following that of Stravinsky, Bartók, and De Falla are a number who also, and for the same reasons, adopt nationalist music as their point of departure. The most noteworthy of them are the Latin Americans Heitor Villa-Lobos of Brazil and Carlos Chávez and Silvestre Revueltas of Mexico.

Latin America is wakening to its spiritual strength. Heirs to Iberian humanistic traditions, its artists direct anxious attention to what remains of Indian civilizations, and take great interest in the style of the Negroes imported by slavetraders. In new climates, faced with forceful and opulent natural surroundings, the Latin spirit in the Americas was infused with fresh vitality of a very particular nature, the development of which we should follow closely. Poetry, painting, and music have taken great forward steps in Latin America.

The most modern trends seem to attract artists to a radical position regarding indigenous sources of inspiration. It is certainly true that musicians like Villa-Lobos and Chávez and a painter like the Mexican Diego Rivera, wanting to express their own particular personalities and create a distinctive style, have formed their attitudes in the primitive image, which they were able to do because of the constant contact they maintained with the peoples of the plains and forests. It is equally true that rediscovering the live sources of artistic sensitivity and expression in a period of mechanization and industrialization must be a powerful stimulus for the creation of new forms.

The position and real value of HEITOR VILLA-LOBOS (born in 1881) have been properly appreciated by Henri Prunières, and we can do no better than to repeat parts of his study of the Brazilian composer:

Villa-Lobos, after acquiring a solid foundation in music, spent four years traveling all over Brazil. He gathered songs directly from the Indians, some of which go far back into history, while others bear traces of European influence. But all, in their variety of rhythms, their modes and their melodic contours, are of great musical interest.

Villa-Lobos was not content simply to write down this precious material. He re-created in himself the soul of a primitive from contact with nature and the natives. The works he designed using these stylized elements can be compared with the paintings and sculptures of a Gauguin in Tahiti.

It is useless to look for logical development here in the sense of European music. Villa-Lobos's work is a sort of sonorous chaos, but a chaos which nonetheless takes shape under the guidance of a very acute sense of balance and proportions. The art of savages knows nothing of strict symmetry or linear perspective, but it has nonetheless created works of undeniable beauty.

In the three Indian poems *Canine-Ioune-Sobalet, Teira,* and *Iàra,* percussion instruments serve mainly as accompaniment. From time to time choruses raise their voices in brief and hard song to mark the rhythm. In the magnificent *Chorôs Pica Paô,* the wild vocalizations of the tenors flow above the unremitting refrain of the basses, scanned on a dance rhythm, while the percussion rages, augmented by a number of Indian instruments.

To concert audiences in Paris in 1927, the *Chorôs*—"a new form of music composition which synthesizes the various modalities of Brazilian, Indian, and popular music"—were a revelation. These pieces are built on a folk theme which disappears and reappears more or less modified. The polyphony is entirely original, and is inspired by the peculiar polyphony of Indian timbres. Villa-Lobos handles combinations and superimpositions of the most complicated rhythms easily. Native percussion instruments are very important in the battery section: gourds to be shaken or scraped, all sorts of xylophones, xuchalhos, caracachas, reco-recos, puitas, caxambus, maracas, and so on.

Chorôs 8, for Orchestra and Two Pianos, along with *Nonetto, Three Indian Songs* and *Chorôs 10,* is indubitably the most striking music we have heard. From time to time, a mad storm breaks out, the voices erupt in startling onomatopoeia, the battery section—a veritable orchestra of percussion instruments— hammers the rhythm with Dionysiac fury, and the orchestra outdoes itself in frenzied violence. The music is a cataclysm of sound, a volcanic eruption, a cyclone.

One may well have a different conception of the art of music, but one cannot remain indifferent to works of such power. One would have to agree with Florent Schmitt that "a truly great inspiration has passed by" [*Example 129*].

Villa-Lobos's work abounds with the exuberance and lush vegetation of the virgin forest, of the *Floresta,* with a touch of the languid grace of the Portuguese *fados.*

The work of the Mexican CARLOS CHÁVEZ (born in 1899) is more austere. It took form on high arid plateaus, in the land of volcanos.

Mexico, the revolutionary country, bold and daring, has seen the mestizo, the Indian-Spanish half-breed, grow in importance since Juarez. Long years of oppression did not lessen the vigor of the Indians of that country, and the revolution begun in 1910 was fought to raise the social and economic level of the Indian population.

Mexican artists strongly identified with the popular movement, and the painting of Diego Rivera is a direct expression of this concern. Carlos Chávez is an orchestra conductor, educator, and composer all in one. He directs the Philharmonic Orchestra of Mexico, has undertaken a broad program of popular music education, and has devoted himself to putting means of mechanical reproduction (recordings and radio) at the disposal of this cultural campaign.

Chávez's most interesting works were composed after 1926. They contain no picturesque writing, nor anything which attracts the ear at first blush. The structure of the melodies, composed in Indian modes, strictly observes modal relationships. The *Ten Piano Preludes* (1937) hold strictly to a two-voice polyphony. The first seven preludes have no modulation. The last three superimpose two different modes. The music is almost skeletal in its bareness. Its powerful vitality does not come across until it has been heard several times. In 1927, Chávez introduced his symphonic ballet, *Sinfonía de Baile, H.P.,* which attracted attention to this unusual talent. In 1934 and 1935 two important works brought him triumphant success, the cantata *El Sol,* and a proletarian symphony, *Llamadas,* for chorus and orchestra.

The *Sinfonía India* (1935–1936) allows us to approach a definition of Chávez's method of development. This method is based on two alternating ideas, one slow and the other lively. Chávez does not utilize these melodic, modal ideas to construct a real polyphony. He remains faithful to the spirit of folk song, which is monodic, and whose essence is, in most cases, badly translated by harmonization. Chávez uses the device of repetition, but constantly varies orchestral timbres, thus varying the accentuation and position of the number of vertical, columnar chords that support the melody. The coda of this symphony is an insistent, pulsating movement, a unison in raucous accents and harsh sonorities, punctuated with unremitting rumbling from the percussion instruments.

The *Sinfonía de Antígona* (1933) rounds out the entire body of woodwinds by calling on often neglected bass instruments of each group: the bass oboe and bass flute take their places beside the bass clarinet. This arrangement insures great fullness in that polyphony of timbres so dear to the composer and, moreover, so characteristic of Indian music. In 1937, Chávez presented his beautiful *Concerto for Four Horns and Orchestra,* and in 1940 a widely acclaimed *Piano Concerto.* Both pieces reflect the austerity of high plateaus where the agave fields are swept by volcanic dust. All these works, rooted in the very nature of Indian art, are free of local color. It is their internal rhythm, as in De Falla's *Harpsichord Concerto,* which makes them nationalistic.

Parallel to these humanistic works, Chávez has composed a number of more obviously Indian works, which he wrote for a particular group: the Mexican orchestra. This orchestra is composed of several wind instruments, usually a small flute, an oboe, a small clarinet, and a trumpet; plucked string instruments (vihuelas, guitars, and harps); and a great variety of Mexican percussion instruments, including various drums and marimbas, and a score of rattles—small, large, made of copper, terra cotta, and so on.[25]

25. In general, Chávez's thought moves in the atmosphere of pre-Spanish America—its great pyramids, its temples and rituals, its arid, sun-baked earth. He was the first, says Otto Mayer-Serra, "to recognize the symbiosis between the contributions of Europe and the indigenous folk art."

His student Silvestre Revueltas (1899-1940) followed the line he laid down. But Revueltas was more interested in the present. He did not seek out the purity and austerity of the plateau Indians. Rather, he sang the pleasures and sorrows of the people composed of the mestizos, Negritos, and Spaniards who swarm through the city streets. Chávez the architect was succeeded by Revueltas the painter, who infused a flamboyant orchestra with the essence

In Europe and Latin America, the phenomenon of nationalism in contemporary music is characterized by the desire to create a specific language which can subsequently be utilized to express humanistic ideas. This concept of nationalism has had brilliant results. The work of Bartók, De Falla, Stravinsky, and to a lesser degree, Hindemith and Milhaud stands in evidence.

The United States has also exhibited a degree of nationalism in music, but it has neither the importance nor the meaning it carries in Europe and Latin America. Around 1910, Americans began to take interest in the music of Louisiana Negroes. The Negroes had preserved French and English eighteenth-century songs, modified and adapted them to their own demands, submitting them to rhythmic distortions corresponding to their fantasy and humor and their sense of dance and musical improvisation. The Negroes had formed little orchestras composed of an assortment of instruments—trombones, clarinets, saxophones, fiddles, trumpets, pianos, guitars. They had imaginatively amalgamated these instruments into a cohesive ensemble, the elements of which were interrelated by percussion devices of differing timbres. The role of percussion instruments was not limited to marking the rhythm, but grew to have an expressive function. The Negroes had succeeded in creating a specific style, a *rag music*, which made a strong impression on the American music world.

In 1912, Irving Berlin composed *Alexander's Ragtime Band*, while William Christopher Handy wrote *St. Louis Blues* in 1914. These two pieces oriented dance music in the direction of the two types of jazz. By 1915, the vogue of jazz had spread throughout the United States. But musicians did not yet consider this folk art, or even Negro spirituals, as serious music. It was in Paris that jazz caught the attention of composers, who discovered all the instrumental and rhythmic resources that this unusual technique put at the disposal of music. They valued the crudeness and openness of this art as an antidote to the

---

of Mexican ardor. His talent had matured by 1936, when he wrote his most significant works: *Homenaje a García Lorca* for orchestra, and a delightful children's ballet, *El Renacuajo Paseador*. In 1938 he published a sumptuous and exuberant symphonic poem, *Sensemaya*.

delicacy of the impressionists. In *Le Coq et l'Arlequin,* Jean Cocteau relates his impressions of his first contact with rag music in the passage quoted above (see p. 220).

Stravinsky wrote *Piano Rag Music* and *Ragtime for Eleven Instruments.* After a trip to the United States, Milhaud composed the *Création du Monde.* The characteristics of jazz were digested and incorporated into their own language.

Works such as these alerted American composers to the fact that they had in their country the elements of a well-defined folklore appropriate for use in serious music. Composers of jazz music themselves went to work to enlarge the framework in which Negro music had evolved, and in 1924 in New York, the first symphonic concert of jazz took place, conceived and directed by Paul Whiteman. The program included George Gershwin's piano concerto, *Rhapsody in Blue,* a highly imaginative work which reflected a sure hand, but which stopped at a compromise between the facile tunes of the music hall and the stringent requirements of concert music. The same year Louis Gruenberg wrote two interesting scores based on texts of Negro sermons—music inspired by both jazz and Negro spiritual styles. These were *The Daniel Jazz,* Op. 21, and *The Creation,* Op. 24. These two works, too little known, constitute one of the boldest and most extreme attempts yet made in the United States to invent an original style independent of European influence. They are only attempts, however, for they progressed no further than a stage which is still too close to folk music, the point of departure.

Another attempt, more hesitant, was made by the Negro composer William Grant Still, who in 1930 presented his *Afro-American Symphony,* for symphony orchestra. In this work Negro spiritual melodies are included in a style halfway between that of Dvořák's *New World Symphony* and that of César Franck's *Symphony.*

If we add opera to these efforts, or rather Gershwin's great operetta *Porgy and Bess* (1935), we will have almost exhausted the catalogue of music which has risen from the foundation of Negro folk art. There is another sort of Americanism which is seeking expression by abstracting from Negro influence. This type of nationalism, less obvious, does not strike the ear on first hearing or first reading. It is not communicated through the bright colors of spirituals or rag style. Composers like Charles Ives (1874–1954), Aaron Copland (born in 1900), and George Antheil (1900–1959) are not concerned with local color. They want to express the spirit of the American Anglo-Saxon, as it has developed within a commercial and industrial civilization. "What is happening to the soul, what is happening to man in this storm-filled life, surrounded by the incessant clatter of machines and motors, obsessed by the pulsing rhythm of the scramble for money? What does he think, what does he want?" These are the questions composers seem to be asking themselves. As in American novels and movies, there is a nostalgic longing for silence in their music, a need for tranquillity, a sometimes painful attraction toward the open horizons of the countryside —a need to bathe, to be refreshed, to forget the city.

CHARLES IVES, of all American composers, was the boldest. He is to America what Schoenberg and Stravinsky are to Europe, but with less impact. His talent was far from negligible, and if his work is little known, it is because the youngest American composers have shown themselves much more hesitant and less free.

Ives thought that music is a living being, and that what the composer notes down is simply an embryo to be developed by the imagination of the interpreter. Music makes frequent demands on the interpreter's improvising skill, giving him a choice between several possible renditions of chords or orchestration. By 1906, Ives had already made the rhythmic and orchestral experiments which would be characteristic of Schoenberg and Stravinsky. In 1906, in fact, he wrote the *Set for a Theatre Orchestra* which broke as radically with every known tradition as *Pierrot Lunaire* or *Le Sacre du Printemps* did later. This free music reveals a rare delicacy of ear. The expression is human, nonindividual and semivisionary. At every turn, this art seems to reunite the irreconcilable, to melt the most heterogeneous elements into a single scheme. The style is rich, and the inspiration, based on the sensitivity of the people much more than on folk songs, is generous and large. In many ways, the unusual and captivating style of Charles Ives makes one think of Walt Whitman. His best works were composed between 1906 and

1915, and it seems that after 1921 Charles Ives did not write at all. Besides the *Set for a Theatre Orchestra,* the *Third* and *Fourth Symphonies* (1907 and 1910–1912) and *Three Places in New England* (1903–1914) are noteworthy, as are the pieces in quarter-tones written before 1915. Ives's unusual artistic outlook should not be underestimated, because it tends to rectify the abuse of the craft by calling more frequently on imagination. This trend has appeared recently in Elliott Carter's *String Quartet,* in which the material developed by the two violins very plainly expressed serenity, while the viola and cello counterpoint this tranquil music with contrasting dramatic violence.

AARON COPLAND and GEORGE ANTHEIL as well take inspiration from Walt Whitman's thought. Their expression is rather particularized, despite the eclecticism in language which is only too common among American artists. Antheil is known for his opera *Transatlantic* (1930), which describes the aspiration for tenderness and love of youth imprisoned between the high walls of skyscrapers. His radical modernism, essentially rhythmic in nature, is too systematic, probably as the result of an immediately noticeable lack of imagination. In Aaron Copland, on the contrary, we are aware of the formation of a harmonious and peaceful style, well adapted to his tempered, and sometimes very distinctive, expression. His orchestral piece *Quiet City* is a melancholy, contemplative image of a great industrial city in the evening when all movement has ceased. A trumpet and an English horn carry the dialogue simply but movingly, against the almost immobile background of a string orchestra. Copland's spirit is filled with the vast horizons of the West. There is something childlike in the vivacity of expression and the naïveté of his pleasure, in the odd combination of a touch of weariness and a communicative graciousness. He draws the portrait of prairie dwellers in firm, supple lines. *Appalachian Spring* and *Rodeo* are delightful representative scores.

There has been some excitement about two operas of Gian-Carlo Menotti, whose *Consul* was enthusiastically received by theater audiences in a number of countries. As his work is a modernized protraction of *verismo,* we need not linger over it.

The period of explosive growth in contemporary music has come to a close. We have examined the liberation brought about by the greatest composers of our time, and have seen how other composers have created new styles by starting with folk music as their source of inspiration.

There remains for us to discuss numerous artists who have utilized the elements of modern expression without themselves contributing anything new in the domain of sound. Many of them have shown evidence of great talent, skill, virtuosity, spirit, and feeling. These are eminent qualities which justify the interest their labors have inspired. But their eclectic art does not have the grandeur that only the creative force of genius can confer, nor the persuasive power that emanates from a very unusual personality. We will limit our discussion to a cursory review of the works of these distinguished composers. Before going on, however, we will examine more closely a few of these eclectic composers whose ideas and art strike our attention.

Like every other approach, eclecticism can nurture the growth of a strong personality. There was a time when eclecticism was decried as the course taken by a man incapable of finding in himself the fresh wellspring of a new language. But the question rises as to whether it is always necessary to seek a new manner of speaking. The necessity was imposed after the romantic period. Stravinsky, Schoenberg, and others took it upon themselves to experiment. They dismantled the mechanism of the old sonant apparatus and built new ones with the parts, each according to his own blueprint. They also showed their contemporaries that the single parts were there for their use if they wanted to build a new structure. When the period of analysis and experimentation was ended, there naturally came a time to think about creating a new style—not to throw distinct personalities into relief, but to establish a common language which would fit the spirit and exigencies of the present. This general language, the formation of which the best trends have contributed to, is the concern of modern eclectics. Their problem is not to take heterogeneous elements and juxtapose them in a language lacking in unity (this is precisely the brand of eclecticism which is reprehensible), but to meld them into homogeneous speech.

KAROL SZYMANOWSKI (1883–1937) is one of the composers who succeeded best in shaping their personalities by assimilating the various influences to which they were subjected. Having felt the influence of Richard Strauss from one quarter and that of Scriabin from another at the outset of his career, and sensitive to the specific qualities of Stravinsky, Schoenberg, and Ravel, he was able to amalgamate these influences without rejecting any, and developed his own features. Kolinski has these apt words on the subject: "After Chopin, Karol Szymanowski is the most representative composer of Poland, the musical genius of which, like the god Janus, has two faces: one turned toward Germany, the other looking toward Russia. Thus, Szymanowski's music, deeply rooted in Polish soil, associates the architectural ideal of German music with the enchanting colors of Russian music. Thought and dreamed in turn, it rarely lets itself be swept into the free interplay of timbres and sonorities."

Between the *Hymn to the Night* which is the *Third Symphony,* Op. 27, and *King Roger,* that eulogy of the dance, there is a void. The composer progressed steadily toward Latin clarity of thought. Kolinski continues:

"The most recent works occur at the high point of these efforts: the *Fourth Symphony,* and his ballet *Harnasie* (1935). Their musical material is reduced to the essential in the *Mazurkas,* Op. 50. Compared to Chopin's, Szymanowski's *Mazurkas* present about the same similarities as the still lifes poetized by Chardin might have with those painted by Cézanne. As much as Chopin's mazurkas are little poems in music, Szymanowski's are pure music. Their form is that of the *Lied,* but enlarged under the influence of the large form—variation, sonata, fugue. The traditional relationships between the tonic and the dominant are disguised in chromatic apparel, full of invention and rich in color. On the *orchestral* side of the mazurkas, the sonorous gamut of the piano becomes that of an invisible orchestra.

"Everything they contain of the meeting of East and West is very instructive for better understanding a theater or symphonic work of Szymanowski, especially in his last manner."

In the *Myths for Violin and Piano,* Op. 30, the composer's personality becomes more luminous and settles more and more into its essential traits, which are clearly perceptible in the

Études, Op. 46, and subsequent works. A splendid series of works follows, whose inner warmth is expressed intensely in a very pure and denuded style: *Berceuses,* Op. 48; the *Mazurkas,* Op. 50; the ballet *Harnasie* (1926); *Stabat Mater,* Op. 53 (1928); *Concerto No. 2 for Violin* (1930); and the *Fourth Symphony* (1935).

Another interesting eclectic composer is the Russian VLADIMIR VOGEL. Born in Moscow, he lived in Germany, where he was one of Ferruccio Busoni's favorite pupils. Leading a very retired life in the Swiss mountains, Vogel published one of his works from time to time. They are characterized by a careful and bare style. Vogel prefers epic subjects, and he has invented a particular choral technique for the recitation of an epic. The chorus intermittently sings and speaks in rhythm. The technique is basically the one Milhaud used in *Les Choéphores.* But Vogel creates polyphony with the spoken chorus, and composes pieces written for it according to the laws of music of fixed sounds. For example, in his spoken choruses, there are sarabands, passacaglias, and fugatos. The preciseness with which the spoken choruses are written allows them to be integrated with orchestral music in such a way as to form a harmonious whole.

Vogel's two most remarkable works are *The Fall of Wagadu* (1935) and *Thyl Claes* (1940–1945). "How Wagadu Fell by Pride" is a story taken from the *Dausi,* the *Book of Heroes,* the Kabyle epic collected by Leo Frobenius. The *Dausi* is devoted to the grandeur and fall of Wagadu, who falls four times—by pride, felony, greed, and discord. Wagadu is not only the name of a region but, as the poet says, "Wagadu is not wood, nor stone, nor earth; it is the force that moves the soul of heroes."

Wagadu is also the story of those minstrels, sons of nobles, who lead a life of adventure and chivalry. It is told how the lute does not begin to sing until it has been sprinkled by the blood of numerous warriors. Lyricism is thus born of human experience.

Vogel wrote his score in 1930. It is almost totally choral, and includes only a few solos. There is no orchestra. The chorus is supported by five saxophones (from soprano to bass) which fill the role of an organ, but an organ whose breath seems almost human. Vogel's inspiration is of uncommon diversity. It makes us feel the bleeding wounds of the heroes, the growl of wild animals in the brush, the great desolation of the plains, the freshness of folk poetry, terror, ardor, wisdom—all irradiated with the pitiless sunlight that dries up the earth and the heart.

This great music, too little known, merits a place among the most beautiful works of our time.

The same epic spirit animates *Thyl Claes,* an important two-part work for orchestra, spoken chorus, reciters, and solo soprano composed around sections of *Tyl Ulenspiegl* by Charles de Coster. This book, a masterpiece in Belgian literature, commemorates the war of liberation of the Flemish people at the time of Spanish rule over the Low Countries.

Vogel prefers to proceed by short motifs, which he weaves in a clear polyphony and treats with variations in timbre, He achieves very winning expressive effects by superimposing major and minor modes.

IGOR MARKEVICH (born in 1912) also falls under the sign of eclecticism. Actually, his choice of means is not as broad as Szymanowski's. His best works are based on a system of rhythm which owes everything to Stravinsky, and on a conception of polyphony which derives from Hindemith. No other influence can be felt in this composer's very irregular works, but he sometimes exhibits a curious angle of vision, at least in three of his compositions: *The Flight of Icarus* (1932), the *Psalm* (1933), and *Paradise Lost* (1935).

Markevich's theory is that until the present, music has been used to translate feelings born of impressions transmitted by the sensory organs. His aim is to show a certain state of perception the image of which none of the senses can transmit. He writes:

"Music is the art of re-creating the world in the realm of sound, We see things from only one angle. But there are other aspects which can only be perceived with the eyes of the spirit, and these are the aspects which I think should be re-created in music. Music proceeds inversely to painting to achieve the same goal. Suppose an artist were to paint a bird. If he is sparked by love of truth in his efforts, we, looking at that bird, should have a feeling of the life that pulses through it, a sense of its warmth, an impression that its wings can carry it. On the contrary, in music one can create the impression of the flight, of the warm and very special throbbing of the little bird body, and in this way communicate the feeling of life. If we consider, therefore, that music can re-create things from within just as all other forms of art do, and thus enrich the spirit by giving it a feeling of life in its purest state—and here purity intervenes—we can then give it the place it deserves. . . . The least that I can say about my work is that it took me a long time to see the most important possibilities of the art I serve. I tried to put these views into effect for the first time in *The Flight of Icarus*."

This *Flight of Icarus* is a fascinating symphony. The orchestra successively presents the *Games of Icarus; Icarus and the Birds; Meditation, Flight, and Fall of Icarus;* and *Death of Icarus.* It presents, but it does not describe. The music really acts in accordance with the ideas detailed by the author. Thus, to give the impression of flight, certain instruments hold a long note punctuated by a few isolated and accented notes emitted by other instruments. This gives an impression of continuity, levelness, and speed which, to be sustained, needs only a few light pulsations and only a small outlay of energy. While the held notes sound in the middle register, the accented notes are scattered in the high or low registers, which provides a measure of the passage of time and a notion of the space through which this suspended body glides. There is no trace of description, and no trace of imitation of a visual impression. We find ourselves immersed in the expression of a perception, knowledge, a music of the spirit.

The death of Icarus is as beautiful as a Balinese gamelan. There is nothing dramatic about the death. It is felt as a state in which nothing moves any longer, and which lasts for infinity. The feeling is translated by notes of equal time values, which destroys dynamism, and by the melodic curves included in a single tetrachord from which all harmonic functions are absent [*Example 130*].

The work is unique of its kind, and makes an indelible impression.

The *Psalm* is also a work of high quality, in which the eternity of the Lord is transmitted by a similar conception of time and a sense of immobility which folds the music back on itself.

In 1935 Markevich published his most important work, *Paradise Lost,* based on Milton's poem, for solo voices, chorus, and orchestra. Markevich, writing about this oratorio, says that he has put greater and greater distance between himself and the myth of Adam and Eve to represent a human being in whom he incarnates the whole of humanity.

As my work progressed, I left Milton farther and farther behind, and when I had finished, I found a real wall between us. First, because we are separated by centuries, centuries during which humanity has taken a decisive step toward intellectual freedom. Perhaps humanity has lost some of the certitude of faith but it has gained faith in the concrete world. This permits it to understand spiritual concepts in their pure state and their inscription in material things much more clearly. This takes on great importance in the question of the evolution of music.

This interesting commentary explains not only the music of its author; it explains as well the impression of concentrated strength, the impression of the musical being realized to the fullest, that are reflected in certain passages of Stravinsky, Schoenberg, or Webern. These qualities make such music appear not as a modern aspect of a way of being which has already been expressed, but as a new state of musical consciousness, of perception through music.

Markevich then details that perception he wants to express:

I must discuss a question with you which is often on my mind: the question of Time, so important in the art of sounds. This question came to me in two forms: first, its material aspect, if I may use the term, which is that of the time that passes, from which I had to cut a piece to breathe musical life into; and then, wanting to fix the meaning of what would give life to this piece of time which is passing, and perceive that truth I was speaking of above which remained to be revealed, I penetrated a second dimension of Time. This is a sort of eternal present, which is, as it were, perpendicular to the time passing. In it innumerable forms of truth exist in their pure state, living forever in relation to perishable things which themselves pass, eternally recommencing, in which these truths are inscribed and are made perceptible to us. The problem was to bring these two times together, and I came to understand that here was one of the potentials of Music which is peculiar to this art and makes it extraordinarily advanced. Since it develops in the time that passes, it is therefore capable of leading us to the light with its divine contents, a piece of that eternal present that I called a second dimension of Time, of being, in other words, *a truth made sound.*

Paradise Lost contains two parts. The first portrays the birth of Man and the repercussions of that event in the world of the Angels. The Evil One and the Angels, generators of the passions and ideas which will stir that life, engage in a dramatic, violent spiritual debate around Man, in which all the characters come face to face. As a result, various expressions are superimposed, creating a striking impression of simultaneity. The chorus sings, speaks, shouts, and whispers in seeming disorder, enveloped by an orchestra that moves in both the low and high registers —the intermediary parts being left to the voices [*Example 133*]. The second part begins with an introduction, static in pace. The variety of characters disappears, and the music, now coherent, seems to be "inspired by the invisible gleam of a Paradise refound" (A. de Graeff).

It is unnecessary to discuss in detail the composing techniques of this score. Its elements can be found in what has been said about Stravinsky's writing. Markevich's language is not essentially personal; it is eclectic. The great originality of his art is due to its spirit. Unfortunately, the most recent works of this exceptionally gifted composer are not illuminated with that spirituality which is the essential worth of *The Flight of Icarus* and *Paradise Lost.* They merely exhibit great orchestral virtuosity, and are ensconced in a position that lacks originality. This retrogression is especially noticeable in the *Symphony with Voice* (1943), based on poems by Lorenzo the Magnificent.

LUIGI DALLAPICCOLA, born in 1904 at Pisino in the province of Pola, began life as an Austrian and became a naturalized Italian citizen in 1918 when the province was attached to Italy. Perhaps the fact of being born in such a contested borderland explains certain traits of his character, notably his combativeness and his habit of taking a stand with the opposition when current ideas become lukewarm or too academic.

Dallapiccola has lived in Florence since 1922, and his first compositions date from 1927. In 1934, he wrote the *Divertimento in Quattro Esercizi,* for solo voice and instruments; in 1936, *Music for Three Pianos;* from 1933 to 1936, *Sei Cori di Michelangelo Buonarroti il Giovane;* 1937, *Tre Laudi,* for voice and instruments, followed by the opera *Volo di Notte,* based on Saint-Exupéry's *Vol de Nuit;* then in 1939–1940, *Canti di Prigionia,* for chorus and instruments; and in 1943, *Sex Carmina Alcaei.* Later there appeared *Il Prigioniero,* a one-act opera; the mystery play *Job;* and *Canti di Liberazione* (1955).

These are his most important works. Dallapiccola's temperament is lyrical. Like Poulenc, Sauguet, Milhaud, or Britten, he is at his best in vocal composition.

We might expect this Mediterranean, bred in Italian culture, to be a melodist. But nothing is further from what is called Italian music than his. He sought the secret of architecture in Schoenberg and Webern, and studied Berg for possibilities of developing lyricism in the framework of new forms.

How often has the opinion been expressed that Schoenberg's ideas lead to an impasse, that those who follow his method of composition are reduced to imitation! Alban Berg alone proves that Schoenberg's technique adapts readily to the needs of a different temperament. Dallapiccola's works are evidence that atonality and Schoenberg's system can be separated from Viennese expressionism to accommodate the clarity of the Latin mentality and enhance the expression of Mediterranean genius.

The twelve-tone system is used by Dallapiccola, sometimes intermittently (*Volo di Notte*) and sometimes strictly (*Sex Carmina Alcaei*). In orchestration, he inclines more and more to the use of a few solo instruments, and in his orchestra, as in Webern's, the various notes of the twelve-tone series are played by different instruments. The relationship is obvious. Dallapiccola belongs to the *Schoenbergkreis.* But what is most important, his music does not have the same sound at all as that of his models. It plunges us into a completely different atmosphere, in which there is nothing somber and no trace of expressionism. We are transported into a luminous and sunlit world, a climate of fervor, faith, and enthusiasm absolutely contrary to the depressing sentiments of the Viennese.

It would be useless to try to explain by stylistic analysis how

Dallapiccola achieves this transposition, this change of climate. A single example is enough to demonstrate it. The series of twelve tones in Dallapiccola's works is usually arranged in such a way that it can be subdivided into groups of consecutive notes related by a clear tonal sense. Furthermore, the succession of notes is made without the wide leaps which create the painful tensions the Viennese need but which do not fit the harmony, tranquillity, and serenity of expression proper to the Mediterranean temperament. The first measures of *Sex Carmina Alcaei* shown in *Example 132* immediately define Dallapiccola's style. We find the *consequente Dürchfuhrung* of the twelve-tone series (*recto tono* in the voice part; *motu contrario* in canon for the instruments and in augmentation for the piano and harp); the tossing of the series from one instrument to another; intervals which do not go beyond the sixth; and the subdivision of the series into tonal groups.

Luigi Dallapiccola succeeded in uniting the architectural element with gentleness of inspiration and elegance of Mediterranean thought. He thus created an art both reflective and expressive corresponding to a specific psychic climate that is comparable in meaning and execution to the art of the Sienese masters and Giotto.

What Markevich represents in the extension of Stravinsky's thought, Dallapiccola brings about in following the Schoenberg school. Both should be cited as examples of what can be done with an eclectic language vivified by a personal and independent spiritual position.

They also bear witness to the fact that there are today no more national schools. There are two or three main trends in European music which are followed by composers of various nationalities. This is one of the aspects of the current evolution of European life. Local influences are making way for great international currents rising from the increasing interpenetration of national cultures.

To end this review of modern music, there remains for us to examine rapidly a few talented artists whose works are recommended by qualities as numerous as they are varied, but whose personalities are not so individual as those of the composers we have been discussing.

In Italy, a century of opera had obscured the most nourishing sources of music. Composers concerned themselves only with facility and superficial effects, and were content to use often rudimentary craftsmanship to exhibit undeniable melodic spontaneity and genuine, but rather elemental, sense of musical drama. Verdi's whole life was a struggle to restore to opera the dignity it had lost, a truer expression, and greater value.

Instrumental music had been neglected. A few precursors, like Martucci and Sinigaglia, had led a campaign to revive enthusiasm for and programing of symphonic music. But until around 1910, their efforts achieved no noticeable results. Busoni was working in Germany, and his activities made no impression in Italy. Also, for a century Italian music had developed in isolation, and composers were almost totally unaware of the evolution of the art in France, Germany, and Russia.

A new generation of artists, finding no teaching in Italy capable of raising the standards of music, left to work in foreign countries. Ottorino Respighi (1879–1936) studied with Max Bruch and Rimsky-Korsakov; Alfredo Casella (1883–1947) went to live in Paris, and Gian Francesco Malipiero (born in 1882) to Germany. Ildebrando Pizzetti (born in 1880) was an exception. He remained in Italy, where he had the good fortune to meet an unusual master, Giovanni Tebaldini. Tebaldini had a clear concept of Italian music of the fifteenth, sixteenth, and seventeenth centuries, and advocated a serious study of this music as the basis for a renaissance. In the absence of Busoni, the influence of Tebaldini's ideas was decisive in determining the postromantic development of music. Respighi was a brilliant orchestrator, but his style is a rather anomalous mixture which shows the influence of Strauss, Rimsky-Korsakov, Stravinsky, and Debussy. *The Fountains of Rome* (1917) is a good example of his talent. Franco Alfano (1876–1954), whose opera *Sakuntala* was very successful, displays just as superficial an eclecticism. Alfano is less of a symphonist than Respighi. On the other hand, he has a more interesting melodic gift. Although we are justified in treating the style of these two composers severely, it should nonetheless be pointed out that their talent has produced some attractive works. Other questions aside, they deserve credit for having been among the first to reintroduce into Italian music the subtlety it had lost. Pizzetti has more charm than Respighi and Alfano, is more inventive, and is endowed with a purer and more homogeneous style. His instrumental works are rather poor, but his vocal works are very interesting. His first songs, especially *I Pastori,* reveal his particular qualities: luminous thought, elegant expression, supple and gracious vocal lines, and sensitivity that shows in his delicate handling of modes. Around 1917, he wrote the remarkable choruses for Gabriele D'Annunzio's *La Nave.* His two best works are the operas *Fedra* and *Debora e Jaele,* uniting real dramatic power and a delicacy of taste which at that time was something new in Italian music.

The composers GIAN FRANCESCO MALIPIERO and ALFREDO CASELLA figured in the most intensely combative period of contemporary Italian music. Malipiero, inspired by the madrigals and dramas of Monteverdi, of which, by the way, he has published an admirable edition, succeeded in steadily discarding the influences which affected his formation. Gifted with a very subtle imagination, and never lacking in ideas, he excels in the shorter forms. He does not have a feeling for large structure. Each time Malipiero tries to expand and work on a large scale, he becomes dull and tedious. But his short pieces are captivating. Among them are suites for string quartets like *Rispetti e Strambotti,* and collections of piano pieces, the best of which is *Poemi Asolani.* His *Stagioni Italiche* for voice and piano soars in marvelous flight, and is both intimate and warm. Malipiero wrote a number of operas. Among the most successful are *Sette Canzoni,* a suite of short, contrasting dramatic scenes, with a song as the subject of each scene; and the lively *Tre Commedie Goldoniane,* wonderfully impertinent and sparkling. Among his symphonies, there are some which are very attractive, especially the third, called *Delle Campane,* and the fifth, *In Echo.*

The chief virtue of Malipiero's music lies in its melodic flow and its ready spontaneity and animation. The incisive vivacity of his notations is charmingly Venetian. These are the qualities that adorn many of his inimitable works, like *Sette Allegrezze d'Amore,* for voice and 24 instruments, based on a poem by Lorenzo de' Medici.

Alfredo Casella's art is basically intellectual. Casella enjoyed a brilliant career as a pianist and orchestra conductor before 1914. He had composed an entertaining collection of piano pieces *À la Manière de* . . . , in which he amused himself with ironic imitations of D'Indy, Strauss, Debussy, and other contemporary masters. It has been said that all of Casella's music was written in the manner of someone or something. The accusation, although exaggerated, is partly true. Casella had the intelligence to understand that Italian music had an excellent means at its disposal to get out of its rut: by reviving the spirit of the masters of instrumental music—Vivaldi, Scarlatti, and Clementi, among others. In these composers he found the clarity and simplicity of construction, and the source of that rather abrupt liveliness, which are properly Italian. He used these qualities as points of departure, and brought them onto the contemporary scene by transporting them into the modern world of harmony.

Of all Italian composers, Casella had the most developed sense of harmony. Acquired during his long stay in France, this harmonic gift is perceptible in some of his pre-1914 compositions, notably *Notte di Maggio*. The crisis in Italian music took place between 1914 and 1918, and was resolved in a unanimous decision to re-establish direct contact with the periods anterior to the nineteenth century. Moreover, *Les Femmes de Bonne Humeur*, a ballet of Scarlatti sonatas orchestrated by Vincenzo Tommasini for Diaghilev's Ballet Russe, appeared at that time. This ballet was evidence of the Italian renaissance. It had considerable influence on young French composers and on Stravinsky. At this time, composers began to take a real interest in conciseness and clarity of form, characteristics that later became a permanent mark of Western European music, and developed a passing taste for brusqueness and impertinence.

Casella was one of the principal craftsmen of that Scarlattian influence. After 1920, he produced a long series of works which had no real depth but showed the composer's rather unusual spirit. He was sensitive to all the trends of the moment, nothing seemed to escape his attention. He understood these influences on his art, and looked upon the fact with irony. He handled them and his own ironic attitude adroitly, in not very original but always carefully constructed forms. All things considered, the result is an art form lively in spirit and remarkably intelligent, which gives pleasure but is soon forgotten.

Casella also furnishes us with the best Italian instrumental music of the time, such as the ballet *La Giara;* the *Concerto for Orchestra;* the *Concerto Romano for Organ and Orchestra;* and the *Serenade for Five Instruments.* His best stage work is a chamber opera, *La Favola d'Orfeo,* in which his attitude toward the lyric theater is rather close to Milhaud's.

Of the next generation, we should retain the name of Vittorio Rieti (born in 1898), who spent most of his life in Paris, and whose goals are the same in some respects as those of Poulenc and Auric. His orchestration is light and transparent, and his ideas are elegant and fresh. His ballets reflect fine taste, especially *Noah's Ark,* in which the rise of the flood is impressively described, and *Barrabau,* written with highly amusing Roman humor. He also has to his credit a good *Symphony,* several concertos, and a good chamber concerto, the *Concerto du Loup.* Giorgio Federico Ghedini writes with clear and moderate expression. Among other interesting works is his lovely *Concerto de l'Albatro,* based on a chapter from Melville's *Moby Dick.*

Finally, passing on to the youngest generation, we find Luigi Dallapiccola (born in 1904), whom we have already discussed, and Goffredo Petrassi (born in 1904), composer of *Salmo IX* and a *Partita* for orchestra which lean toward the Stravinsky of the 1930's. More recently, Petrassi has succeeded in expressing himself more independently. *Coro di Morti* and *Notte Oscura* are great dramatic madrigals for chorus and orchestra, admirably planned and executed. Monteverdi's lesson was not lost on Petrassi. His opera, *Il Cordovano,* overflows with tumultuous but orderly life.

The youngest Italians have all been more or less influenced by dodecaphonism. Looking to it as a means of disciplining the melodic temperament with which they are so generously endowed, it threatens to lead them to exaggerated expression. For the Italians, serial composition is often the best antidote for *verismo*. Mario Peragallo, for example, after great success with traditionally conceived operas, began to follow the Schoenbergian school, a healthy exercise which enabled him to write beautiful works like the opera *La Collina* and the *Concert for Piano*, among others. More recently he composed a very beautiful *Violin Concerto*, and an enchanting chamber opera, *La Gita in Campagna*. Guido Turchi also benefited from the teaching of the Viennese masters, and is noted for a powerful choral composition, *Invective*. Bruno Maderna oscillated between Schoenberg and Dallapiccola in his *Tre Liriche Graeche*. His *Orchestral Etudes* for Kafka's *The Trial* brings him nearer to independence. He is followed by Luigi Nono, who shows undeniable talent in a series of compositions forming the *Epitaph for Garcia Lorca*.

The renaissance of music in England is analogous to the Italian renaissance. The two movements were contemporaneous, sprang from similar causes, evolved in the same way, and achieved comparable results.

In England, there was no period in which bad, melodramatic taste had degraded music, as was the case in Italy. But after the last masters of the eighteenth century, like Arne, Boyce, and Pepusch, a long silence ensued. In the nineteenth century, there is but one bright light: the collaboration between W. S. Gilbert and Arthur Sullivan (1842-1900) for the composition of some fifteen operas which sometimes have a distinctly popular flavor, like the *H.M.S. Pinafore*, created in 1878. The popularity of these operas has not been exhausted even today.

Yet the English people love music, and during the nineteenth century concert societies flourished. The same is true today, and this enthusiasm was certainly in large part responsible for the maintenance in England of a fairly high level of musical composition. But English taste is very conservative and cautious. Boldness is considered folly, and even today Tchaikovsky and Dvořák, along with Beethoven and Brahms, and with Sibelius, are the favorites of the Anglo-Saxon public. This temperate climate, too temperate for our taste, and this preference for a gentle lyricism which does not involve the soul of the listener too deeply explain the success of a postromantic musician like Edward Elgar (1857-1934) whose works, although sincere, meet with indifference in continental Europe. There is nonetheless profit to be had in listening to a score like the symphonic study *Falstaff*, which is probably the best of Elgar's works, and which portrays precisely the character of English music as it was before the appearance of the most recent generation.

Gustav Holst (1874–1934), Granville Bantock (1868–1946), John Ireland (born in 1879), Arnold Bax (1883-1953), Eugene Goossens (born in 1893), and Frank Bridge (1879-1941) should be considered as belonging to a period prior to Debussy, despite the various influences the composer of *Pelléas* may have exercised on these composers. The impressionist Frederick Delius (1863-1934) would be excellent if his art were a little less sugary. Of these composers, Holst is the most noteworthy, on the whole. His symphonic poems *The Planets* have a certain élan and are not uninteresting. There is one great point to his credit. He drew the attention of the younger generation to the English madrigalists. Holst was the musical director of Morley College in London, where the techniques of Byrd, Bull, Morley, Gibbons, Dowland, Weelkes, and then Purcell were taught. The study of old English vocal music proved salutary. The English language distributes its accents in a very special way, and the quality of its sound is therefore very different from that of Germanic or Latin languages. Sixteenth-century madrigalists held these peculiarities in mind and built their vocal style around them. Holst pointed out this source of native style, and the new generation, discarding the outdated romanticism which was in fashion, lent an attentive ear to the teachings of the masters of the Elizabethan period. William Walton (born in 1902), Benjamin Britten (born in 1913), and Michael Tippett (born in 1905) especially devoted their attention to the originality of the old masters, as did the dean of English music, Ralph Vaughan Williams (1872-1958).

Before these men, there were, however, some talented artists who were the first to break with romanticism and join the renaissance movement which vitalized Parisian musical life. These were Arthur Bliss (born in 1891), Constant Lambert (1905-1951), and Lord Berners (1883-1950).

Lord Berners, a cultured and witty man, was strongly attracted by the humor of Satie and Stravinsky. Around 1920, he wrote several very gay short works which had the virtue of reacting against the overly conformist and ceremonial spirit of the romantics. His ballet *The Triumph of Neptune* was well received by Diaghilev.

Bliss could not resist extending his eclecticism to too diverse sources, and his style has remained unindividual and composite. The music he wrote for the movie *Things to Come* is, however, well carried out, and his ballet *Checkmate* is an attractive score.

Constant Lambert is the most interesting of these three composers. His ballets *Pomona* and *Romeo and Juliet* abound in beautiful details.

RALPH VAUGHAN WILLIAMS is to England what Kœchlin is to France. Like Kœchlin, he watched several generations pass by and held himself aloof from the movements they provoked until, in his old age, he felt himself in harmony with twenty-year-olds. And again like Kœchlin, he wrote audacious and sometimes reckless pieces, and other compositions in which he sought serenity and balance. His production is bountiful and encompasses all genres. He is curious and ever alert, and concentrates his attention on the use of modes, the liberation of harmony, and a melodic style based on folk music. The personalities of these two composers are remarkably alike.

A fine example of his simple and knowledgeable, natural and cultivated style, of his reflective and sensitive art that sometimes makes Vaughan Williams' expression so captivating, is his famous *Fantasia on a Theme by Thomas Tallis,* for string orchestra, which echoes the spirit of sixteenth-century motets. His romance for violin and orchestra *The Lark Ascending* and his overture *The Wasps* have become almost as popular as *The Sorcerer's Apprentice. Hugh the Drover* is one of the rare English operas which shows individuality. However, the core of Vaughan Williams's work is his symphonies and the ballet *Job.*

The *First Symphony* or *Sea Symphony* (1903–1910) is written for solo voices, chorus, and orchestra, and is based on poems by Walt Whitman. Like the two symphonies following it, it is rather descriptive. The four movements do not express contrasting feelings. Rather, they should be considered as four aspects of a single region of feeling. This is the case, moreover, for

Vaughan Williams's other symphonies. The *First* was followed by the *London Symphony,* a portrait of the great city. The *Third* is the peaceful *Pastoral Symphony.* After these evocative works, in 1935, appeared the *Fourth Symphony,* more introverted, and written under the sign of revolt. After the first performance of this work, the author is supposed to have said: "I had to get it out of my system." This violent outburst, as from one who has reached the end of his patience, this sudden need to shout after so much reserve, is characteristic of the English temperament. In William Walton's *Belshazzar's Feast,* we also find one of these brutal and surprising eruptions. A critic said of this cantata: "It is Walton's great bulge."

The ballet *Job* is as powerful as the *Fourth Symphony.* This again is an act of revolt, a protest against what so often prevents the English soul from crossing boundaries, against that innate sense of propriety which brakes the most powerful impulses. The *Fifth Symphony* was written in 1940, and develops on a range of gentle and serene emotions.

WILLIAM WALTON's music is bright and frank. *Portsmouth Point* is a rapid and spirited overture. The *Viola Concerto* develops passionate ideas, and a youthful work, *Façade,* partakes of Satie's and Stravinsky's humor. Walton has also composed good film music, like the *Spitfire—Prelude and Fugue* for the movie *The First of the Few,* and a score for *Henry V.*

BENJAMIN BRITTEN, born in 1913, is at present the most original of the English composers. Gifted with rare animation, he has arrived on the scene at a time when all the foreign influences have been assimilated and a common language of our time is being formed. He is attempting to extract by elimination something more essential from this international language, which is threatening to create a uniform style. He has brought nothing new to it, but has chosen the sonorous elements which best suit his particular sensitivity, and has thus achieved extreme precision in characterizing his expression. In short, his case is comparable to Henri Sauguet's. A great admirer of poetry, Britten takes the nature of the English language as his point of departure to find his rhythms, melodic inflections, and vocalizations

[*Example 131*]. Hence it is not surprising that, like Poulenc and Sauguet, his talent is best applied in vocal works. Britten is as prolific as Milhaud and Hindemith, which implies that his work has not been uniform in quality. Among his first works, the collection of songs *On This Island* was inspired by the noble expression of Purcell and Handel. *Our Hunting Fathers,* a suite for soprano and orchestra based on old texts, has a very distinct flavor. Humor and grandeur are joined in a complex emotion admirably expressed in musical form. More recently, Britten has put some of the poems from Rimbaud's *Illuminations* to music. Several of these poems are very impressive. We should also draw attention to the lovely *Serenade for Tenor, Horn, and String Orchestra.*

In 1945 *Peter Grimes* was first performed. This opera, composed of a prologue and three acts, is a great experiment. The idea came from reading a poem by George Crabbe entitled *The Borough.* Crabbe tells of the life of a little fishing village on the east coast of England. All the characters represented, who belong to different classes of society, gravitate around the central figure of the fisherman Peter Grimes, an enigmatic boy, morbidly sadistic, and sometimes brutal, who is pictured in his isolation rather as a victim of the village petite bourgeoisie. All the action is enveloped in a sort of obstinate theme—the sea is everywhere.

Britten wrote the libretto for his opera from this poem. He wanted to give the opera a character of its own, through inner feelings, without alluding to folklore. He was partially successful. All the lyric passages have the particular character desired. On the other hand, the style of the more specifically dramatic portions is not completely free of conventionality. The relationship between the voices and the orchestra is not too different from that established by Verdi in *Otello.* Britten uses simple orchestral techniques to create the atmosphere and avoids burdening the drama. He concentrates primary interest on the voices. The orchestra thus is deliberately held to a range of rather neutral colors. It depicts that gray luminosity of the North Sea very well. *Example 134* shows how exact are the notations for creating the atmosphere in *Peter Grimes.* The gentle swell of the sea is expressed in a succession of diatonic thirds and a descent to the perfect chord of the major, which is fleeting, however, because the melodic design moves in the minor. This design recurs repeatedly, and sets the scene, under the voices, before the action has been specified. The second scene, with a superb arioso by Peter Grimes and a round, a continuous canon in diabolical rhythm, is perfect, as is the end of the last act in which Peter Grimes's ballad is sung with no orchestral support, while at regular intervals a tuba holds a long note to give the effect of a foghorn. At such moments, the listener senses all the pull, all the strength of Britten's lyricism. We have the feeling that the young composer will one day produce a masterpiece if he will lay aside external action to seek expression in pure lyricism. Because of his inclinations and independence, he stands alone in English music, and his is the most solidly developed talent.

MICHAEL TIPPETT is more traditional. But he follows the most fruitful of traditions, that of Holst and Ralph Vaughan Williams. Tippett succeeded Holst as musical director at Morley College, where he continues to teach and practice sixteenth-century choral music. This music serves him as a model, or rather, an example, for the outlines of his own works. His oratorio *A Child of Our Time* (1945) has excellent qualities. The subject is the drama of the youth of our time, the despair of youth in the face of mechanical civilization and horrifying rivalry between nations.

The originality of this oratorio lies in the substitution of a Negro spiritual for the Protestant chorale. The choice was not made in the interests of local color—the action takes place in Europe. The composer considers the Negro spiritual as the song of distress and hope of our time. The chorale was popular in origin, and corresponded to a particular state of mind which no longer exists today. The Negro spiritual is popular, as well, and expresses the helplessness of our soul in a world crushed under material concerns. Recently, another young composer, Alan Rawsthorne, has drawn notice with a sprightly *Concerto for Piano*.

The Italian and English movements, in their search for a national tradition, show obvious cohesion. Several musicians of other countries deserve to be mentioned.

Tibor Harsányi (Hungarian), Marcel Mihalovici (Romanian), Alexandre Tansman (Polish), and Bohuslav Martinů (Czech) made up an amicable group between 1925 and 1939 under the name of the École de Paris. Martinů was the most interesting. He was a prolific composer, and his writing is always serious in quality. Martinů is the archetype of the modern composer who uses a cosmopolitan language formed of the fusion of all the contemporary harmonic discoveries. Very adept and fluent, he is also one of those musicians whose music one calls *workmanlike*. But that is all we can say. Martinů is the Saint-Saëns of contemporary music.

Around 1920 the Catalan Fedérico Mompou published a number of collections of piano pieces. His *Cants Magics* and *Suburbis* have retained all their freshness. Oscar Esplá of Madrid followed in the tradition of Albéniz and De Falla.

The Romanian Georges Enesco had considerable success with his *Oedipe,* first performed at the Paris Opera.

In the Low Countries, Heink Badings has come under the influence of Alban Berg, while Willem Pijper has been somewhat swayed by all the great modern masters. Badings's work has solid qualities, as shown in his symphonies and interesting concertos, as well as in some of his convincing dramatic works. Jean Absil of Belgium was attracted by the virtuosity and arabesques of Ravel. His *Concerto pour Piano* and *Chants du Mort* are good examples of his fresh talent. Marcel Poot has written the pleasant and successful *Ouverture Joyeuse.* Raymond Chevreuille is presently the hope of Belgian music. His symphonies, concertos, and quartets bear witness to deep and unpredictable emotions, and he shows true mastery in expressing his ideas. Chevreuille is more and better than a skillful musician; he has the gift of poetry, and it is hard to understand why his work is so little known outside of his native country. *Évasions,* a cantata for soprano and orchestra, is full of mystery. It is one of his best works. The *Concerto pour Cor* does not find its equal in any other country, and his *Symphonie des Souvenirs* shows great feeling. The new generation, notably Louis de Meester, David van de Woestijne, Victor Legley, and Renier van der Velden, is improving on the unfruitful romantic period, which, for Belgium, was of little importance. Progress, in this case, has a special meaning. It refers to an affirmation of autonomy which was completely unknown to preceding generations.

In Switzerland, it will suffice to single out Conrad Beck, whose symphony *Innominata* caused some stir; Willy Burkhard, whose outstanding work to date is the oratorio *Das Gesicht Yesaias,* and who is having difficulty throwing off the influence of Hindemith; Frank Martin, who set passages of Bédier's *Tristan* to music under the title *The Drugged Wine;* and Jean Binet, who has composed some pretty and at times exquisite rustic songs.

The fact that since 1939 many celebrated European composers —among them Schoenberg, Stravinsky, Milhaud, Hindemith, Křenek, Martinů, Tansman, and Rieti—have been living in the United States has helped American musicians develop a feeling for composing. We have already discussed the nationalist trends ruling the country. But in the United States, besides Ives, Copland, Antheil, and Gruenberg, there are a great number of more eclectic composers who can be divided into rightist and leftist, or progressive and conservative, groups.

Among the experimental stands Edgar Varèse, French-born, who has attempted curious effects in instrumental polyphony. His *Octandre* is intriguing. John Cage is presently experimenting with percussionist music based on the use of very small intervals of undetermined notes, hoping to achieve by this method a more radical solution to the problem posed by the use of quarter-tones. Among the conservatives we find Ernest Bloch (who left his native Switzerland long ago), Douglas Moore, Samuel Barber, and Roy Harris. William Schuman has the most developed sense of grandeur; actually, his symphonic works are a little too spectacular. But his choruses *A Free Song, a Holiday Song* are particularly free and youthful. The works of Walter Piston and Roger Sessions are equally noteworthy.

The artists whose names have been mentioned in this rapid enumeration are all what we would call *sound musicians.* The only criticism we can make of their works is their lack of effective range, of communicating power, and the absence of necessity—qualities which are innate in composers of the first rank.

CONCLUSION

THE STUDY which has been the object of this book shows that musical production was abundant between 1910 and 1955. This production is notable for high quality in writing and a remarkable broadening of musical language, which allow us to rank this period among the greatest in the history of music.

When such works as *Pierrot Lunaire, Le Sacre du Printemps, Parade,* and *Les Choéphores* were being published one after the other, the world naturally spoke of the rupture with the past, revolutionary art, and anarchy. This is what was said of Debussy in the days of *Pelléas;* of Wagner, when *Tristan* appeared; of Beethoven when his last quartets were first heard.

Actually, all the great composers of our time did no more than develop in their own way the potential of musical language, assist in its emancipation, and work for liberation of its elements in order to use them as they wished and according to their own designs.

There were moments when the evolution developed step by step, slowly and peacefully. There were other moments when it proceeded by abrupt leaps and bounds. These were generally periods when artistic problems were caught up in the tide of great social upheavals; at such times the world sees phenomena analogous to what in biology are called mutations. We are living in such a time.

If we make an inventory of the contemporary body of works, and if we ask ourselves which, in the final analysis, is the best part, we are struck by the fact that since 1930 a good many symphonies have been composed. But we could count on our fingers those of sufficient beauty and originality to pass on to posterity. Ours does not seem to be a period of symphonies. Our composers seem to feel more at ease in handling free forms, in which the individual may most clearly express his particular message. This fact perhaps explains the importance given to symphonic ballet.

The best and purest part of contemporary instrumental music is chamber music, and especially string quartets and music for orchestras of solo instruments.

But it would certainly seem that our period has expressed itself most fully in vocal music. The art song and folk song have been particularly cultivated, as have the oratorio and cantata. And in the same breath that opera is pronounced dead, we are given *Erwartung, Wozzeck, The Nightingale, Mathis der Maler, Christophe Colomb, La Chartreuse de Parme, Peter Grimes,* and *The Rake's Progress*—in short, a whole series of meritorious and noteworthy works which are obviously not of just passing interest, but all of which reappear periodically in theaters or concert halls.

Need we mention "mechanical music," that novelty of our time? With the introduction of radio, some composers thought that special music should be written for that medium. Experience has shown the uselessness of such an undertaking. Music which is good to the ear is good through the microphone. Besides, broadcasting and receiving equipment is gradually being perfected, and a time will come when sound can be transmitted with no distortion or deformation.

The problem of sound tracks for films is different. Here it is a question of creating music which is heard without dominating the spoken text, which sets the atmosphere discreetly and quickly. Little by little, movie producers are coming to understand that for films of quality it is worth their while to seek out good composers. The art of movie music is still in its infancy.

Movies, phonographs, and radios are only electrical means of reproducing sound. There also exist electrical apparatus for producing sound. These are of more direct interest to composers. At present, the only instrument in wide use is the electrical instrument called the ondes Martenot. At present, it can produce seventy-five different timbres. This instrument enriches the orchestra, and a number of composers, notably Honegger, Milhaud, Messiaen, and Jolivet, have had success in combining its timbres with those of other instruments.

It is surprising to realize that the great interest taken in specific timbres, a result of the increasing importance of solo orchestra instruments, has not spurred composers to use new instruments. The Eb clarinet has indeed come into common usage; the flute in G can be found in some scores. But practically no use has been made of the magnificent bass oboe, also called the Heckelphone, which fills out the family of oboes in the lower registers. And although the bass clarinet is today a permanent addition to the symphonic orchestra, the contrabass clarinet has not yet made its appearance, except in Schoenberg's *Five Pieces for Orchestra*. It emits a clear and expressive timbre in very low registers which could make a considerable contribution to the body of sound.

Percussion has been appreciably enriched as a result of the influence of jazz, oriental music, and South American music.

And now, we might ask, after this contemporary period, after Stravinsky and Schoenberg, what will happen? Where will music go? It will go where it is led by the fantasy and imagination of those who have great enough genius to bring their vision to bear. This will be very interesting to see, as it always has been when music has started on an adventure. For one of the most precious qualities of art is its diversity; its evolution, as a human manifestation, never comes to a halt.

At the immediate moment, as we conclude this study, which in principle should be restricted to the period between the World Wars, new research is in progress. This time, it is correct to use the word *research* in the strict scientific sense. Systematic labors are in question here, undertaken by common consent by artists and engineers for the purpose of discovering new means of expression in technical methods of sound recording.

The first experimental undertaking was that of John Cage, which we have already mentioned. In 1946 he presented *Three Dances for Prepared Piano* at Carnegie Hall. He "prepared" the pianos so that they were detimbred, relieved of their capacity to make measured intervals heard, and transformed into percussion instruments with very varied effects. Cage addressed himself to the problem of the architecture of form without falling back on either tonality or thematic development. On close examination of the question of the architecture of time, he succeeded, he claims, "in separating the concepts of musical anatomy from their psychological union with the expressive contents." Lou Harrison, in presenting the *Three Dances*, tells us:

At first sight, his principle of architecture is faintly reminiscent of the medieval mysticism of numbers. . . . In principle, his idea of form is simple, so simple that it is difficult to grasp. It involves only the prismatic use of temporal schemas. For example, let us imagine a composer who begins with an idea discovered spontaneously and continues for ten measures. These ten measures are articulated in smaller groups. Let us suppose that this idea can be subdivided into three groups: four plus three plus three measures. Let us now take the square of the idea—ten times ten. This number of measures will be chosen as the length of the piece. Each phrase will therefore include the small subdivisions four-three-three, but the whole piece will have the same proportions, the first section of the hundred measures thus being worth four times ten, the second, three times ten, and the last, three times ten. In this way, each phrase and all the sections will be articulated in the same way, according to the same proportions, which will be audible in their augmented form as well as in their diminished form. . . . In nontonal music, this method allows for delicate proportioning of the structural balance and, at the same time, for freedom of the poetic spirit which could not be had in applying classic means of development to the use of new material, percussive in nature.

Listening to Cage's pieces, a pleasure in places, facilitates the understanding of this explanatory text, which is less theoretic then it appears at first glance. The plan here is still entirely preconceived. The music exists without psychological impulse. In other words, this is an art in which the role of the intellect reduces the role of inner life and the subconscious to a minimum, and in which mathematical precision replaces the capricious meanderings of human methods.

The concert of Cage's dances took place in 1946. Hardly two years later, in 1948, Pierre Schaeffer was caught up in the same sort of experimentation. He enlisted the services of Radiodiffusion Française to try to reserve grooves or parts of grooves on records and, by repeating, retarding, or accelerating them and mixing them with other parts of grooves, to create sounds with an entirely new timbre and dynamism. By combining them, he invented *musique concrète,* so named because it is engendered by concrete musical objects—the grooves of records. Contrary to the preconceived schematizing of a composition which is John Cage's method, the composition of *musique concrète* is done empirically, by experimentation or successive trials. At present, the results are not very satisfactory. Hearing pieces thus composed almost invariably makes the listener think of the concerts of noise as conceived by the futurists prior to 1914, and such pieces do not possess the musical traits which can be recognized in John Cage's work.

Serge Moreux defines the qualities of *musique concrète* in these words:

The material of *musique concrète* is sound in its original state as nature furnishes it, machines establish it, and handling transforms it. Between these particles and their multiplication, there are no other affective or acoustical relationships besides those which govern the scattered and twinkling physical universe. The space filled by *musique concrète* is the space commanded by the machine and its by-products, that world of vibrations, colors, and volumes unknown to our musician's ear as yet imprisoned by mechanisms. It is astonishing that a man should have wanted to use that world to build works of the spirit. Despite the numerous imperfections of these first attempts, the works impress on us their own logic, their psyche bordering on our own, their dialectic of chance. There was a Middle Ages of stone; it was sculptured. There is a Middle Ages of waves: they are being captured.

There is no reason to be alarmed at experiments like Cage's and Schaeffer's. Our post-World War II period has been completely dominated by mechanical, chemical, and electrical forces. Our culture is no longer agricultural: it is urban. It is no longer based on literary notions, but falls under the sign of the physical sciences. Whether we want it or not, our thinking is being increasingly affected by the scientific disciplines, whose formative faculty is progressively replacing that of the old discipline of letters.

Let us turn to a commentator, René de Obaldia: "We must nonetheless point out here the exceptional degree of pathos and tragedy which these first attempts involve us in. And for good reason. Here we stand before the reproduction of that mechanical universe which has become ours and which gains more power over us daily. Undeniable evidence. The drama of our times is etched on this honeyless wax."

But beyond the drama inherent in every intellectual revolution, we will again strike a balance. Gaston Bachelard says, "Having formed reason in the image of the world as its first effort, the scientific spirit of today is beginning to construct a world in the image of reason. Scientific activity is achieving *rational wholes* in the full meaning of the words."

There is nothing wrong with the principle of *musique concrète*. It is an outgrowth of the new scientific spirit that in great measure represents our age. Everything depends on what will be done with this principle, on the real or illusory capacity of its application to insure the continuity of the function of music —to be the relationship between the phenomenon of sound and the listener who perceives it.

In his book *À la Recherche d'une Musique Concrète* (Paris, 1952), Pierre Schaeffer insists on the fact that "the concrete experiment in music consists of building sonorous objects, not with the play of numbers and seconds of the metronome, but with pieces of time torn from the cosmos [these pieces of time being grooves of records]. What is torn from time is done nonetheless with time, in giving form to time." Two recent works of *musique concrète, Symphonie pour un Homme Seul* by Pierre Schaeffer and *Le Voile d'Orphée* by Pierre Henry, seem to indicate that the proper domain of this art is drama.

In addition to the experiments in *musique concrète*, research in electronic music has been carried on since 1950 at the studios of the Nord-West Deutsche Rundfunk in Cologne by Werner Meyer-Eppler, Herbert Eimert, and Fritz Enkel. This research does not involve instruments like Trautwein's monochord or the wave instruments of Theremin or Martenot. The aim of the work undertaken in Cologne is to furnish composers with sounds produced by electronic instruments. It is the composer's task to arrange and coordinate these sounds harmoniously. Electronic music is not played by instrumentalists, it is not produced before a microphone (except for radio transmission), and no method of writing could actually be used to put it down in notation. Contrary to *musique concrète,* which works with the microphone, electronic music uses exclusively sounds of electro-acoustical origin. The sound, produced by a generating apparatus, is placed on a magnetic tape. The composer creates his music by simultaneously manipulating a number of tapes, each carrying a given sound. A whole new world is disclosed. Herbert Eimert observes:

The timbre of the sounds thus produced, which are rich in harmonics, can be modified due to electrical filtering networks. Fundamentals, upper partials, or whole bands of frequencies can be muffled or fully sounded at will. In this way, the timbre of the sounds becomes an element that can be shaped freely. By the same procedures, a noise made by a noise-generator, spread throughout the range of audibility (white sound), will be transformed into "colored" sounds. The approach can be changed, within large limits, with the help of a tape recorder equipped with a constantly variable range of speeds. With an electronic controlling mechanism, the sonorous process can be rhythmically transformed as desired, with no need for manual skill. In the same way, resonances of very long duration can be created synthetically. To compose a work, a musician would use an installation of tape recorders which would allow for simultaneous recording of a number of voices, independently of each other. . . . The vibration of the electrons produces a quantity of sounds that is impossible to master, from the simplest sound to the most fantastic formations. Selecting, arranging, and working them into a composition, to show the superiority of the Muses over technique, is the task of electronic music.

The first attempts at composing electronic music naturally still sound like experimental research, since this was a totally unknown domain until recently. This is true of pieces like *Klang in unbegrenztem Raum* and *Ostinato-Figuren und -Rythmen,* composed by Herbert Eimert and Robert Beyer. Young composers of talent are now taking up the composition of electronic music. Among them are Karlheinz Stockhausen, who has already created some stir with works of very new spirit and imaginative form, *Kreuzspiel* and *Nr. I Kontrapunkte,* and Karel Goeyvaerts, trained in the schools of Messiaen and Milhaud, who has discarded all other forms of composition to write only electronic music.

Some worthy people have taken alarm at the trends contemporary music is following—Stravinsky's objectivity, atonality and dodecaphonism, *musique concrète,* and electronic music. Ernest Ansermet notes that Stravinsky introduced a new attitude of the composer toward his music, according to which the composer separates his own interior life from the musical object he is creating. In 1948, Ansermet wrote:

Judging by their behavior, it is impossible to say whether composers no longer know how to proceed, or whether they no longer know what to do or how to do it. Creative action has lost its sense of necessity. So they invent. They set up a working hypothesis for themselves, and everything produced between the two World Wars is an immense aspiration to music, a desperate search, by way of the unauthentic, for lost time. The composer devotes himself less to a work to be done than to a new way of doing it, a new technique, a new type of object, resulting in that rapid succession of unprecedented, if not absurd, forms which have so disconcerted the public and which no longer correspond to aesthetic projects but to fads. . . .

When its incentive has disappeared, art can give its dicta no substantiality other than dogmatism and formalism. This is the orientation of most aesthetic systems today, and it is also the orientation of the two most striking creative movements of these times, that of Schoenberg and that of Stravinsky.

Such statements, from an artist who has spent most of his career defending contemporary art, are not to be taken lightly. They contain some truth. But we must add that, in our opinion, the current state in the evolution of music is not voluntary, and that, if there are fads, they always correspond to deep needs.

We have mentioned the strange fact that although many symphonies have been composed by contemporary musicians, there is not one of lasting significance. They are performed or heard once, they are found to be interesting and well written, and then they are forgotten. We must realize that the sonata and the symphonic spirit as they were understood a century ago decidedly belong in the past, and that it is useless to regret their passing or prolong their existence in the midst of modern compositions. Neither one nor the other can serve any longer as the framework for expressing modern sensibilities and conscience. The sonata and the symphony were appropriate for a hundred and fifty years. Used by us, they are not appropriate. They are a travesty.

The drama of our time lies in the fact that we have not yet found a means of replacing them with other forms. It is too early for a new classicism to take root. All classicism, to develop, needs a calm, stable time. For forty years, the world has lived in economic, political, and spiritual chaos. Numberless and contradictory hypotheses are proposed daily in every domain. None can predominate, for none represents a sufficiently large and general body of facts. The positive or physical sciences alone continue to develop in a coordinated and irrefutable way. It is therefore not surprising that the physical sciences, more than arts and letters, have taken the responsibility for forming modern culture. The concepts we form of life and the universe are infinitely better expressed by the structure of the atom and reflections on matter and energy than by works of art.

The latter, as Ansermet correctly states, have lost their sense of necessity, and have not at present succeeded in conceiving forms suited to the greatest spiritual revolution since the invention of writing.

In the process of an evolution which began in the thirteenth century and is now ending, music has progressively moved away from its natural function. It has gradually become involved in formalism, which has ended by submerging music at the moment when it no longer expressed the human, but only the man who was writing it. We say *writing* instead of *composing* because without writing, without notation, exaggerated formalism would have been impossible.

The immeasurable importance of the concern with form on the one hand and anarchy on the other has muddled understanding of physical, biological, and psychological realities of music because tonal functions have been denied and the natural limits of auditory and cerebral perception have been forgotten. The composer, whose work represents himself alone, has lost all sense of responsibility. This is the state we are now in, due to an excess of individualism and the incapacity of music to keep up with the demand for new means of expression created by great and rapid transformations of cultural bases.

Individualism is a consequence of the cultural state we are now abandoning. Concerning the new forms which must be found, we should give credit to the young composers. We have no right at this moment to ignore the progress, such as it may be, toward the discovery of new foundations for music and the restoration of its natural function.

Young composers are eagerly taking up the marvelously rich and diverse sounds furnished by electronic music and new and yet unknown techniques. They are fumbling, not yet knowing how to use the new potentials and the new attitude suggested by our times. They find themselves in exactly the same situation as primitive people discovering for the first time that a cord stretched by a bow vibrates and makes sounds, and that a gourd, a hole in the ground, or a cavity in the cheek can modulate sound.

Primitivism, of course. This did not prevent the musical bow from being the basis of the development of music, nor did it prevent the delight taken in the sounds it makes from leading rapidly to the use of these sounds for signaling, identification, and then magic and religion. The analogy between absolute primitiveness and our modern version, if not carried to the extreme, is so obvious that in itself it explains the passionate interest many young people take in the native music of peoples all over the world, in that music not written but recorded which is functional and has so remained since its first utterance. The study of its nature has now become part of our music education, and will help us rediscover the function of communication, temporarily lost, which new music must possess.

And yet we must not lose sight of the present cultural situation. Modern music that is truly representative of its time is not and cannot be the same in different parts of the world. Even within a single culturally homogeneous area, there will be different paths because many complexes of ideas and expression can coexist. In Western Europe, for example, there are at present two distinct cultural currents.[26]

One of these currents follows the values that have been the basis of society for the last seven or eight thousand years: the values of agricultural peoples, whose musicians and poets even today sing of roses, nightingales, spring, and summer. Their con-

26. By *culture* we mean the behavior of the individual in a specific society.

ception of time is patterned on the movement of the sun, and their rhythms obey the pulsations of nature.

The other current, of recent origin, represents the urban and industrial culture which is still in the process of forming. For city people, who know nothing of the country except what they read in books, whistles and automobile horns replace the murmur of the woods and the water. A curve to them is an asphalt road; their rhythms translate rows of mercury lamps and the flickering of neon lights. Their sense of time does not reflect the passage of the seasons but rather the speed of automobiles and airplanes. Caught in a metallic frenzy, the industrialized man is under constant and intense pressure. Interior tranquillity and meditation are forbidden to him. If this man is a musician, he will think like Stockhausen or Boulez; it is natural for him to seek new means of sonorous expression through electronics in order to represent a cultural condition humanity has never before experienced. Good-by, clarinet, good-by, violin; sing of roses and grassy trails. Our life is a dance in the cement streets, the smell of gasoline, and masses of people. We need other sounds to clothe our dreams.

Le Marteau sans Maître is representative of this new culture. In another direction, so are *La Symphonie pour un Homme Seul* and *Le Voile d'Orphée*. In the one the electronic music (and related types) and the *musique concrète* in the others have arisen from the same modern phenomenon, though their means of expression are different.

Let us therefore be sympathetic to the work of Stockhausen, Boulez, and Nono, and to that of Pierre Schaeffer and Pierre Henry. But let us avoid the common mistake of thinking that theirs is the only path possible. There are still and there will always be people who have nothing to do with city life and who are not subjects of the industrial empire. We can even say that the great majority of men are not touched by the painful tensions of our machine age. Their daily reality is still composed of blossoming apple trees and nocturnal calm. And they too have the right to express themselves, and their music has nothing in common with the works that tell of our new anxiety. Their calm is a blessing, as we know from Boris Blacher's lovely *Zweites Konzert für Klavier und Orchester*, Op. 42, Werner Egk's *Sonata for Orches-*

tra, and the delightful *a cappella* composition *Mörike Chorlieder-buch,* Op. 19, by Hugo Distler, dead before his time. They deserve our gratitude for their fresh spontaneity and their purity of soul.

MUSICAL EXAMPLES

MUSICAL EXAMPLES

EXAMPLE 1

Très lent

_ rer an _ non _ çant _____ U _ ne ro _ se dans les té _ né _ bres.

EXAMPLE 2

EXAMPLE 3

EXAMPLE 4

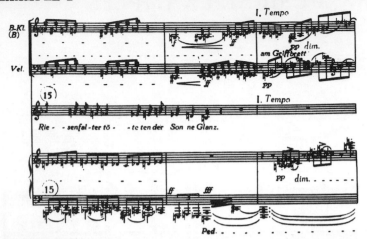

EXAMPLE 5

Original Row (Grundgestalt)

Inversion

Retrograde

Retrograde Inversion

EXAMPLE 6a

Langsam (♩ = ca 54)

EXAMPLE 6b

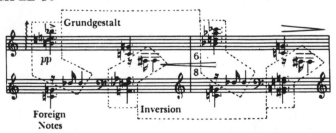

Grundgestalt

Inversion

Foreign
Notes

EXAMPLE 7

Grundgestalt

Retrograde

Inversion

Retrograde Inversion

EXAMPLE 8a

EXAMPLE 8b

EXAMPLE 8c

EXAMPLE 9

EXAMPLE 10

EXAMPLE 11

EXAMPLE 12

EXAMPLE 13

Mäβig (moderato) ($\flat$ = ca 100)
etwas langsamer anfangen

EXAMPLE 14

EXAMPLE 15

EXAMPLE 16

EXAMPLE 17a

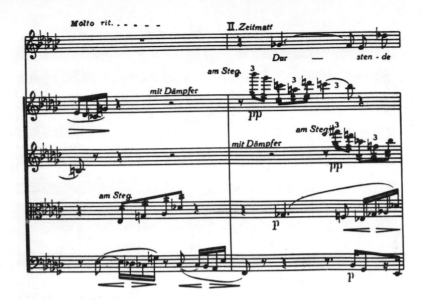

EXAMPLE 17b

EXAMPLE 18

EXAMPLE 19

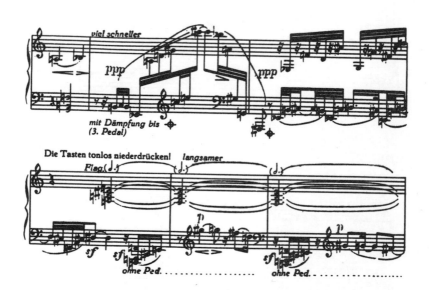

EXAMPLE 20

EXAMPLE 21

Da mei - ne Lip - pen reg - los sind und bren - nen.

EXAMPLE 22

Sa - get mir auf wel - chem pfa - de heu

EXAMPLE 23

EXAMPLE 24

EXAMPLE 25

Ruhig schreitend (♩=ca 50)

ANTON WEBERN, OP. 21

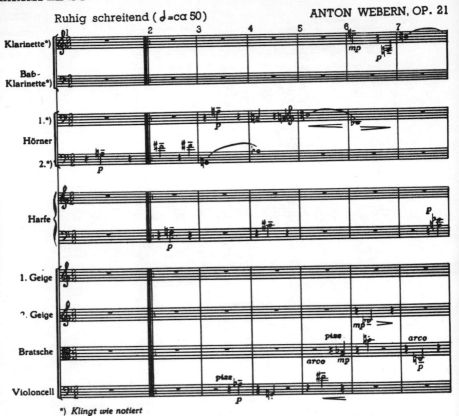

*) Klingt wie notiert

EXAMPLE 26

Sehr schnell ♩=ca 160

EXAMPLE 27

EXAMPLE 28

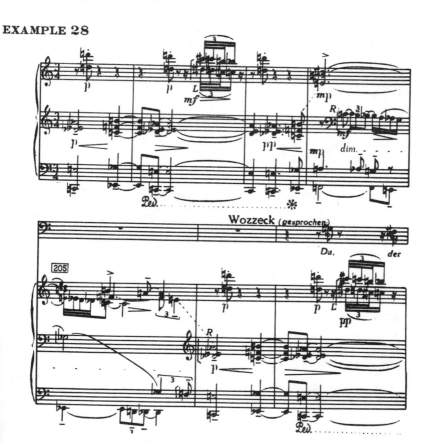

XAMPLE 29

EXAMPLE 30

EXAMPLE 31

EXAMPLE 32

EXAMPLE 33

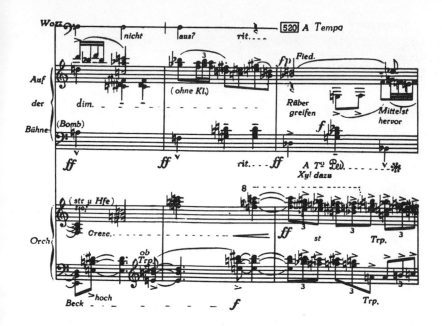

EXAMPLE 34

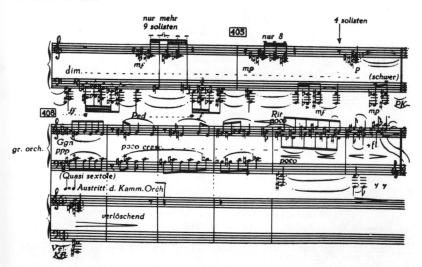

EXAMPLE 35

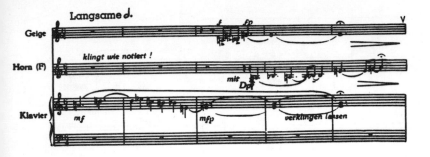

EXAMPLE 36

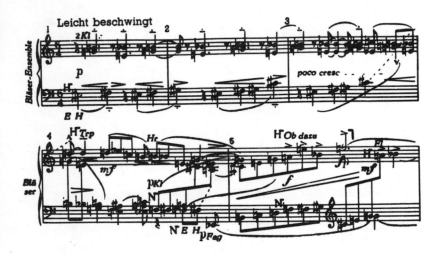

EXAMPLE 37

EXAMPLE 38

EXAMPLE 39

EXAMPLE 40

EXAMPLE 41

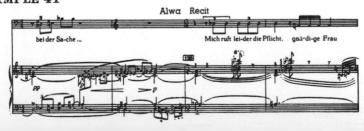

EXAMPLE 42

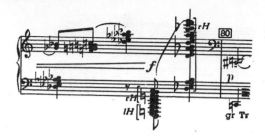

EXAMPLE 43

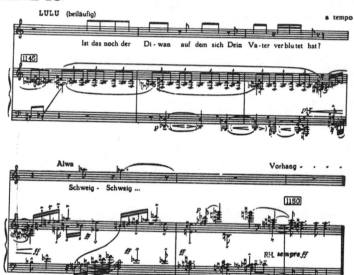

EXAMPLE 44

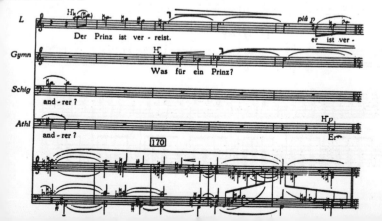

EXAMPLE 45

EXAMPLE 46

EXAMPLE 47

EXAMPLE 48

EXAMPLE 49a

EXAMPLE 49b

EXAMPLE 50

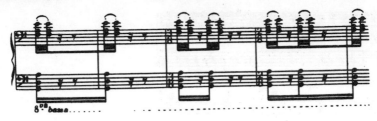

EXAMPLE 51

EXAMPLE 52

EXAMPLE 53

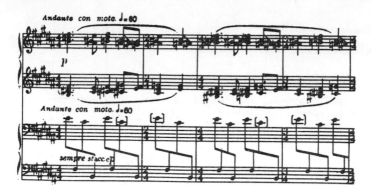

EXAMPLE 54

EXAMPLE 55

EXAMPLE 56

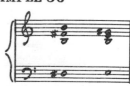

EXAMPLE 57

EXAMPLE 58

EXAMPLE 59

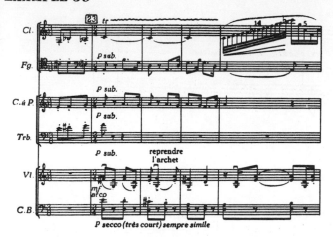

EXAMPLE 60

EXAMPLE 61

EXAMPLE 62

EXAMPLE 63

Ma chie - re dame, a vous mon cuer en - - voy
Que li - e - ment et hum - ble - ment con - - joy

EXAMPLE 64

EXAMPLE 65

EXAMPLE 66

EXAMPLE 67

EXAMPLE 68

té, Je n'ai pas sa-vou-ré tou-te la vo-lup-té De sa pa-ro - - le tendre èt de son fier vi-sa-ge Et qu'un

EXAMPLE 69

EXAMPLE 70

EXAMPLE 71

EXAMPLE 72

EXAMPLE 73

EXAMPLE 74

EXAMPLE 75

EXAMPLE 76

EXAMPLE 77

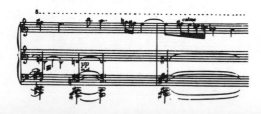

EXAMPLE 78

EXAMPLE 79

Lent, soutenu et lumineux

EXAMPLE 80

EXAMPLE 81

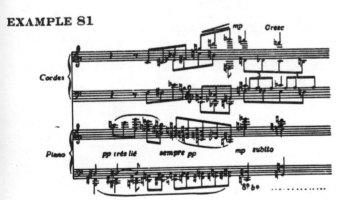

Cordes

Piano

pp très lié   *sempre pp*   *mp subito*

mp   *Cresc*

EXAMPLE 82

Modéré (♩=84)

Piano

EXAMPLE 83

EXAMPLE 84

EXAMPLE 85

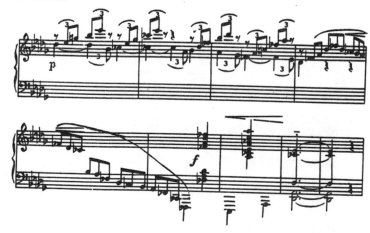

EXAMPLE 86

EXAMPLE 87

EXAMPLE 88

EXAMPLE 89

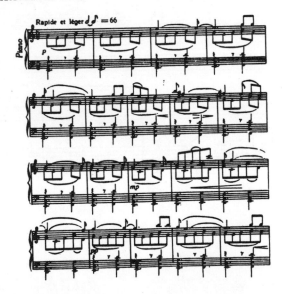

EXAMPLE 90

EXAMPLE 91

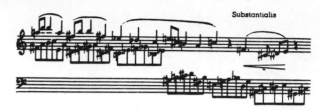

EXAMPLE 93

EXAMPLE 92

EXAMPLE 94

EXAMPLE 95

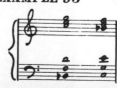

EXAMPLE 96

Le lys naît blanc comme o-deur Sim-ple - ment je le pré-fè-re

EXAMPLE 97

C'est vous qu'au Pa lais de Tau - ri - de, Fu - nes - te pri - vi -

EXAMPLE 98

Re gar dez ce Mon sieur qui va Mon - ter en li mou - sine Et

EXAMPLE 99

- rai Il me se-ra beau de mou - rir en -

- sui - te Deux a - mis re - po - se - ront côte à côte a - près ce cher

EXAMPLE 100

EXAMPLE 101

EXAMPLE 102

EXAMPLE 103

EXAMPLE 104

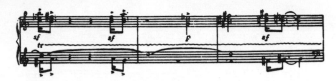

EXAMPLE 105

EXAMPLE 106

EXAMPLE 107

EXAMPLE 108

EXAMPLE 109

EXAMPLE 110

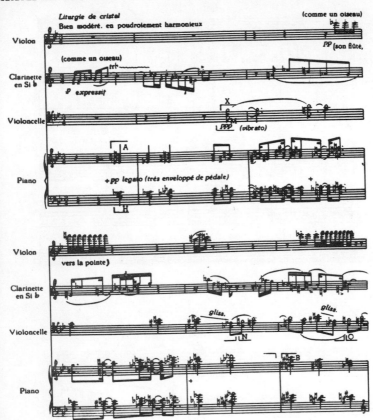

EXAMPLE 111

Mode 2, First Transposition

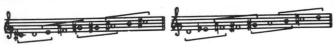

EXAMPLE 112

EXAMPLE 113

Mode 2, Fourth Transposition

EXAMPLE 114

Mode 2, First Transposition

EXAMPLE 115

EXAMPLE 116

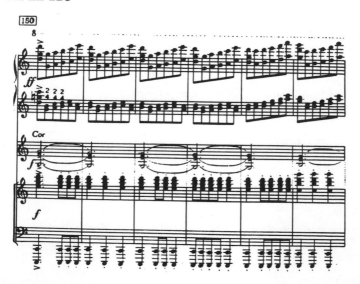

EXAMPLE 117

EXAMPLE 118

tat er's. Sie ver - stand es spä - ter, wie sie ihn in sei - nen Weg -

EXAMPLE 119

Gesang

Der ſel - - be gro - ße En - - gel, wel cher einst ihr der Ge - bä -

Piano

sempre legato

(Basso ostinato)

EXAMPLE 120

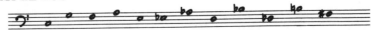

EXAMPLE 121

EXAMPLE 122

EXAMPLE 123

EXAMPLE 124

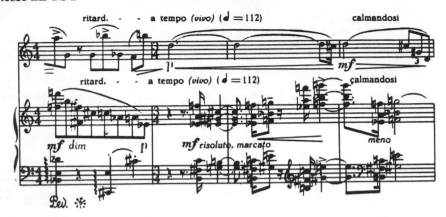

EXAMPLE 125

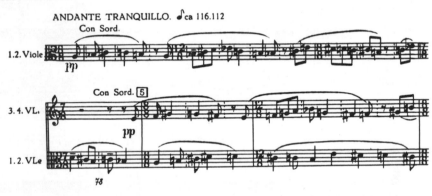

EXAMPLE 126

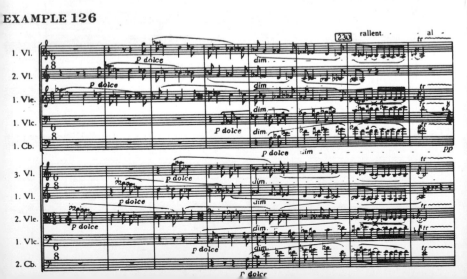

EXAMPLE 127

EXAMPLE 128

EXAMPLE 129

EXAMPLE 130

EXAMPLE 131

EXAMPLE 132

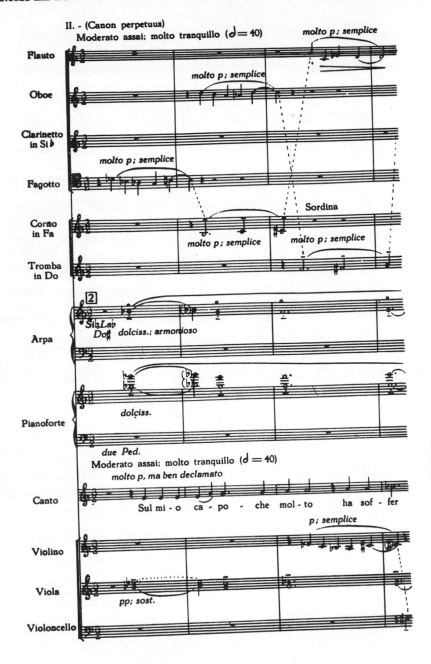

EXAMPLE 133

EXAMPLE 134

MODERN MUSIC AND LYRIC THEATER

DURING THE Festival of Music in the Twentieth Century, which took place in Rome in 1954, a seminar was held on opera, present and future. On the basis of a study presented by Henri Sauguet, a discussion developed between music critics, theater directors, and composers of the most diverse inclinations. Participating in this seminar, we introduced some ideas we had already brought up at the Florence Congress of Music in 1937.

Contrary to the widely held opinion, it seems that opera is not a form of musical thought belonging to the past with no place in today's culture. Many contemporary composers write operas, or want to write them. There are some very beautiful twentieth-century lyric works whose musical worth has been recognized. But they are better known through published scores, concert performances, and recordings than through their infrequent stage performances.

There are many indications that composers and theatrical directors are not adapting to the exigencies of our times. Modern opera poses an important problem that needs elucidating.

During the nineteenth century, lyric theaters gave performances every evening. The works in the repertory were intended only to entertain and to provide material for beautiful voices. They did not inspire the spectators to profound reflection. The opera or operetta gave them a more or less agreeable evening's diversion. Text and music were conceived so that the general public could understand and appreciate them; composers held in mind the fact that the average cultural level of a population was not very high.

The social role of the opera in the nineteenth century was taken over in the twentieth by the movies, which have the advantage of offering a more captivating visual aspect than opera.

Besides, music is not of primary importance to the public at large.

Since Wagner, lyric theater has tended to adopt forms bearing deeper meaning. It expresses certain mental attitudes, certain conceptions of life and the world. It requires sustained attention from the listener and a capacity for understanding and rapid adaptability which are found only in limited circles of highly cultivated people. Because of its new significance, modern opera has become an exceptional thing, a festival performance. It is not suitable for daily fare, and cannot be incorporated into current repertories, which are aimed at entertaining the masses. The most noble works of the modern lyric theater, staged in the largest cities, attract only the elite. They can only be performed three or four times, and cannot be revived for a number of years. Such is the case with the *Ring der Nibelungen, Elektra, Pelléas et Mélisande, Pénélope, Love for Three Oranges, Wozzeck, Christophe Colomb, Cardillac, La Chartreuse de Parme,* and *Padmâvati.*

The expense incurred in presenting these grand operas is too great in relation to the uncertainty of a reasonable return. Almost always, the director of a theater will present such a work knowing that he will lose money. If he does decide to produce the work, he does so out of artistic persuasion and because he knows that it will bring his theater prestige.

Given the fact that in a single city the public is not large enough to allow a sufficient number of performances to cover expenses, and that from another point of view the success of a fine modern work is no less real or deserved because it has had a short run in a single city, the problem consists of finding a larger audience by sending a worthwhile production, created in a given theater, on tour to a number of cities. This problem can be resolved if authors, composers, producers, and theater directors agree to follow certain basic rules.

Artists who want to address and be understood by the public of different countries with different languages, different concepts of life and cultural values, and varying tastes and customs, must meet certain unavoidable requirements. We outline them below in schematic summary as we think they should be distinguished:

1] The subject must be of sufficiently broad human interest to affect the most diverse groups. *Wozzeck* is a good subject, because it corresponds to an experience most people have had. *Lulu* is too specialized, too individual. *Les Malheurs d'Orphée, Antigone, Elektra, Christophe Colomb,* and *Peter Grimes* are good subjects. *Maximilien* is not, because it includes too many elements of local history.

2] Artists should avoid burdening the music with too much textual material. The text, difficult enough to grasp in its country of origin, becomes practically incomprehensible in countries where other languages are spoken. Excessive text is, moreover, almost always the result of a poor choice of subject, and comes from the need to give explanations. Narration does not suit opera.

3] The plot should avoid complications, episodes, and diversions. These belong in spoken theater. The development of the music is too slow to keep pace with the complicated action. An overly detailed plot is boring in lyric theater, because it inevitably causes the music to stagnate. Attention should be drawn to well-centralized, simple action, and should at no time be distracted from the more broadly human plane. This condition is indispensable for making the musical-dramatic intention clear.

4] For the same reasons, and as a consequence, the music should avoid recitatives, above all the continuous recitative which has replaced the melodic line, in a good many musically interesting works. It is improper to camouflage a continuous recitative under the name of continuous melody in order to satisfy this principle. The melody is a very specific musical form with distinct limits in time and a characteristic structure. The sinuousness of its line differs essentially from that of the recitative, which is mortally tedious if it is prolonged because it becomes monotonous and lacks character in its delivery. True melody must be restored to primacy. True melody, moreover, can be engendered by dodecaphonic language as well as by diatonic language.

5] Since the opera must be able to travel and maintain its high quality, a simple, solid décor should be created which will adapt to any stage, even that of a concert hall. This planning of décor should have as its counterpart a careful study of the performances of the actor-singers. The movies have taught us to be intolerant of bad actors or stereotyped direction. The traveling opera should take advantage of the chamber orchestra, which would be confined to its normal role, the accompaniment of song.

6] There does exist a possibility of creating a form of modern opera, representative of our times and capable of interesting a cultivated public in many areas. Suppose that at a given moment four or five theaters have the means of showing, each for its own gain, a modern creation of quality, with a good expectation of returns. It would seem that they could come to an agreement on exchanging these spectacles. Each city would therefore have an opportunity to see and hear a series of four or five modern works, which would be the subject of a special subscription and would be launched with the publicity such an effort merits.

In principle, the establishment of a project for an itinerant lyric theater festival is not utopian. But there are difficulties to surmount. First, the choice of works: it is obvious that success can be anticipated only for an extremely limited selection, excluding any influence of friendship, national sentiment, or private interests. Quality alone must be the sole criterion. There can be no question of tolerating works which are mediocre or purely experimental in character. And even with every precaution taken as to the quality of the works chosen and their production, there no less remains the fact that certain types of expression and certain styles may be disqualified because they would not be understood by foreign audiences. Even in the most cultivated groups, not everyone has the flexibility to adapt quickly and easily to aspects of thought foreign to the character of his own culture.

There is as well the question of languages. Some countries

and some audiences like works to be presented in their original language, while others require translation into their own tongue.

The problems concerning the life of opera in the twentieth century are numerous. But the difficulties they present are not insurmountable. The question is one that deserves attention and discussion.

INDEX

Index

Index

Index

Thomas, Ambroise, 224
Thomson, Virgil, 44
Tinchart, 203
Tintoretto, Il, 148
Tippett, Michael, 44, 47, 382, 384
Tolstoi, Aleksei, 307
Tolstoi, Count Leo, 307
Tommasini, Vincenzo, 120, 379
Trakl, Georg, 89, 90
Trautwein, Friedrich, 394
Turchi, Guido, 45, 381

Unamuno, Miguel de, 354

Valéry, Paul, 89, 123, 129, 260
Varèse, Edgar, 44, 283, 388
Vaughan Williams, Ralph, 43, 382-4
Veden, Renier van der, 387
Verdaguer, Mosén Jacinto, 358
Verdi, Giuseppe, 275, 317, 377, 385,
Verhaeren, Émile, 191
Verlaine, Paul, 163, 164, 201, 248
Victoria, Tomás Luis de, 354, 359
Villa-Lobos, Heitor, 43, 338, 340, 360-2
Ville de Mirmont, Jean de la, 170
Villon, François, 167
Viñes, Ricardo, 224, 266
Vitruvius, 141
Vivaldi, Antonio, 149, 379
Vogel, Vladimir, 44, 54, 87, 370
Voisins, Gilbert des, 193
Vuillermoz, Émile, 138, 185, 186, 188
Vyshnegradski, Ivan, 278

Wagenaar, Bernard, 44
Wagner, Richard, 13, 15, 49, 59, 60, 75,
  79, 93, 96, 103, 124, 131, 137, 160,
  194, 209, 219, 256, 263, 308, 310, 312,
  313, 317, 328, 389, 402
Wahl, Jean, 242
Walton, William, 44, 47, 53, 382, 384
Watteau, Antoine, 148
Weber, Karl Maria von, 132
Webern, Anton, 18, 43, 45, 48, 54, 57,
  58, 75, 76, 87, 88-91, 92, 104, 105, 109,
  113-14, 151, 153, 154, 312, 327, 373,
  375
Wedekind, Frank, 94, 97, 106, 109, 111
Weelkes, Thomas, 382
Weill, Kurt, 44, 53, 327-9
Weiss, Paul, 287
Wellesz, Egon, 44, 58-9
Werfel, Franz, 244
Weterings, Joseph, 198
Weyden, Roger van der, 88
Whiteman, Paul, 44, 365
Whitman, Walt, 326, 366, 383
Widor, Charles Marie, 255
Wiesengrund-Adorno, Theodor, 88
Wilde, Oscar, 93, 225
Willaert, Adrian, 85, 151
Witkowski, Georges Martin, 43
Woestijne, David van de, 387

Zemlinsky, Alexander von, 62
Zimmerman, Bernd Alois, 45, 337
Zurbarán, Francisco de, 358

A SELECTED LIST OF *Universal Library* TITLES

History and Political Science

Literary Criticism, Drama, and Poetry

Titles of General Interest